Dead Men Tapping

Dead Men Tapping

The End of the
Heather Lynne II

Kate Yeomans

International Marine / McGraw-Hill

*Camden, Maine • New York • Chicago • San Francisco • Lisbon • London • Madrid • Mexico City
Milan • New Delhi • San Juan • Seoul • Singapore • Sydney • Toronto*

The McGraw·Hill Companies

2 3 4 5 6 7 8 9 0 DOC DOC 0 9 8 7 6 5 4

The Library of Congress has cataloged the cloth edition as follows:
Yeomans, Kate.
  Dead men tapping : the end of the Heather Lynne II / Kate Yeomans.—
1st ed.
        p.   cm.
Includes bibliographical references. (p.   ).
  ISBN 0-07-138034-5 (hardcover : alk. paper)
  1. Heather Lynne II (Fishing boat). 2. Shipwrecks—Massachusetts
—Gloucester Region. 3. United States. Coast Guard—Search and
rescue operations. I. Title.
  G530.H39Y46 2003
  910′.9163′45—dc21   2003013533
Paperback ISBN 0-07-144546-3

Illustration pages ii–iii by Stephen L. Davis, based on a photo from Corbis. Map
on page vi by International Mapping Associates. Lyrics from "Angel" by Sarah
McLachlan on page 384 © 1997 Sony/ATV Songs LLC/Tyde Music. All rights on
behalf of Sony/ATV Songs LLC and Tyde Music administered by Sony/ATV
Music Publishing, 8 Music Square West, Nashville, TN 37203. In Canada, rights
administered by Nettwerk Management. Used by permission.

For the crew of the Heather Lynne II
Kevin Foster
Jeffrey Hutchins
John Michael Lowther

May they never be forgotten

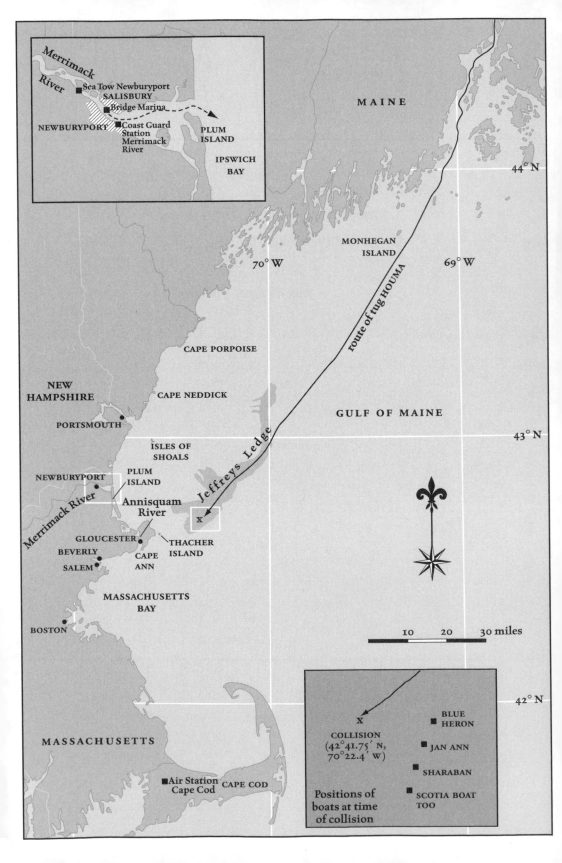

MAINE

Merrimack River

Sea Tow Newburyport
SALISBURY
Bridge Marina
NEWBURYPORT
Coast Guard Station Merrimack River
PLUM ISLAND
IPSWICH BAY

MONHEGAN ISLAND

44° N

70° W

69° W

route of tug HOUMA

CAPE PORPOISE

NEW HAMPSHIRE

CAPE NEDDICK

GULF OF MAINE

PORTSMOUTH

43° N

ISLES OF SHOALS

NEWBURYPORT

PLUM ISLAND

Annisquam River

Jeffreys Ledge

Merrimack River

GLOUCESTER

BEVERLY

SALEM

THACHER ISLAND

CAPE ANN

MASSACHUSETTS BAY

10   20   30 miles

BOSTON

MASSACHUSETTS

42° N

BLUE HERON

X

COLLISION
(42°41.75′ N,
70°22.4′ W)

JAN ANN

SHARABAN

Air Station Cape Cod

CAPE COD

SCOTIA BOAT TOO

Positions of boats at time of collision

Contents

The greatest obstacle to being heroic is the doubt whether one may not be going to prove one's self a fool; the truest heroism is, to resist the doubt; and the profoundest wisdom, to know when it ought to be resisted, and when to be obeyed.
                                                    —Nathaniel Hawthorne

Prologue

« *Saturday, August 4, 2001* »

UNDER AN IVORY AUGUST SKY twenty-eight miles at sea, I stood on the aft deck of our 42-foot charter fishing boat, *Erica Lee*, and worked to pry a rusty hook from the tough jaws of a cusk. Sticking my thumb in one eye and forefinger in the other, I pinched the bone between them to get a better grasp. As the fish slapped my leg with its tail, thick blood slipped down my orange rubber coveralls and mixed with shimmering seawater and gritty, putty-colored fish feces.

On this greasy calm day, isolated by invading fog, we were drifting over a rocky pocket of Jeffreys Ledge off the northeast coast of Massachusetts that was home to plentiful large cusk. The sixteen charter fishermen on board laughed and shouted in Spanish as they hauled in fish like gold coins from a slot machine. I could hear Rob, my husband and cocaptain, muttering his annoyance at a few of these anglers who, hungover, continued to vomit into the toilet and clog it despite our repeated pleas to toss their cookies over the side. Alone in the small head compartment down below, he attended to the brimming white porcelain bowl.

Though not yet noon, it had already been quite a day—for everything that had gone right, something else had gone wrong. We had been heavy into fish all morning—cod, haddock, and pollock as well as big cusk—but the VHF marine radios on board kept blowing fuses and we were out of cell phone range, the head looked to be terminally clogged, and I had dropped not one but two gaffs over the side while snagging the fish our customers were reeling in. Though these fishermen were happy, Rob, our deckhand April, and I faced continuous chaos.

I swore under my breath to no one in particular, too frustrated to appreciate the ugly cusk wriggling in my hand. Light brown, and without the distinctive fins and features of a cod, it had risen to the surface looking like a long, smudgy, muck-colored eel—even down to its extended, eel-like dorsal fin. As it squirmed, suspended, its soft air bladder protruded from its mouth like a pink balloon. The remarkably thick, firm white fillets of this sluggish bottom scavenger would be delicious, but at the moment its strong jaws and muscular cheeks—built to eat brittle stars, crabs, and lobsters—were its most notable features. It was not pleased about my efforts to pry a hook from its mouth with a pair of pliers.

Seven slippery cusk wriggled on deck unattended while our clients reeled still more to the surface. I focused my attention on the stubborn fish in my hand and tried not to be rattled by the impatient angler waiting for me to return his hook so he could resume fishing. I don't know why, but I paused at that moment and looked up to the east. Though we had nineteen people on board, I was the only one who noticed the dark blue, distinctively Nova Scotia–built fishing boat steaming out of the enveloping fog straight toward us.

White water furling off her bow made a frothy splashing sound. Her diesel engine hummed above the chatter that surrounded me. I watched as she drew near. She held her course and speed. I couldn't see anyone in her wheelhouse. The cusk landed on deck with a thud as I scrambled past charter fishermen and over their coolers to reach our helm. Keeping one eye on the approaching boat, I turned two keys to start our own engine. Its growl propelled Rob up on deck to ask what was going on.

"I'm getting ready to get out of his way," I said, pointing at the boat that was now about fifty yards off.

Rob and I stared at the boat. Our passengers grew silent and followed our gazes. We wondered aloud what this boat was doing and waited for her to change course. Time was running out. We did not know that the boat had lost her bearings on her maiden trip from Nova Scotia to Kittery, Maine, 24 miles to the northwest. We did not know that although the captain had radar on board, he had not yet installed it. All we knew was that we were adrift in his path with sixteen monofilament lines, some attached to fish, under our boat. We didn't want to risk tangling fishing gear in our propeller, not to mention needlessly killing hooked fish. But we didn't have a choice.

"Fuck this!" Rob barked as he pushed the gearshift into forward.

Everyone on board the *Erica Lee* lurched and grabbed the mahogany railing. Rob blasted the air horn at least five times and screamed at the oncoming boat, his voice rising in urgency, "Hey! Hey! Hey!" Our passengers yelled Spanish curses and waved their fists in the air.

A man popped up at the phantom boat's helm and turned right as if to intercept us, still steaming at what looked to be a good twelve knots. Rob threw our boat into hard reverse. The *Erica Lee* cowered astern as our growling diesel spit clouds of acrid black exhaust smoke. Cold water gurgled in through the scuppers and set the decks awash. The Novi boat, still not slowing down, followed our move, turning back to the left as if it were a torpedo locked in on us. The gap closed. Then, at the last moment, the boat veered again to the right and passed twenty feet ahead of us, gliding through our footprint.

"Hey! Wake up!" Rob yelled.

The man in the wheelhouse waved. Though between us Rob and I had accumulated more than thirty years at sea, our hearts pounded as we stared at the Novi boat in disbelief. How, in this vast ocean, could one boat have set up on a course hundreds of miles away that would take it through the exact spot 28 miles offshore, no larger than a 42-foot radius, where we happened to be fishing? Although it wasn't the first time in her twenty-one years that the *Erica Lee* had had to scramble out of the way of an oncoming boat, it was the closest call we'd ever had.

TWELVE HOURS LATER and a hundred miles to the east, the 541-foot Russian tanker *Virgo* emerged from the fog, possibly with no one in the wheelhouse, and plowed over an 83-foot trawler, *Starbound*, that was headed home to Rockland, Maine, with 275,000 pounds of herring on board. The *Starbound*'s captain, Gloucester fisherman Joe Marcantonio, had been asleep but woke up when his first mate, James Sanfilippo, yelled, "We're gonna get rammed!"

Sanfilippo said he had tried to avoid the ship. Marcantonio told him to go below and wake the other two deckhands, Mark Doughty and Tom Frontiero. As Sanfilippo raced down the companionway, the enormous red bulbous bow of the *Virgo* struck the *Starbound*'s port side and knocked Marcantonio down. The deck dropped under his feet. Seawater rushed in. Marcantonio leapt overboard and surfaced in time to see the lights on the *Virgo* fade into the distance. He found *Starbound*'s life raft, which had deployed automatically, climbed inside, and watched his *Starbound* sink in less than ten seconds. He clutched the activated emergency position-indicating radio beacon that alerted his distress to the U.S. Coast Guard. Alone in his life raft, he spent the next three hours screaming over the dark, still waters for his crew.

No one answered.

Peter Begley, captain of the lobsterboat *Eulah McGrath*, heard the Coast Guard's report of a vessel in distress 15 miles from him. Arriving on the scene, he found Marcantonio, dressed only in his underwear and a thin exposure suit, adrift in *Starbound*'s life raft. The lobsterboat *Jacqueline Robin*, one of several fishing vessels that assisted in the search for survivors, found the lifeless body of Sanfilippo adrift. Doughty and Frontiero would remain lost at sea.

Coast Guardsmen, on the day the agency called off its 250-square-mile search for Doughty and Frontiero, said this accident was "extremely rare." They could not recall the last time there had been a deadly collision like this off the New England coast.

They must have forgotten about the *Heather Lynne II*.

»The Collision

O N A RAW TUESDAY MORNING IN LATE APRIL, in a small federal courtroom on the Boston waterfront, a fisherman sat alone on a witness stand and tried to remember the September morning he'd spent three years and seven months trying to forget. He folded his hands and looked past the lawyer to the water-blue and blood-red stencil rolling along the dark wooden arches on each of the room's white walls. The arches signified the equal contributions of everyone—judge, lawyers, litigants, and onlookers—to the events that would unfold upon the blue carpet. But to the fishermen who would gather here to add their shards of memory to the emerging mosaic of a tragedy, the wooden curves resembled the lingering image of a capsized boat.

Sitting opposite an empty jury box was Richard Burgess. He wore dark blue jeans, an olive button-down shirt, and brown deck shoes. Embroidered on the back of his royal-blue jacket, which he had slung over a nearby chair, were his boat's name, *Scotia Boat Too*, and a bluefin tuna. His forty-six-year-old, clean-shaven face held the weathered lines of a seasoned fisherman, while his trimmed black hair, black mustache, and silver-rimmed eyeglasses suggested a soft-spoken, contemplative man.

Plaintiffs' attorney Bradley M. Henry asked him what he did for a living. Burgess explained that he owned five boats and now spent many of his days ashore running his fishing business rather than going to sea. He wasn't asked about the hours he spent advocating for Gloucester's commercial fishermen as vice-president of the North Shore Community Tuna Association and chairman of the Gulf of Maine Fishermen's Alliance. He didn't mention that he had once been appointed by Governor William Weld to the Massachusetts Fish Recovery Commission and had served as a member of the board of directors of the Massachusetts Fishermen's Partnership.

Burgess also didn't mention that he spent much of his time ashore worrying about his boat crews working offshore—more, probably, than he would worry if he were with them. He didn't tell the judge that every time the phone rang late at night he hesitated to answer it, afraid something could be wrong aboard one of his boats. That's when his wife would tell him to pick up the phone, saying, "You have to find out what's going on."

"You don't fish anymore?" U.S. District Court Judge Patti B. Saris asked him.

"Just a little bit in the summertime, maybe," Burgess said.

"Why is that, Mr. Burgess?" Bradley Henry asked.

"I just have a hard time sleeping at night on the vessel."

"And why is that?"

"From this incident."

"How long have you been a fisherman?" Henry asked.

"Twenty-five years."

RICHARD BURGESS had had his feet in fishing boots for as long as he could remember. As a kid, he'd spent every summer with his uncles, commercial fishermen who lived on New Brunswick's Campobello Island. He tended fish weirs alongside them at seven years old and later joined them on longlining and herring seining trips. At the end of each summer, he returned to Manchester-by-the-Sea, a small coastal town a few miles south of Gloucester. After graduating from high school, he had headed to sea full-time. Now married, he had two young daughters and had named one of his gillnetters, *Heidi & Heather*, after them. When his girls asked where he had gone to college, he told them he'd attended North Atlantic University. When they asked where that was, Burgess drove them to the beach and pointed out at the horizon.

After working more than twenty-five years at sea, he figured he'd seen and experienced just about all the ocean could throw at him. He bought his first Nova Scotia–built boat in 1976 and took it lobstering and Scottish seining for gray sole and yellowtail flounder. He bought other boats and went dragging, gillnetting, and tuna fishing. He'd seen weather in the Bay of Fundy blow the windows out of the wheelhouse of a 55-foot seine boat. On a night the wind blew a hundred miles an hour atop New Hampshire's Mount Washington, he'd been caught fishing on Jeffreys Ledge, 40 miles east of Gloucester, in seas that laid his 42-foot Bruno lobster-style boat over on one side and forced her wheelhouse windows into the water. Suspended on the whims of wind and waves, he prayed his boat would right herself instead of capsizing. Finally she did. After one successful fishing trip his 50-foot dragger rolled over and sank at the dock. On a winter day he had to retrieve his nephew from frigid waters after the younger man was snatched overboard by a lobster trawl—a string of twenty traps on a single line—that was dropping to the ocean bottom. Burgess had helped other fishermen and been helped by them. He had seen rough seas and calm seas. He had seen boats sink and boats almost sink.

But he had never seen anything quite like what he saw in the early morning hours of September 5, 1996.

If Burgess could have gone beyond what was humanly possible and recalled the events of that day in crystalline order and photographic detail, if he could have told a tale unaffected by hindsight, and if trial procedure had allowed him uninterrupted scope and time, this is the story he would have told.

He met his crew in Gloucester and untied the lines of his 42-foot black gillnetter, *Scotia Boat Too*, at around two o'clock that beautiful September morning. As they slipped past the Gloucester Coast Guard station and out of the protected harbor, Burgess set up on a northeasterly course toward the spot fifteen miles away where they'd caught a bluefin tuna the day before. He noted the bright night sky, flat calm seas, and good visibility. The lights on the Cape Ann shoreline lingered for a long while astern.

About four miles off the coast, Burgess found the visibility good enough to warrant shutting off one of his two radars, turning on the autopilot, and putting his feet up on the dash while he listened to his gillnetting friends talk on the marine radio. They all worked together, keeping in touch throughout the day by monitoring VHF channel 10. He reached for his personal logbook and began making notes about the successful day before: anchor coordinates, weather (a southeast wind blowing 10 to 15 knots), what enticed the tuna to bite his hook (a live whiting suspended in

110 feet of water at 3:20 P.M.), and how the day ended (a 306-pound tuna worth twelve dollars a pound tied up alongside the boat by 4 P.M.). He paused and looked out over the inky calm sea.

Maybe they'd be lucky again.

Stephen Smith and John Gilson were sleeping down below. Gilson was a family friend who had never been tuna fishing; at Burgess's invitation, he had taken a week off from work as an investment salesman and joined the *Scotia Boat Too* crew. Smith was Burgess's thirty-one-year-old nephew, the one who had fallen overboard while lobstering with Burgess that frigid winter day. Smith had grown up in Manchester-by-the-Sea and had owned his first boat, which he used to fish fifty lobster traps, when he was fifteen years old. After high school he enrolled in Burgess's North Atlantic University and had worked with his uncle since 1983.

When they arrived in the vicinity of the southern end of Jeffreys Ledge, ten miles east of Cape Ann, at about 4 A.M., Smith crawled out of his bunk and joined Burgess in the wheelhouse. They found the 32-foot *Sharaban* anchored on the exact coordinates where Burgess had caught his tuna the day before. They noticed two more boats—*Jan Ann* and *Blue Heron*—anchored within a half mile. The small fleet set up in a line that followed the contour of the underwater ledge; below them a sliver of the gray sandy bottom was beginning its rise from a depth of about 250 feet to 180 feet in less than a half mile. The assembled fishermen knew that bluefin tuna liked to cruise the edge of the ledge and chase the smaller baitfish that feed on the nutrient-rich waters forced upward by deeper, colder ocean currents.

Smith dropped the anchor on its 40 feet of chain and 300 feet of line to the ocean bottom about 240 feet below. Once secured to the ledge with his bow facing south, Burgess shut off the engine. He again looked behind him at the *Sharaban*, about an eighth of a mile away, and took one last look at the radar, which was set at a half-mile range to monitor the boats around him. Then he and Smith went below to catch an hour of sleep. Gilson had stayed in his berth the whole time.

The fishing would begin in earnest with the sunrise at 6:14 A.M. Burgess set the alarm for 5:30 A.M., but woke up a few minutes after five o'clock to a still, dark morning. He climbed down from his top bunk, unwittingly waking Smith, who had been dozing in the berth below him.

Burgess slipped on his shoes, climbed up into the wheelhouse, and turned on the white wheelhouse light. He looked at the radar and saw the *Sharaban*, the *Jan Ann*, and the *Blue Heron* still anchored in a line stretching a half mile behind him. It appeared that nothing had changed since he'd gone to sleep about forty-five minutes earlier. The time was between 5:06 and 5:10 A.M.

Then a blasting air horn hammered the peaceful morning air.

Loud.

Quick.

Sharp.

Burgess shot a glance through the open door behind him and saw a tugboat illuminated by amber deck lights perhaps a mile to a mile and a half north and a little west off his starboard aft quarter. He could see both its red and green running lights and realized it was headed straight toward him.

After about twenty seconds of intermittent blasts, the horn stopped. A diesel engine roared like thunder as it slowed to what Burgess assumed was a dead stop. Three distinct crashes—two sharp bangs and one soft boom—followed quickly.

"You should have heard the noises I heard," he said three years later. "I still have nightmares about that."

Down in his berth with his ear next to the fiberglass hull, Smith heard the amplified rumbling of an approaching boat through the water. He heard the horn blast. Sharp crashes. A few soft, repetitive bangs.

"It was like a boom, boom, boom," he said later. "It was boom, boom, boom."

Gilson awoke from a dead sleep to a loud scraping, metal-on-metal sound, one you don't hear very often.

"Hey! Did you hear that?" Burgess screamed, as he started up the engine. "Someone's been hit!"

Smith jumped out of his berth and ran up to the bow to release the anchor line, which was tied to an inflated orange ball—as tuna fishermen routinely do, so they can leave an anchor and find it on their return. They sped toward the tug to see if they could help, something any fisherman does when suspecting another fisherman is in trouble.

"Your first reaction is to go and try to save a person, or two, or three," Burgess said later. "You hear a noise and scream to your crew to get ready, whether they're in their underpants or full dress. You go and see what you can do to help."

Burgess turned north and steamed toward the tug at about eleven knots, as fast as he could go. It would take less than four minutes to cover three-quarters of a mile. As he approached the tug, the thought crossed his mind that it might have run them down if it had not hit another boat first. He figured that this tug with a barge in tow was trying to make its way through the fleet of anchored tuna boats, and his boat had been next in line.

"We were fifty to seventy-five yards away from the same thing happening to us," is how Gilson remembered it. "It looked like he was trying to thread a needle."

On board the *Sharaban*, the crew felt the same way. They heard the horns, saw the tug, and started their two engines just in case they had to get off their anchor and scramble out of the tug's way. Then they saw the tug start to turn as Burgess sped toward it.

When Burgess approached the tug at 5:18 A.M., it was turning hard to port—to the east—so Burgess too veered east, then slowed down. He heard a man identifying his vessel as the tug *Houma* call the U.S. Coast Guard via the marine radio. When a watch-stander at Coast Guard Station Gloucester answered, the man on board the *Houma* reported in a slow, shaken voice, "Yeah, we've got a Mayday situation. We're at latitude, uh, 42 41.75 North, 70 22.4 West. We're right off Cape Ann. [A] fishing boat just crossed right in front of the barge we're towing and went under it and apparently sunk. We're looking for survivors in the water."

"Roger," the Coast Guard watch-stander said. "Stand by."

Burgess hailed the tug *Houma* on the radio.

"Skipper on the tug," Burgess said, "you still on here?"

The tug did not reply. After twenty seconds, the Coast Guard called the tug and asked for the length of the vessel that went under the barge.

"It was about a fifty-foot fishing vessel," the *Houma* said. "He cut right between the [tug] and the barge. Tried out the course of blowing the whistle for him. Uh, he went right in front of the barge."

"Roger, sir," the Coast Guard said. "Stand by."

Burgess again tried to call the *Houma*. "Skipper on the tug, you still on this channel?" Burgess heard no reply and instead heard the Coast Guard call the *Houma* to confirm its position.

"That's correct," the *Houma* said. "We're trying to round up, see if we can see survivors."

"Roger, sir," the Coast Guard said. "Have you found anybody in the water?"

"I'm trying to get ahold of my barge," the *Houma* said. "I think I still see something floating back there. It's a little hazy here. We've got six or seven hundred feet of hawser out," he added, referring to the towline. "We'll see if we can get back in that area."

Houma answered a call from its barge *Essex* and asked, "Do you see anyone in the water back there?"

"No, we've been looking," the *Essex* said. "The boat is right here though, right behind us, Mike."

As Burgess drew closer to *Houma*, a man on board hailed him on the radio. "The *Houma* to the fishing vessel off my starboard bow."

"Yes, sir," Burgess replied in a soft, calm voice. "We've just come over here to give you a hand if we can."

"OK," an agitated voice replied. "This guy just cut right in front of the barge, went right under us, and, uh, it looks like he is still floating right there. I don't know what the situation is. They're looking, back on the barge."

"All right," Burgess said. "Well, if you can put your spotlight down that direction there, we'll be right over to 'em there."

"OK," *Houma* said. "We're rounding up to come [to] port, all the time, Cap. Just watch around by our bow. You see where I've got my port spotlight there?"

As Burgess idled along the beam cast on the water by the tug's giant spotlight, a school of herring skittered through the sea surface. Sunrise was still an hour away, and several fishermen later recalled that during the first half hour after the collision it was "pitch-black dark." In fact, nautical twilight had begun at 5:10 that morning off Cape Ann. At morning twilight, which begins when the sun is still 12 degrees below the eastern horizon, faint outlines of objects begin to materialize from the darkness, though the horizon remains indistinct.

Smith grabbed two life rings and climbed onto the roof of the *Scotia Boat Too*. He stood there with Gilson, who could feel the hair standing up on the back of his neck. They each held a life ring in one hand and hollered into the dark. They could not see the barge except for one small, red light on its port bow. "I don't know what we're going to see," Burgess had told them, "so keep your eyes out. Be prepared for anything."

What Burgess saw next was a green shadow emerging on his radar screen. He looked out the pilothouse window and saw a smudge of light rise from beneath the water a fair distance away, behind the barge. He realized it was the stricken fishing boat—her lights momentarily still aglow—returning to the surface amid a field of debris. There was a lot of debris in the water at first, Smith remembered, but then it just disappeared.

"Yep, I gotcha," Burgess told the *Houma*. "I just want to stand in tight, not get near the cable, so we'll come around easy. I got them on the radar here."

Coast Guard Station Gloucester broke into their transmission to hail the *Houma*, but the tug told the Coast Guard to stand by and nervously hailed Burgess.

"The fishing boat," *Houma* yelled. "Skip, just keep away from me, skip! I'm coming around. We don't want another problem. Just stay away from my bow, OK?"

"Yep," Burgess said in a calm voice. "I got you there fine, sir, yep."

"You see me coming around there?" *Houma* repeated. "I'm coming around also to see if I can see anybody in the water. I've got six hundred feet of hawser out."

"Yep, that's right," Burgess said. "I understand."

As Burgess eased toward the overturned boat on the edge of the spotlight's beam, Coast Guard Station Gloucester again called the *Houma*, which was circling back on itself as it prepared to haul in its hawser and secure its barge.

"Let me get back to you after a couple of minutes," *Houma* replied. "We're coming up to the boat and we're a hundred, two hundred feet from it, and I'd like to see if I can't see anybody in the water. I'll get right back to you."

"Roger, sir," Coast Guard Station Gloucester said at 5:27 A.M. "Be advised we've got a vessel underway [to] your position."

After three minutes of radio silence, *Houma* called Burgess and asked, "Cap, can you get up to this capsized boat and see if you can hear or see anything?"

"Yeah, we're trying to get right on it, Captain," Burgess said softly.

"We're gonna—we just didn't want to hit anybody in the water, you know?"

"I hear that," a man on board the *Houma* sighed.

Burgess eased alongside the target that had emerged on his radar screen. The still, ghostly forest-green hull of an upside-down fishing boat took substance from the enveloping darkness. Gilson struggled to process the image, so simple in outline yet so profound in its implications. A landsman, he fell back to the Hollywood movie *Jaws* for a frame of reference, as when the marine biologist and the police chief approach a lifeless, half-sunk fishing boat in the murky night and, with wide eyes, whisper, "What happened?" About the same size as his *Scotia Boat Too*, this turtled boat looked to Burgess like his own boat upside down. Her keel faced the fading stars. He wanted to know her name, so he worked his way past her stern. On her transom he read large, upside-down white letters painted above a white handlebar mustache: "*Heather Lynne II*, Newbury MA."

Seeing that name was heart wrenching. He and Smith knew the *Heather Lynne II*. She was what they considered a highliner, a boat that stands out among the fleet as a top producer, captained by a seasoned, skilled fisherman. Burgess had known her owner, Ted Rurak, for several years. As they idled alongside her, just inches away, they saw smoke or steam rising from a through-hull fitting on the starboard side. Her propeller was not moving. They did not hear her engine. Bubbling air purged from the hull. A high-flyer buoy such as would be attached to a gillnet stuck out from under the boat and clung to the surface. Any lights that had been on were now extinguished.

Smith shined a deck light into the water. A strobe light from the *Heather Lynne II*'s emergency position-indicating radio beacon (EPIRB) flashed under the surface. A yellow, $5/8$-inch-diameter polypropylene line floated from the bow to a nearby orange ball—what these fishermen assumed had been an anchor ball. From there, the line ran straight down into the depths.

"Oh, my God," Burgess said to his nephew. "They must have been on anchor."

Burgess reached for his marine radio and called, "Yeah, tugboat, you on here?" When *Houma* answered, Burgess said, "Yep, we know the guys there. Yeah, we know the boat. We just, uh, I don't know what to do. I—" He paused and sighed. "There's not much we can do here."

"Can you get anywhere close to him so you can see if you can hear any noise or anything?"

"We're right alongside of it here. Hang on. Stand by a second. We're almost touching it here."

Smith reached for a harpoon and started hitting the hull in a systematic way that would sound like help and not another collision to anyone trapped within. He heard no reply. He banged on the hull some more. Gilson wondered if they weren't listening hard enough for a response, or if someone might be alive but no longer conscious.

At 5:34 A.M., 16 minutes after the Mayday call, Coast Guard Station Gloucester called the *Houma* and announced that a helicopter was en route from Air Station Cape Cod.

"OK," the *Houma* said. "The name of the fishing vessel is the *Heather Lynne*. It's capsized. *Scotia Boat Too* is right at it now, putting the boat up on it to see if they can see anyone. I don't see anyone in the water around here." A minute later he asked, "Is the [Coast Guard vessel] that's coming going to have divers on board?"

"Negative," the Coast Guard said. "The helo has a rescue swimmer."

"OK," *Houma* said. "Well, this vessel *Heather Lynne* is capsized. Uh, there may be survivors in the hull."

At 5:36 A.M., Burgess called Coast Guard Station Gloucester, which he had overheard talking with the *Houma*. "Did you say there's a helicopter on its way?"

"Roger, Cap," came the reply. "En route from Cape Cod."

"Yeah, I got you. We're touching it here. It's right upside down, bow's in the water, stern's coming up here. I—." Again Burgess paused. "There's not much we can do."

"Roger, sir," Coast Guard Station Gloucester said at 5:36 A.M. "Be advised, we're gonna call some divers."

"OK," Burgess said. "Very good. Thanks."

Nineteen minutes after the Mayday call, Coast Guard Group Boston issued an Urgent Marine Information Broadcast (UMIB) on hailing and distress VHF channel 16:

> Pan Pan, Pan Pan, Pan Pan, hello all stations. This is the
> United States Coast Guard Boston Massachusetts Group,
> United States Coast Guard Boston Massachusetts Group.
> Break quote. Time 0936 Greenwich Mean Time. The Coast

Guard has received a report of a vessel capsized in position 42
41 decimal 75 degrees north, 070 22 decimal 4 degrees west,
approximately ten nautical miles off Cape Ann. All vessels
are requested to keep a sharp lookout, assist if possible and
report all sightings to any Coast Guard unit. Unquote break.
This is the United States Coast Guard Boston Massachusetts
Group, out.

Burgess heard this broadcast aboard the *Scotia Boat Too* while Smith
continued pounding on the thick fiberglass hull of the *Heather Lynne II*
with his harpoon. He'd yell, "Hello? Hello? Is anybody there?" They'd
pause and listen for a response. Again he'd pound and they'd shout. Then
Gilson said to Smith, "Dude, I think I hear something."

"Really?" Smith said, and banged again. They heard someone cry out.
Gilson heard a thudding. He believed there was definitely more than one
person alive. He remembered, "I could hear the panic. I could hear
screaming, but not their words. It was muffled."

Smith banged again. Up forward, by what would be the port corner
of the wheelhouse, he heard someone bang back.

"They're alive!" Smith shouted. He and Gilson yelled to the trapped
fishermen, "Help is on the way! Help is on the way!"

Smith considered what he could do. He kept thinking, "Jeez, somebody has got to do something here." He wanted to jump in and try to
lead the trapped men to the surface. He again shined a deck light down
into the black water to have a better look. Talking it over with Burgess, he
realized he would be putting himself in extreme danger. Although he
knew the boat, he had never been aboard. He knew enough about the nature of boats to realize that swimming into or out of her upside down, underwater, in the dark would be nearly impossible without scuba gear. Gillnets were hanging down like a giant spider web, and he knew trying to
swim through them might be deadly. Also, they didn't know what the
boat would do. She hung perilously at the surface, without any indication
when—or if—she would sink. The best thing they could do, the crew of
the *Scotia Boat Too* figured, was try to stabilize the boat in some way to
buy time for the divers they hoped would arrive and to preserve whatever
air pocket still lingered inside the *Heather Lynne II*.

At 5:40 A.M., John Frawley, a tall, thin, blond fisherman who had
been listening to the marine radio aboard his 36-foot tuna boat *Blue*

Heron—one of the three boats anchored near the *Scotia Boat Too*—approached the scene and backed up to the *Heather Lynne II*. He had met her crew the day before at the fish pier in Newburyport. Frawley and his deckhand banged on the hull by the forecastle and yelled. Two voices yelled back. He recognized one as belonging to John Michael Lowther. One voice yelled, "Help! Help! Help!" while another yelled, "Get us out of here!"

"Just hang on!" Frawley shouted back. "The Coast Guard is coming! We're real close to shore, so it shouldn't be but a few minutes!"

Frawley, a longtime commercial swordfisherman, who also owned the 65-foot *Haddit*, remembered when the Coast Guard once successfully rescued him off the coast of Puerto Rico. While they were swordfishing in rough seas, a mate had dropped a 250-pound bait table on Frawley's head; it crushed his spine. After waiting for the towering seas to subside, the Coast Guard airlifted him to a naval hospital in Guantánamo Bay, Cuba, and, later, to a Florida trauma center. He credited the Coast Guard's professional actions for his recovery and his return to fishing and expected the Coast Guard would soon rescue these trapped men. He told the pleading voices to just hold on.

"The Coast Guard is coming!" Frawley yelled.

A voice he believed to be Lowther's screamed, "Get me the fuck out of here!"

AT 5:41 A.M., *Houma* CALLED Coast Guard Station Gloucester. "Yeah, *Scotia Boat* says that they hear a knocking on the hull of the *Heather Lynne*. They're right there alongside. We're pulling our hawser in now [and] we'll see if we can assist them."

"Are you pushing or pulling your barge?" the Coast Guard asked.

"We were towing, and we'll have it right up short behind us now."

"Are you still on scene with the subject vessel?"

"That's correct," *Houma* said.

"And right now the only resources you have is yourself and the *Scotia Boat Too*?"

"Uh, and another vessel that just arrived on scene also."

At the same time—five minutes after being told the helicopter was en route—an angry Burgess called the Gloucester Coast Guard station and asked, "Can you tell me where the helicopter is, please?"

Coast Guard Station Gloucester did not answer Burgess and instead asked the *Houma* to again confirm its position and report the on-scene weather. It was still 31 minutes before the sun would rise over these waters ten miles east of Cape Ann. *Houma* reported that the seas were calm and the morning sky was a bit overcast with a half-mile visibility, though Burgess had noted fine visibility hours before and twenty minutes earlier had watched the *Houma* from a mile away. A light haze rendered the horizon indistinct in photographs and videotapes shot later that warm and humid morning, and eyewitnesses would recall a predawn haze. There was a predawn ground fog over Cape Cod to the south. Yet other testimony and witness accounts suggest a visibility of two miles or more. Perhaps the most that can be said with certainty of the visibility in that morning twilight is that it was neither bell-clear nor poor.

Other fishing vessels had begun to congregate a few feet away from the overturned *Heather Lynne II*.

"I just want to confirm," Coast Guard Station Gloucester asked the *Houma* at 5:43 A.M., "you heard a faint knocking on the hull of the capsized vessel?"

"Yeah, *Scotia Boat Too* heard the knocking. He's trying to call you right now on [channel] 16."

After a minute of calling each other back and forth on different radio channels, first on the Coast Guard's working channel 22 and then on marine distress channel 16, Burgess still did not connect with the Coast Guard and instead, at 5:45, called the tug, which had been pulling in its hawser to place the barge on a shorter tow. Burgess and Smith could hear air continuing to escape from *Heather Lynne*'s hull. They believed she was sinking and knew that although the Coast Guard was en route, something had to be done now. Burgess considered trying to lash the stricken vessel to his own boat, but thought better of it.

"[The *Heather Lynne II*] was the same size as my boat," Burgess said later. "And if it loses air, there was going to be two of us on the bottom. But then you've got a big, giant steel tug and that boat won't bother it a bit."

Burgess told the *Houma*, "It's starting to go down by the bow. Is there any possible chance we can get that tug alongside and tie this thing on by the skeg and everything that's sticking out of the water here?"

"Yeah," the *Houma* replied after a pause of several seconds. "I'm going to do that right now."

"Yeah, all right," Burgess said with a hint of hope in his voice. "A guy can come up on the stern, uh, guys can walk right on the stern right to the rudderpost and the wheel and the shaft and stuff there because, uh, you can cinch it up real tight, you know. They won't lose any more air than they got there."

"OK," *Houma* said. "You hear a solid knocking there or whatta ya got?"

"Oh yeah," Burgess said, raising his voice for emphasis. "They're in there. They're banging on the hull under the galley."

"OK, Cap, we're gonna let the barge go right now," *Houma* said.

"All right," Burgess said. "I'll get the other guys away from the stern here so you can pull right alongside there nice and gentle."

Coast Guard Station Gloucester called the *Houma* and asked if they could see anyone inside the *Heather Lynne II*. *Houma* said no one was visible but that the *Scotia Boat Too* heard banging on the hull. *Houma* reported that he planned to drop the barge so he could maneuver alongside the *Heather Lynne II*, tie a line on her, and keep her afloat, "so they don't lose any more air or sink completely." The Coast Guard asked if Burgess could talk to the trapped men and find out how many people were on board. *Houma* said he didn't think Burgess could do that, but he'd check.

"Captain, did you hear, were you able to talk—," *Houma* asked Burgess, "the Coast Guard wants to know, were you able to talk to anyone on there?"

"We can hear knocking," Burgess said at 5:48 A.M., thirty minutes after *Houma* placed the Mayday call. "We can hear people banging on the inside of the hull."

Houma called Coast Guard Station Gloucester and reported, "We can hear them, [but] I don't know how many people are in there."

"They're yelling 'Help! Help! Help!' They're yelling for help!" Frawley added, aboard the *Blue Heron*. "Coast Guard, you don't have a chopper where you can come out here and drop somebody in the water to get these boys out of there?"

The Coast Guard did not answer him. Frawley had grown up in Rockaway Park, near the waters of New York City, and was used to seeing

NYPD helicopters drop divers into the water on a regular basis. He expected, and hoped for, a similar response here.

Houma called the *Scotia Boat Too* and asked if he knew how many people usually fished on board. Ted Rurak, owner of the *Heather Lynne II*, had been monitoring the communications and talking with other fishermen while he raced to the scene aboard a friend's tuna boat, *Retriever*. He broke into the marine radio traffic and hailed the Gloucester Coast Guard, but heard no reply. Coast Guard Group Boston, which was in command of the rescue but had been letting the Gloucester station handle the communications, answered Rurak.

"I'm the owner of the boat," Rurak told Group Boston. "There's three people aboard."

"You said there were three people on board?" the Coast Guard asked.

"Yeah," Rurak said. "That's right."

Group Boston asked Rurak to call via his onboard cell phone, possibly to keep the VHF channel clear or to conduct a more private conversation on the identities of the trapped fishermen.

"I'm three quarters of a mile from where they're at," Rurak said. "So let me get there first."

"We do have vessels en route," the Coast Guard said. "If you could call us [on your cell phone] and give us some more information, we'd really appreciate it."

"I'll get back to you in five minutes," Rurak said.

"Coast Guard," Burgess interrupted. "Give me the phone number. I'll call you right now."

At 5:51 A.M., Burgess called Coast Guard Group Boston on his cell phone and spoke with the search-and-rescue mission coordinator, Petty Officer Richard Barone.

"This is the *Scotia Boat Too* standing by on the accident scene," Burgess said.

"*Scotia Boat Too*, OK," Barone said. "We got a helicopter heading out over there."

"I hope it's fast because these guys are screaming from inside the boat."

"OK, they're getting there as quick as they can. We're trying to get some divers together from Gloucester, gonna zip out there [in] the 47-footer we have. It's a matter of getting them to the station, but they're doing it as fast as they can. The helicopter is in the air en route to the position. They have a rescue swimmer on the boat." (In fact, the rescue swimmer was on the helicopter, while the crew of the 41-footer, which had been underway since 5:23 A.M., were qualified as surface swimmers. Neither was permitted by Coast Guard regulations to try an underwater rescue. It's unclear which of them Barone was referring to. Though Barone hadn't said so, Burgess now believed that the helicopter would pick up the divers in Gloucester—certainly a reasonable assumption.)

"OK. Where is the helicopter now?"

"It's, uh, leaving Cape Cod. It's probably midway [there] or a little less."

"All right."

"It's about a 20-minute run once they get up into the air."

"OK."

"Can you give me a little description of the situation, of what you see there?" Barone asked.

"Yep, we have a 44-foot fishing boat, gillnetter, upside down," Burgess said.

"Are you one of the ones that was fishing with this boat?"

"Well, we're all doing the fishing here."

"What, are you tuna fishing?"

"Yup. It's totally upside down, rudder and propeller sticking out of the water right up to the bow."

"The whole thing's up on the surface?" Barone asked.

"Yup, it started to take on water at the bow where the men are. We're trying to get the tugboat alongside to hold the stern tight with a hawser."

"OK. Anything else?"

"I don't know what to tell you," Burgess said. "There's an anchor ball out. It looks like they were sitting on anchor. I'm not sure, but that seems to be the look of things here."

"Really? OK. I'm writing this down. So you can hear them screaming, right?"

"Yes, that's right. They're screaming for help and knocking on the hull."

"Can you communicate with them? Can they hear you?"

"We're trying right now. The tug's going alongside there to try and hold it up."

"OK. I'll try to get an estimated time of arrival for the dive team. My [41-foot rescue boat] there yet?"

"Uh, no."

"OK, they'll be there shortly. Does it look like it might go down or stay afloat? Can you tell?"

"Well, it started to go slowly down to the bow. Right now, the tug's pulling up to the bow as we speak," Burgess said. "It's definitely sinking. It's afloat so far, but it's definitely taking on water at the bow. We can see air bubbles coming out."

"OK, is there any way you can tie on without jeopardizing the stability of it?" Barone asked. "Is there anything you can tie to it? If it starts to go down, the divers can follow the buoys down or something."

"Yep, we're going to try. The skipper of the tug is going to get a line to tie to the stern of the boat. I'm going to put my guys on the stern and try to secure this, all right?"

"OK," Barone said. "I'll let you go."

Burgess hung up the phone and prepared to help the *Houma* tie alongside the *Heather Lynne II* just as the *Retriever* arrived on scene with Ted Rurak on board. He had taken the *Retriever* out tuna fishing that morning and was heading to a spot near Burgess when a fisherman called his cell phone and told him his *Heather Lynne II* was in trouble.

"Teddy," Burgess called on the radio. "Do you want to take that line from [the tug and] secure it to the rudderpost there?"

"Definitely, yeah," Rurak said.

"OK," Burgess said at 5:54. "I'll back off for you. If you can, you ought to go alongside the stern there and fix her up tight, you know. The 41's on the way and the chopper's trying to get a dive crew together."

Burgess eased away and watched as Rurak drove the *Retriever* alongside. Rurak's deckhand climbed onto the slippery bottom of the *Heather Lynne II*, passed a thick nylon line through her skeg and handed it back to the tug crew, who tied it to the tug's starboard quarter bitt. Burgess idled a couple of boat lengths away. He didn't like the way the *Heather Lynne II* was floating lower at the bow. He called out to the men on the tug that they should get a second line under the bow, but they said they didn't know what the bow looked like underwater. "It's the same boat as mine, just look at my boat," hollered Burgess, but he got no response. He took his spot in the gathering fleet that would soon swell to about a dozen fishing boats. He figured there was nothing more he could do. He would wait for the Coast Guard to bring the divers who Barone had assured him would soon be en route.

ATTORNEYS DID NOT GIVE Burgess an opportunity to tell his whole story from his seat on the witness stand on the first day of the trial, April 25, 2000. Testifying against the U.S. Coast Guard on behalf of the trapped fishermen's families, he was instructed to answer only those questions that were asked, according to his best recollection three and a half years later. He would have preferred not to testify at all. It wasn't that he didn't have his own concerns about the Coast Guard's rescue response that day. What worried him was that, once they learned of his testimony, the Coast Guard might hassle his five boat crews during random fisheries law enforcement inspections. As a matter of normal Coast Guard procedure, Burgess and his captains, on more than one occasion, had been boarded by the Coast Guard at gunpoint. At Burgess's request, no Coast Guardsmen were allowed to hear his testimony inside Courtroom Thirteen.

On this raw Tuesday morning, rivulets of rain rolled down the hundreds of thick panes of glass that gave the new John Joseph Moakley Federal Courthouse a striking northwesterly view of downtown Boston and its waterfront. Outside were the Coast Guard's First District Headquarters on a neighboring street corner, and tugs and tows passing by. Spanning nearly four hundred feet, the glass wall was curved like the foot of a billowed sail. This transparent facade was meant to imply that the courts were open to all. People inside could look out, while the public outside could look in and be reminded that the courts are both, as one reporter wrote, "a part of and apart from the community."

Each morning inside Courtroom Thirteen, five attorneys representing the families of *Heather Lynne II* captain Jeffrey J. Hutchins and first mate John Michael Lowther spread their notes on a small table to the left and in front of Judge Saris. The family of Kevin Foster, the third crew member, had opted not to join the suit when their lawyer told them of the near impossibility of winning a judgment against the Coast Guard. The plaintiffs' attorneys would gather around the table, huddle and whisper, read documents, wiggle yellow highlighters, flag information with Post-its, and make notes on legal pads. They appeared to be in a state of constant preparation.

At the opposing table sat one lawyer representing the U.S. Coast Guard. Department of Justice Attorney Stephen Campbell wheeled in four brown cardboard boxes filled with documents each morning, but most of the time he left the boxes stacked and unopened. He sat back in his chair, one leg crossed broadly over the other, his hand on one knee, his large eyes magnified by glasses as he looked up at the overhead lighting. Sometimes he smoothed his gray beard or ran one hand through his thinning hair. He turned his head slowly from right to left and back again every few minutes, as if relieving a neck cramp. Campbell did not appear concerned about what might unfold before Judge Saris in the hours and days to come. He had successfully defended the Coast Guard before. To him, the proceedings were a formality, and he expected to prevail. The Coast Guard expressed no interest in settling this case because it did not believe it had performed any negligent acts on that September morning for which it could be held liable. Judge Patti Saris, Campbell expected, would agree.

Reporters from the *Newburyport Daily News*, the *Boston Globe*, and the Associated Press attended the first day of the trial; two from the Newburyport paper attended each of the seven days thereafter. The family of the *Heather Lynne II*'s captain and two experts who would testify later watched from hard wooden benches arranged in three rows. Several Coast Guardsmen would show up for a later day of testimony, but otherwise the courtroom, which could comfortably seat up to ninety spectators, was mostly empty.

This maritime case was not a criminal action but a civil one—the sort of proceeding normally used by a victim of alleged negligence. A civil trial usually turns on a failure to fulfill an assumed or imposed obligation and furthers a community's expectations of justice while seeking the resolution of legal conflict. Since 1789, Congress has made the federal courts available for civil lawsuits in maritime, or admiralty, cases. Some victims can bring maritime cases in state courts, but this was a suit against the federal government. Most national and state governments are immunized from suit by the doctrine of "sovereign immunity," which is drawn from the ancient concept that "the king can do no wrong." The United States government is no exception. Several federal statutes do provide a partial waiver of sovereign immunity, but in order to take advantage of that waiver the *Heather Lynne II* family members had to bring their suit in federal court, to be decided by a federal judge without a jury. The families of the *Heather Lynne II*'s captain and first mate believed that the Coast Guard had negligently failed to fulfill its obligation to rescue their loved ones and that the judge's ruling would profoundly affect how the Coast Guard conducted its search-and-rescue operations.

"The Coast Guard has become rather smug and arrogant in its operations," Attorney Brad Henry said during an interview after the trial. "They think of themselves as 'the cops' of the waters rather than 'the rescuers.' We hope that this suit will make leaders in the Coast Guard think twice about what their real job is and how they should act on a daily basis to fulfill that mission."

In front of the spectators, with a wall of black law books behind her, sat Judge Saris, who had once presided over the historic Essex County Superior Court in Newburyport, whose interior Courtroom Thirteen was designed to resemble. The court stenographer took a seat halfway between Judge Saris and the witness. Law clerks came and went, but Saris paid little attention to them and instead focused on the witnesses, the attorneys, and the clock on the wall above the courtroom entrance.

Just after nine o'clock on the first morning of the trial, Attorney Brad Henry asked Burgess what kind of communication equipment he had on board his boat. Burgess said he had a VHF marine radio, a single-side-band radio, and a cell phone. Like all gillnet boats, he usually monitored VHF channel 10.

"What kind of channel is that?" Saris asked, interrupting Henry.

Burgess explained that there were about eighty-eight channels on a marine radio, and that the local gillnet fleet happened to monitor channel 10.

"Is it a safety channel or is it golden oldies? I mean, I don't know much—" she said as some laughed.

"No," Burgess said quietly. "I'm a gillnetter by profession, and that's what gillnetters stand by on, channel 10."

"So you talk to each other on that channel?" Saris asked.

"We talk to each other on channel 10," Burgess said. He explained that about a hundred gillnet boats hailed from ports along the coast from Provincetown, Massachusetts, to Portland, Maine. On his *Heidi &*

Heather, his gillnets were each about three hundred feet long and, when deployed, stood like a chain-link fence about eight feet off the ocean floor. Fish swam into the wall of nets and were tangled by their gills. When he was gillnetting, as opposed to fishing for tuna with rod and reel, Burgess would set about ten strings of fifteen nets each at daybreak, then work all day to haul them back. The *Heather Lynne II* also spent most of her time gillnetting, though she had been after tuna the morning of the collision.

After establishing that Burgess's was the first boat to reach the overturned *Heather Lynne II*, attorney Henry asked Burgess to describe what he'd seen. Burgess recalled how first he saw some debris in the water, and then the boat itself emerged.

"So it was totally submerged and it began to re-emerge?" Saris asked, trying to picture in her mind what the scene looked like.

"It came up under the center of the barge. It was totally submerged."

"Under the barge?" Saris asked.

"Under the barge," Burgess said, though what he meant was that the capsized boat returned to the surface *behind* the barge and had obviously *been* under it. He would later say that the barge was half a mile away when he approached the *Heather Lynne II*, which was consistent with the turn Captain Breen on the *Houma* was making.

"When you first saw the vessel coming up behind the barge, what did it look like?" Henry asked.

"The same boat as mine," Burgess said. "It looked like my boat upside down." He rubbed his palms together gently and explained how closely he approached the overturned boat. "I very slowly went alongside of it, just went by the stern until I saw the name, and then we backed up and we were actually barely rubbing each other."

Burgess explained that they wanted to see if anyone was alive inside the boat, so he told the court how his nephew began to tap on the hull. He slowly rapped his knuckles on the wooden desk in front of him and sent a hollow echo through the courtroom.

Tap.

Tap.

Tap.

On a wooden bench in the middle row of Courtroom Thirteen, Captain Jeffrey Hutchins's mother, Diane Fondow, dressed in black, sat next to her two daughters. She wiped away silent tears.

"What happened at that point?" Henry asked.

"I started calling the Coast Guard," Burgess said. "We were just at the time pleading with the Coast Guard, trying to get them to get someone on scene, and it just went on from there, just kept going, calling and calling and calling."

Later, Henry asked Burgess why he wanted divers to arrive on scene.

Burgess paused. "Because there was no way possible that we could help these people."

Before concluding his questioning, Henry needed Burgess to confirm that the Coast Guard had taken charge of the accident scene and in so doing had compelled or instructed other would-be rescuers to refrain from helping. Henry hoped to prove that the Coast Guard's response—and the initiative-robbing effect of its intervention—had worsened the condition of the trapped men. Burgess said there was no question that the Coast Guard was in charge of this rescue.

"When they showed up," Burgess said, "they took control."

Campbell stood up to begin his cross-examination. He asked, "While the 41-footer was on scene with the *Heather Lynne*, were any of the other vessels in that general location doing anything to assist in rescuing any survivors inside the *Heather Lynne*?"

"As soon as the Coast Guard showed up," Burgess said, "they took charge and told us all to back off."

"That wasn't my question, sir. Were any other vessels in the vicinity doing anything to rescue possible survivors on the *Heather Lynne*?"

"We were just doing what we were told," Burgess said. "We were sitting there watching."

"Prior to the Coast Guard arrival, what was anybody doing to rescue the survivors of the *Heather Lynne*?" Campbell asked, his voice raised. Burgess resented Campbell's implication that he was more to blame than the Coast Guard.

"I called the tug over—"

"What else?"

"—to try to bring the boat up, and there was essentially nothing we could do."

"OK. And the other vessels that were in that location of the accident, were they doing anything?"

"They probably felt the same way I did," Burgess said. "There was not much you could do."

"When the 41-footer arrived, [it] shooed these other vessels away from the *Heather Lynne* is what you're saying, right?"

"Yes."

A few minutes later Campbell asked, "Did you know any other divers that you could have called yourself?"

"No."

"Did you feel constrained from calling other divers, had you known them?"

"You mean, if I had known, would I have—is that what you're asking me—if I had known, would I have called someone else?" Burgess asked.

"Yes."

"I'm sure I would have."

"Did the Coast Guard prevent you from seeking any other help?" Campbell asked, his voice again raised.

Burgess shook his head. He glanced over at Jeffrey Hutchins's mother. He looked at Judge Saris. He said quietly, "I didn't know where else to go."

»The Crew

ON SEPTEMBER 5, 1996, thirty-year-old Jeffrey Hutchins snapped awake at 1:30 A.M. and dressed in a pair of faded Levi's, a T-shirt, and a blue plaid flannel shirt. He had hazel eyes, a sharp nose, short, coarse auburn hair, a mustache, and a stubble beard. Sometimes he wore a green corduroy cap on which his boat's name—*Heather Lynne II*—was embroidered in white letters. One inch short of six feet tall, he carried most of his 216 pounds as muscle built up from his days at sea. A black and green tattoo of a mermaid riding a dolphin was etched onto his upper left arm, covering the tattooed name of a former fiancée to whom he had twice been engaged. A rugged and charming bachelor, he could turn heads.

Although he usually took the 45-foot *Heather Lynne II* eighty miles or more offshore for multiday gillnetting trips in search of cod, haddock, and other groundfish, this was bluefin tuna season. His sister, her son, and his girlfriend, with whom he shared his new house, could expect him home for dinner each night. Hutch, as his closest friends called him, loved tuna fishing. He once told a friend after a day in the woods hunting deer, "I don't know what gives me a bigger rush, killing a deer or catching a tuna." Whenever he caught a tuna, he said, "I don't know what gives me a bigger rush, catching a tuna or killing a deer."

HUTCHINS KNEW, when he woke up that Thursday morning, that he had to make the day count, because bluefin tuna fishing was a highly competitive, internationally regulated fishery in which catching just one fish—a thrilling experience in itself—meant a big payoff. He would not be alone out on Jeffreys Ledge. At least four hundred other boats would be spread around him as far as forty miles away. As he dressed, he might have been strategizing about the day ahead: he would have to choose the right spot, get there at the right time of day, offer the best bait, and set out the best tackle at the right depth. Once at anchor with his lines in the water, he would have to keep a constant watch on the fish-finder and note when a tuna swam under the boat and at what depth and then adjust his lines accordingly. Beyond being vigilant to what was going on around and underneath him, he would just have to wait and hope to get lucky.

One of the largest and most powerful fish in the ocean, Atlantic bluefin tuna can live thirty years and grow to 1,400 pounds and 15 feet long. They have dark, steel-blue backs, silvery, opalescent sides and bellies, two dorsal fins (the leading one of which can retract), and seven yellow finlets the size of half-dollars behind the second dorsal and anal fins. *Thunnus thynnus* (from the Greek, meaning "to rush") can pursue herring, whiting, mackerel, and squid at bursts of speed approaching ninety miles an hour or cruise across the Atlantic in sixty days.

Before 1970, bluefin were sold to domestic manufacturers of cat and dog food at a nickel a pound. Then a market developed among Tokyo restaurateurs for use as sushi and sashimi. Japanese buyers would meet boats at wharves along the New England coastline, slice a raw, red steak from the tail, and taste the fish before offering a price. As a Japanese delicacy, New England bluefin fetched as much as a dollar a pound in 1973; by 1986 the landed price per pound was twelve dollars, and thereafter it fluctuated with the market. In 1994 it ranged from two to forty-two dollars per pound, averaging about eight.

By 1996, a passionate debate was swirling through the booming Atlantic bluefin tuna fishery. Because bluefin are a highly migratory species, and many scientists had a hunch that the eastern Atlantic-Mediterranean population mixed with the western Atlantic fish (this was finally verified in a 2001 tagging study), the United States was among a handful of nations that in 1969 had created the International Commission for the Conservation of Atlantic Tunas (ICCAT) as a means of coordinating international research and fishery management. Each year, ICCAT would recommend harvest quotas, catch limits per trip, and minimum size limits. The National Marine Fisheries Service (NMFS) was charged with divvying up ICCAT's suggested U.S. bluefin quota—1,311 metric tons in 1996 versus the 39,331 metric tons allotted for the eastern Atlantic and

Mediterranean. NMFS allocated a percentage of the U.S. quota to each of five main groups. In 1996, "general-category" fishermen like Jeffrey Hutchins, who caught the fish using handlines or rod and reel, were given the largest share, about 41 percent (541 metric tons) of the total.

The 1995 season had been a mixed blessing. The money was good—prices at the Yankee Fishermen's Co-Op in Seabrook, New Hampshire, had averaged $17.26 per pound for the 132 fish landed during the month of July. The exchange rate with the Japanese yen was favorable, good-quality bluefin were landed, and the fish seemed plentiful. While ICCAT and NMFS argued that the bluefin population was declining, the East Coast Tuna Association paid for aerial surveys showing that the population was more than four times larger than government scientists believed. The general-category fishery, which opened on June 1, 1995, closed abruptly on September 12 because fishermen caught the quota faster than NMFS had expected and exceeded it by 112 tons. Many fishermen feared that NMFS would respond with a smaller quota for the 1996 season.

By June 1996, general-category tuna fishermen, many of them full-time commercial fishermen like Jeffrey Hutchins who relied on tuna as a critical part of their livelihood, were seeing threats everywhere. Overfishing in the eastern Atlantic and Mediterranean might deplete the overall resource; mismanagement of the recreational angling category would unfairly jeopardize the U.S. quota; increasing pressure from North and South Carolina fishermen to let them in on the fishery that had popped up off their coast could lead to too many fishermen chasing a limited allotment of fish; and lobbying by environmental groups, who insisted the bluefin population was in dire straits, could bolster NMFS efforts to cut quotas further. Internationally, nations were divided on who should catch how many tuna; at home, various user groups within the fishery waged bitter fights against NMFS and each other to win a larger share.

The profitable seasons of the early 1990s had not gone unnoticed. More and more fishermen were entering the fishery despite the fact that only a small percentage of permit holders actually caught a tuna. Just one good tuna, worth maybe $5,000 or so, would pay for the countless gallons of fuel, boxes of herring, spools of monofilament, and expensive tackle purchased in the hope of a big score, like the lucky fisherman who, in 1991, sold a single 708-pound bluefin for $68,503, or $96.65 per pound. With so many fishermen playing this bluefin lottery, the tuna fleet stretching along the coast of New England in early September 1996 was larger than it had ever been.

Because there were so many general-category boats vying for so small a quota, further management measures were implemented to prolong the season. The best-quality fish, bringing in the biggest bucks, were known to arrive off New England in September and October. To ensure that the quota wasn't eaten up before then, NMFS in 1996, as it had in 1995, issued the same mandatory days off from fishing—Sunday, Monday, and Tuesday—and further divided the 541-metric-ton quota into monthly subquotas. Once the quota for a month was filled, or reported landings suggested it would be filled soon, NMFS would shut down the fishery for the month, sometimes with as little as twenty-four hours' notice. In August 1996, the fishery shut down after nine fishing days, opening again on Sunday, September 1.

LIKE MOST GENERAL-CATEGORY TUNA FISHERMEN, Jeffrey Hutchins knew that in this derby-style fishery—in which the legal fishing days were decided months ahead of time and no allowance was made for dangerous weather or sea conditions—he had to fish hard every day that first week of September 1996. Derby-style fishing made an already-dangerous profession even more perilous, forcing tuna fishermen to take additional risks. Some fishermen left the dock early in the morning or slept overnight on the fishing grounds; some fished right through the weekend's Hurricane Edouard, which had kicked up fifteen-foot swells. Every decision about every fishing day that first week in September had to be weighed carefully. If Hutchins didn't catch a fish or two quickly, he could be shut out for the rest of the year, and who could be sure what the fishery might offer next year? (As it turned out, NMFS closed the fishery on September 9 after just six days of fishing.)

Hutchins had fished every day that week. On Monday, September 2, he anchored on a part of Jeffreys Ledge known as the Second Island, about twenty miles east of the *Heather Lynne II*'s homeport in the Merrimack River. He noted in his log that a friend had caught a fish there the day before and that Sunday evening, as Hurricane Edouard passed off the coast of Nantucket on an easterly course, weather forecasters had predicted northeast winds gusting to ninety knots and large swells. Before leaving that Monday morning, Hutchins's deckhand, Jimmy Bashaw, had told his wife, "You'll probably see us all over the news." While at anchor, Hutchins watched the fish-finder and noted in his log what was going on beneath him. He had blue dogs—blue sharks measuring about ten feet long or less—"big time" around the boat. He started marking tuna at 11:15 A.M., and every five to ten minutes marked them again 19 to 24 fathoms below the boat. At least a dozen fish, or maybe the same two or three, made several passes beneath him. He must have sensed that any second a line might go off. At about 12:10 the marks on the fish-finder started to disperse. He marked tuna off and on for the next half hour, and then they were gone. Monday night, tied up back at the dock, Hutchins, John Michael Lowther, and a few friends sat around the boat and shared some Miller Lites. At 12:22 A.M. someone ordered a Domino's pizza.

On Tuesday, a no-fish day in the tuna fishery, he took the boat to the far northern end of Jeffreys Ledge to gillnet for herring to use as tuna bait for the next few days. He made and received fourteen cell phone calls in the course of twelve hours; the last call he placed Tuesday was at 7:39 P.M. to Concord, New Hampshire, to ask his friend Kevin Foster to fish with him the rest of the week. A deckhand, dissatisfied with what Hutchins paid him, had quit and left Hutchins shorthanded. Hutchins spent Tuesday night at sea and by 6:03 A.M. Wednesday had called the home of Bob Campbell, manager of the Tri-Coastal Seafood Co-Operative, to report that he was on his way home with a tuna on board. By ten o'clock in the morning he had docked in Newburyport and sold his 591-pound bluefin to the highest bidder. John Frawley, aboard the *Blue Heron*, was tied up nearby with his own tuna on board, and he and Hutchins engaged in the congenial banter of a successful day.

After his crew helped his sister, Jennifer, load groceries for the next three days—all open tuna days—Hutchins moved the *Heather Lynne II* across the Merrimack River to her slip at Salisbury's Bridge Marina. On his way home he stopped at the Neptune Veteran Firemen's Association with his crew for a beer. They laughed and joked about the fish they had caught and shared the tale of its capture with the bartender and a fellow patron. When the bartender offered Hutchins a second beer, he said, "Nope. We're heading out early."

At 7:15 P.M. Wednesday, just before going to bed, Hutchins had to decide where to fish the next day. He dialed the cell phone aboard the

Retriever and talked to his boss, Ted Rurak, owner of the *Heather Lynne II*. Rurak reported to Hutchins that he had just started home from a spot on the southern end of Jeffreys Ledge where he'd seen a few tuna boated (including the one landed by Richard Burgess aboard the *Scotia Boat Too* just after 4 P.M.). Rurak said that might be a good place for Hutchins to start in the morning, adding that it was 21.45 miles from the Merrimack River entrance. Hutchins said he'd have to figure out what time to leave in the morning to get there before daylight. If he left his dock at about 2 A.M., traveled three miles against the flooding tide downriver, cleared the jetties, and set his boat's engine running at about nine knots, he'd arrive in the area just before 5 A.M. He'd have a good hour before the 6 A.M. tide change and the 6:14 sunrise to set out his bait nets—to catch some live bait—cut up a bucket of chum, and anchor in a good spot before the tuna fleet filled in. Without mentioning how many deckhands he'd have on board or who they would be, Hutchins told Rurak he'd probably head that way in the morning.

Just to be sure it was his best bet, Hutchins also called the cell phone aboard the *Jan Ann* and reached his friend Dean Holt. Hutchins trusted Holt's opinion. They had both attended Newburyport High School, where Hutchins graduated in 1984.

NEWBURYPORT NESTLES along the southern bank of the Merrimack River, which flows 177 miles from its headwaters in the White Mountains of New Hampshire to meet the Gulf of Maine just three miles east of town. Once home to the Pawtucket Indians, Newbury, as it was first known, became a bustling seaport after its settlement by European immigrants in 1630. Shipyards cropped up along the shore, and ships built there went fishing as far away as the Grand Banks and Labrador or participated in the rum and spice trade with the West Indies. In a book of local reminiscences from older residents, Sarah E. Mulliken noted, "Those were the days when our town had more distilleries and churches than any other community in the commonwealth." After a catastrophic fire in 1811, the downtown was rebuilt of brick—no building more than three stories high—that had been used as ballast in ships returning light of cargo from Asia.

During the American Revolution and through the War of 1812,

Newburyport privateers were licensed to attack British merchant ships wherever they met them. Just before the Revolution, local seafarers sank pilings in the Merrimack River channel to endanger enemy ships. A small boat stood by at all hours to pilot friends through. One captain, Offin Boardman, used to venture out through the river entrance and fool ships loaded with supplies for the British army into thinking this was Boston Harbor. When a British ship allowed itself to be piloted into the harbor, Newburyport privateers captured it.

The city considered itself the birthplace of the clipper ships, 317 of which were built along the Merrimack River between 1831 and 1883. One of the most famous, the 212-foot *Dreadnought*, was launched on October 6, 1853, with a red cross painted on her foretopsail. Built for the governor of New York for trade between Liverpool and New York, she made the transatlantic trip in a record time of nine days and thirteen hours, earning the sobriquets "Wild Boat of the Atlantic" and "The Flying Dutchman." Her captain, Samuel Samuels, was so certain of her speed that he guaranteed delivery dates, a practice to which few other captains submitted.

Minnie Atkinson, another local author, wrote that Newburyport during the nineteenth century smelled of a salty east wind blowing "odors of tea and molasses, of spice and rum, of oakum and new lumber, of bales of Indian cotton and French silks, of brandy and wine, of tar and brown sugar, of coffee and salt—the blended odors of merchandise from all the world." By 1880, more than 1,600 vessels large enough to be used for foreign trade, as well as numerous small craft, had been built on the Merrimack River.

With so many ships setting sail, it was inevitable that some would not return. The town was filled with widows and fatherless children. Young boys who had learned geography by following the courses of their fathers' ships often put to sea themselves. Meanwhile, one orphanage in town was nearly filled with daughters of lost sailors. Despite losing so many seamen—after one such loss, a memorial service drew 2,500 mourners—the city had never erected a seafarers' memorial. Small tablets were placed in churches and cemeteries for a few lost ships and crews, but no one created a monument dedicated to all the sailors who had left the Merrimack River to die at sea.

By 1996, the seafaring town had gentrified into a marvel of urban renewal and attracted many tourists who browsed the shops along State Street and dined in local seafood restaurants. Staying at one of the handful of federal-style sea captains' homes that had been turned into inns, visitors might learn that George Washington slept in what was now the library (also visited by John Quincy Adams, Benedict Arnold, and Aaron Burr) in late October 1789; that President William McKinley's wife, Ida, danced at the 1897 inaugural ball wearing silk slippers made for her by the Newburyport Shoe Company, one of eighteen shoe manufacturers then in town; that Ben Franklin came to town to examine the spire atop a meetinghouse that had been struck by lightning; that Newburyport patriot Eleazar Johnson organized a "tea party" in Market Square in March 1773, nine months before the Boston Tea Party; or that the bell rung at the Old South Church—at which a sea captain once sat at the head of every pew—was made by Paul Revere. Visitors could walk down a cobblestone street and make their way to the waterfront lined with pleasure boats and sailboats, a few deep-sea passenger fishing boats, a whale-watch boat, and a harbor tour boat. If they looked hard enough, they might spot one of the town's nine commercial fishing boats, including the *Heather Lynne II*, scattered across the wharves.

The city by 1996 was beginning to fill with Boston commuters, who were driving up real-estate prices and displacing long-time residents. Starbucks had not yet come to town, though, nor had the upscale restaurant Black Cow yet replaced the more casual, walk-into-the-bar-with-your-fishing-boots-on Captain's Quarters. The fishing community in Newburyport remained small and tightly knit, and unless you knew someone personally, you might not have paid much attention to the draggers and gillnetters and the men who worked them.

As FORMER CLASSMATES at Newburyport High and members of this small fishing community, Jeffrey Hutchins and Dean Holt's paths often crossed, so it was natural that they would be working together eleven years later, through the summer and into the fall of 1995, as co-captains of the *Heather Lynne II*. A few hours after he and Holt had tied up the boat for the day on Friday, October 13, however, Hutchins had found himself rolling across highway asphalt after an accident with his 1995 Fat Boy Harley-Davidson, license plate "H-Dog." He broke his left foot and sprained his right ankle, but he felt lucky to have escaped worse. He mentioned this to his sister Jennifer one afternoon as she wrapped his ankle. He remembered that a substitute teacher had once read his palm and told him, "You'll die in a tragic accident when you're thirty." He would turn thirty on April 30, 1996, just a few short months away—her words echoed in his memory. He told Jennifer he was grateful to be alive, even if it meant not going fishing for a few months.

His accident didn't stop him from deer hunting that November with a group of older men who called him "Hutch Dog" because he was so good at tracking deer. With his leg in a cast, he made himself a special pair of boots with his toes sticking out. His friends would carry him through the woods and he would sit on a plastic bucket, waiting for a deer to cross his path.

"He killed more deer then than ever," remembered Jim Bashaw, who often went fishing with him. "He was a hard man. He'd sit there and just freeze, but he wouldn't move."

By February 1996 Hutchins was ready to go fishing again, despite the fact that his ankles still bothered him after he had been standing on a hard deck for long hours. A few months later, Holt left the *Heather Lynne II*. Two captains working one boat was like too many cooks in the kitchen. They remained friends, however, and on the telephone that Wednesday evening, September 4, Holt told Hutchins that he planned to spend the night at anchor close by the coordinates Rurak had given Hutchins, a small edge of southern Jeffreys Ledge just ten miles off the coast of Cape Ann. Holt confirmed that it looked like a good bet for the next day. Before he hung up, Hutchins told Holt, "Well, we'll see you out there."

Just after eight o'clock, Hutchins's mother called him. Jennifer answered the telephone and said that her brother had already gone to bed. Their mother told Jennifer not to wake him; she would talk to him in the morning.

FAMILY MEMBERS KNEW young Hutchins wanted to be a fisherman when, at eight years old, he drew crayon seascapes. On one he wrote in bold, misspelled letters that he hoped to grow up to be a fisherman who sailed the seas and caught tuna. At about the same time, his parents divorced. He sought to fill his father's absence by becoming the family's spark plug, the one who took care of his mother and assumed a fathering role to his younger sisters. When Jennifer needed a place to live, he invited her to share his home. He would say that someday he wanted a hundred kids of his own. In the meantime, he played with his nieces and nephews and posted their pictures near the helm in his wheelhouse.

Hutchins earned money during high school digging steamer clams from local mudflats, then steered a straight course to sea following graduation. In the spring of 1985 he traveled to Florida and took a three-month Professional Mariner Training course at the Chapman School of Seamanship, in which he learned about the nautical rules of the road, piloting and coastal navigation, safety, weather, first aid, and boat handling and maintenance. He returned home ready for a job on a commercial fishing boat, so his father took him to the Boston Fish Pier, where they found the swordfishing boat *Terri Lei* unloading her catch. Hutchins introduced himself and was hired. His first trip took him off the coast of Newfoundland, where during the summer of 1985 and into 1986 he went longlining for swordfish on thirty-day trips. In his first six months, with a 9 percent cut of the profits, he made between $25,000 and $30,000.

Nelson Beideman, owner and captain of the *Terri Lei*, would sometimes invite young Hutchins, whom he nicknamed "the clammer," to fly home with him to New Jersey from Newfoundland. Beideman was well known and well liked in the commercial fishing community. A graduate of the Maine Maritime Academy with thirty-three years at sea, he served as president and later as executive director of the Blue Water Fishermen's Association, based in Barnegat Light, New Jersey. On behalf of the association's more than 250 fishermen, buyers, and processors of highly migratory species like tuna and swordfish, Beideman often testified before Congress, was quoted in the press, and attended regulatory meetings to advocate for the longliners. In 2001 he would serve on the advisory committee to ICCAT. He was a good man for a young fisherman to know.

Beideman knew right away that Hutchins loved fishing and was a fast learner. It was only a matter of time before this nineteen-year-old novice fisherman would captain his own boat. Although it came as no surprise when Hutchins later told Beideman he was leaving to work on a smaller boat that fished waters closer to home, Beideman was disappointed to see him go.

"We liked him a lot," Beideman said, pausing in thought. "He was a good kid when he was here, a hard-working straight shooter. He was a tremendous fisherman."

Hutchins left the *Terri Lei* to learn how to gillnet aboard the *Barbara & Lynn*, a boat based in Newburyport. By then he had learned how to open his own doors and find opportunities to apprentice under the area's best fishermen. Within ten years he had established a reputation as one of the best fishermen on the northeast coast, a highliner, someone who knew how to put fish in a boat. A common aphorism is that ninety percent of the fish are caught by ten percent of the fishermen, and by 1996 Hutchins was without dispute among the top ten percent. Many people said that any boatowner would gladly have hired him to run a boat. His father claims that Hutchins even held the Newburyport record for bringing in the most fish in one trip: 42,000 pounds of cod and haddock. The *Heather Lynne II* under his command was one of two boats that sustained the local seafood co-op through the winter. As captain, he took his job seriously.

"The biggest thing is responsibility," he once said. "Just a lot more responsibilities. Finding the fish. Got to get everybody a pay check."

Hutchins was a hard worker, and he also liked to play hard. His mother and sisters liked it when he went to sea because there, they figured, he could stay out of trouble. At sea, he was safe. He liked to drink Miller Lite, sometimes drinking a six-pack in one night and sometimes not drinking any alcohol for a week or more, depending on what he was up to. He loved to surround himself with friends; his closest friends said they could talk about him for days and never tell the same story twice. And he loved to host impromptu parties at his new house, which was built with plenty of windows to watch deer in his backyard.

Hutchins had spent a lot of time planning that house. He bought the land abutting a state forest in his hometown of Byfield, Massachusetts, for $69,000 in 1991, when he was twenty-four years old. Then, working entirely as a commercial fisherman, he saved enough money to build himself a $200,000 home in the summer of 1994. He had also wanted to build himself a boat, and he couldn't decide which to build first. Friends encouraged him to build the house; he could build a boat later.

"He had his goals and he met them," Dean Holt said. "He wanted to build that house, and he did."

In 1996 he still had a few unattained goals. He had always wanted to go salmon fishing in Alaska and had begun talking with an Alaskan boat-owner over the summer. Hutchins said he would go only if he could be the captain and earn his requested percentage of the profits. That was his offer, take it or leave it. In the meantime, he was content to fish his home waters. He also wanted to start a family. He hadn't been quite as lucky dating as he had been fishing and hunting, but things were looking up. He had been seeing Jeanne Huberdeau, a local independent landscaper, for almost two years. Stray pieces of his life were starting to come together.

WHILE HUTCHINS WAS FISHING in the Gulf of Maine, his first boat, Beideman's *Terri Lei*, was lost at sea on a swordfishing trip ninety miles off the coast of South Carolina. She was under the command of a relief captain from Massachusetts, thirty-four-year-old Adam Randall, who two years earlier had planned to go fishing on board the *Andrea Gail*, but changed his mind when he pulled into the fish pier. That decision saved his life—the *Andrea Gail* was lost a few weeks later during what became known as "the perfect storm." But Randall's luck did not last.

On the morning of April 7, 1993, searchers, alerted to the *Terri Lei*'s distress by an activated EPIRB, found nothing but a debris field that included a life raft with no survivors on board (and no evidence they had ever been on board), orange longline buoys (found upwind of the first EPIRB signal location), a wood drawer with chrome handles, a longline tackle box, a notebook, white plastic cups, a hat, milk crates, bait baskets, a package of hot dogs, and a funnel.

Speculation surfaced that she had been rammed by the passing 666-foot container ship *Edyth L*, but the evidence was inconclusive. Following an investigation, the Coast Guard could only surmise that what happened to the crew of the *Terri Lei* must have been quick and traumatic. There were no distress calls, and no survivors were found, even though all four crew were good swimmers and had survival suits and the life raft had floated free. Beideman believed the *Edyth L* had collided with his *Terri Lei*, but he couldn't prove it. What he did know is that other fishing boats had collided with merchant ships in the past, accidents that he figured "happen a bit too often."

Hutchins was aware of the inherent risk of collision at sea. His crew knew that whenever they were on watch, above all else they were to pay attention to boats around them and notify Hutchins if they were ever unsure of a developing situation. Friends said he often talked about tugs and barges and that colliding with them was what he feared most. He would say that many boats lost at sea without a trace had likely been run over by a tug and barge that just kept on steaming and didn't know, or didn't care, what they had hit. Tugs and barges and merchant ships were on tight schedules, and so were fishermen, who had to make the most of every day and who worked wherever bottom depths, water temperatures, and the whims of fish dictated. As one fisherman, who himself narrowly escaped a collision in July 1998, reported in a Coast Guard journal of safety at sea, altering course could put merchant ships behind schedule and therefore, "This becomes an issue of safety versus schedules, in which safety is often compromised." Hutchins figured there were probably a lot of boats sitting on the ocean bottom because of unreported collisions. Boats disappeared and it was just not mentioned or was written off as a storm, but they probably got run down and sank within seconds. No one knew what happened except, maybe, the dead fishermen.

And dead men don't talk.

Dressed for tuna fishing in the early hours of September 5, Hutchins left his girlfriend, Jeanne Huberdeau, asleep in his bed and went downstairs to wake thirty-eight-year-old Kevin Foster, who was asleep on the couch. Foster had spent part of the night trying to contact his girlfriend, Beth, back home in Pembroke, New Hampshire. She had said she didn't want him to go fishing on this trip. He told her he had agreed to go fishing one last time to help out his friend Hutch.

Foster was from a small town near Concord, New Hampshire, where he had lived with his father, a cabinetmaker and owner of a trailer park, ever since his parents divorced when he was fifteen years old. His two sisters had moved out to live with his mother. A mild-mannered man with a large upper body and belly, he often wore jeans and sweatshirts with cut-off sleeves. In family photographs he had a bushy brown beard, a wispy mustache, and a hat to cover his thinning brown hair. He had an electric twinkle in his eyes.

Foster had met Hutchins in 1989 while Hutchins was running the *Ann Marie*, a gillnetter out of Portsmouth, New Hampshire, owned by

Foster's brother-in-law, Steve Lord, and named after his wife, Foster's sister Ann. The *Ann Marie* was built within a year after Lord's 42-foot gillnetter *Karie Ann Nicole* sank on May 4, 1987, 57 miles east of Gloucester. The crew of the *Heather Lynne II*, fishing nearby, had rescued her adrift crew.

Over the course of five years aboard the *Ann Marie*, Hutchins and Foster developed a solid friendship filled with practical jokes. Both men liked to laugh and they liked to eat. Foster knew that whenever he napped at sea, Hutchins would rummage through his lunch bag and eat whatever he liked. He did it in part because he knew it annoyed Foster. One day, Foster decided to get even. He asked his sister Ann, who made his lunches for him whenever he stayed at her house, to make a tuna sandwich out of cat food. Thinking that was a little too mean, she resisted. Instead, she and Foster bought some beef jerky dog treats and put them in a plastic bag. Later that morning, Foster made a point of telling Hutchins about his special snack. Ann remembered, "He told Hutch, 'Now look, I've got some homemade beef jerky in my lunch, so don't you go near it.' " Foster knew this would spur Hutchins to dive in. When he woke up from a nap, Hutchins had eaten his "beef jerky" but said it was a little dry. The crew called Hutchins "Scooby Doo" for the rest of the day. Of course Foster knew there would be a payback, like dog crap smeared under his truck door handles, or worse. It was only a matter of time.

Foster was eight years older than Hutchins, but he didn't mind letting Hutchins be responsible for finding the fish and taking care of the boat. Foster was happy to be crew. Ann described him as a "wimp at heart," someone who hated the inherent dangers of fishing, wouldn't take unnecessary risks, and would always speak up when a perplexing situation confronted him. When he lost his driver's license after driving while intoxicated, he didn't bother to get it back (Hutchins had also once lost his for the same reason but did get it back). Foster's friends didn't mind driving him around. Although he preferred backstage to center stage, he stood out as a friendly guy who enjoyed making people laugh. He should have been a comedian, friends said, not a fisherman.

On board the *Ann Marie*, Foster took pride in stacking the fish and icing them down in a special way that he was sure would fetch them a better price at the dock, where, after a good trip, they would come in with a load of fish that sank the stern below its painted waterline. Foster enjoyed watching the sun set at sea, and he liked being outdoors, but fishing wasn't the work he loved. What he loved was stacking wood, clearing land, cutting logs, making woodpiles, and burning brush. He loved fire so much that his sister Ann would name her golden retriever "Pyro" after him. He liked to stand back at the end of the day and look at the wood he'd stacked, feeling a great sense of accomplishment. After going fishing this one last September day with Hutchins aboard the *Heather Lynne II*, Foster planned to return to Concord, marry his fiancée, and sell firewood.

Foster sometimes accompanied Hutchins on hunting trips for rabbits, turkey, or deer with a group of men who had taken Hutchins under their wing. Hungering for father figures in his life, Hutchins had gravitated to these older Byfield men, who at first saw him as a young kid they didn't want anything to do with. But it wasn't long before they grew to love him.

"We really didn't want any newcomers," Dave Morse, one of his older Byfield friends, remembered. "But we got to know him and said, 'oh, all right.' And then he became like a son to me. I'd come home and there'd be no one here until I walked into the house and saw Hutch with his head in the fridge looking for something to eat."

Late at night, his Byfield friends would hear Hutchins holler to them through the still night air as he roared by on his Fat Boy. Then he'd slow down, turn up his driveway, open the sliding glass door, and drive into his basement. When the night fell silent, they would know he was home safe in his new house anchored by a grand stone chimney and cocooned by leafy maples, tall pines, and a broad lawn, in the corner of which he kept a few chickens in a small cage.

ON THE MORNING OF SEPTEMBER 5, 1996, Hutchins and Foster left the house a little before 2 A.M. and climbed into Hutchins's 1987 blue-and-white Ford pickup. Hutchins forgot the truck keys and had locked himself out of the house. Standing under the stars, he knocked softly on the glass-panel door. Huberdeau walked over to the second-floor bedroom window.

"I forgot my keys," Hutchins whispered.

"I'll be right down," Huberdeau said. She came downstairs and handed the keys to him. He thanked her, gave her a quick kiss good-bye, and turned to walk to his truck. After a few steps, Hutchins turned, looked back at Huberdeau and asked, "Can you feed my chickens?"

Hutchins joined Foster in the truck and drove down the tree-lined gravel driveway of his home. He turned left onto Forest Street and followed the winding road until it reached Main Street, where he again turned left and drove through rural Byfield toward the waiting *Heather Lynne II*. His truck had a rattle in the rear axle and, if his friends were awake, they would hear him headed down the paved street as it became Scotland Road, under Interstate 95, past the state police barracks on his left, past the Colby pig farm, through the industrial park until he came to Low Street, where he would take a right and then, at the lights, turn left onto U.S. Route 1 and travel north over the Merrimack River on the Andrew J. Gillis Bridge, which connects Newburyport to Salisbury. Hutchins probably looked east toward the mouth of the river for running lights signifying boats on the move. The orange glow of lights on the central waterfront cast a shadow over the boats moored in the still harbor. He turned right at the bottom of the bridge and into the parking lot of Bridge Marina, where he found his *Heather Lynne II* ready for another day at sea in search of a giant bluefin.

Hutchins and Foster walked across the long wooden pier, down a ramp, and onto the dock where the dark green-and-white *Heather Lynne II* was tied. She was a pretty boat, custom-built in 1987 by Atkinson Boatbuilders in Clarks Harbor, Nova Scotia. According to a marine surveyor who examined her in the spring of 1995, her replacement cost was at least $200,000. Her fiberglass hull was a typical Novi design, with a proud stem rising straight up from the water, pronounced bow flare, and a deep keel. She was 45 feet long, 17 feet across, and drew 5½ feet of water. She was a rugged boat that barely twitched when someone stepped onto her deck, which was built of two layers of ¾-inch plywood. Standing on her deck felt like standing on a battleship, as if she were ready to face whatever the sea could throw her way and didn't plan on losing.

"It was *not* a boat you weren't comfortable on," Hutchins's sometime deckhand Jim Bashaw said, "or I wouldn't have been on it."

Those who fished the *Heather Lynne II* said she was indestructible. Dean Holt remembered the winter day he fished aboard her ninety miles offshore in the worst seas he'd ever encountered. During the long, slow, pounding ride home against a raging northwest wind, her through-hull fittings bounced loose, debris in the engine's dry exhaust pipe was pummeled to powder, zinc anodes were shaken free and dangled from her hull, and fish-finder transducers were dislodged to hang by their sensor wires. The boat was sinking with a load of fish on board—but not enough to make the beating worth it—as she headed toward the Merrimack River. Despite the rising doubt among the crew, who had their survival suits within arm's reach and thought the breaking waves might tear the deckhouse right off, she made it home safely. The *Heather Lynne II* also survived not one but two fires on board. Though she had an unlucky history, she could catch fish, keep her crew safe, and find her way home.

To get on board, Hutchins and Foster had to step over the 27-inch-high bulwark and walk forward past the starboard aft steering station and nearby 4-foot-wide wooden bin that held a hundred 6-inch-mesh gillnets (she also had four 2½-inch-mesh bait nets on board). Behind them was the work deck, beneath which was a hold big enough for twenty tons of fish and four or five tons of ice. Ahead of them was the pilothouse; if its wooden door were closed, it would take two hands and some oomph to slide it open. The interior of the pilothouse was painted white with oak trim. The deck was carpeted to cut down on noise from the boat's generator and single Caterpillar 3406 Turbo engine, which turned a 3-inch shaft and an extra-large 40-by-30-inch four-bladed bronze propeller. The engine had been rebuilt just four months earlier—it had 8,519 hours on it —and ran well that summer; the only mechanical problems they had from time to time were blown hydraulic hoses connected to the steering, but these had just been replaced. Inside the pilothouse with the engine running, it was fairly quiet, and the crew could talk in normal speaking voices.

Before getting underway, Hutchins and Foster might have descended the four wooden steps that led below to a forward cabin with a carpeted sole, white painted walls, and oak trim. She had two oak bunks on each side—Hutchins claimed the lower starboard bunk as his own. Overhead, a 2-by-2-foot Lexan escape hatch, like a tinted skylight, let in fresh air when opened. The head was to starboard and the galley counter was to port; it included a microwave, a coffeemaker, a sink, and a cell phone. A stove was mounted against the aft wall a little to starboard. Most striking was the headroom. A six-foot person could stand there comfortably and not worry about bumping his head.

Back at the helm on the starboard side of the pilothouse, or wheelhouse, Hutchins could look out of the five half-inch-thick, brown-tinted Lexan windows that spanned the front. The windows were virtually bulletproof, built to withstand a heavy sea. Instead of a windshield wiper, the window in front of the helm carried an inlaid rotor that would spin to shed spray, offering a clear view even when heavy seas were shipping over the bow. On the dashboard around him, Hutchins had at his fingertips a full complement of navigation and fishing equipment: two compasses, a clock, a Koden color fish-finder, a radar, two Loran-C units for navigation (but no GPS, which was still a relatively new technology), two VHF radios, a single-sideband radio, a cell phone, and an autopilot. There were also some creature comforts at hand: a refrigerator, a 21-inch color television with a VCR, and a cushioned helm chair. For safety gear, the crew could access a flare kit, a four-man inflatable life raft mounted on the pilothouse roof, an EPIRB, a 30-inch life ring, four survival suits, four life jackets, a first-aid kit, and six dry-chemical fire extinguishers. On the roof was a 9-foot-tall mast to which were welded two radar reflectors; more radar reflectors were attached to the gillnet buoys standing on the aft deck. The boat could carry plenty of fuel for long trips offshore: there was a 350-gallon tank on each side and a third 250-gallon tank in the lazarette, the aftermost compartment on the boat, although it was usually empty.

Hutchins probably started up the generator so he could turn on the running lights and several of the *Heather Lynne II*'s seven spotlights before leaving the dock. Four halogen spotlights lit up the work area of the deck, spanning the center of the boat behind the pilothouse, where they picked fish out of the gillnets. Two more spotlights illuminated the stern, and another, mounted by the hauling and steering station on the starboard side, could light up the water when they hauled in gillnets over a 24-inch-diameter stainless steel hydraulic net lifter. Fishermen aboard other boats could recognize the *Heather Lynne II* instantly at a distance because she was always lit up like a Christmas tree. All these lights, which some said were always kept on partly to maintain a base load on the generator (which was needed periodically for other purposes), also made her easy to spot at night, but her small red and green running lights could be less easily distinguished in the glow. While an observer on any nearby boat could see her, he might not be able to determine quickly in what direction she was headed or what she was doing.

As Hutchins eased the *Heather Lynne II* out of her slip, through a field of moored boats, past the silent waterfront of downtown Newburyport, and down the Merrimack River, it was just after 2 A.M. When he passed by the stone jetties and tolling red number 2 bell buoy, he probably had the boat cruising along at about nine knots. He likely set a course of 105 degrees, turned on the autopilot, and said, "I'm going to bed." Foster may already have been asleep in one of the upper bunks below. Hutchins would have retired to his lower starboard bunk where he would try to catch a little more sleep before turning out once they were a few miles from their destination. In the meantime, he would leave the helm to his first mate, John Michael Lowther, who sat in the dark brown cushioned chair and watched the black night smother the lights of Newburyport, and home, on the horizon behind them.

A FEW HOURS EARLIER, twenty-seven-year-old John Michael Lowther had walked into the kitchen of his grandparents' Newburyport home, where he ate all but two doughnuts from a full box. He was a big guy with a boyish face—dark brown eyes, short brown hair, a thin mustache, short stubble beard, and a charming smile. A tattoo of a grizzly bear standing on its haunches spanned his right arm from elbow to shoulder. He told his aunt it gave him courage.

Knocking on his grandparents' bedroom door, he found his grandmother sleeping while his seventy-four-year-old grandfather, John Lowther, watched a John Wayne movie. John Lowther saw himself and his grandson in John Wayne, someone who was straightforward and plain-spoken. The elder Lowther had collected 182 John Wayne videos—almost every movie Wayne ever starred in—some of which the younger Lowther would put into a Ziploc bag and take with him aboard the *Heather Lynne II*. When he returned early from tuna fishing on Wednesday, September 4, Lowther had brought some of these videos home because the VCR on the boat wasn't working.

Now, standing in the bedroom doorway, John Michael asked his grandfather for a ride to the boat.

"At what time?" his grandfather asked.

"We have to be there at two," John Michael said.

"Well, I don't really want to stay up that late," his grandfather said.

"How about I take you now and you can sleep on the boat tonight?"

They climbed inside John Lowther's blue Ford Crown Victoria, which had a bumper sticker that he figured summed up his life's history: "Been there, done that." The elder Lowther usually wore a blue long-sleeved cotton shirt buttoned to the top, blue cotton Dickies, a wide brown belt, two pens in his left breast pocket and four in the right. On his hat was a dime-sized pin that said, "It's OK to say no." He had quit school in the eighth grade and landed his first job as a taxi driver when he was sixteen so that he could get his parents—his father had worked in a shoe factory—off welfare. He and Eleanor, married in 1952, had seven kids. In his lifetime as a cab driver and family man, he had delivered seven babies on his own, including one of his own children at home.

His grandson, John Michael, had lived with him ever since birth. John Michael's mother never told anyone who the father was. A few years later she had a daughter, whom she took with her when she moved out of her parents' home, leaving John Michael behind. John and Eleanor raised John Michael as if he were their own son. They took him to baseball games, and his grandfather coached his Little League team at Pioneer Park, where John Michael usually played catcher or center field.

Lowther, whose friends called him "Johnny" or "J'Mike" to distinguish him from his grandfather, graduated from Newburyport High School in 1988. At the time, his goal in life was to finish his term with the army—he had joined the local National Guard unit because he wanted to do something with his life—and then move to Hawaii. He was proud of the National Guard and often wore his uniform even when he didn't have to. Friends would tease him by calling him "G.I. J'Mike."

When he wasn't performing National Guard duties, he worked odd jobs, often in the kitchens of local restaurants or unloading fish at the local seafood co-op. One day after high school he went fishing with his friend Dean Holt. He liked the lifestyle, the sea, and the money he could make, and Holt liked having him on board.

"He had what it takes," Holt said. "When you get someone new, you can tell whether they have it or they don't pretty quickly, and he looked like he was going to make it. He got sick the first few times, but he stuck with it."

John Michael told his grandparents that he was going fishing to earn some money for them. He wanted to buy books for his cousin's college courses. He told his grandmother, "I gotta fish because you and Papa need my help. I'm here to help." She told him that eventually he would get married and have a family of his own, and he shouldn't worry about his grandparents. He told her he didn't plan on getting married for a long time. He just wanted to fish, enjoy life, and do whatever came along.

John Michael wanted to help others, like the time he helped a neighbor push a couch through a window or stopped to help a woman who had just been in a car accident. Like Foster and Hutchins, he loved to laugh, too. He often had a smile, a wave, and maybe a wisecrack.

"If something bad happened, he'd laugh about it," his grandfather remembered. "That was his way of dealing with sad times."

Lowther loved the sea and would rather be offshore on extended trips than on land, where, after a few days, he'd get restless. Maybe that's why he'd received fifteen speeding tickets. At sea, his family understood, he could relax and be himself and make a good day's pay. Lowther tagged along with Holt and worked on the two boats in the Merrimack River that caught the most fish, the *Sara Jean* and the *Heather Lynne II*. They went out the farthest, stayed out the longest, and came back the fullest. And Lowther didn't mind doing his share of the work.

"Johnny was a good worker," said Ric Littlefield, owner of the *Sara Jean*. "He was always there when you needed him."

Of course, Lowther had moments when he questioned whether this was the career for him, like the time he was gillnetting on the northeastern part of Jeffreys Ledge, a good forty-five or fifty miles from home, in howling wind and heavy seas. He called his grandfather on the cell phone and said "Papa, I want to come home." That was the trip that taught him to respect the sea, and it will respect you. Once he lived through that, he figured he could live through anything.

He called home on good tuna days, too.

"Everytime he got a fish, he called me," the elder Lowther said. "He'd say, 'Papa, I got a fish,' and through the static I'd say, 'what?' And he'd say, 'I got a fish' and I'd say, 'how big?' and he'd say, '500 and I'll be in in two hours.' "

Those were the calls his family liked.

The elder Lowther and his grandson drove now along Water Street and through downtown Newburyport, past the empty brick sidewalks illuminated by colonial-style streetlamps that cast an orange glow on the town. They crossed the bridge over the Merrimack River into Salisbury, turned into Bridge Marina, and headed toward the wooden pier. As he opened the car door and stepped out, John Michael said he hoped they would catch another fish. Then, before shutting the door, he looked his grandfather straight in the eye.

"The sea is not going to take me," John Michael said. "I drive too goddamn fast." His words caught his grandfather off guard. Uncertain how to respond, he smiled and mentioned the tuna John Michael and the *Heather Lynne II* crew had caught the day before.

"Your luck is with you," his grandfather said. "You've been doing good the last three years. What time do you think you'll be in?"

"I don't know," John Michael said. "If we get a fish, I'll give you a call."

"All right," the elder Lowther said as he watched his grandson start to walk away. "I'll see you later."

"Yes," John Michael said. "I'll see you soon."

John Lowther watched his grandson walk down to the empty *Heather Lynne II* and climb on board. He turned the car around and drove home. He began to cry as he crawled into bed. Eleanor asked what was wrong.

"John Michael just said something that hit me square between the eyes," he told her. "He said, 'The sea is not going to take me.' Now why would he say that?"

Recalling the conversation several years later, John Lowther figured his grandson must have had a reason for those parting words.

"People get a premonition, and that's not superstition, that's pure feeling. There's something about people who make a living on the sea that gives them premonitions people with a normal life like you or I don't have," he said. "They have an inkling that something is going to happen, and ninety percent of the time they're right. That man knew something was going to happen."

At 4:15 A.M., when the *Heather Lynne II* was just under six miles from her destination on southern Jeffreys Ledge, Rurak's deep gravelly voice boomed in over the VHF radio. Lowther answered right away. Rurak could hear a little engine noise in the background, but it was pretty quiet.

"Where's Jeff?" Rurak asked. "Sleeping?"

"Yes," Lowther said.

"Don't bother waking him up right now," Rurak said. "I'll talk to him later in the morning."

As a rule, Hutchins liked to be waked up once they were five to ten miles from their destination. Not long after talking to Rurak, Lowther would have had to wake up Hutchins and Foster so they could get their gear ready. They had four tuna rods on board; each was as thick and long as a broomstick and weighed about eighteen pounds. Onto a reel the size of a volleyball were spooled hundreds of feet of 300-pound-test monofilament line. A sharp Japanese-made hook was attached to the line with a plastic thimble and crimped metal sleeve. One rod and reel setup cost about $1,500; like most boats in the fleet, the *Heather Lynne II* often had at least four rods on board. Given the cost of the gear and the intense strain placed on it while fighting a bluefin, great care was taken to keep it in top-notch shape. The crew was careful not to step on the monofilament because one nick in the line could cause it to break off with a giant fish. Periodically they'd wind fresh monofilament onto the reels. Before setting the rods into stainless steel rod holders strategically bolted around the stern of the boat, they would check for wear and tear on each one. A small nylon safety line attached to the boat would be clipped to the reel to prevent it from falling over the side if a tuna struck.

When they reached the area where they planned to fish, they would look around for a school of herring and set at least one net to catch live bait, no matter how much dead herring they had on board. Then they'd find a spot to anchor, sit there for an hour or two, and then go back and haul the bait net. Because Hutchins had some bait on board he'd caught two days before, he would have Lowther or Foster cut some up into chum. Once back at anchor, they would stand by the starboard net hauler and throw the chum over the side in a steady stream. The anchor line would be attached to an orange ball so that if they hooked up on a bluefin they could slip the anchor by freeing the line from a midships cleat, then come back to it later. That way, they would be able to drive the boat so as to ease some of the strain of the fighting fish off the rod. On this morning, they had chum to cut, tackle to inspect, and bait nets to set before they could start fishing by sunrise, which would be at 6:14 A.M.

That was what the men were planning, but fate had other plans. Sometime just after 5 A.M., and about a mile northwest of the coordinates Rurak had given Hutchins the previous evening, the *Heather Lynne II* crossed paths with a tug and a barge.

The next time anyone talked to Lowther it was after 5:30 A.M., and he, along with Hutchins and Foster, was trapped inside the capsized *Heather Lynne II*. Minutes earlier a thick steel cable had sawed across the stem of the boat, wrenching her bow to starboard, then snapped up over her roof as it snaked past. The cable was shackled to a chain bridle that snagged the tall mast and antennas and plucked them from the roof. In the next instant the forward-sloping wall of a massive steel barge loomed over the port side and delivered a powerful blow, its impact crushing and tearing away a 3-foot-square section from the forward port corner of the pilothouse roof. Hitting the *Heather Lynne II* at nine or so knots, the 1,250-ton barge pushed the fishing boat sideways like a truck pushing a plow, at the same time rolling her down onto her starboard side. For a few heartbeats the *Heather Lynne II* was shoved deck first into the black sea, captive to the overriding steel wall above, water rushing at her under tons of pressure. Then, almost mercifully, she rolled further and was forced under the empty barge. Upside down, the *Heather Lynne II* bumped along under the flat steel bottom of a barge six times her length and four hundred times her weight as it passed overhead. Though the bottom of the barge was no more than three feet underwater, the fishing boat was probably forced down repeatedly as deep as ten feet before rising to be bumped again. At nine knots the 272-foot barge would have passed overhead in about fifteen seconds except that the *Heather Lynne II* was now moving in its direction, pulled along by the momentum of the initial blow and the suction that entrained her. At the same time the fishing boat was slowing the barge, prolonging her own imprisonment. It was probably at least thirty terrifying seconds, perhaps even a full minute, before the barge released the boat to its dwindling wake and slowed to a temporary drift not far away. More minutes passed before the *Heather Lynne II* resurfaced, upside down, several hundred feet from the point of first impact.

Now the men, if still conscious, found themselves blinded by total darkness. Sixty-four-degree seawater mixed with diesel fuel and dead herring flooded in like a tidal wave and shocked them into gasping for whatever air they could find in the dark. Buoyant gear like pillows, foam cushions, plastic cups, and wooden boards blocked air pockets, while heavy equipment like tools, fire extinguishers, and the stove in the cabin tumbled past and sank to the ceiling. The escape hatch now pointed straight down and was covered by five feet or more of foul water. The electrical system shorted out, and sparks and smoke shot through the boat. The 2-inch-thick wooden pilothouse door with its Lexan window was obstructed by an anchor chain that hung taut across it.

Even if they could have opened the pilothouse door, they probably would have feared the unknown hazards that awaited them on the other side. It would be just a few yards to the surface, but it would be risky. In underwater darkness they would have to navigate their way through dangling lines, chains, floating boards, plastic boxes, and a hundred gillnets. If they got stuck in a net, with no eyewear to help them see through the oily black water, with no air pocket to pause in, no confidence in their ability to swim, and no way of signaling for help, they would drown.

As the trapped men fought against a shrinking window of time and air, they may have heard the engine noises of approaching boats and the bubbling and hissing of air escaping from their own. But at least John Michael Lowther may have had hope. He could hear muffled voices shouting. He heard someone banging on the hull. As he banged back with his fist, he probably knew that three inches of rock-solid fiberglass separated him from his rescuers. He might have heard someone say the Coast Guard was coming. He might have heard someone say just hold on, it wouldn't be long before divers would come and get him out. He would have to do his best not to panic.

"He was upside down and it was dark," John Lowther, who had once suffered a panic attack, said of his grandson's peril. "The first thing that takes over is fear. There's no control over fear, and if things get progressively worse, then panic, and if panic sets in, you lose control of your faculties."

And then all you can do, trapped in the dark at 5:30 A.M. in fuel-filled cold water, is wait.

» *Codseeker*
May 9, 1877

H UNDREDS OF MILES to the east and 119 years earlier, two other fishermen found themselves similarly trapped in a capsized vessel, praying for help to arrive.

The 58-foot two-masted schooner *Codseeker* had been two days into her maiden voyage under the command of Captain Philip Brown and twelve crew before she foundered on shoal ground east of Cape Sable Island and southeast of Bacarro Light. Captain Brown, who had fished the Grand Banks for twenty-six years, had planned to take *Codseeker* from Halifax to his homeport of Barrington, Nova Scotia, where he would load bait before sailing out to the Grand Banks. *Codseeker* surged along on a west, southwesterly course with empty fishholds in the following seas of a northeasterly gale. Time after time, heaving swells picked up her starboard stern quarter and forced her bow to plunge down into the troughs. In the last hour of that stormy Wednesday, just a few miles from Barrington, one freak wave rolled *Codseeker* onto her side, and she stayed there. By midnight, she was swaying like a wooden half moon in sixty feet of icy water, half her decks awash, her keel facing the freshening wind.

Captain Brown found some of his men gathered at the stern, struggling to launch a boat that had been suspended over the transom. He saw that two of the four 14-foot dories stowed on deck amidships had washed away. The cook and a young sailor were trying to free one of the remaining dories, and Captain Brown helped them and climbed aboard. They started bailing water with a bucket and a sou'wester hat, but as the dory lightened, it drifted away from the schooner and they could not row back against the wind and sea to rescue any of their shipmates. Captain Brown could see the beacon of Bacarro Light and helped his two dory mates row toward it.

The men left aboard *Codseeker* lashed themselves to her railing and shrouds while breaking waves pounded over them, but the new ropes they used were stiff and could not hold knots as well as older, softer lines would have. Perhaps this was why the knots slipped and caused eighteen-year-old Ansel Crowell Nickerson to fall from the shrouds and drown among the folds of a wet sail. As dawn approached, the men looked down and watched as Nickerson's body billowed in the submerged sail.

One sailor, William E. Kenney, began to sing a century-old hymn: "Jesus, lover of my soul, let me to thy bosom fly. While the nearer waters roll, while the tempest still is high." Then he began again, singing the same two lines over and over again. Slowly, the others joined him.

The men did not know that sometime during the nine hours they had been lashed to the side of a heaving wreck amidst a howling nor'easter eight miles at sea, Captain Brown had reached shore. He combed the fish piers of Clarks Harbor—from where, 110 years later, the brand-new *Heather Lynne II* would depart for her maiden voyage to Newburyport. At least thirty schooners lay tied up to ride out the storm. When he discovered a cluster of fishermen, Captain Brown announced *Codseeker's* peril and asked if anyone was willing to rescue her. Twenty-four-year-old Captain Job Crowell asked Captain Brown if he figured the men could still be alive, considering *Codseeker's* condition and the brutal weather and seas. Captain Brown said he didn't know.

But he wanted to find out.

By ten o'clock that morning, *Matchless* was underway in search of *Codseeker*. The two-masted schooner, which had been built in Gloucester's neighboring town of Essex, Massachusetts, was owned by Captain Crowell and his father. As he cleared the harbor and broke into the roiling open sea, Captain Crowell feared the seas were too rough for their success. Maybe it wasn't worth putting himself and his crew at risk. He vowed to press on just a few more miles before turning back. Then, barely eight miles from Cape Sable Island, they spotted the low-lying black hull of *Codseeker*. As *Matchless* approached, Captain Crowell and his crew saw lifeless figures tied to the rigging. After several blasts of the foghorn, the *Matchless* crew saw a head lift. A weak arm waved.

Several volunteers from *Matchless* rowed over in an eight-oared seine boat and attached a line to the *Codseeker*. Three of her tired wet crew leapt down into the boat, leaving two men tied together in the rigging. One of the remaining two leaped successfully, but the second man, Ziba Hunt, a fifty-three-year-old father of eight, lost his footing in a crashing wave. He disappeared beneath the sea.

The four rescued crew—Jesse Smith, Jeremiah Nickerson, William Goodwin, and William Kenney—climbed aboard the waiting *Matchless* and gathered around a hot fire burning in the stove below. Captain Crowell asked the men if there might be any more survivors aboard the *Codseeker*. The men all agreed: that was impossible. The *Matchless* sailed away.

But they were wrong.

Just before the foundering, James Edwin Smith, the eighteen-year-old stepson of *Codseeker's* owner, had ducked below to fill a tin cup with water. Just as he dipped his cup into the cook's bucket, the deck dropped out from under his feet as the schooner rolled on her side. He was thrown against a bulkhead, and splashing water extinguished the oil lamp. In darkness, he reached for the companionway. In a frantic effort to escape, he stepped on the bottom step, but lost his grip on the rail when a violent rush of seawater forced him back below. He hit his head and fell unconscious.

When he came to, he was awash in frigid water and absolute darkness. He searched for something solid to grab as he forced his way through flotsam. Panicked, he tangled in blankets, but fought his way free until he finally reached the sideboard of a top bunk and clung to it. There he began to wait, for what he wasn't sure. The *Codseeker* wallowed in the waves. She threatened to roll completely over before swaying back on one side. Smith struggled to stay inside the air pocket that shifted with the motion of the boat. He dozed off and woke up ensnared in the companionway ladder. As he freed himself, he thought he heard a weak voice.

Samuel Atwood was also trapped but had managed to grab hold of a bunk. They yelled to each other, finding a sliver of comfort in the sound of another voice. As Thursday dawned, daylight revealed debris floating all around them. The air pocket increased and diminished as the *Cod-seeker* shifted in the seas. And then Smith saw Atwood. They shouted to one another about how to escape. They considered swimming through the hatchway but feared that once on the surface they'd find nothing to hold onto and would be washed away. Neither knew how to swim.

Smith cried. He and Atwood were unaware that there were fellow crewmen lashed to the railing outside, and that these others were rescued at midday. Night passed. On Friday morning, they assumed the storm had passed them because *Codseeker* no longer felt so restless. They were hungry and fixed their thoughts on a nearby food locker, where they found and ate doughnuts soaked in kerosene and seawater. Smith considered a second submerged food locker. As he looked below, he saw the drowned face of a fellow sailor who had been trapped when the galley stove fell onto his leg. That sight put an end to their search for more food. Another night passed. Smith wondered whether he'd die of starvation or suffocation, hypothermia or drowning.

On Saturday morning, more water poured in and threatened to flood the forecastle. Then Atwood and Smith felt *Codseeker* shift again. She was sinking and she sank for what seemed like a long time before stopping with a thud on the ocean bottom.

Confined in shoulder-high water, the sailors in their small air pocket tried not to lose hope, but they were trapped alive at the bottom of the sea—how could it get much worse? They braced themselves as *Codseeker* shifted from time to time. Hours later, after shifting again, *Codseeker* miraculously floated back up to the surface, where she returned to her original position, listing to one side. Smith and Atwood assumed she had sunk due to the weight of the salt kept on board to cure any fish they had hoped to catch. Once the salt dissolved, she regained some of her buoyancy.

Another night passed. They were thirsty, cold and desperate, but alive. It was now Sunday morning, and the men had been trapped since Wednesday night. Lost in feverish thoughts, they watched sunlight slip through small cracks and cast shadows about them.

Then they heard a sharp clang. And voices.

Outside, the schooner *Ohio* had been sailing from Belfast, Maine, toward the Grand Banks with Captain Edwin Dorr at the helm. Captain Dorr had glanced toward the horizon and spotted something low and black in the water. He figured it was a whale, but the whale never sounded. He took out his telescope and realized it was a derelict ship. He sailed closer, noticed she was nearly brand-new, and decided to see what he could salvage from her. He sent a crew of sailors over to strip her. He was especially interested in the new ropes. After the crew stepped aboard, two young men walked forward and swung axes at the rigging, but one of them missed his mark and hit an iron strap. That was the loud clang the trapped men heard.

The men on deck heard muffled shouts inside the abandoned schooner.

"Ghosts!" they shouted.

A skeptical middle-aged fisherman walked forward to investigate. He listened and heard the voices for himself. They yelled over to Captain Dorr, who told them they were crazy. If they were hearing voices, Dorr shouted, then they were hearing live voices. Dorr climbed aboard the *Codseeker* and yelled to the voices: "Below there!"

They heard a reply. Captain Dorr grabbed an axe and tapped on the hull again. He heard two knocks. Captain Dorr tapped a few more times to determine where the men were, then he and a fellow fisherman set about chopping a hole. They knew they had to work fast. Once the hull was punctured, air smelling like bilge water hissed out. The fishermen shaped an oval hole about twenty inches across, then reached in and pulled out an ashen-faced Atwood. Smith's shoulders were too broad, so they worked at the hole again until, with his arms over his head, Smith could be yanked through the hole and into the fresh afternoon air, scraping his ribs along the way.

Smith and Atwood had survived being trapped alive inside their fishing boat for eighty-nine hours.

At eight o'clock Monday morning, the *Ohio* delivered the two sailors to a grateful community who had thought them long dead. A few days later, two salvage schooners towed the abandoned *Codseeker* to Port Maitland. There she was pumped out and righted; the bodies of the three drowned men trapped aboard were removed. A crew set about repairing her wounds, and in July, two months after her foundering, she again set sail.

On board was James Edwin Smith, who slept in the same berth he once feared would entomb him. His rescue that spring day in 1877, and that of fellow sailor Samuel Atwood, proved that while being trapped inside a fishing boat was a terrifying ordeal, it did not have to be fatal.

»The Tugboat Mate

ECAUSE THE TRIAL focused on the rescue efforts that followed the Mayday call from the tug *Houma*, none of the events leading up to the collision were reviewed in court. Judge Saris did not hear testimony from any of the tug and barge crew, and no one painted a picture for her of what may have unfolded on the dark waters off Cape Ann before 5 A.M. on September 5, 1996.

If he had testified, *Houma*'s mate Mike Simpson, like Richard Burgess, would have said it was a pretty night. He had been on watch four hours in the dark wheelhouse of the 87-foot tug as she growled southwestward along the coast of Maine and New Hampshire at about nine knots. The 7-inch-circumference nylon towline, or hawser, stretching 700 feet behind him was shackled via a 15-foot-long wire pendant to a chain bridle from the bow of the empty and engineless 272-foot petroleum tank barge *Essex*. The dark sky washed into the sea and concealed the horizon like a black velvet curtain. Simpson could feel *Houma* sway in the lazy one- to three-foot ground swell rolling in from the east, the last remnants of Hurricane Edouard as it tracked farther offshore. Small white anchor lights—and sometimes red or green running lights—appeared like lightning bugs as far away as three or even five miles. He knew his was not the only boat out there.

Six days later, he would sit at a table before Coast Guard investigators and a panel of lawyers, including his own, and sketch his version of the events that led up to the collision.

Houma's journey had begun at noon on Wednesday, September 4, just a few hours after the *Heather Lynne II* had landed their tuna in Newburyport. After delaying for a day due to the passing hurricane, *Houma* departed the Webber Fuel Terminal in Bangor, Maine, and traveled down the Penobscot River and Penobscot Bay and out through Two Bush Channel. She approached Monhegan Island, ten miles offshore, near 9 P.M. While Simpson slept, Captain Allen Breen looked at the nautical chart covering the Bay of Fundy to Cape Cod. Bound for the Cape Cod Canal and home to New York Harbor, Breen had two choices.

He could take his tug and barge from a position three miles west of the red whistler buoy off Monhegan Island to the red-and-white bell off Provincetown's Race Point, where he would then set a course for the entrance to the canal. This direct route would take him thirty to forty miles offshore and five to ten miles east of the congested fishing grounds of Jeffreys Ledge, which was prominent on Breen's chart. The ledge was a crescent moon of submerged granite four to eight miles wide and some twenty miles offshore, with one end near Cape Neddick, Maine, and the other forty miles southwest off Cape Ann, Massachusetts. There, on any late summer day in 1996, one could expect to encounter a few dozen deep-sea passenger fishing boats, a handful of whale-watching boats, several commercial fishing boats, and numerous sailboats and recreational powerboats heading to and from the Maine coast. Breen knew the anchored tuna fleet, made up of two or three hundred boats, would be scattered among them.

Captain Allen Breen, fifty years old in 1996, was a New Jersey native who had spent thirty years in the merchant marine. He was qualified to serve as a captain of vessels up to 1,600 tons as well as a pilot—someone with local knowledge who navigates merchant ships into and out of rivers, bays, and harbors—on vessels up to 500 tons traveling New York–area waters from the Hudson River to Weehawken, New Jersey. He had started working for the Eklof Marine Corporation, owner of the *Houma*, in 1975 and, with the exception of a few months with Mobil Oil, had worked for Eklof since. He had been a captain on tugboats running between Maine and Virginia, trips that took him to Portland, Portsmouth, Boston, New Bedford, Narragansett Bay, Bridgeport, New York Harbor, up the Hudson River and to the Great Lakes, down the coast to the Delaware Bay, upriver to Camden, New Jersey, through the Chesapeake & Delaware Canal to the Chesapeake Bay, and down to Norfolk, Virginia. In his year aboard the *Houma*, he had traveled this northern route three or four times. He had seen fishing vessels all over the Gulf of Maine and expected them to be anywhere.

Captain Breen also knew that his office might call in the morning and ask him to take the empty barge *Essex* into Boston to pick up cargo for the trip back to New York or possibly even for Maine or New Hampshire. It would depend on what could be lined up and when. He didn't want to be far offshore, or even at the Cape Cod Canal, when the call came in and then have to waste time turning around and backtracking to Boston Harbor. Standing over the chart in the wheelhouse, Breen chose a more coastal route that would take him from the Monhegan whistler to a way-point 3½ miles east of the red whistler off the tip of Cape Ann. This direct course to Boston, what Breen regarded as a standard route, would take the tug and barge at 9 to 9½ knots right over Jeffreys Ledge and through the tuna fleet.

When Simpson entered the pilothouse to relieve Breen of his watch at about 11:30 P.M., Breen told him to maintain a course of 215 degrees true. The autopilot kept *Houma* on a straight course while two VHF marine radios monitored radio traffic, the Loran-C receiver and a global positioning system, or GPS, receiver tracked the tug and tow's progress, and a radar scanned out to twelve miles all around them to detect any nearby vessels. Breen had been trying to call the home office in Staten Island but hadn't had any luck. He asked Simpson to try calling later.

Breen and Simpson had worked together for about six months. They held the same Coast Guard captain's license and respected each other's judgment. Breen trusted Simpson's boat-handling ability and knew him to be an experienced captain and mate. The only improvement he felt Simpson could make was to change the way he talked to his deckhands—he would raise his voice a little bit, sometimes too much. Other than that, Breen would tell Coast Guard investigators, Simpson was "a fine boatman." He believed that Simpson, when on watch, knew he was authorized to make any course changes necessitated by prudent seamanship without consulting Breen. If Simpson felt he could avoid a heavy traffic area by altering his course several miles, he "absolutely" had the authority to do so without waking up Breen. Simpson, for his part, liked Breen, considering him an easy-going guy with a good sense of humor, and figured he had learned a lot from him.

Before turning the helm over to Simpson and leaving the pilothouse, Breen made some small talk to pass the time while Simpson's eyes adjusted to night vision. After a few minutes, when Simpson felt he was ready, he took over. Breen then left the bridge, walked down to the galley, made a sandwich, and drank a glass of soda. He entered his room, undressed, brushed his teeth, and crawled into his bunk, where he read for a while. Then he put in earplugs to drown out the engine noise, since he slept right behind the exhaust stack, and fell asleep at about 12:45 A.M.

Meanwhile, Simpson took a seat in the wheelhouse and settled in for the long ride south. Lights from the electronics cast shadows on his square, boyish face, dark brown hair, and hazel eyes. The same age as Kevin Foster, thirty-eight, he had been working on tugboats since his early twenties. A friendly guy with a broad smile, he liked to spend his spare time doing tree work for extra cash, mountain biking, and roller-blading; in the winter, he had worked for a while on the ski patrol at a New Hampshire ski area. He had grown up with three brothers and two sisters in Beverly Farms, Massachusetts, and now lived in nearby Essex, not far from where the schooner *Matchless* had been built and where *Houma* would be passing near sunrise. His mother was a nurse, while his father sold machinery parts on weekdays and on weekends enjoyed woodworking and woodcarving. His father also had a Coast Guard license and sometimes took friends and family fishing. Simpson had gone tuna fishing years before, back when the fish were used for cat food, a time when it was more a rich man's sport than a working man's gamble on a several-thousand-dollar score. As a kid Simpson had wanted to be a cabinetmaker, but his first job after high school was working for his older brother's tug company, Simpson Towing and Salvage. He liked the work and stuck with it.

He took navigation courses in New Orleans and studied at home to pass Coast Guard exams that eventually led to a 1,600-ton master's license, which qualified him to run tugboats on inland and coastal waters. He had worked on tugboats in the Great Lakes, along the New England coast, south to Norfolk, Virginia, and even to the Caribbean. For the past seven years he had been employed by Eklof, six of those years as a mate on tugs towing barges along the coast and in New York Harbor. In late March 1996, Simpson had first stepped aboard the *Houma*, one of twelve tugs owned by Eklof.

Eklof, which in 1999 would change its name to K-Sea Transportation Corporation, had been in business since 1910, the year Carl Eklof and his son started selling used rope from a rowboat in New York Harbor. By

1996, Eklof Marine operated forty-two vessels, including twenty-two tank barges and six tank ships working the waters of the East Coast, inland waterways, the Gulf of Mexico, and Central and South America. The early months of 1996 had not been good to the company. A fire on board its tug *North Cape* in January led to the grounding in Rhode Island of a barge carrying 4 million gallons of home heating oil. As much as 828,000 gallons spilled, causing immense environmental damage, fines topping $7 million, a $10 million settlement in a lawsuit brought against Eklof by 110 lobstermen, and the loss of the tug (estimated at $1.5 million) and barge (estimated at $3.6 million).

Simpson had traveled the route to Bangor, Maine, at least twenty times by the spring of 1996, but this was his first trip on the route aboard the steel tug *Houma*. He liked *Houma* because she was comfortable, quiet, and had excellent visibility from the high wheelhouse. Built in 1970 at the Jakobsen Shipyard in Oyster Bay, New York, *Houma* stretched 30 feet across and was 87 feet long from the shaggy brown bow pudding hanging over her black stem to her low, rounded black stern. Big black tires were chained in a string along her midsections. Her hull extended 11 feet down in the water. The red deckhouse had round portholes and steel doors; inside, a stairwell led up to the wheelhouse, or bridge, which measured 10 feet wide and 8 feet fore and aft. A waist-high console extended about 3 feet aft from the forward square windows. Instead of a steering wheel, a lever rode on a long bar that spanned the bridge on the edge of the console. Using the lever, the captain or mate could drive the tug while looking out either side window as required. The helmsman could also maneuver the tug using a toggle switch attached to a small handheld box as he walked around the wheelhouse. There were duplicate engine throttles at either end of the console, and a compass was mounted in the center. The radar display was to port and the GPS to starboard. Behind the helm was the chart table. There were windows on all four sides of the bridge. Outside, below the square windows, a wooden sign hanging against the white painted wheelhouse announced "HOUMA" in bold, white capital letters.

She was equipped with two 645E2–AMD diesel engines offering 975 horsepower each. With a barge in tow, Simpson estimated she'd make about 8½ knots. He told investigators he could not go more than a knot or two slower than that or the barge would not track well behind the tug (an opinion at least one expert would later dispute). On the morning of

September 5, 1996, he was traveling at full cruising speed. Simpson saw no reason to slow down because, as he later said, the whole point is to make your best possible speed to the next waypoint.

Simpson knew his primary responsibility was the safety of his tug and tow. He had to keep a constant vigil over the radar screen and out the windows for boats that he approached or that approached him. He also had to consider his maneuverability. It would take a mile (and about five to eight minutes) at a minimum to come to a complete stop, but neither he nor Breen believed it would be safe to stop so quickly. If Simpson were suddenly to take his two diesel engines out of gear, the momentum of the huge barge would carry it forward, possibly to collide with the tug. Further, a sharp turn, which Simpson defined as any abrupt course change greater than ten degrees, could introduce enough angle and slack in the 700-foot towline to foul a propeller, knocking out an engine and leaving the tug in jeopardy from the surging barge. Even if that didn't happen, the barge's forward momentum would keep it tracking on its original course until it swung far outboard of the turn, possibly transmitting enough torque to the tug's stern quarters to capsize or "trip" it. The point of the chain bridle extending from the bow of the barge was to help the barge follow straight behind the tug, but the danger of a sharp turn still existed.

Breen would later explain to investigators that a far safer maneuver would be to slow down gradually, over several minutes, while hauling in the hawser to put the barge on a shorter tow. This would then enable the helmsman to make a sharper course change to an alternate heading. Better still, of course, would be to alter course well ahead of time or to reduce speed slowly and early to let an approaching vessel cross far ahead. Simpson understood all this. He knew he needed to respond to any risk of collision several miles ahead of time, because the safety of his tug and tow hinged on his making no sudden changes to course or speed. To stop or turn quickly would jeopardize not just the *Houma*, but any other vessels close by.

In the early hours of September 5, 1996, Simpson watched the radar the way a stockbroker watches the ticker on a computer terminal. In the dark night, the radar offered his best information on the positions of nearby vessels and whether they were underway, adrift, or at anchor. Sometimes he would look through his binoculars and search for red or green running lights to determine whether a boat was headed toward or away from him. Many times he spotted white lights, signifying boats at anchor, clustered like constellations.

He hoped nearby boats saw his own red and green running lights and amber deck lights. Three white masthead lights and a yellow-over-white stern light indicated to others that he had a barge in tow more than 200 meters astern. His black barge had its own running lights—a small red light on the port bow, a green one on the starboard bow, and a small white light on the stern. Simpson knew that at night, when no shapes are distinguishable against the blackness, the lights of his tug and tow were his first defense against any other boat that impeded his course or was trying to decide who he was and where he was headed. He hoped no one would mistake his tug and tow—spanning a total of about 1,000 feet from the bow of the tug to the stern of the barge—for two separate vessels and try to pass between them.

Of course, if any boat threatened to come too close, Simpson would probably see the situation unfold on the square radar screen. As the radar antenna rotated on the roof, it was sending a signal over the water. Whenever the signal struck another boat, it would bounce off and return to the antenna, which would translate it into a target on the screen. The larger or denser the object, the stronger the return signal and the sharper, larger, or brighter the displayed target. A cruise ship, for example, would show up like a lightning bug in a night sky, while a small sailboat or a small, fiberglass, low-to-the-water fishing boat might show up like a small mosquito, if at all. As a safety precaution, some boatowners elected to install radar reflectors, like the two welded to the nine-foot-tall aluminum mast on the *Heather Lynne II*'s roof, to increase the likelihood that their boat would paint a strong image on someone else's radar screen. *Houma*'s radar had a daylight screen, meaning that targets would remain on the screen even after the antenna swept past. This constant picture, renewed and updated with each rotation of the antenna, was a luxury compared with older-model radars—like the back-up radar Simpson had on board but was not using—which showed targets only during the instant they were highlighted. Simpson knew a prudent mariner keeps a constant watch over the entire screen and evaluates the motion of his own vessel relative to the targets around him.

All night Simpson had been watching clusters of boats enter and leave his radar screen, but he wasn't concerned about their proximity to his tug and barge. He could have reduced speed from time to time or altered his course several miles to the east or west to try to avoid some of the traffic, but none of the boats he'd been seeing looked as if they would pose any problems. Besides, he was used to having dense traffic around him, and it was common to see vessels approach too close, day and night, in harbors, in Long Island Sound, and in the open ocean.

"We were sticking to the plan," he later remembered, "and I didn't see a need to alter course. There was just as much boat traffic five miles west as there was east."

AT ABOUT 3:30 THAT MORNING, not far from the waypoint off Monhegan Island where the *Houma* had turned to the southward some six hours before, Captain Raymond "Kelly" Benner snapped alert to the sound of his 57-foot trawler shaking all around him. As he told one reporter, "It made a big rattle at first. Then there was a roar, like a cannon going off next to my head."

His fishing vessel *Kristen & Erin*, named after his daughters, had collided nearly head on with the *Hitra*, an 803-foot Norwegian oil tanker headed out to sea. The *Hitra* hit the trawler's outrigging on her starboard side and bent the steel rigging in half. This spun the *Kristen & Erin* around, slamming her bow into the tanker's side and shattering her bow and wooden deck rails. On the *Hitra*, the only sign of damage was some scraped paint. The *Hitra* called the *Kristen & Erin* and asked if they needed assistance. Benner declined and limped back to port as the *Hitra* continued on its course.

The Coast Guard's investigation later found that no one was at the helm of the *Kristen & Erin* at the moment of impact. Evidence suggested that far greater damage or even loss of life would have occurred had the *Hitra* not altered course seconds before the collision to soften the blow. Ultimately, Coast Guard investigators suggested this collision could have been avoided with prudent seamanship on board both vessels.

"These days, the ocean is a busy place," said Jeff Ciampa, a Coast Guard Fishing Vessel Safety Coordinator. "It's sort of like a highway with no lamps."

AT ABOUT 1:00 A.M. AND AGAIN AT 3:15, Simpson's deckhand, twenty-nine-year-old Shawn Richter, visited Simpson in the wheelhouse, where he remained for a half hour to an hour each time, looking out at the white lights of nearby boats. At about 3:15, when the *Houma* was about halfway down the length of Jeffreys Ledge and about twenty-seven miles due east of Portsmouth, New Hampshire, Richter glanced at the radar screen and asked Simpson why there were so many boats out there at that hour. Simpson told him they were probably tuna boats, since it was tuna season.

Richter was not from the area. He had grown up in Babylon, New York, and after high school had attended a marine vocational school in Louisiana. In 1986 he had taken his first maritime job, working for a supply boat company serving the Gulf of Mexico. A year later he gained certification as an "able-bodied seaman" and worked for a tug and barge company in New Orleans. In time, he also earned a Coast Guard license that qualified him to be a captain on boats up to 100 tons and a mate on boats up to 1,600 tons. Like Captain Breen and Simpson's licenses, Richter's also carried an endorsement as "radar observer," a Coast Guard qualification requiring classroom study and successful completion of a test showing a certain level of skill at using radar to avoid collisions and to fix a vessel's position. In 1994 Richter joined Eklof and worked on board *Houma* as a deckhand. He had no navigational responsibilities, but instead would spend his watch doing what he was told by the captain or mate. He would walk around the tug and see that everything was as it should be. He cooked and cleaned and, when asked, would serve on the bridge as a lookout or helmsman.

At 4 A.M. Simpson asked Richter to come up to the wheelhouse and keep an eye on things while he went below to grab a slice of pizza. Ten minutes earlier, Simpson had placed an X on the chart, circled it, and penciled the time next to it: 0350. It marked their position twenty-six miles east of Hampton, New Hampshire, on an edge of Jeffreys Ledge known to local fishermen as the "northern end of the curl." Before leaving the wheelhouse, Simpson told Richter to maintain a course of 215 degrees true and a speed of about 8½ knots and to track some radar targets that didn't seem to pose an immediate problem. Six to eight miles away, groups of boats appeared to be drifting or anchored along Jeffreys Ledge.

When Simpson returned to the bridge at 4:10 A.M., he noticed that the twenty or so targets on the radar had drawn a little closer, but still nothing was crossing the bow and no targets required a course change. A few small boats surrounded him seven to eight miles away. At about the same time that John Michael Lowther on the *Heather Lynne II* was answering a radio call from Ted Rurak, Simpson and Richter talked again about why there were so many boats in the area so early in the morning. Simpson would later tell investigators that the boats he saw were "power-driven vessels"—an all-encompassing term under the rules of the road for any vessel traveling under engine power alone—and that he couldn't be sure what they were doing. Richter, however, told investigators that on two occasions, first at about 3:15 A.M. and again at about 4:15 A.M., Simpson told him the boats were probably out there chasing tuna.

Simpson knew that under the international maritime rules of the road, he was required to use every navigational instrument and all knowledge available to him at all times to evaluate what was going on around him and determine if a risk of collision existed. He was required to monitor his radar and use its various plotting tools—including an electronic bearing line that could be placed over an approaching target and a cursor that would measure the distance to a target—to scan the waters several miles ahead for other vessels and track their movements relative to his own course. Further, the rules of the road specifically instruct that "assumptions shall not be made on the basis of scanty information, especially scanty radar information." Instead, mariners should understand that a risk of collision exists if the compass bearing on an approaching vessel does not appreciably change with time, and that a risk may sometimes exist even when an appreciable bearing change is evident, especially when approaching a large vessel, a tow, or a vessel at close range. Most notably, the rules warn mariners that, "If there is any doubt, such risk shall be deemed to exist."

Simpson knew that in an open-water crossing situation between two power-driven vessels—regardless of whether either was a military ship, merchant ship, fishing boat, or recreational boat—the vessel to the right, showing a red light on its port side at night, was the "stand-on" or "privileged" vessel and was expected to maintain its course and speed. The other vessel, showing only the green light on its starboard side, was "burdened" and was supposed to give way by altering course or speed in a manner early and obvious enough not to confuse the stand-on vessel. While he had to be aware of all the vessels around him, Simpson had to pay particular attention to those on his right.

With Richter posted as lookout and Simpson watching the radar and GPS, *Houma* steamed southwestward, pulling *Essex* along behind her as the pretty night rolled into early morning. While Richard Burgess recalled essentially unlimited visibility that night, Simpson told investigators that he had a visual range of only about two miles. He also said, however, that he often saw other vessels as the predawn hours wore on. The sea was dead calm. Simpson noticed it would soon be nautical twilight, a time when the sky begins to lighten yet the stars are still bright enough to be used for celestial navigation.

Simpson looked at the chart on the table behind him, turning his back to any boat that might be approaching on his starboard side, to which he would have to give way. The white sixty-watt bulb on the chart table was dimmed to about half its full-rated illumination in order to protect his night vision, though a red bulb is generally considered more effective. Simpson showed Richter the charted outline of Cape Ann. Even though he was about twelve miles offshore, would still have about thirty minutes of darkness before nautical twilight, and would later report having about two miles of visibility, Simpson would insist to investigators that he could see the tree-covered hills of Cape Ann just before the collision.

"If we had a car," Simpson said to Richter. "We could be at my house in ten minutes."

Richter looked at the clock in the wheelhouse. It was 4:48 A.M. He told Simpson he was going below to make a pot of coffee for the oncoming watch, whom they'd wake at 5:30. Richter walked down the steps of the bridge and into the galley. Setting out some cups, sugar, and cream, he dumped out the stale coffee and started to brew a fresh pot.

At 4:50 A.M., a blip on the radar screen caught Simpson's eye.

Simpson would tell Coast Guard investigators that the target wasn't strong enough to paint a consistent image on his radar screen at its 12-mile-range setting, but it did show up often enough over the next several minutes to convince him that a boat was out there, five miles to his right. It showed a bearing of 65 to 70 degrees relative to the *Houma*'s heading, placing it near the two-o'clock position. Simpson did not consider changing his course or speed.

Ten minutes later, at 5 A.M., Simpson turned the range on the radar down to 6 miles. He believed the boat to starboard was now about 2½ miles away at a bearing that he remembered as 70 or 75 to 85 degrees at different points in his testimony. He picked up his binoculars and saw bright white halogen deck lights and both the red and green running lights, indicating that the boat was headed in his general direction. Although the vessel was approaching from starboard and the *Houma* was therefore the burdened vessel, Simpson held his course and speed.

Having decreased the range on the radar to get a better look at the boat closing from starboard, Simpson did not sketch out any concrete calculations or use the plotting features on his radar to determine the other boat's course and speed relative to his own. Instead, he made a rough mental estimate based on experienced observation that the vessel would pass behind his barge within an eighth to a quarter of a mile. When the boat was 2 miles away its relative bearing had increased to 80 degrees (or 75 to 85 degrees, according to Simpson's later testimony). He never expected that a collision was imminent.

Besides, he had to consider other boats around him.

"I felt that he was going to fall astern of me," Simpson later told Coast Guard investigators, "and that my best course of action, considering the proximity of other vessels in the area, [was] that I should hold my course and speed while I was maintaining a close watch on him."

Simpson switched off the autopilot, grabbed the small metal box with its toggle switch for hand steering so that he would have better control of the *Houma* as she traveled through the half-dozen or more boats he could see ahead. He also knew that as the *Houma* was approaching the waters off Cape Ann, he would have to change course at his next waypoint, now 4½ miles away.

A minute or two later, Simpson dropped his radar down to a 3-mile range to take an even closer look at the vessel that was now just under two miles away.

"It's kind of a general rule that I think a lot of people use," Simpson said, "that you want to make sure when someone is that close to you that you double-check and make sure that things are what you think."

He looked at the range rings on his radar to see how long it took the vessel to travel a given distance, from which he could calculate her speed. He guessed it to be about ten knots. He first testified that he timed the vessel from 2 miles to 1.5 miles out, which would have taken 3 minutes at 10 knots, but later he testified that he watched her for a mile, or 6 minutes. He also moved a cursor over the target to establish a fixed electronic bearing line and watched to see if the actual bearing to the target would increase relative to the unmoving electronic line. As seconds passed he was convinced that it did so, which confirmed his belief that the other vessel would pass safely, though closely, behind his tug and barge.

As Simpson watched the smaller vessel through his binoculars, another reason for his belief that no risk of collision existed was that he figured she was far more maneuverable than he was, and could, in an emergency, make an abrupt course change or stop to avoid him. The rules of the road require that a stand-on vessel take any action necessary to avoid a collision—but only when the give-way vessel cannot or will not take the necessary steps itself. Also, there were other vessels ahead of him and to port that he needed to consider; though he didn't know it at the time, these included the *Scotia Boat Too*, *Sharaban*, *Jan Ann*, and *Blue Heron*. To starboard, he had just the one vessel, and he had already waited too long to give way by turning to starboard and passing with his barge in tow behind the approaching vessel; to do so would require, in his opinion, sharply turning the tug back and crossing in front of the boat's bow, because the tug was already ahead of the boat, but the barge was not. The turn would be dangerous, and the barge would swing wide. Besides, he still believed the oncoming boat would pass safely behind the barge. He held his course and speed.

"Given the close proximity of other vessels," Simpson told investigators, "and the fact that I could be creating more of a problem by making a course change and creating a dangerous situation with other vessels . . . my best course of action was to hold my course. . . . If I came left, the barge would swing out to starboard and compound the problem more than eliminate it. And if I came [to the right], I was afraid that all I'm going to do is close [in] with the vessel more than I was."

When the boat was a mile and a half away, Simpson estimated its relative bearing at 85 degrees. He now considered himself restricted in his ability to maneuver, though he did not adjust his masthead lights to indicate as much. He believed that any move he made would have caused a problem with the vessels that surrounded him.

A tug and its tow are not legally considered restricted in their ability to maneuver unless the tug is displaying the appropriate light configuration of red, white, and red in a vertical stack. This is a gray area, however, since a tug with a tow is, by commonsense definition, less maneuverable than an ordinary power-driven vessel. If formally designated as such, a vessel restricted in her ability to maneuver has the right of way over any other vessels in motion around her—even those working their nets or otherwise engaged in fishing. But Simpson, by not altering course or speed well ahead of time, had created this close-quarters situation (a conclusion he would have disputed). Now backed into a corner in which any course change would worsen the situation and it was not safe to come to an abrupt stop, he believed these other vessels should give way to him— even the one to starboard—despite the fact that the rules of the road explicitly warn against any insistence on right of way.

Over the next minute or two, he would later claim, as the boat closed to under a mile away, its bearing increased appreciably to as much as 110 degrees relative to the *Houma*'s course (the estimates in his testimony ranged from 90 to 110 degrees). At the same time, Simpson told investigators, the approaching boat's course seemed to change from northeast, to east, to southeast, so that even as she was falling behind his starboard beam both her red and green running lights remained visible. While this would indicate that she was turning to the south even as the *Houma* traveled past on a southerly course, he still believed the boat would pass astern of the barge. (Since the *Heather Lynne II* had presumably followed a course of 105 to 110 degrees from the Merrimack River, the suggestion that she was traveling northeast is difficult to accept. Simpson later testified that the boat's course was about 110 degrees and did not change.)

Through his binoculars, he could now see under the halogen deck lights a green fishing boat rolling in the trough of the easterly swell. He could not see anyone on deck. Ahead and to his left, Simpson saw the deck lights of anchored vessels.

When the boat to starboard closed to within a half mile away, Simpson believed that although they would not collide, "it was going to be very close." (In fact, if the *Heather Lynne II* had been closing from roughly abeam, on a course roughly at a right angle to the *Houma*'s and at approximately the same speed as the *Houma*, the tug would have moved a half mile south by the time their courses intersected, and the barge would have been more than a quarter mile *past* the fishing boat.) He told investigators that, with his VHF radio set at low power, he hailed "the green boat on my starboard side" first on channel 13 and then on channel 16. But Coast Guard recordings contain no evidence that such a call was made, and a test conducted by the Coast Guard the following day at the scene, on channel 16 at both high and low power, suggested that a call on 16 on low power would have been recorded. Further, Richter told investigators he never heard Simpson call the boat, nor did Simpson tell him he had tried to do so. If Simpson did call, the vessel did not respond. Simpson held his course and speed.

Next, Simpson said he turned on one of the two bright spotlights mounted on the roof of the *Houma*, each of which could cast a beam nearly two feet in diameter for two miles. Simpson directed the blinding light onto the boat to get someone's attention. He could not see through the tinted windows and into the wheelhouse and, therefore, still could not determine whether anyone was in the wheelhouse or on the aft deck. He shined the spotlight on the white-painted bow of the barge behind him in an attempt to signal impending danger, then again turned the light onto the green fishing boat. Then back to the barge. Then to the fishing boat and back to the barge. Simpson held his course and speed.

Standing in the aft starboard corner of the wheelhouse, Simpson reached overhead with his right hand and pulled the red handle on the cord that sounds three air horns. He blew five blasts—the international danger signal.

With his left hand he directed the spotlight back and forth.

Fishing boat.

Barge.

Fishing boat.

Barge.

Again, five loud blasts.

Fishing boat.

Barge.

Fishing boat.

Barge.

Five loud blasts.

Simpson said he blew the air horns so much that he almost lost throttle pressure. He couldn't believe the green fishing boat did not change course. Though he saw her wallowing in the trough of the easterly swells, he insisted to investigators that she was speeding along at about ten knots, because she was pushing a lot of water, showing what mariners call "a bone in her teeth."

RICHTER WAS CURIOUS, but not alarmed, when he heard the air horn blasting. He stepped out of the galley and onto the starboard deck. He later told investigators that it was a few minutes past five o'clock when he saw the tug's spotlight lighting up an entire fishing boat. He saw a green hull and a white cabin on which was painted, in large black numbers and letters, MS 20A. He could clearly see its green starboard running light and a little bit of its red port running light, but after a few seconds he saw only the green light. He remembered the boat approaching the hawser in front of the barge at nearly a 90-degree angle and guessed that it must have been traveling at about ten to twelve knots. Richter stood on deck and watched for about twenty seconds. He couldn't see anyone on deck on the fishing boat, did not even see any deck lights, and could not see into the wheelhouse. He walked fast up to the bridge, where he stood at the top of the steps. He saw Simpson staring aft with one hand on the spotlight and one hand on the horn. He would later guess it was about 5:10 A.M. Simpson was holding his course and speed.

"Holy shit!" Simpson yelled. "What's this guy doing?"

"Should I get the captain up?" Richter asked.

Simpson didn't answer him. It was too dark to see Simpson's face, but Richter knew he was focused on what was happening. After about ninety seconds, Richter heard the tug's engines shut right down to an idle. Simpson hoped this last-ditch maneuver would put enough sag in the hawser to let the fishing boat pass safely over, but it did not. Ten seconds later, Richter and Simpson watched the bow of the fishing boat hit the thick wire pendant 15 feet in front of the barge. The fishing boat stopped and bounced back, then moved forward against the pendant. The pendant carved a notch in the bow of the *Heather Lynne II* as it smoked past, wrenching the bow of the boat away from the oncoming barge. Antennas and the mast on the fishing boat's roof tangled in the chain bridle and were yanked out by their roots. The front wall of the empty barge, raking forward to a height of 16 feet, loomed overhead, then struck. The green fishing boat rolled over and disappeared beneath the barge's port bow.

"Get the captain," Simpson said.

THAT WAS THE STORY Simpson told Coast Guard investigators and eight attorneys—three representing Captain Jeffrey Hutchins's estate, one representing Michael Simpson, two representing the Eklof Marine Corporation, and two representing Ted Rurak, owner of the *Heather Lynne II*—during two and a half days of sometimes contentious testimony a week after the collision. Simpson was one of sixteen witnesses to testify in thirteen days of hearings, part of a formal Coast Guard investigation that would last six months and gather ninety-five pieces of physical evidence. Coast Guard investigations such as this, while not always as lengthy, are routinely conducted following significant accidents at sea. Their purpose is not to assess civil or criminal liability but instead to determine the cause of the casualty and whether any misconduct, negligence, or equipment failure caused or contributed to it. Federal laws prohibit any part of an investigation from being admitted directly into evidence in a court proceeding, but the questions raised and conclusions reached in an investigation can nevertheless profoundly influence subsequent litigation. Thus, attorneys were there to gather information for the inevitable future lawsuits, and were permitted to intervene when their clients' interests might be jeopardized.

When repeatedly asked by Attorney Peter Black, who represented the family of Jeffrey Hutchins at the Coast Guard hearing, whether or not, as he watched the *Heather Lynne II* from two miles away, Simpson could have expected a close-quarters situation with her to worsen, stay the same, or improve, Simpson could not answer and instead insisted that he could not be expected to predict what the *Heather Lynne II* was going to do. The international rules of the road agree that no mariner can ever be absolutely sure what an approaching vessel's intentions are, but, in accordance with these rules, Simpson was expected to eliminate all uncertainty by taking early evasive action. The rules clearly state that when there is any doubt, risk of collision shall be deemed to exist and vessel operators must do whatever is necessary to avoid a collision.

Many people have questioned the plausibility of Simpson's summary of the events leading up to the collision. One Coast Guardsman close to the investigation remembered that Simpson was not considered a reliable witness and that his testimony appeared rehearsed. Since Simpson was alone in the wheelhouse until just before the collision, Coast Guard investigators even considered it possible, though certainly not proven, that he was asleep at the wheel and woke up just in time to see—but not to avoid—the imminent collision.

In late 1996, attorneys representing the owner of the *Heather Lynne II* asked retired Coast Guard Captain James Kelly to evaluate Simpson's story. Captain Kelly had graduated from the U.S. Coast Guard Academy in 1952 and had served in the Coast Guard for twenty-nine years. He had commanded three Coast Guard cutters, including the training bark *Eagle*, and had taught navigation and coastal piloting to Academy students, emphasizing a prudent mariner's obligations to do radar plotting and follow the rules of the road. While Simpson's testimony was drawn from memory, Kelly used the *Houma*'s logbook and courses as plotted on the chart taken from her wheelhouse to work backward from the point of impact and reconstruct the events leading up to it.

Kelly assumed for the sake of argument that the *Heather Lynne II* was traveling at a speed of 9 knots on a course of 111.5 degrees true, based on a course line drawn from the Merrimack River entrance to the accident scene, when she was within five miles of the *Houma*.

Kelly also assumed that the *Houma* was traveling at a course of 215 degrees true. ("True" courses are referenced to the north pole; magnetic courses are relative to magnetic north. Off Cape Ann in 1996, magnetic north was 16 degrees 41 minutes west of true north.) Although Simpson said *Houma* was moving at about 8 to 8.5 knots, Kelly determined, based on the times of two fixes Simpson had plotted on *Houma*'s chart earlier that morning, that her speed before the collision had to have been 9.5 knots. Kelly concluded that, had the *Houma* been traveling at 8 knots since the last plotted fix as Simpson claimed during his first day of testimony, the tug and tow would have been more than a mile north of the collision site at 5:15 A.M., and the collision would never have happened.

Instead, Kelly concluded, Simpson failed to keep a proper watch on the radar and carry out his duties under the rules of the road. Basing his conclusions on the plausibility of the scenario Simpson described—that the *Heather Lynne II* was in fact underway at 9 knots—Kelly believed the collision happened a lot faster than Simpson suggested.

When the *Heather Lynne II* was abeam of *Houma*, Kelly believed it was 250 yards away, not a half mile away as recalled by Simpson. If the *Heather Lynne II* was on a bearing of 90 to 110 degrees from the *Houma* when it was a half mile away, Kelly said, the collision would not have happened unless *Heather Lynne II*'s speed far exceeded 9 knots, which her owner said was her top speed.

During the investigative hearing, Simpson said that he took no action to avoid a collision until it was clear the *Heather Lynne II* would not pass astern. When the *Heather Lynne II* was about a half mile away and about three minutes before the collision, Simpson said he began his efforts to warn the *Heather Lynne II* by first trying to call the boat, then shining the spotlight, and in the last seconds slowing the engines to put sag in the hawser in the vain hope that the *Heather Lynne II* would pass over it.

Kelly concluded this could not be so. Instead, Simpson probably began his last-ditch efforts to warn the boat—efforts that culminated in dropping the engines to an idle—when the *Heather Lynne II* was 250 yards and about forty seconds from collision.

Kelly believed Simpson should have begun a gradual 30-degree course change at least ten minutes before the collision, in which case he would have passed a half mile behind the *Heather Lynne II*. Instead, Kelly said, Simpson maintained his course and speed until it was too late.

"Based on a comparison between an accurate reconstruction of the situation and what Mr. Simpson testified to," Kelly concluded, "it is obvious that Mr. Simpson misinterpreted every important aspect of the situation as it developed—so much so that one might legitimately question his motives for testifying as he did as well as to raise doubts as to whether or not he was, in fact, at all times in the tug's wheelhouse before collision. Regardless, this collision could easily have been avoided had Mr. Simpson properly used his radar equipment and his eyes and had he carried out his responsibilities under the rules of the road, as the person in control of the burdened vessel in a crossing situation."

The report of the Coast Guard investigation, which was written by Lieutenant Paul King, asserts that neither vessel altered course or speed prior to the collision despite Simpson's testimony that the *Heather Lynne II*'s bearing and course changed appreciably as the two vessels drew near. Like Kelly, it notes that the *Houma*'s speed was in fact a knot faster than Simpson had said. Lieutenant King also agreed with Captain Kelly's assertion that Simpson should have determined more precisely the course, speed, and closest point of approach of the *Heather Lynne II* and, since the *Houma* was the give-way vessel, taken clear and appropriate action to avoid a collision. King also determined that Simpson, regardless of the initial course set by Captain Breen, "failed to adequately take into consideration the maneuverability of the *Houma* and *Essex* tow configuration prior to knowingly entering a concentration of fishing vessels." King agreed that the evidence showed that Simpson made no attempt to avoid a collision until thirty seconds before the collision took place.

King concluded that Simpson failed to determine whether a risk of collision existed, imprudently traveled at 9.6 knots until ten seconds before the collision, failed to avoid a collision, and failed to sound the danger signal in time. He found that the crew of the *Heather Lynne II* also contributed to the collision by failing to maintain a proper lookout, failing to use all available means to determine if risk of collision existed, failing to take evasive action, and failing to correct their impaired ability to see through tinted and weathered wheelhouse windows.

Simpson stopped working for Eklof in early July 1997. On August 13, 1997, he pleaded no contest to Coast Guard charges of misconduct (for failing to determine if a risk of collision existed) and negligence (for failing to avoid a collision and following an imprudent course and speed through a concentration of fishing vessels). His license was suspended for four months and he was placed on probation for one year, during which time any additional mishaps would have resulted in his license being revoked. He was also instructed to take a bridge management resource course. By 2003 he had returned to sea and was running tugs for a Massachusetts towing company that, among other duties, escorted giant liquefied natural gas tankers into Boston Harbor.

IN AN INTERVIEW five years after the accident, Simpson said the morning still haunted him, and that fishing boats terrify him the most.

"Now, I'm very wary of fishing boats doing screwy things. I always was, but now I'm petrified," he said. "You can't predict that they are going to do the right thing."

He insisted that his account of the events leading up to the collision was based on the facts, and that he had nothing to hide.

"I did everything right," he said. "I know how to do my job. And you can't control what other people are going to do—or not do. You can say all you want, but the rules of the road only work when there is someone running both vessels."

James A. Ruhle, a fisherman who narrowly avoided a collision with a merchant ship off the coast of North Carolina in 1998, might agree with Simpson, but in an article he wrote for the Coast Guard's journal of safety at sea, he reminded mariners that there's no guarantee that there will be someone in the wheelhouse of both vessels, and one captain may be left by default to determine the best course of action. In Ruhle's case, as the merchant ship had passed him, he had looked into the bridge and had seen no one there. He had been trying to hail the approaching ship for six miles. In fact, the rules of the road take this variable into account; one can't always expect an operator to be at the helm of another vessel due to a myriad of reasons ranging from physical (falling unconscious or asleep) to operational (the helmsman helping with nets, plotting a course, or investigating a mechanical malfunction). Further, the rules of the road clearly state that a collision is everyone's fault.

Simpson insisted that anyone in his shoes would have done the same thing.

"I did everything I could, based on the knowledge I had," he said. "If I had known no one was running that boat, then I would have gone five miles to the east to get away from it. Anybody would. If you knew a torpedo was coming at you, you'd do what you could to get out of its way."

Simpson said those who had suggested the boat was at anchor, like the crew of the *Scotia Boat Too*, were dead wrong.

"The boat was *not* anchored," he said, his voice raised, "or, if it was, that was the fastest anchored boat I've ever seen."

As for those who reconstructed—and then found fault with—his actions, Simpson said it was unfair of them to judge.

"Of course someone could plot something backward based on calculations, and it all looks good on paper, but it's different at sea," he said.

"Everyone in my industry knows it could happen to them. What's that saying? 'There but for the grace of God go I?' Anyone who's ever towed up and down the coast has innumerable stories of close calls. Everyone thinks, 'It wouldn't happen to me, because I would have done something different.' But you don't know what you would do—or could do—unless you've been there.

"I know what I saw, and I know I did nothing wrong. People like to think of the big bad tugboat running down the little fishing boat, but that's just not what happened."

» Linda E
December 11, 1998

FOR MORE THAN A YEAR, no one could verify whether the fishing vessel *Linda E* had been run down the day she disappeared. When a foreman at the Smith Brothers Food Service called the *Linda E*'s cell phone at 9:46 A.M. on December 11, 1998, deckhand Scott Matta reported that they were still hauling nets and would be in later that afternoon with about a thousand pounds of chub. With the bright sun shining, they could see seven miles across the calm waters of Lake Michigan. The temperature climbed from below freezing to a mild 48 degrees near noon. There was a light, four- to six-knot southwest wind. It was a pleasant, ordinary day, just one more day in the string of years, nearly thirty, that Captain Leif Weborg and his crew had worked these waters to catch fish for Smith Brothers.

Weborg had left Port Washington, Wisconsin, near Milwaukee, at about 5:15 A.M. aboard his 42-foot gillnetter *Linda E* to haul her nets a few miles to the south. Friends said he typically fished two sets of gillnets that were four feet high and as long as two miles. Weborg would head west while hauling the nets, a job that took at least three people. Then he'd turn to the east as his two deckhands set the nets back out to fish overnight. Sitting in the pilothouse he'd eat a lunch packed earlier by his wife, then he'd put the boat on autopilot, head at about 8½ knots for home, and go below to help clean fish.

Burger Boats, in Manitowoc, Wisconsin, had built the steel gillnetter in 1937. In 1996 she was replated with ³⁄₁₆-inch steel plates welded over her original hull, which made her especially appealing for use during the winter, when ice damage was a concern. Her deckhouse, no more than eight feet off the water, was completely enclosed. The only way to see the lake around them was through portholes or one of the five sliding metal doors the crew would open to haul or set gillnets while staying out of the weather. They would retrieve the nets through two forward doors (one on each side) and set the nets through three doors at the stern. (Two other doors were considered service doors and were not used for fishing.) Every five to ten minutes while they worked, the crew would take turns looking out the portholes and doors to see what was around them.

The *Linda E*'s navigation and safety equipment included a VHF radio, cell phone, radar, magnetic compass, autopilot, life jackets, ring buoy, and survival suits. She did not carry an EPIRB. The Coast Guard in 1995 had granted Captain Weborg's request to be exempt from such a requirement.

Weborg, a sixty-one-year-old fisherman of Norwegian descent, had two men on board with him: a longtime friend, forty-five-year-old Warren G. Olson Jr., and Weborg's son-in-law, thirty-three-year old Scott T. Matta. Weborg's father, uncles, and grandfather had all been commercial fishermen; Weborg figured fishing was in his blood. Earlier that week, a friend had asked Weborg why, at his age, he didn't retire from fishing. He said he probably should, but, "You know, I love what I'm doing."

Olson was just as passionate about commercial fishing. His father had worked at Smith Brothers and had once fished with Weborg, to whom he introduced his son. For the next twenty years, "Warnie," as his family called him, fished alongside Weborg. A quiet and even-tempered father of four, he, like Weborg, was as passionate about stock-car racing as he was about fishing, and the two often attended races together. Matta, Weborg's son-in-law, did not love the fishing life. To him it was simply a job, but he was a hard worker who was known to have an engaging and occasionally disarming sense of humor. Like the others, he was a family man, devoted to his wife and two young daughters. The three worked long, hard hours together and would come home soaked in the odors of boat and fish. Weborg told his kids it was "the smell of money."

Although Matta had said during the 9:46 A.M. call that they'd be home midafternoon on December 11, just two weeks before Christmas, the *Linda E* was never heard from again.

WEBORG'S WIFE WAS TRIMMING their Christmas tree with their grand-children when she and her daughter, Matta's wife, realized that the *Linda E* was overdue. Coast Guard Group Milwaukee, upon being alerted, began a two-day search that encompassed 3,000 square miles of Lake Michigan and turned up nothing. One friend of the fishermen, who joined in the search with his own boat, said it looked like the lake had been raked clean. Searchers found no sign of the boat. No debris. No pollution. No oil slick. No recorded distress calls. No reports of anything out of the ordinary. Nothing.

She had just disappeared.

On the day the Coast Guard called off its search, it told the family there was nothing more it could do to locate the missing boat because the Coast Guard does not do search and recovery, leaving that job to com-mercial salvors. Instead, the agency launched an investigation to try to fig-ure out what had happened to the *Linda E*, a mystery the family argued couldn't be solved without finding the boat. Coast Guard investigators in-terviewed forty commercial fishermen, family, friends, and others to un-derstand the routines of the crew and the handling habits of the *Linda E*. They studied similar boats and created computer models to understand her stability and strength characteristics, finding that even if her bilges were full of water and she were iced up, she'd still be fairly stable. They learned that her hull did not contain watertight compartments that, if one portion of the hull began to flood, could be sealed from the rest of the boat to retain positive buoyancy. If she began flooding through a 2½-inch hole, she'd sink in about an hour. If she began flooding through an open stern door, she'd sink within eight seconds.

COAST GUARD INVESTIGATORS identified twenty-six commercial vessels that had passed through the area where *Linda E* was last reported at about the time she would have been there. One merchant ship, the tug *Michi-gan*, pushing the barge *Great Lakes*, passed through the area—and over the *Linda E*'s submerged nets—sometime between 11:20 A.M. and 12:05 P.M. This integrated tug-and-barge unit, in which the tug hooked into a notch on the stern of the barge to push instead of tow it, had an overall length of 454 feet, was 60 feet wide, and extended 13 to 14 feet down in the water. The *Great Lakes* had a reinforced bow so that she could break ice while operating year round on her usual route carrying fuel oil from Whiting, Indiana, to Cheyboygan and Traverse City, Michigan. From the *Michigan*'s wheelhouse 42 feet above the water, the crew would have been able, on a clear day, to see the *Linda E* up to eleven miles away. The crew of the tug *Michigan* told investigators that they had not seen the *Linda E*, or any debris from her, when they passed through the area. Nor did they see any other vessels on their radar.

Investigators found white and black marks indicative of a collision on the sharp stem and forward starboard bow area of the barge *Great Lakes*, extending 2 to 8 feet above the waterline. Paint samples were compared with paint believed to have been used by Weborg on the *Linda E*, but the paint did not match. The tug's crew, who said the boat usually docked on the port side, could not explain the fresh scrapes on the barge's starboard side.

At a press conference, Coast Guard investigators said they had repeatedly interviewed Scott Gorney, the thirty-seven-year-old first mate on the tug *Michigan*. Gorney said he'd been alone in the wheelhouse during the time the two could have collided. There had been a watch change at 11:30 A.M., after which Gorney, facing aft, had stood at the chart table—as Michael Simpson had done on board the tug *Houma*— and had made corrections on the chart. He looked up at one point and noticed an unusual number of gulls pass behind him, but other than the gulls, he insisted that he didn't see or notice anything out of the ordinary.

Because there were no known witnesses or concrete evidence to the casualty and the *Linda E* remained missing, Coast Guard investigators could reach no conclusion as to what had happened to the boat and her crew. In their report, investigators suggested she might have collided with another vessel, hit a submerged object, or experienced some structural failure. The report recommended that the Coast Guard examine its EPIRB exemption policies and distribute the report as a safety advisory to all commercial vessels operating on Lake Michigan. The report also said the Coast Guard would open the investigation again if any new information surfaced.

FAMILY MEMBERS WERE NOT SATISFIED. After more than a year, the Coast Guard's investigation had only turned up more unanswered questions. At least five private salvagers tried unsuccessfully throughout the year to locate the boat. Family members refused to let the mystery go unsolved. They believed there had been a maritime accident, and only a conclusive investigation would prevent similar accidents from happening again, thus ensuring their loved ones hadn't died for nothing. Desperate to persuade the Coast Guard to reopen its investigation, the family sought the help of U.S. Representative Mark Green.

Green arranged a meeting with Admiral James Loy, the commandant of the Coast Guard, to ask him to use sonar equipment to locate the sunken *Linda E*. That summer, the family watched news accounts during which the Coast Guard announced it was conducting what would become a $492,000 search and recovery mission—something it had told the *Linda E* family it didn't do—to find the lost plane of John F. Kennedy Jr. President Bill Clinton assured the country that the initial rescue efforts were "consistent with what would have been done in any other case." Clinton's assertion was echoed by a spokesperson for the Coast Guard, who told an Associated Press reporter: "It doesn't matter to us if you are John F. Kennedy Jr. or John Q. Citizen. We are in the business of saving lives. We will launch whatever resource it takes. Only when we have ruled out any chance of a survivor, and usually it's reluctantly, will we suspend the search."

The family of the *Linda E* crew wondered why the Coast Guard had given up its search for the missing fishing boat and her crew far sooner than it was willing to give up the search for Kennedy's missing plane and its passengers.

ON DECEMBER 16, 1999, Representative Green gave Admiral Loy letters from fifty-four family members, forty-three friends, thirty-five state representatives, and fourteen state senators. He also handed Loy a petition initiated by Olson's aunt and signed by 1,052 people urging the Coast Guard to keep the investigation open and resume a search for the *Linda E* by calling in Navy salvage resources. After a meeting that lasted about an hour, Loy still wouldn't budge. He told Green that after investigating for one year, to do more than the Coast Guard already had would be exceeding its Congressional mandate. A Coast Guard spokeswoman told the *Milwaukee Journal Sentinel*, "We have done the investigation to the extent that's appropriate for this agency. We are not in the salvage business."

Loy said the Coast Guard would offer its resources only in support of investigations conducted by others. Green, vowing to find some other agency willing to help search for the *Linda E*, contacted the National Transportation Safety Board, which said it would consider investigating only if asked to do so by Congress. Normally, the NTSB doesn't investigate marine accidents unless more than six people die, the accident involves a large vessel, or significant monetary loss or environmental damage occurs. About the same time, Wisconsin Governor Tommy G. Thompson sent a letter to Transportation Secretary Rodney Slater requesting a joint Coast Guard–NTSB investigation. By summer 2000, a year and a half after the *Linda E*'s disappearance, the family had started to lose hope. Their requests were mired in bureaucracy despite the efforts of Congressman Green and Governor Thompson.

Then they heard the Navy was coming to town.

In June 2000, the Navy minesweepers USS *Kingfisher* and USS *Defender* planned to be in the area for a Great Lakes recruitment cruise. Representative Green asked if they'd look for the *Linda E* as they passed through the area. Admiral Jose Betancourt, commander of the Navy's Mine Warfare Command, considered it a good training exercise. Friends of the family who had conducted their own searches gave the Navy charts that depicted where they figured the boat might be. On the day of the search, Coast Guardsmen pulled aside Green, who was aboard the Coast Guard's 41-footer with family members, and told him they probably weren't going to find the boat. Green said they at least had to try.

Late in the evening of Father's Day 2000, the *Linda E*, which had been missing for eighteen months, was found by minesweeper sonar sitting 260 feet underwater in mud up to her waterline, seven miles from Port Washington and two-tenths of a mile west of where Weborg's northern gang of nets had been found. Video taken of the wreck by a University of Michigan submersible robot on loan to the Coast Guard showed extensive damage on her starboard stern quarter, the most significant of which was a wedge-shaped indent similar to what would be caused by the sharp bow of a vessel. Several creases ran aft of the indentation; portions of her aft upper deck were crushed. A small tangle of nets could be seen extending out of the open aft, port service door. Three of the five doors used for fishing were closed; two starboard stern doors were open, through which, if the crew looked in time, they may have seen a 60-foot-wide, three-story-high black steel wall bearing down on them.

IN OCTOBER 2000, the Coast Guard issued a supplemental investigation report. Analysis showed that the wedge-shaped bow of the barge *Great Lakes* was consistent with the damage done to the *Linda E*. The Coast Guard determined that the vessels would have intersected at about a 90-degree angle on the *Linda E*'s upper deck, starboard side. The downward force of the collision would have forced her to heel 51 degrees to port, submerging the whole port side. Since two stern doors were open, two seconds of downflooding would have sunk her stern first. Flooding would have forced the crew forward where, with the forward doors closed, escape would have been nearly impossible. The damage also suggested that when the *Linda E* collided with the barge she would have been spun about 150 degrees, so that she sank facing northeast even though, at the moment of impact, she was probably on a southwesterly course. A crime lab also found that paint samples taken directly from *Linda E*—as opposed to a sample from a can of paint that Weborg was *assumed* to have used on the *Linda E*—were consistent with samples taken earlier from scrapes on the starboard side of the barge *Great Lakes*.

The Coast Guard determined that during the late morning of December 11, 1998, the bright sun was just off the port bow of the tug *Michigan*, shining right into the wheelhouse as she headed on a southerly course. It was also likely that the *Linda E* was off the port bow of the tug and barge. The sun glare would have made it difficult to see her. Further, due to the size and configuration of the tug-and-barge unit, once the *Linda E* was close she would have been obscured from the pilot's vision. In the last seconds leading up to the collision, the helmsman would not have seen her; nor, upon collision, would he have felt her.

As for the *Linda E*, her portholes did not offer a clear, unobstructed view from the deckhouse. The crew would have had to look out multiple portholes from multiple angles to get a complete view of what was going on around her. Under that morning's clear weather conditions, the Coast Guard determined that her crew should have been able to see the tug and barge for twenty to thirty minutes before the collision.

Based on the location of Weborg's gillnets, the Coast Guard figured her crew was not fishing when the collision happened, although they may have just finished hauling a string of nets. Coast Guard investigators were unable to determine if she had been moving or stationary at the time of collision; the damage could have occurred either while drifting or while cruising along at 8½ knots. Finally, the Coast Guard suggested the collision would not have happened if both vessels had been keeping a proper lookout. Instead, both boat crews had been busy working. The *Linda E* crew was probably cleaning fish (or possibly, stray evidence suggested, working on a broken engine), while the tug's mate was making corrections on the chart.

The owner of the tug and barge, BP Amoco Corporation, denied in January 2001 that a collision occurred between its tug and barge and the *Linda E*. It sought a limitation of liability for the $8.7 million value of the tug and barge. (Limitation of liability is an admiralty law concept that relieves a shipowner from liability for acts done by his crew without his knowledge and limits the consequent damage award to the value of the offending vessel, its equipment, and the freight it was carrying when the accident occurred.) A judge denied that request in May 2001. Family members of the *Linda E*'s crew sued BP Amoco Corporation. Matta's widow and two young daughters settled with the company on October 2001 for $3.3 million. The Olson family settled in December 2001 for $1.3 million. Captain Leif Weborg's widow and estate settled in June 2002 for an undisclosed amount.

Meanwhile, the Coast Guard sought to revoke the licenses of the tug's captain and mate rather than press criminal charges through the Department of Justice. In April 2001 it dropped its attempt to revoke the license of the captain. The tug's mate, who had been on watch during the collision, agreed to a two-year license suspension and consented to undergo additional training.

THE *LINDA E* STILL RESTS on the bottom of Lake Michigan. Family members decided they did not want to raise her because they knew some of the crew would want their ashes scattered over the lake in any event. It was better to let them be.

On September 21, 2001, Smith Brothers Food Service, a family business that had operated in Port Washington for 153 years, closed down. It reached this decision in part, it said, because of the loss of its commercial fishing fleet in Port Washington, including the *Linda E*. Part of the Smith Brothers building has now become office space for an advertising firm, whose staff meets in a conference room that once served as storage for fishing gear belonging to the *Linda E*.

The loss of the *Linda E* was one more reminder that collisions between commercial ships and fishing boats happen more often than one might think, just as *Heather Lynne II* captain Jeff Hutchins had claimed. Had she not been found, the *Linda E* would have been another footnote in the long list of vessels mysteriously lost at sea, but there was no mystery—just a mate alone on watch with the sun in his eyes or his head bent over a chart, the crew of a fishing boat cleaning their catch or fixing an engine, and neither vessel keeping the vigilant lookout prescribed by the maritime rules of the road. Or perhaps there was a mystery, after all—that strange conjunction of circumstances that, over and over again, puts two vessels in the same small patch of water at the same time.

»The Barge Crew

O N BOARD THE empty oil barge *Essex*, John McLernan was on his midnight to 6:00 A.M. watch. There wasn't a lot to do on the 272-foot barge traveling down the New England coastline. When he had come on watch, he had prepared himself a cup of hot chocolate before stepping out on deck to walk around. He made sure the port and starboard running lights were still lit. He looked over the raked bow to make sure the chain bridle and wire pendant connecting the barge to the towline weren't dragging in the water.

When the barge was loaded to capacity with 35,000 barrels of oil, it weighed about 6,000 tons and sat 12 feet deep in the water, its sides rising just 6 feet high. It reacted more slowly and was less maneuverable when full. But when it was empty, as now, the deck rose 16 feet above the water, while the flat bottom of its 1,250-ton hull was a mere 2 feet underwater. The empty barge, though more affected by wind, was otherwise easier to maneuver. McLernan walked aft to check the stern light, then looked forward one last time to make sure the tug was still towing him.

He walked inside the small cabin and picked up a book. Neither the television nor the AM/FM radio was on. The marine radio was tuned to VHF channel 5 in case the tug needed to hail him. The only sound he heard was the hum of the diesel generator. After reading several hours, he took off his glasses and shoes, put down the book, closed his eyes, and fell asleep in his chair.

By September 5, 1996, McLernan, a tall forty-four-year-old with brown hair and brown eyes, had been working for Eklof for fifteen years, the last three and a half on board the *Essex*. His father, an oil salesman who had moved his family to Staten Island, New York, knew Carl Eklof Sr. and had found his son a job working on Eklof oil barges. Before that, McLernan and his brother had operated a lawn care and landscaping business in New Jersey. He was not interested in tugs and navigation. He was, rather, a self-described "cargo guy" who pumped oil on and off the barge. He kept the deck lines in order, kept the place clean, and maintained the three pumping engines and the generator, which supplied electricity to the small living quarters located on the port corner of the stern. Inside this deckhouse, which measured about 18 feet long and 9 feet across, were a small galley and a separate, decent-sized bunkroom with lockers and two bunks. The metal door to the deckhouse, which was usually closed, opened toward the stern. There were two portholes on the port and starboard sides.

On board the barge with McLernan, asleep in the bunkroom, was forty-eight-year-old barge captain Barry Beretta. He had joined the merchant marine in 1973 after serving four years in the Navy, which included a tour as a gunner on a 32-foot riverboat patrolling the waters of Saigon during the Vietnam War. Beretta started working for Eklof in 1976, first on tugboats and later on barges, and had worked on the *Essex* for about eight years. As barge captain, he was responsible for loading and discharging the cargo and for associated paperwork, as well as machinery maintenance. His watch schedule alternated with McLernan's. On the morning of September 5, having unloaded their cargo in Bangor, Maine, Beretta figured all they had to do was to "cruise on back to New York."

On watch and asleep, McLernan didn't know there was a problem until he heard the tug *Houma's* air horn blowing the danger signal. He heard more blasts as he jumped out of the chair.

"I went outside onto the stern, and I was looking," he told Coast Guard investigators. "And I seen the tug off our starboard side. It had its spotlight on."

McLernan walked to the starboard side of the barge and saw the tug about 300 to 400 feet ahead and about 150 feet to starboard of the barge, in about the two o'clock position. The barge was not tracking in a straight line behind the tug. To him it appeared the tug was heading almost perpendicular to the barge's track, as if the *Houma* were making a hard right turn.

McLernan saw the spotlight on the tug shining a slow arc from side to side on the water behind it. He would later tell Coast Guard investigators that he had a bad right eye and wasn't wearing his glasses, so he had a hard time seeing what was happening. He couldn't be sure what the tug was doing, because the spotlight was blinding him.

"I was trying to focus on what was going on," he told investigators. "And I was looking at the tug. And for several seconds. And I was looking. And all of a sudden, I caught a glimpse of the fishing vessel that was going past. And it went in between the tug and the barge."

He couldn't be sure of the fishing vessel's course or the direction from which it was coming, but it was off to the starboard side of the barge. He couldn't guess its speed other than to say, based on the few seconds it took to pass the tug, that the fishing boat was going "pretty fast." He thought it would hit the hawser, not the side of the *Essex*, and then the barge might trip over the boat.

McLernan ran back to the cabin, opened the door and looked at the clock straight ahead on the wall. It was about 5:15 A.M. He wanted to put on a shirt and shoes and grab a flashlight. While he was putting on his shoes, he neither heard nor felt any evidence of a collision. No crash. No bang. No shift or shudder of the barge. Recalling these events before Coast Guard investigators weeks later, he choked up remembering that moment when, in desperation, he just wanted to help out.

As McLernan bent over to tie his shoes, barge captain Barry Beretta opened the bunkroom door and said, "Something must be wrong." He had been sleeping when the tug's horn blasting in through the open port-hole woke him up. McLernan looked up at Beretta and said, "I think we hit something." Beretta walked out the back door and over to the starboard side of the *Essex*. He saw the tug offset a little to the right. He saw its spotlight moving back and forth. He went back inside and grabbed two big flashlights inside the galley door. Handing one to McLernan, who was on his way out, he said, "Start looking." As Beretta walked to the port side of the barge, he cast his flashlight beam fifteen to twenty feet into the darkness. He found a capsized fishing boat off the port stern quarter. He could hear a slow revving sound of the still-running engine, its propeller turning a slow putt-putt-putt.

"Here it is," he called to McLernan.

Beretta walked back inside the cabin and called the tug at 5:21 A.M.

"*Essex* to the *Houma*," Beretta called on the marine radio. He could hear the tug talking to the Coast Guard. At 5:24 A.M. he tried again, saying, "*Essex* to the *Houma*."

Mike Simpson answered him.

"Yeah, it's the *Houma*," Simpson said. "Do you see anyone in the water back there?"

"No, we've been looking," Beretta said. "The boat is right here, though. Right behind us, Mike."

"OK," Simpson said.

Beretta walked back out on deck. He told McLernan to take the starboard side and he'd take the port side and start looking for anyone in the water. They didn't notice right away that the assemblage of antennas and gear ripped from the roof of the fishing boat now hung in their bridle. A minute or two later, they met up along the stern of the barge and again shined their lights on the turtled boat afloat behind them.

Its engine had died. The propeller was still.

ON BOARD THE *HOUMA*, deckhand Shawn Richter raced down the steps of the wheelhouse and through the corridor to wake Captain Allen Breen. He knocked on the door and then opened it. The room was still dark.

"A fishing boat just tried to cut in front of the barge," Richter said.

"Did we hit it?" Breen asked.

Richter later thought he said yes.

Captain Breen would later explain to investigators that he woke up when he heard the tug's horn blowing an alarm. It wasn't something he could hear easily underway; it was only because the engines were slowing down that he was able to hear the horn blasting. When the engines dropped down to an idle, about 300 RPMs, the horn stopped. As he gathered his senses, he thought, "Jeez, I hear the alarm going off, which does happen in the course of a trip, but maybe it's time to get up and maybe I ought to go up to the bridge."

Within five seconds, Richter entered his room with the news.

Breen jumped up, threw on a pair of pants, his boat shoes, a flannel shirt, and his hat, and ran up the stairs to the bridge. He later figured it took about twenty seconds. He found Simpson using one of the searchlights and talking on the radio to the Coast Guard. Breen asked what had happened.

"A fishing boat went underneath the bow of the barge," Simpson said.

"Are you sure?" Breen said.

"Yes."

Breen looked at the radar and said, "Where are they?"

"They're behind somewhere," Simpson said.

Breen searched the radar screen for a target. Simpson had put the engines back in gear and was just starting to turn to the right. Breen wanted to be sure the barge, which he found off his starboard side, wasn't going to run into the tug. Simpson was near tears.

Breen looked at the radar to see if the tug had enough room to turn around. He didn't want to hit any other boats. Taking the helm, he first turned more to starboard and then gradually swung around to port so as to keep the barge behind him on a reciprocal course back to the capsized boat. He later told Coast Guard investigators that he made a much tighter turn than he would normally make, because all he wanted to do was get back to that fishing boat. He saw a radar contact and then looked up to see a small fishing boat coming toward him from the south, maybe a thousand feet away. (This was the *Scotia Boat Too.*) At the same time, Breen and Simpson were also playing the two searchlights over the area of the collision. They saw something off the port stern of the barge and shut the searchlights off to see if, using their night vision in the first hints of a predawn twilight, they could get a clearer view.

That's when they saw a silhouette of something in the water.

Breen told Simpson, "I have it."

"Watch out," Simpson said to him. He wanted to make sure they didn't hit anyone who might be in the water. Breen started heading in the direction of the object while the crew prepared to haul in the hawser. He called the approaching boat, the *Scotia Boat Too*, and told Richard Burgess, whom Simpson had known from their boyhoods on Cape Ann, to stay clear as the tug was turning to port. The *Scotia Boat Too* veered off and then headed for what looked like the capsized fishing boat. As Breen approached within 100 feet of the *Heather Lynne II*, he walked to the aft controls to pull the hawser in. He told Simpson to stay in the pilothouse and keep looking for anybody in the water.

Breen initially planned to stay near—but not too near—the capsized boat and keep the *Essex* on a short tow. From where he was standing at a set of duplicate helm controls on deck as they hauled in the nylon hawser, he looked toward the capsized boat and noticed the *Scotia Boat Too* nearby. A few more fishing boats were steaming over. Feeling that his tug and tow could prove a hindrance, he stayed about 150 yards from the

Heather Lynne II. When Breen returned to the bridge after hauling in the hawser, Simpson told him the gathering fishermen needed them.

"They're calling for us to come over and help them," Breen remembered Simpson saying to him at 5:45 A.M. "They believe they heard tapping on the hull and for us to come over there and try to see about getting a line on them and holding them up."

Until then, Breen had no intention of helping the *Heather Lynne II*. He had not heard the call from the *Scotia Boat Too*, who made the request.

"I wasn't going to go over there," Breen told investigators. "I was going to hold my hawser because I knew other boats were coming on scene, and I didn't want to go into that area with a barge on my stern." Simpson remembered that he had to talk Breen into going over to see if they could help, because Breen didn't want to be pushed into any rash decisions.

BERETTA COULD SEE from where he was standing on the *Essex* that the crew was assembling on the *Houma*'s stern and preparing to haul in the hawser. He walked forward and started up the engine that ran the hydraulics needed to pull in the bridle and pendant and disconnect from the tug. McLernan worked the capstan, operating a single lever to drive, stop, or reverse the drum used to haul in the bridle and pendant. He followed Beretta's commands as he wrestled with the hawser: slack it down, pick it up, slack it down, pick it back up.

It wasn't easy going. Beretta looked over the bow of the barge and saw a mast, radar, radio antennas, lines, small white buoys, a square section of the *Heather Lynne II*'s roof, and a cluster of net tangled in the bridle and pendant. The pendant wouldn't budge; something else appeared to be holding it down into the water. Minutes later, the *Houma* arrived alongside the bow of the *Essex* and tied another line to the entangled gear. They used this line to take the strain off the hawser, which was undamaged, so they could disconnect it from the barge. Beretta left the chain bridle dangling and dropped anchor. The work had taken about twenty minutes.

IT WAS JUST BEFORE SUNRISE, with the thick morning air hanging heavy on the glassy sea, when Breen, his tug still lit up for towing, drifted alongside the silent *Heather Lynne II*. He placed his bow parallel to her stern. As they prepared to tie a line to her, the *Retriever* appeared with Ted Rurak on board. He backed up to the *Heather Lynne II*, and his deckhand climbed onto the slippery green bottom and helped pass a line through her skeg and back to the *Houma*. At least now she wouldn't sink and take her crew with her.

Simpson, Richter, and tug deckhand Joe Koch stood on deck along with *Houma's* engineer, Rexford Touse. Simpson grabbed a crowbar, ran to the *Houma's* stern, and hung out over the tires so that he could bang on the hull of the *Heather Lynne II* up near her bow.

Someone rapped back.

Simpson banged again. Back and forth they banged. Simpson yelled to whomever was banging. Richter found a long boathook and handed it to Simpson. Breen had told the Coast Guard they'd need to get divers on scene. Now, they figured, there wasn't much they could do. Some thought about diving in, but they didn't have any dive gear on board, so Simpson, Richter, and Koch banged on the hull of the *Heather Lynne II*. At intervals Simpson would walk up to the wheelhouse to listen to the radios and see how the rescue was progressing. Then he'd go back to the stern. At one point, Simpson climbed onto the overturned hull of the *Heather Lynne II* and sat there, yelling to the men trapped below, just three inches of fiberglass between them.

Excruciating, Simpson later said, was a good word to describe the exchange. And the wait.

What appeared to Simpson to be the same voice from the same general location in the boat repeatedly yelled: "Help me! Help me! Get me out of here! Get me out of here!"

Simpson told him to take it easy, that a Coast Guard helicopter was on its way with divers. He told the voice to try to save air. At the Coast Guard's request, he asked how many people were on board, and the voice kept saying, "Three. Three. Three."

It went on like that.

The urgency in the trapped man's voice never changed. Simpson tapped on the hull of the *Heather Lynne II*. A muffled voice hollered something about losing air. He and Richter both cried. Then Simpson chain-smoked cigarettes and paced the deck. Low, milky clouds smothered the emerging daylight. They saw other fishing boats gather near them and idle there. Somber tuna fishermen watched and listened as Simpson yelled to the trapped men, whose pounding on the hull and cries for help rippled through the gathered fleet.

"There's not much air in here!" the trapped fisherman yelled. "Get me out! Get me out!"

The boat was shifting as time wore on. Initially, it was exactly upside down, resting on its waterline with about a third of the hull exposed, in the first few minutes it rolled perceptibly. Then it seemed to stabilize. Unknown to onlookers, however, the turtled *Heather Lynne II* was straining against the increasingly taut line that held her to the tug.

Breen looked down at the fishing boat tied alongside him and thought about what they could do to help. He thought about a number of different things to try, even going into the water himself. The whole crew wanted to jump in.

"When you're a seaman like that, you're willing to take more chances than you had to," Breen told Coast Guard investigators. "We all wanted to go in. I thought about that. I thought about a number of different things to assist in this capsized vessel. But at that time, it was later on, I was expecting help to arrive. . . . I didn't know what would happen if I did or didn't do anything. With help coming in, I didn't want to ruin their chance by doing something."

So, the captain decided it was best to do nothing but wait for the Coast Guard to bring a dive team to the scene.

Simpson said the crew felt helpless.

"Once the Coast Guard gets on scene, they're in charge," he said. "But there was nothing the Coast Guard could do, either. Everyone was pretty helpless until we had the right assets there. We told them we needed divers right away, [which] was obvious with a capsized boat. No one was going to swim in there like Lloyd Bridges in *Sea Hunt*. This is real life. No one could hold his breath that long. Everyone out there would have done anything they could to help. But it was obvious no one could do anything."

Breen kept talking with the Coast Guard throughout the morning. "They were letting me know as the time was going on . . . that divers were on the way," Breen said. "And then I would come back and ask again every few minutes, or five minutes, 'Any more word? Any more word?' I kept on asking."

He believed that at one point he was told the divers would arrive in twenty minutes, or by about 6:30 A.M. Breen said that at first he didn't consider how the tug's ability to generate compressed air might be used to assist the trapped men. The thought hadn't occurred to him until one of the deckhands mentioned it. Breen then considered the idea but decided against it.

"It was hollered up on deck about using air," he told investigators. "And at that time, we thought that any minute the divers were coming."

It was Joe Koch, Rexford Touse remembered, who suggested trying to force air inside the *Heather Lynne II*. Touse, at fifty-four years old, had been in the merchant marine for twenty-six years and the chief engineer on board the *Houma* for the past seven years. In the early morning hours of September 5, 1996, he was asleep in his cabin, which was above and just slightly ahead of the main engines. He woke up between 5:05 and 5:15 because he heard the engines slow down. It wasn't a gradual, normal slowdown like he'd hear when it was time to pull in the hawser. It was quick, and that's what woke him up. He sat up in bed and turned his light on, knowing it was about time to get up anyway. He wasn't a ball of fire that morning, but it didn't take long to dress. He wasn't concerned until he heard Richter running through the passageway a minute or two later. As Richter banged on Joe Koch's door, Touse opened his door and looked at Richter.

"We've got to pull our hawser," Richter said. "A boat went over the hawser."

Touse grabbed his work vest and climbed down to the engine room to start the other generator so that they could use the capstan to pull in the hawser. Then he went up on deck. In all, this took maybe a minute. Once on deck, he saw nothing but the barge behind him. He didn't converse with Simpson about what had happened, but he could tell Simpson was agitated. They all were.

At some point, while Simpson banged on the hull and yelled to the trapped men, Joe Koch suggested making use of the *Houma's* two air compressors (used for needle guns and chipping hammers) and about 150 feet of hose. Koch wanted to tie an air hose to a boathook and stick it down into the water and under the boat. If the bubbles didn't reach the surface, then they'd know the air was under the boat. But the air intakes were located on the compressors, which were in the aft lower engine room, and Simpson said this wouldn't be clean air. It was engine room air that you wouldn't want to breathe. Years later Simpson would say, "You don't take your scuba tanks to the gas station to fill them up."

"Do you think there's any way we could get a hose up in there to them?" Koch asked Touse, who stood beside him.

"How are we going to get it in there to them?" Touse replied. "Who's going to take it in there to them?"

Dissatisfied with Touse's reply, Koch looked up and yelled to Breen, who was watching from the open wheelhouse window. He asked, "Should we try to use compressed air?"

"Help will be here very shortly," Breen shouted down. "They'll be here any minute."

Koch was twenty-five and had grown up in Jersey City. Simpson considered him a quick learner and a nice kid from a tough background. Some of the crew worried that they might make the situation worse, and then who'd be liable? Koch didn't care about liability. He only cared about saving these guys' lives, but he was the low man on the totem pole and his suggestions didn't go far. Nobody pursued the air hose idea any further. Nobody got out the hoses and hooked them up to give it a try. No one considered using the tank of compressed oxygen that was kept on board for welding. Breen later remembered that someone suggested using a fire ax to chop a hole in the hull. Rurak said they'd never be able to do it because the hull was three inches thick. That made sense to Breen, who was worried that once they pierced the hull, air would escape and that might cause the boat to sink. Breen worried that if the *Heather Lynne II* started to sink, she'd try to take the *Houma* down with her, but Simpson wasn't worried about that because he had the fire ax ready and could cut the line connecting the tug to the fishing boat if he had to. In the end, the best thing to do, the tug captain resolved, was wait. The Coast Guard had assured him that divers were on their way.

ON BOARD THE *ESSEX*, now anchored several hundred yards from the scene with a rat's nest of antennas and lines dangling from its bow like a scarlet letter, Beretta and McLernan couldn't see what was happening to the *Heather Lynne II*. As they sat and waited for orders, they avoided trying to puzzle together what had happened. McLernan wept as the rising sun cast hazy shadows across his face. The morning wore on, while the two somber bargemen watched fishing vessels arriving on scene like a gathering chorus.

»The Gathered Fleet

ORD THAT THE *Heather Lynne II* was in trouble spread like a gust of wind across the waters of Jeffreys Ledge. Twenty-two miles to the northeast, thirty-one-year-old Mike Leary was at the helm of his *Meghan & Ryan* navigating around tuna boats as he searched for his submerged gillnets. He had two radios on board, and one was locked into VHF channel 16, the hailing and distress channel. As he approached the flagged PVC pole on the high-flyer buoy marking one end of his nets, Leary half listened to Richard Burgess talking about a collision. Then he heard Burgess say that the boat was the *Heather Lynne II.* Leary reached for his cell phone and at 5:37 A.M. called Ted Rurak.

"Hey," Leary said, "your boat got hit."

"Where are they?" Rurak asked.

Leary said he didn't know, but he could hear the Coast Guard talking about it on channel 16. Leary had worked for Rurak on board the *Heather Lynne II* from 1988 to 1990 and knew she was a rugged boat because she had taken him through steep seas with winds topping fifty knots. He also knew she had a history. One winter morning he had arrived at Bridge Marina to find that a two-acre ice patch had forced the *Heather Lynne II* off her berth and into the pier. Leary slid through a roof hatch, started the boat up, and backed her away. The insurance company declared the accident an act of God—something of an omen in itself, he thought. Twice he had taken freak waves over the bow and blown the windows out of the wheelhouse, so Rurak had installed heavy-duty, unbreakable Lexan windows. After that her heater caught fire and filled the wheelhouse with smoke, and when a firefighter tried to break the Lexan windows with a fire ax it only bounced back and nearly hit him in the forehead. The firefighter instead managed to rip a hole in the forward port corner of the roof through which the smoke could escape.

Leary also knew her crew. Jeffrey Hutchins had once been his room-mate and was late to Leary's wedding because his deckhand had fallen asleep at the wheel and driven the gillnetter *Ann Marie* several miles past their destination. Hutchins had been furious. Leary said one of every captain's biggest fears is that his helmsman on watch may fall asleep at the wheel.

As Leary listened to the Coast Guard talking to the *Houma* and the *Scotia Boat Too*, he thought of going to the scene, but he knew it would take his boat about two hours to get there. By then, he expected, the men would be rescued. So, with the radios turned up loud enough to be heard on deck, Leary began to haul a string of nets.

ALONG THE WESTERN part of the ledge between Leary and the accident scene, Bob Yeomans and his son Rob, on board the *Erica Lee*, had just reached their chosen tuna-fishing spot about three miles north of the tip of Cape Ann, having left the Merrimack River in early-morning darkness. Idling on the flat calm sea, they were sniffing out the best spot to set up for the day. Rob stood by at midships and held the 40-pound anchor on the gunwale while he waited for his father, who was watching the fish-finder, to tell him when to let it go. Bob, forty-eight years old with blond hair, blue eyes, and a graying beard, looked preoccupied with what he was hearing on the marine radio, something about a collision between a fishing boat and a tug and barge off Cape Ann, not too far away. Bob turned up the volume on the VHF, and they listened for a few more minutes to get a sense of what was going on. They considered whether to drop anchor or drop their plans. Then they heard the boat's name: the *Heather Lynne II*.

Bob Yeomans turned to the southeast and sped toward the scene. He had been fishing these waters for more than thirty years and had known Ted Rurak almost as long. When Yeomans had enlisted in the U.S. Coast Guard in 1966, his four-year tour of duty included time as a third-class boatswain's mate at Coast Guard Station Gloucester, where he was a coxswain of a 40-foot search-and-rescue boat. In 1980 he'd built his *Erica Lee*, a black-hulled, 42-foot Bruno with a 20-foot-long pulpit and a 20-foot-tall aluminum tuna tower. For a while he took her commercial fishing and had her rigged as a dragger. In 1996 she had spent her summer weekdays hauling kids around as part of a marine educational program and her weekends deep-sea charter fishing. On days off and on every open day after Labor Day, Yeomans took her tuna fishing.

As they sped to the scene, Yeomans and his son continued listening to the marine radio. Yeomans called Rurak at 5:38 A.M. and again at 5:45 A.M. to be sure he knew his boat was in trouble and then to find out what he could do to help. On another radio channel he heard a raspy-voiced fisherman advising John Frawley on the *Blue Heron* to shine lights in the water so the trapped fishermen could find their way out. Frawley thought that was a good idea and said he'd see what he could do. Just before six o'clock, the Coast Guard's 41-footer announced on the radio that it would soon be on scene and asked for an update. The *Houma* said they had lines on the stern but that the *Heather Lynne II* appeared to be sinking.

Rurak called the Coast Guard boat. While he was waiting for a response, a friend on board the Merrimack River–based *Robyn Ann* called him. The *Robyn Ann*—a dragger, or trawler—was pulling an otter trawl over the bottom on Jeffreys Ledge to catch groundfish. Rurak's friend asked, "Teddy, you want us to come out and put some cables under it?" Rurak, who might not have heard the offer, instead asked the Coast Guard 41-footer when they would be getting on scene. It was 6:06 A.M. The 41-footer said it was about two miles away.

"All right," Rurak said. "My guys are still banging on the inside of the hull."

"Roger that, sir," the 41-footer replied.

Seconds later another dragger from the Merrimack River called Rurak, saying, "Hey, Teddy, this is Jimmy. If I can help you, give me a holler. I'll do anything you want." Rurak told him no, there were plenty of boats there, but thank you.

When Bob Yeomans heard that the men were alive and trapped in the overturned boat, the first thing that came to his mind was that they'd need a diver.

They needed Michael Goodridge.

EARLY IN THE FIRST WEEK OF THE TRIAL, Bob Yeomans told plaintiffs' attorney Brad Henry that Goodridge, who had done diving work for him, had been a diver for at least the past twenty years and was very well known.

"Well known in the Merrimack area?" Judge Saris asked.

"Yes, in that—Merrimack, Newburyport, Gulf of Maine, Jeffreys Ledge—that whole area," Yeomans said. He explained that as he was headed to the scene, he picked up his cell phone and called Goodridge at home. It was 6:05 A.M. He told Goodridge the *Heather Lynne II* had been hit and the guys were trapped inside. Goodridge asked Yeomans for the loran coordinates. And then the phone dropped.

"Excuse me," Saris interrupted, leaning forward. "What do you mean 'dropped'? Did he hang up on you?"

"Well, I think that phone came down and he was on the way quickly."

AFTER HE HUNG UP HIS CELL PHONE, Yeomans called Rurak at 6:07 A.M. to report that Goodridge was on his way. He said, "I don't know how fast he's gonna be, but I just got ahold of him. He'll be out there in a bit."

"Thanks, Bobby," Rurak said.

"Yeah, Bobby, you copy me?" Goodridge asked. It had taken him less than four minutes to go from sleeping in his bed to his boat, docked a mile away. Goodridge wanted to know if the guys were still trapped inside.

"Yeah, everybody is inside," Yeomans said at 6:08 A.M. "The boat is still upside down, you know. . . . I guess the Coast Guard is trying to get a dive team together, there, and they're going to drop them off by helicopter, but I don't know any more than that."

"OK," Goodridge said, then asked for confirmation of the loran coordinates. "How far offshore are they?"

"Ten miles east of Thachers [Thacher Island]. The [loran] numbers are 680 and 740, about somewhere around there," Yeomans said. "I don't know the exact numbers, but we're heading in that direction. I think you're going to be close to it."

At 6:10 A.M., while Goodridge was leaving the marina from which the *Heather Lynne II* had departed four hours earlier, the Coast Guard 41-footer was arriving on scene. *Houma* asked if it had a diver on board. The 41-footer said it did not, but that the Coast Guard had contacted an "underwater recovery team." A helicopter was also on its way from

Cape Cod, the 41-footer said, "And we're gonna go from there."

"Yeah, OK," *Houma* said. "There's banging in the hull, Cap. And we're gonna need someone here as soon as possible."

"Roger that," the Coast Guard's 41-footer said.

By 6:15 A.M., the crew of the *Heather Lynne II* had been trapped for at least one hour.

At least one fisherman could still be heard screaming for help.

WHEN BOB YEOMANS ARRIVED on scene at approximately 6:30 A.M., he stopped about fifty yards from the *Heather Lynne II* and faced the stern of the *Erica Lee* toward her. He stood with his son, Rob, in the cockpit and tried to make sense of what he saw. Looking at the *Heather Lynne II*, he told Attorney Brad Henry—upside down with only her stern tied to the tug—bothered him.

"Very commonsense rule about her being tied up," he said. "There's not a boatowner here that wouldn't tie a stern *and* a bow."

"Did you attempt to go into the scene to tie up the bow?" Henry asked.

"There was two or three of us that were trying to get in closer, wanting to do something," Yeomans said. "The man on the tug, whether it was the mate or the skipper, waved us off. He said that the Coast Guard is going to take care of this case. The Coast Guard is involved. Wait for the Coast Guard."

Attorneys representing the families of Jeffrey Hutchins and John Michael Lowther hoped the testimony of Yeomans and the fishermen who would follow him would convince Judge Saris that there had been more than one person alive and trapped inside the *Heather Lynne II*, that the Coast Guard was in charge of the scene, and that its presence—at once reassuring and intimidating—compelled others not to help. These others had included boats on scene and boats in nearby radio range, one of them a big scalloper rumored to have been heard on the radio offering to help. The attorneys hoped to establish that the only reason fishermen stood by and did not attempt to save their trapped friends was because the Coast Guard had told them to stay away, and in so doing had worsened the plight of the trapped crew of the *Heather Lynne II*.

Attorney Henry asked if Yeomans had heard a scalloper offering to help. Yeomans said that he had not, but that boats right on the scene wanted to tie up to the *Heather Lynne II* to stabilize her and prevent her from sinking or rolling and losing any more trapped air.

"There were comments going on between all of us that were right there, pretty close to each other," Yeomans said. " 'Let's get in there and tie up to it.' "

"And if you had been allowed in there," Henry said, "what did you expect to tie up to?"

"The bow of the boat, tie that bow up. Anything to—the bow was going down, the men were in the bow. Anything to buy time."

"And who waved you off?" Judge Saris asked Yeomans.

"The guy on the deck of the tugboat and then [someone on] the radio was—was saying that the Coast Guard—'fishermen stay away' or 'let's keep people away'—I don't know if that was the captain of the tug or the Coast Guard." Either way, Yeomans said, he believed he was being waved off because "the Coast Guard was involved [and] taking the case. They were in control."

On his cross-examination, Department of Justice Attorney Stephen Campbell asked Yeomans about his wanting to tie a bow line on the *Heather Lynne II*.

"And you were told to go away by someone on the tugboat?" Campbell asked.

"Yes."

"Now, other than the mate or the master of the tugboat telling the vessels to stay away because the Coast Guard's there," Campbell said, "you said you overheard something on the radio. You don't recall the exact words?"

Yeomans recalled the words were something like " 'The vessels around the area of the tug and the boat to stand clear.' "

"You don't know who said that?"

"No, I don't."

"They didn't identify themselves as Coast Guard Group Boston or Coast Guard vessel 41399 [the 41-footer]?"

"I'm not sure," Yeomans said. "I wouldn't want to say that and not really know for sure."

"There was just a voice on the radio?"

"Yes."

"One final question, sir," Campbell said, looking at Yeomans. "I think you testified—I just want to make sure this is correct—that when you heard there was a capsized vessel, the first thought you had was to get divers and that's why you called Mike Goodridge?"

"Yes."

BY 6:30 A.M., Mike Leary had been hauling his gillnets for an hour. Voices booming across his deck from the VHF radio insisted that while the Coast Guard assured the men on scene that divers were coming, time was running out. Maybe, the assembled fishermen were telling each other, they should do something. Maybe they should pass cables under the boat to hold her up high on the surface. Maybe a big scalloper could lift her up with its powerful winches. Maybe they should try to chop a hole in the boat. Maybe someone should jump in the water and try to swim in, underneath the turtled boat. Maybe they should take matters into their own hands, despite the Coast Guard's presence. He remembered hearing a lot of confusion on the radio because, as he later said, "everyone wanted to assist but no one knew what to do."

Leary had debated similar ideas a short while earlier when he looked up from hauling his nets and saw the *Scotia Boat* approaching alongside. On board was Billy Muniz, age thirty-one, a fellow gillnetter who had been anchored for tuna fishing nearby. Muniz had bought the *Scotia Boat* from Richard Burgess, owner of the *Scotia Boat Too*, but he had always wanted a boat like the *Heather Lynne II* and would later copy her layout when he built his 45-foot gillnetter *Lady Shannon*. He particularly liked the net bin on the stern where the gillnets could be left ready to be flaked out at any time rather than stored in grain bags. The *Heather Lynne II* was a boat Muniz respected and, on this morning, wanted to help.

On board the *Scotia Boat* with Muniz was deckhand Charlie Rine, who was a diver and had his gear with him. Muniz asked Leary if he thought he should race down to the scene. Nearby was a 25-foot Mako, a center-console fiberglass fishing boat with twin 225-horsepower outboards on it that Muniz had driven before. He knew he could borrow the boat and arrive on the scene in less than thirty minutes, but would it accomplish anything? After some conversation, Muniz and Leary decided the Coast Guard already had divers on the way, and Jeff Hutchins,

Kevin Foster, and John Michael Lowther would be rescued before Muniz could get there. Or, worse, the boat would sink before anyone could save them. Either way, Muniz and Rine wouldn't change the outcome, so Muniz returned to his anchor and resumed tuna fishing while monitoring the events that unfolded on the VHF radio.

"The *Heather Lynne* morning went on for hours," Muniz later remembered. "Any second, we were waiting to hear that it was over, but the drama just kept going on."

THREE AND A HALF YEARS LATER, Muniz sat on the edge of his seat in the witness stand, leaned forward, and watched Attorney Brad Henry. A good-looking, slender man with large brown eyes and dark brown hair, Muniz looked as if this courtroom were the last place he wanted to be. Henry could see that Muniz was nervous, so he started with easy questions. He asked how long Muniz had been a fisherman. Muniz said he had grown up in Gloucester and had been fishing nearly twenty years, since he was sixteen years old. He had tried swordfishing, lobstering, gillnetting, tuna fishing, herring seining, and Scottish seining for flounder.

"Scottish seining?" Judge Saris asked.

"They've outlawed it," Muniz told her.

"They've outlawed it?" she repeated, eyebrows raised.

"It was too effective," Muniz said.

"I see," Saris laughed.

Henry noted that on the morning of September 5, 1996, Muniz was fishing aboard his *Scotia Boat*, a 42-foot Bruno.

"So your boat was called the *Scotia Boat*?" Henry asked.

"Yeah."

"And that's different from the *Scotia Boat Too*?"

"Yeah."

"Do you know who owned—"

"Richard Burgess," Muniz said.

"—that vessel?"

Henry smiled, paused, and asked Muniz to try to wait until he finished the question so it would be easier for the court stenographer to follow.

"I was just trying to get out of here," Muniz said, causing laughter to fill the courtroom.

"Well, that's honest," Saris said, smiling. Henry asked Muniz where he was fishing on the morning of September 5.

"A place called the Narrows."

"And where's the Narrows, roughly?" Henry asked.

"13465 and 25765," Muniz said, recalling the loran coordinates as easily as he would his home phone number.

"Let me ask that again," Henry said. "Where is it in relation to Jeffreys Ledge?"

"It's on the top of it."

Muniz explained that he was tuna fishing with two other men, Daniel Sullivan and Duane "Charlie" Rine. He learned of the collision sometime around 5:30 A.M. when his deckhand woke him up and said Richard Burgess was on the marine radio talking about a fishing boat that was going down. Burgess called Muniz and told him that a boat had been run over by a tug and barge. It floated back up, and there were people trapped alive inside. That was Burgess's main concern, Muniz said, that somebody was still inside.

Muniz told the court that he had dive gear onboard: a drysuit, two air tanks, weight belts, regulators, mask, and flippers. He had been a recreational diver but had quit after a bad experience—he once almost didn't make it back to shore—yet he knew that if he had to, he could still jump in. But Rine was a more experienced diver. He had taken courses in commercial diving at the Divers Institute of Technology in Seattle, Washington, as a first step toward becoming a Navy diver. Rine had been diving for fifteen years and knew that even if he couldn't enter the turtled *Heather Lynne II*, he could swim around her and help rig up extra lines to stabilize her.

Muniz had heard the Coast Guard issue its urgent marine information broadcasts, but he didn't interpret them as a general alert requesting any and all available divers to respond to the scene. After reading a verbatim transcript of the broadcast, he told the courtroom, "That's what they say every time they put a distress call out." He noted that the position and possibly the nature of the distress will change, but otherwise it's pretty standard language. On the morning of the collision, he believed the Coast Guard had found its own dive team. Henry asked Muniz if he would have responded had the Coast Guard broadcast a request for divers.

"In seconds," Muniz said.

"Did Mr. Burgess ask you to come?" Judge Saris asked him.

"No, because we didn't think it was going to last this long."

"Say that again?" Saris asked.

"We didn't think the boat was ever going to stay afloat this long."

"Why is that?" Henry asked.

"I've been down twice," Muniz said. "Two boats I've sunk in."

"You've had two boats sink from under you?"

"Yes."

"How long in each of those occasions did the boats take to sink?"

"Ten to fifteen minutes."

"So is that your basis for thinking that the boat was going to sink fast?"

"Yup."

Muniz had been aboard the 40-foot *Harmony* when she rolled over and sank one winter night off Cohasset, Massachusetts. She had been herring seining during the day and at night would tie up to the stern of the *St. Peter III*, a 62-foot wooden boat that traveled with them and held their catch. On this trip, four men and one twelve-year-old boy rounded out the *Harmony* crew. Two adults were in the wheelhouse while the other two—including Muniz—and the boy were asleep down below. No one knows for certain what happened—Muniz thought it might have had something to do with the bilge pumps and the load of herring they had on board—but the next thing Muniz knew, he woke up to yelling and screaming as the boat listed to starboard. In that situation, he said, a fisherman is so scared that he figures out pretty quickly how to get out of the boat.

"Like if you were in a building and suddenly the lights went out," Muniz explained. "You'd know how to find your way out based on your understanding of how you got into the building in the first place."

He insisted that if a fisherman can't escape a capsizing boat, there's a good reason for it.

Aboard the sinking *Harmony*, he had crawled through the dark engine room and stepped on the running engine to find his way out. Someone grabbed him from above and helped him the rest of the way. Standing on the listing deck, the fishermen yelled, but no one aboard the *St. Peter III* heard them, so fisherman David Sullivan jumped into the icy water, swam over to the *St. Peter III*, and climbed on board to wake up the crew. Meanwhile, the *Harmony* rolled and all hands were tossed into the frigid sea, where the *St. Peter III* crew rescued them. Muniz said if Sullivan hadn't jumped in and swum over to the *St. Peter III*, he and the men with him would all have drowned. (Sullivan's heroic act—jumping in the water to save his fellow fishermen—is mentioned in Sebastian Junger's *Perfect Storm*, as Sullivan would lose his own life a few years later aboard the *Andrea Gail* on her ill-fated final voyage. He had agreed at the last minute to fill the spot that Adam Randall, who would be lost at sea aboard the *Terri Lei*, had vacated on a hunch.)

In July 1988 Muniz was on board the *Lancer*, coming home from swordfishing on Georges Bank, when the boat took on water and sank. Everyone abandoned ship and climbed into the life raft; they shot off a flare, and a nearby Gloucester fishing boat picked them up. Muniz had never been rescued by the Coast Guard because it had never arrived on scene in time—he was always picked up by other fishermen. Muniz thought of all this as he sat in Courtroom Thirteen and answered questions about why he didn't try to save the trapped fishermen aboard the *Heather Lynne II*.

Henry asked Muniz if, as he listened to the radio that morning, he heard a scalloper offer to help.

"There was some big boat at the scene," Muniz said. "I'm not sure who it was, if it was a scalloper, dragger, or somebody. But he wanted to hook onto a winch. He was talking about hooking a main wire onto his boat."

"Now, how do you know this?" Saris asked him.

"Because they were talking on the radio," Muniz said.

Henry asked if Muniz knew whether or not the scalloper traveled to the scene, but Campbell objected and Judge Saris sustained the objection. Muniz answered it anyway, saying, "He was somewhere in the area."

Campbell again objected. Saris told Henry that Muniz only knew what was recorded in the radio transmissions since he had not actually traveled to the scene. Muniz looked at Saris and furrowed his brow.

"Why, are you saying he wasn't there?" Muniz asked, thinking no one believed him. Henry told him that Campbell was objecting to his questions and not to Muniz's testimony.

"I feel like I'm on TV," Muniz said. Laughter again broke the silence in the courtroom.

Henry tried to rephrase his question, but again Campbell objected on grounds of hearsay. Henry instead asked if Muniz knew when the scalloper was available. Despite Campbell's continued objections, Muniz answered that he couldn't be sure. He only knew that it wasn't at the beginning or end of the rescue attempts but instead was somewhere in the middle.

Judge Saris interrupted Henry to ask Muniz, "So why didn't you respond if you had a diver on board?"

"Who would ever have thought it was going to last this long?" Muniz said.

Henry asked Muniz to list all the reasons why he did not jump onboard the smaller, faster boat with Charlie Rine and his dive gear and speed to the scene.

"The first one—the chances of a boat ever staying up this long, a million to one," Muniz said. "And then, the Coast Guard took over. Burgess wasn't really in charge no more. It's out of your hands."

"Had the Coast Guard not been involved in obtaining divers," Henry said, "would you have gone to the scene yourself?"

"If I thought the boat was going to last that long," Muniz said, "we would have already been there."

During his cross-examination, Campbell took issue with Muniz's interpretation of the Coast Guard's Urgent Marine Information Broadcast. At Campbell's request, Muniz confirmed that he had talked with Burgess and knew that there were people trapped inside the capsized *Heather Lynne II*.

"And when this [UMIB] message came out," Campbell said, "the Coast Guard said that we have a capsized vessel at that general position there and requested that all vessels assist if possible?"

"Yeah."

"So the Coast Guard was asking for assistance for the capsized vessel that you knew had people trapped inside?"

"Yeah."

"And you did not feel it necessary to come down from where you were because you didn't think the vessel would stay up that long?" Campbell asked.

"I didn't think the boat was going to stay up that long."

"Now, no one in the Coast Guard told you not to come down, is that correct?"

Muniz said that was true. The Coast Guard did not ask for his help, but neither did it tell him *not* to help.

As LEARY HAULED HIS NETS, listened to the radio, and paused to talk with Muniz, he remembered that just a couple of years earlier something like this had happened to a boat called the *Lady Lynn* down in Connecticut. It was a frigid late February morning in 1994. The northwest winds dropped the wind chill below 0°F, while the water temperature hung at 32°F. Thirty-three-year-old Captain Robert Conrad aboard the 80-foot trawler called the New London Seafood Dock at around 5:30 A.M. to report that they were icing up and had stopped twice to deice. Conrad knew how quickly ice on deck and in the rigging could destabilize a boat. He expected to arrive by 6 A.M. with a load of whiting. As that hour approached and daylight started to creep in, David Yerman, who owned the boat with partners and had been waiting inside an office on the fish pier, stepped outside, glanced a few hundred yards downriver, and saw his *Lady Lynn* rolled over on her port side, nose down, bow underwater. He yelled to his crew. They clung to her iced-up hull and yelled back. His business partners ran outside. Someone called 911.

Chris Gagnon, a seaman walking his Sunday morning rounds three hundred yards away at Coast Guard Station New London, heard the hollering, looked up, and saw the capsized boat. Coast Guardsmen launched their 41-foot boat at 6:08 A.M., arrived alongside the trawler within six minutes, and rescued four fishermen. Two were pulled from the frigid water and two had been clinging to her bottom. That's when they learned two other men were trapped inside. They could hear them banging on the steel hull and screaming, "Help! Get us out! We're freezing!"

After being plucked from the frigid Thames River, Captain Conrad told Yerman that he'd noticed *Lady Lynn* had felt sluggish from severe icing, and he hadn't been comfortable with the way she was riding on the way home. Built in 1985, the rugged boat had been through every kind of weather. As Conrad maneuvered her toward the dock, thirty-eight-year-old David Mushinsky had been standing on the bow with a boathook in hand, ready to grab a dockline. Todd Rana and Garrett Drake, two deckhands in their early twenties, were standing on the aft deck, preparing to tie up. They'd been dressed in foul weather gear in anticipation of unloading their catch. William Lietke, twenty-three years old, had been down in the galley. The sixth crewmember, Frederick "Rick" Iasiello, had been on deck near a door to the mudroom, a 4-foot-deep by 22-foot-long storage area where extra gear was housed.

"The fellas were pretty relaxed," Yerman remembered. "Everybody was pretty casual and they didn't feel there was a high level of danger. They were approaching the dock. They could see it. They figured they were home safe."

Captain Conrad, in order to come alongside the dock, raised the iced-up outriggers, which had been down during the trip to make for a more comfortable ride home. With the outriggers overhead, the boat felt top-heavy. As he turned to port, he felt *Lady Lynn* roll to port and hang there, listing. Conrad figured maybe a load had shifted, so he told the crew to move some gear over to the starboard side. He tried unsuccessfully to lower the icebound outriggers. *Lady Lynn* continued to list to port, her rail submerging. Conrad told his crew to grab their life jackets; but time had run out, and she rolled over. The three deckhands preparing to tie up at the dock were flung into the Thames River. Captain Conrad escaped from the wheelhouse into the water. Lietke, down in the galley, was swamped by the frigid river water. Iasiello, standing by the watertight door in the mudroom, tried to escape, but shifting gear and rushing water forced him forward and pinned him in the mudroom, which was already chock-full of extra lines, fishing equipment, and shackles. When *Lady Lynn* came to rest in fifteen feet of water, Iasiello found an air pocket.

And started banging.

"Hearing your crew tapping on the hull," Yerman said, "is a horrible, horrible thing to experience."

At 6:20 A.M., the Coast Guard began its search for divers who could rescue these trapped men. They reached the state police dive team as well as divers from the Naval Submarine Base in Groton. At 6:55 A.M. state police divers were on board the Coast Guard's 41-footer. Yerman and his partners tried several times to explain to the divers what the boat would look like underwater and where they'd probably find Iasiello. While there were two divers, only one was qualified to enter a submerged boat. He swam inside *Lady Lynn* but got lost and ended up in the fishhold before returning to the surface. Time was running out.

Rescuers—nearly sixty had gathered from state and local police and fire departments, the Coast Guard, and Navy—decided to cut a hole in the hull. Careful to avoid the fuel tanks, they cut through steel and found a drowned Lietke in the galley just after 8:00 A.M. They still couldn't reach Iasiello. Yerman drew more diagrams and the divers descended in search of him. They found Iasiello near 10:45, entangled in line and cables and gear. He had tried to swim free but drowned during the attempt.

ASIDE FROM THE TRAPPED CREW of the *Heather Lynne II*, there was probably no one on scene who was more aware of what it's like to survive a collision than Dean Holt. He had spent the night at anchor on board the *Jan Ann* near where Hutchins had been headed. The night before, after Hutchins had called him from home and said, "Well, we'll probably see you out there," twenty-nine-year-old Holt and his thirty-three-year-old deckhand, John Cyr, went below to their berths and fell asleep. At some point during the night, a tug and barge passed through the area. Holt figured he would have slept better if the tug had gone farther offshore, but aside from that, it was a beautiful night.

Dean Holt was tall, thin, and witty, with a striking resemblance to Ben Affleck. Working on boats out of the Merrimack River since he was fourteen, he could find fish whenever trouble ashore didn't find him first. By 1996 he was one of the best fishermen in town. He had a kind heart and a rugged work ethic, and he knew how to have a good time. But he also had his share of hard times. One rainy night he watched a car slam into and kill his best friend while he was trying to cross Merrimac Street in Newburyport. On the morning of September 5, 1996, he took a spot in the spectator fleet and listened as his friends struggled to survive getting run over by a barge.

Holt knew John Michael Lowther probably wouldn't even have been aboard the *Heather Lynne II* had Holt not been the first captain to take him fishing. Lowther was only two years younger than he, and they had often run into each other at high school parties. He later agreed to let Lowther crew on the 45-foot gillnetter *Sara Jean* for a day to give it a try. Right away, Holt could tell Lowther had what it took to be a good fisherman. And Lowther wasn't much of a partier, so in the morning he could keep the boat running while the rest of the crew slept off the previous night's festivities.

"He was the one you could rely on to drive," Holt said. "He was someone you could count on. If I could get the boat out of the river, he could take it while you slept."

Two years earlier, Lowther and Holt had been sleeping down below when a deckhand fell asleep at the wheel and drove the *Sara Jean* into the side of a Coast Guard cutter. The *Sara Jean* under the command of Holt and others was a highliner like the *Heather Lynne II*; together the two boats brought in the bulk of the landings for the Newburyport seafood cooperative, Tri-Coastal. The crew of the *Sara Jean* had left the Merrimack River at 3 o'clock on the morning of August 15, 1994, to go bluefin tuna fishing. Underway at six to seven knots, she was 2½ miles south of the Isles of Shoals, a group of islands off the coast of New Hampshire, when, at 5:08 A.M., she ran into the port stern quarter of the 210-foot Coast Guard cutter *Reliance*, which was headed home to Newcastle, New Hampshire, after a ten-day patrol.

A young ensign had been at the helm of the *Reliance* under the supervision of another young ensign, who had qualified for his position less than two months earlier. At about 4:30 A.M., the two ensigns spotted the *Sara Jean* on their radar and noted she was about three and a half miles away. They figured, according to the radar's plotting aid, that she'd pass down the port side and about eight hundred yards astern. The officers did not calculate her true course and speed or determine her closest point of approach. As they watched her draw near on the radar, they noticed she was drifting slightly to port. They then realized that a crossing situation existed. Because the *Reliance* was on the other boat's starboard side, they knew they were the privileged vessel, and the other boat should give way. The officers did not try to hail the *Sara Jean*.

At 5:05 A.M., the ensigns made visual contact with the *Sara Jean* off the port side, just forward of amidships. Now they doubted her intentions. An operations officer who happened to be on the bridge and overheard the ensigns talking walked over to the port side, looked at the *Sara Jean*, and realized a collision was imminent. He first tried to alter course to starboard to avoid a collision, but that didn't look like it would work, so he turned to port and swung the stern away to soften the impact between the two boats.

Even so, the collision tore open the stem of the *Sara Jean*. Lowther had been sleeping down below on the top bunk but woke up when the deck overhead collapsed. Cold seawater rushed in through the bow and splashed on his face. Holt awoke and raced up on deck. He grabbed the wheel, spun the boat around and headed for home as fast as she could go, realizing that if he slowed down, the bow would fill with water and she'd sink in seconds. He called the cutter and said he was headed for home, "and I ain't stoppin'." Holt drove her full speed up the Merrimack River all the way to the dock—a harrowing trip of almost two hours—where a waiting Travelift hauled her out of the water. With his hands shaking while trying to drink a can of soda, Lowther would tell this story to a few fishermen who gathered around him on the pier. With a nervous laugh, he'd keep shaking his head, saying that was the last thing he had expected to happen to him that morning. While the collision shook them up, it didn't keep Lowther and Holt off the water.

The cutter *Reliance* suffered minor cosmetic damage, and the story was swept under the rug. Both boats had failed their responsibility to avoid a collision. Holt registered above the legal blood-alcohol limit when tested ashore after the accident; he had to find another boat to work on, which eventually led to the *Heather Lynne II*. A short time later, Lowther joined Holt because he liked fishing with him.

That summer of 1994, Hutchins was building his house instead of fishing. When *Sara Jean* needed a captain to replace Holt, Hutchins filled in for a few months before leaving her to work the winter on the *Bridgette Mary* out of York, Maine. In July 1995, Hutchins joined Holt on board the *Heather Lynne II*; they worked as cocaptains through the summer and fall until Hutchins hurt his ankle in the motorcycle accident. Holt ran the *Heather Lynne II* with Lowther the rest of the fall, but in mid-February 1996, after Hutchins returned, Holt left to find himself another boat. Lowther stayed behind.

Holt thought of all this that morning as he watched the upside-down *Heather Lynne II*, lapped by early morning ripples while her stern pulled against the line holding her tight to the tug. He knew he quite easily could have been on board with them. More than a few "what-ifs" crossed his mind. But he also knew it was possible to survive a collision with another boat.

"It's like if you come across a bad accident on the road. You feel bad and you want to help. But then if it's your brother or your sister, the things that go through your mind," Holt said later as he sighed and looked skyward. "And then you start thinking about who might have been on the boat instead, and then how it would have been different if they had been."

ATTORNEYS PETER BLACK and Brad Henry were counting on both Holt and his deckhand, John Cyr, to testify that at least one person—and probably more than one—had been alive and trapped inside the overturned *Heather Lynne II*. One might suffice, but two would be better. If Judge Saris didn't believe that two or more men had survived the collision, their case would be weaker—how could they allege a negligent rescue on behalf of the families of Jeffrey Hutchins *and* John Michael Lowther if at least one of the men was probably killed right away? They hoped to convince the judge that the Coast Guard had made the condition of at least two of the three men worse.

Holt testified first. He had wanted no part of it, but Brad Henry had found him one rainy Sunday morning down on his dragger, *Katie Mae*. He remembered parts of that September day, he told Henry as they stood together in his soggy wheelhouse, but he tried not to think about it much. He wasn't sure how much help he could be.

"It's hard to know what to say, because sometimes you hear things and you can't remember if you saw it or heard it or someone else reminded you of it," he said. "And you don't want to say anything unless you're absolutely sure."

Dressed in a navy blue striped shirt, Holt sat in the witness chair and told Henry that he and Cyr had spent the night aboard the *Jan Ann* at anchor right near the *Blue Heron*. They had been fishing the day before but hadn't had any luck, so they decided to sleep on the fishing grounds instead of driving all the way home. It would take so long in his slow boat, he figured, that by the time he got home it would be time to turn around and head out again.

Henry asked Holt if he had been fishing on September 4, an open fishing day.

"Actually, I think it was—" Holt said in his deep voice. He looked up at the ceiling, searching for the best truth his memory could give him. "I believe it was closed, but we were fishing, but we weren't supposed to be fishing—well, we could have fished, but we weren't allowed to keep the fish, or something to that effect."

Those who listened in the courtroom laughed. Holt was mistaken—September 4 had in fact been an open day—but it was a good icebreaker.

"Don't go there," Judge Saris said, smiling.

"On the day of the accident," Henry asked, smiling, "were you allowed to fish?"

"Yes, we were," Holt said without hesitation. He then described the *Jan Ann* as a 37-foot lobster-style fishing boat. On board he had a cell phone, a CB radio, a VHF marine radio, and a single sideband radio. Before going to sleep, he had put the marine radio on channel 16, then talked to John Frawley on the CB radio. He was anchored close enough to see the lights on Frawley's *Blue Heron*. They agreed that whoever woke up at 4:30 the next morning would call the other guy to make sure they both got out of their bunks and started their day. At 4:30 A.M. on September 5, 1996, Holt heard Frawley calling him on the CB.

"I got out of my bunk and went up into the wheelhouse where the radio is," Holt told Henry. "And I answered him back. And he just said it was 4:30, and I said, 'Yeah, thanks for the call,' and I turned right back around and went right back down and got in my bunk again."

Saris joined the laughter that filled the courtroom.

Holt told Henry that the next thing he remembered was hearing voices on the radio. John Cyr was awake and had heard something about a collision. Then they heard Richard Burgess on board the *Scotia Boat Too* talking on the radio to the tug, and sometime during that conversation they heard that the tug had been involved in a collision with a fishing boat, which had capsized. They knew the *Scotia Boat Too* had been fishing right near them the day before, and it dawned on them that this accident might be close by. That's when they got up and took down the plywood screen they'd set up the night before to keep the wind off while they slept. As soon as they took it down, they could see searchlights on the tug and realized it was all happening right behind them.

"We looked around," Holt said, "and we saw the lights and they were fairly close by, so we knew where the accident had taken place was right there. And then I think a little more conversation on the radio led to the name of the vessel that had been capsized."

"And what was that?" Henry asked.

"And that was the *Heather Lynne II*," Holt said quietly, his head down.

"And you were familiar with the *Heather Lynne*?"

"Yes I was."

"And did you know the people that usually operated the *Heather Lynne*?"

"Yes, I do."

CYR UNTIED THEIR ANCHOR LINE and Holt backed away from their anchor ball. They headed at a slow crawl over to the scene less than a mile away, a trip that took between ten and fifteen minutes. They could smell diesel fuel hanging over the water. That's when they heard the *Scotia Boat Too* call the tug *Houma* and say that he had the capsized vessel in sight: *Heather Lynne II*. Holt and Cyr were taken aback. Cyr had worked on the boat for a few months that summer and had known Hutchins since 1989.

As Holt crept slowly and carefully by the tug, which was dropping its barge, he got his first glimpse of the *Heather Lynne II*. One of his first thoughts when he saw her was that Rurak would not be pleased when he learned what had happened to his boat. He thought, "Teddy's gonna tear into these guys for what they did, with his boat upside down." Holt could hear the banging from inside the hull and knew that at least one guy—if not more than one—was alive. He expected they'd be rescued.

He kept telling himself that his friends would be OK.

ATTORNEY HENRY ASKED HOLT IF, when he took his place in the gathered fleet about forty or fifty feet from the *Heather Lynne II*, he heard anything. Holt said he heard banging.

"Do you know whether Mr. Cyr heard any of the banging?"

"Yeah, yeah, he definitely heard what I was hearing, because I remember talking to him about it."

"What did you see happening at the scene next?"

"I'm having a hard time recalling the whole incident," Holt said, pausing and looking up at the ceiling. "I remember somebody was trying to holler into the boat, from the tugboat, I believe. . . . I think there was some conversation, that somebody wanted to know—we knew somebody was banging on the inside, but we wanted to make sure that whoever was on the inside knew that there was somebody on the outside."

Henry asked Holt to read a statement he had made on October 29, 1996, to a private investigator hired by Hutchins's family's attorneys. Holt had said he heard banging that sounded like it was from the bow of the boat and that someone on the tug was hollering to someone inside the boat. He had told the investigator, "The person on the tug said that everyone was alive inside the *Heather Lynne*, but I cannot be sure of that at this time."

Henry asked Holt if he could elaborate on this statement.

"I don't know if he said there was three people that were alive or there was three people aboard. All I know, I heard him say something about three people. And it says in my statement there that I still 'cannot be sure' at this time to that. So if that's what I [said] then, that's what I'm saying now. He said something about three. But I'm not going to testify to the fact there was three people alive or he said there was three people aboard."

Henry asked Holt if he remembered hearing anything about a scalloper offering to help.

"Sometime throughout that time, when everybody was waiting for divers or the Coast Guard to do whatever they were going to attempt to do, I recall hearing something about a scalloper that wasn't right on scene, but was within a few miles or something, that could have came to maybe give some assistance, but they never came," Holt said. "I don't know why, or if they were told not to, or what. But I do remember hearing something about that."

"Where did you hear that?" Judge Saris asked.

"It could have been from the radio. It could have been from—we were close enough to other boats at the time. We could have talked, like we're talking right now, from boat to boat, to a few different boats that were there."

When Department of Justice attorney Campbell questioned Holt, he asked if Holt had heard voices coming from inside the *Heather Lynne II*. Holt said that he had not. He had only heard the banging. While several of the gathered fishermen heard the trapped fishermen tapping on the hull, the ones who heard voices—the crew of the *Scotia Boat Too*, John Frawley, Mike Simpson, and Holt's deckhand John

Cyr—generally agreed that initially there were at least two voices shouting, but that as time wore on, one voice seemed to dominate.

"With regard to this scalloper," Campbell continued. "I'm not sure if
I really understand what you may have heard. Is it possible you could have
heard about the scalloper after the incident, talking to other fishermen?"

"No, I heard about it while we were still there at the scene," Holt said.
"Somebody had said—like I said, I didn't know if I heard it on the radio
or where I heard it, but . . . "

"Did you get a name of the scalloper?" Campbell interrupted.

"No."

"Did you get a location of the scalloper?"

"No."

"Did you talk to the scalloper?"

"No."

"Do you know if anybody told the scalloper not to show up?"

"No."

Campbell sat down as Holt stepped away from the witness stand and
walked to the back of the courtroom. He sat in a hard wooden chair and
listened to his deckhand, John Cyr, elaborate on the events they had witnessed that morning. Cyr told Henry he had heard some yelling and
pounding coming from inside the *Heather Lynne II*'s hull before it was tied
off to the tug *Houma*. Once the Coast Guard boat arrived, its crew asked
someone on the tug to ask how many people were on the fishing boat.

"And then that was relayed to the boat," Cyr said. "And I'm quite sure
we all heard it. There was three."

Campbell objected.

"That's how many people were on the boat or how many people were
alive?" Judge Saris asked Cyr.

Cyr was not sure of that, but he remembered that the exchange went
on for a couple of minutes as they tried to determine how many people
were on board the *Heather Lynne II*.

"Was that communication with someone inside the boat?" Judge
Saris asked.

"Yes, right. They were tapping on the boat. The guy on the tug was
tapping on the boat, yelling, 'How many guys—How many guys are
you?' I believe was the question."

"Did you hear the response?" Saris asked.

"Yes, I did."

"You heard somebody from inside the boat yell, 'There are three of us in here?' " Saris asked.

" 'There's three,' " Cyr said. "Right."

"And was it three of us alive or three of us on board?" Saris asked.

Black objected to Judge Saris's question, but Saris persisted. "Do you know?" she pressed.

"I don't know."

Henry asked Cyr to read his signed statement given on October 9, 1996, in which he said, "I was close enough to hear a guy inside the hull say that there are three. I heard a voice say 'Get me the fuck out of here.' The response given to the trapped man was to hold on, 'Coast Guard divers were on the way.' "

"And you heard the word 'three'?" Saris asked, leaning forward, looking straight at Cyr.

"Absolutely."

"If ever there was an excited utterance," Judge Saris sighed as she sat back in her chair. "Now, what ["three"] means, I don't know . . . " Her voice trailed off, leaving the sentence unfinished. Whereas most hearsay testimony is inadmissible to a court proceeding under the rules of evidence, an "excited utterance," made under conditions of extreme stress or shock, may be considered as lacking all guile and therefore admissible.

Henry wanted to know who Cyr believed took charge of the scene.

"I would assume the Coast Guard would be in charge of the scene once they arrive," Cyr said.

"And was that your perception, once they did arrive?"

"It didn't seem like it, no. There just didn't seem at the time to be a whole lot going on."

"Did the Coast Guard do anything when they arrived?" Henry asked.

"Other than maybe keep some boats back a little bit and keep the area clear of congestion, no," Cyr said, later adding, "I don't remember them specifically talking to anybody. You know, the Coast Guard wasn't answering everybody's questions."

MIKE LEARY REPRESENTED the plaintiffs' last chance to convince Judge Saris that a scalloper had offered to help but was told not to because the

Coast Guard had taken charge of the scene. Leary took the witness stand wearing a dark green shirt and black denim pants. First, Henry asked him to walk over to a large sheet of white paper on an easel and draw a picture of the *Heather Lynne II*'s layout. As Leary sketched and talked, Judge Saris followed closely and asked several questions.

When Leary returned to the witness stand, Henry asked him where he had been fishing on the morning of September 5, 1996.

"Do you want the loran numbers?" Leary asked. Henry shook his head no and smiled, remembering how Muniz had rattled them off, giving the coordinates a level of importance that didn't resonate with the nonmariners in the courtroom. Leary explained that he was gillnetting on Jeffreys Ledge near Muniz, twenty-two miles northeast of the accident. He had six strings of nets in the water, each one holding twenty 300-foot-long by 12-foot-high nets; when deployed on the sea bottom, each string spanned about a mile. It would take him about an hour to haul a string. Leary explained that at some point soon after the tug's Mayday call, Muniz pulled up alongside and asked if he should run to the scene.

"And I said, 'No. The Coast Guard said they're on their way, they'll be there shortly,' " Leary told Henry.

"Did he express agreement with that conclusion?" Henry asked. "That the Coast Guard divers were on their way?"

"Yes."

Henry asked Leary if he remembered hearing anything about a scalloper offering to help, possibly even suggesting it could haul the *Heather Lynne II* up its stern ramp and out of the water. Leary said that he heard it on the radio, but that he was scanning multiple VHF channels and could not be sure which channel he heard it on.

"It was very chaotic," Leary said. "Everybody wanted to help, and the Coast Guard just kept saying: 'Hang on, hang on. The helicopter—it's on its way with the divers.' And as time progressed, it got longer and longer. More people wanted to help."

"That was your understanding, that people were trying to get to the scene to help?"

"It was almost so many people wanted to help, it was chaotic."

Leary said he didn't remember who responded to the scalloper's offer. Henry asked Leary to read the statement he'd given on October 3, 1996, in which he'd said, "I heard a scallop boat which was four miles from the scene tell somebody that their boat could hoist the entire boat up its ramp. I heard the Coast Guard tell them not to touch the boat and that divers were on their way."

"Does that refresh your recollection as to who told the scallop boat not to touch the boat?" Henry asked.

"I don't recall, but reading this, it says the Coast Guard told him not to touch the boat," Leary said. "I don't still remember the Coast Guard saying that, but it's written here, so . . . "

When Leary had given the statement a month after the accident for a lawsuit the families were bringing against the tugboat company, he had not yet heard the Coast Guard could be considered liable. He had read a transcript of his statement and made four corrections to be sure the facts were right; he had not changed what he'd said about the scalloper.

Campbell began his cross-examination by asking Leary if he knew the name of the scalloper. Leary said he did not.

"Have you ever been on a scalloper before?"

"I have."

"Do you know what the speed of a scalloper is?"

"Basically?" Leary asked.

"Yeah, roughly."

Leary said the average scalloper traveled at about nine knots.

"And just so we're clear, a knot is a nautical mile an hour. Is that your understanding of what a knot is?" Campbell asked.

"A knot is a knot. A nautical mile is 1.17 statute miles," Leary said. A wry smile crept across his face, his eyebrows raised. "Roughly."

Campbell explained that he was trying to make it clear for the court that a nautical mile is longer than a statute mile. Leary said that he was right, and that if a boat traveled at nine knots, it could cover nine nautical miles in an hour.

"With regard to the scalloper, again, the boat didn't identify itself?" Campbell asked.

"No."

"And you don't recall when this happened in the scenario?"

"No."

"Was it right at the beginning, when you were talking to Teddy Rurak—"

"No."

"—about this boat?"

"No."

"With regard to the response to that offer," Campbell said. "Did the caller identify themselves?"

"I don't recall."

"Do you recall whether they specified a name or a unit?"

"I don't recall."

"Do you have any recollection at all of what exactly was said in response to that transmission you said you heard from the scalloper?"

Leary said his best recollection was based on the statement he had made in 1996, which was a summary of what he believed had been said over the VHF radio that morning. Campbell asked again if he knew which Coast Guard unit answered the scalloper's call.

"It's probably Group Boston," Leary said. "They took over communications after the first five minutes. And they ran the show."

"But you don't know?"

"No, I don't. That would be speculation."

"So let me ask you this," Saris interjected. "If the scalloper were four miles away, is that what you remember?"

"I do."

"Is that based on something the scalloper said?" Saris asked.

"Yeah," Leary said. "He must have given numbers . . . where the scallopers work on Jeffreys is roughly four miles from there."

"Since you know this nautical mile terminology," Saris said, "how long would it take him to get to the scene of the accident?"

"To go four nautical miles at nine knots is twenty-six minutes," Leary said.

Campbell asked if the scalloper gave his coordinates over the radio.

"Well, if he said he was a scalloper on Jeffreys, I know where he would be, because there's always scallopers in one small area."

"Well, did he say he was four miles from the incident?"

"If I wrote that at the time, he must have said that. I didn't make it up."

"Do you recall exactly what the scalloper said?" Campbell pressed, his voice raised.

Leary said he could no longer remember.

Campbell's purpose was plain. If the scalloper remained a phantom boat, the Coast Guard could not be shown to have told or compelled it not to help, thereby worsening the condition of the men trapped inside the *Heather Lynne II*. No witnesses had been able to pinpoint the scalloper's identity, its location, or the exact nature of its offer to assist, nor could anyone say for certain who had turned its offer down. Through his attempts with each fisherman to highlight the confusion about the scalloper, Campbell sought to suggest that the alleged scalloper was nothing more than a rumor that had circulated through the fleet.

The plaintiffs' lawyers had found no other witnesses to the scalloper's transmissions. As far as Campbell was concerned, this phantom scalloper just did not exist.

»The Search and Rescue Mission Coordinator

I NSIDE A TALL brick building overlooking Boston Harbor, Petty Officer Richard Barone had been sleeping when a Coast Guard watch-stander called to wake him at 5:20 A.M.

"Hey, Rick," Wendy Long said. "Can you come in here? Some guy just hit a vessel and they went down. They can't find the vessel."

"OK," he said. "Be right over."

It was Thursday, September 5, 1996. Barone, a boatswain's mate first-class, had started his 24-hour watch midmorning Wednesday, while the crew of the *Heather Lynne II* was waiting for a buyer to bid on their tuna. After standing duty all day, a day in which nothing major had happened, he had gone to sleep around midnight in a room down the hall from the telecommunications center. His watch-standers monitored communications while he slept, as he was expected to do during a 24-hour watch. He'd be relieved of his watch at midmorning.

As the Group Duty Officer and Search and Rescue Mission Coordinator (SMC), Barone coordinated search and rescue operations for the five Coast Guard stations in Group Boston's area of responsibility, including Coast Guard Station Gloucester. A year younger than Jeffrey Hutchins and two years older than John Michael Lowther, twenty-nine-year-old Barone, of average height, with short brown hair and a soft voice, had been in the Coast Guard eleven years. After serving on cutters and at stations in Alaska, Maine, and Massachusetts, he had been based at Group Boston for a little over two years. His training included coursework at the National Motor Life Boat School, Marine Law Enforcement and Marine Law Enforcement Fisheries School, Small Boat Operations School, Prospective Officer in Charge School, and Marine Safety Petty Officer School. He also had taken a Coast Guard Search and Rescue correspondence course and held a 100-ton near-coastal captain's license. With that and his two months of on-the-job training to become a group duty officer, Barone felt ready for whatever this morning's search and rescue mission might demand of him.

Barone dressed quickly and ran to the telecommunications center. The room's beige walls were covered by sound-absorbent black foam, a white board showing the status of various cutters and other Coast Guard assets, and navigational charts depicting Group Boston's area of responsibility. There were two small desks, a countertop where classified work was handled, two computers, one digital voice logger for radio and telephone recordings, and six radios. There were no windows. For the most part, Barone would make decisions alone, with only a watch-stander nearby.

Wendy Long, the watch-stander, had been listening as Station Gloucester talked with the tug *Houma* and prepared a 41-foot rescue boat to get underway to the scene. She brought Barone up to speed while he consulted a checklist on what to do for "persons in the water," because he did not believe one existed for "persons trapped in a hull." At 5:22 A.M., Barone walked across the white tiled floor, picked up one of four telephones, and placed the first of thirty-three telephone calls—interspersed with radio communications—that he would make and receive during the next three hours. He called the District One Command Center, located down the street, to request a helicopter launch.

THE U.S. COAST GUARD divides itself into nine geographic areas, or districts. Each district encompasses several Coast Guard Group Commands that oversee an assemblage of Coast Guard stations, boats, cutters, and aircraft. There are also some integrated search and rescue and marine safety offices that are called Activities. District One, based in Boston, encompasses the waters and 2,000-mile coastline of Maine, New Hampshire, Massachusetts, Rhode Island, Connecticut, eastern New York (including Lake Champlain), Vermont, and northern New Jersey. It is home to six Groups, Activities New York, thirty-four Coast Guard stations, and twelve patrol boats as well as other support units such as marine safety offices and aids to navigation teams. In 1997 District One was supported by a crew of 13,000 active-duty, reserve, and Auxiliarist Coast Guard men and women who oversaw the care and operation of thirty cutters, a dozen aircraft, and 200 small boats. In the 1990s District One handled an annual average of 10,000 search and rescue cases and maintained roughly 9,000 buoys, day-beacons, and other aids to navigation. One air station on Cape Cod provided aircraft for the district.

Because Barone feared someone from the stricken vessel might have been tossed overboard during the collision, he wanted a Jayhawk helicopter to respond to the scene. The helicopter was one of the best search assets he had; its bird's-eye view would provide his best bet to locate a drifting survivor who might not be visible to the vessels gathering around the turtled boat. To initiate a helicopter launch, however, Barone needed permission from a SAR (pronounced "sar") Controller at the District One Command Center; two controllers typically stood watch together. If a controller agreed a helicopter was necessary, the controller would patch the call into Air Station Cape Cod and brief an officer there, who would then rally the helicopter crew.

"Just got a situation that I'm gonna need the helo for [that] I'd like to brief you on," Barone told assistant SAR Controller Petty Officer Eric Ashwell at 5:22 A.M. "Got very little information right now. Just got the call. The tug *Houma* was off of Cape Ann towing a barge."

"Tug *Houma?*" Ashwell asked.

"Right. He believed that a 50-foot fishing vessel went between the barge and the tug. And they can't see it now. It's gone," Barone said. "Got a position of 42°41.75′ N and 70°22.4′ W. That's about all I got right now."

"OK," Ashwell said. "Tug saw a fishing vessel go in between [its] tow?"

"Yep."

"OK, and they no longer see it?"

"Right."

"OK. What are you guys doing?"

"Well, [Station Gloucester is] getting underway," Barone said. "At least one boat, if not two."

Ashwell put Barone on hold, called Air Station Cape Cod, and then asked Barone to explain what he knew to the Air Station officer who had joined them on the line.

"Got a situation to brief you on," Barone said.

"How far off Gloucester?" the officer asked, cutting him off.

"It's not that far," Barone said, "probably just about ten miles off."

"OK, I'll call you back."

The officer hung up, leaving Ashwell and Barone on the line. Barone expected a helicopter would scramble immediately, meaning that the duty officer at Air Station Cape Cod would alert the sleeping crew, who would then make flight preparations, start up the helicopter, and prepare to take off. He told Ashwell that he was going to try to get more information, but any help or advice Ashwell could offer would be welcome. Ashwell told him an on-scene weather report was a good place to start.

At 5:30 a.m., the officer of the day at Coast Guard Station Gloucester, Petty Officer Kevin Angerstein, called Barone and confirmed that the accident scene was ten miles northeast of the Cape Ann sea buoy.

"I assume we have a helo?" Angerstein asked.

"It's on the way," Barone said.

Angerstein, who answered to Barone in the SAR chain of command, asked Barone if he wanted to take over the communications for the case. Angerstein was thinking they would need to send a second Coast Guard boat to assist the 41-footer, and he'd be the one to drive it out there. Barone agreed and asked, "Think you got the people for it?" Angerstein said he did, and wanted to know if there was anyone else they should call. Barone said he'd see about getting a Coast Guard cutter to the scene. A cutter—any Coast Guard vessel over 65 feet long—was typically commanded by a senior officer, who could assume the role of on-scene commander in the event of a long search for victims. The nearest available cutter, however, was at the Coast Guard Group Portland Maine station.

"I've been running around trying to get the helo and stuff," Barone told Angerstein, "but they think about a 50-foot fishing vessel [went] between the tug and the tow?"

"Yeah, that's what it looks like right now."

"And they can't see the fishing vessel?"

"They can see the boat," Angerstein said. "Apparently it's just floating. Just barely under the surface or something to that effect, but they have no idea about people on board."

"OK, they don't know which boat it was, do they?" Barone asked. He hadn't heard much of the conversations with the *Houma* and wanted to make sure he knew everything Station Gloucester had learned.

"No," Angerstein said. Barone could hear Angerstein asking someone nearby for any other information. Angerstein hadn't heard Mike Simpson's initial Mayday call from the bridge of the *Houma* to Coast Guard Station Gloucester in which he had said, "[A] fishing boat just crossed right in front of the barge we're towing . . . "

Barone heard Angerstein say, mistakenly, "All right, pushing the barge."

"It was pushing?" Barone asked when Angerstein returned to the phone.

"Apparently this fishing vessel went right in front of the barge," Angerstein said.

"All right," Barone said.

"The barge plowed the fucking thing right over," Angerstein said, not understanding that the tug was ahead of the barge and that the *Heather Lynne II* surfaced in the barge's wake. "They can see part of the boat by the stern of the tug. And there's another fishing boat on scene right now, and they don't see any people."

Barone said he'd take over the communications for the case. He asked for the name of the tug and was told *Houma*.

"I have no idea what the tug *Houma* was pushing or anything like that," Angerstein said.

"OK, so where are you right now? Are you in the station right now?"

"I'm in the [communications center]. My 41's already en route."

"OK."

"I'm doing this official plotting bullshit," Angerstein said, referring to the chart plotting that was required by Coast Guard policy but was irrelevant when there were bystanders to guide rescuers to the accident scene.

"All right," Barone said. He hung up the phone as Long, his watchstander, handed him a draft she had written of an Urgent Marine Information Broadcast (UMIB), something Barone considered a "blanket broadcast" that the Coast Guard issued to notify other mariners of a situation and, sometimes, to solicit their help. Barone agreed it was a good idea to issue the broadcast. At 5:37 A.M. she read the UMIB over VHF channel

16, and fishermen like Richard Burgess aboard his *Scotia Boat Too* heard it:

> Pan Pan, Pan Pan, Pan Pan, hello all stations. This is the
> United States Coast Guard Boston Massachusetts Group,
> United States Coast Guard Boston Massachusetts Group.
> Break, quote. Time 0936 Greenwich Mean Time. The
> Coast Guard has received a report of a vessel capsized in
> position 42 41 decimal 75 degrees north, 070 22 decimal 4
> degrees west, approximately ten nautical miles off Cape
> Ann. All vessels are requested to keep a sharp lookout, assist
> if possible and report all sightings to any Coast Guard unit.
> Unquote break. This is the United States Coast Guard
> Boston Massachusetts Group, out.

She and the watch-stander who came on duty after her would read this broadcast five more times on channel 16 that morning—at 5:52, 6:03, 6:22, 6:33, and finally at 6:50 A.M. The text of the standard-language broadcast never changed, even as more information about the nature of the distress became available—specifically, that there were people trapped inside the overturned *Heather Lynne II* and that divers were needed.

PLAINTIFFS' ATTORNEY Peter Black wanted to know why Richard Barone had never requested that the UMIB be updated to include new information. Barone said doing so was an option, not a requirement.

"Sir, isn't it true that the dissemination of information is critical in a SAR situation?" Black asked.

"Yes, sir," Barone said.

Black referenced the National Search and Rescue Manual, from which the Coast Guard took guidance on conducting SAR missions. " 'SAR communications may be the most important, and often the weakest, link in the SAR system,' " Black read aloud from the manual. He looked up at Barone. "You knew that?"

"Yes, sir," Barone said. "That's why we broadcast the Urgent Marine Information Broadcast."

"And is that why you never bothered to update it to provide information both up and down the SAR chain as additional information became known?"

"The chain was updated continuously," Barone said.

"Sir," Black asked a few minutes later, "the SAR system contemplates use of resources that are outside the operational control of the Coast Guard, correct?"

"Yes, sir, it does."

"And that includes police units, correct?"

"Yes, sir."

"And that includes commercial units?"

"Yes, sir."

"And that includes pleasure boats at sea?"

"Yes, sir, it does."

"And isn't it true, sir, the only way you can be reasonably assured that non–Coast Guard units would be aware of the need for, let's say, divers, would be to update the Urgent Marine Information Broadcast to include that in the broadcast?"

"No sir," Barone said. "There was numerous communications going on. Anybody could have heard that information. It was very obvious."

"If they were listening?"

"If they were listening to the UMIB, they would have heard the [other] communications."

"And you assumed that they understood, people who might be out there listening, that the Coast Guard was seeking divers to get to the scene as quickly as possible, is that correct?" Black asked, his voice raised.

"No, I didn't make that assumption."

"OK, but you certainly didn't put that in the Urgent Marine Information Broadcast, did you?"

"No, I didn't."

Black noted that the SAR manual suggests that alerting ships at sea is frequently the most immediate source of help for people in distress situations. Barone was not willing to agree with this statement until he looked at the manual placed before him. After reading the paragraph to which Black referred, he acknowledged that to be the reason the Coast Guard issues UMIBs. Black repeated the manual's assertion that communications may be the most important and yet the weakest link in a SAR event. Barone agreed, though he hadn't recalled reading that in the manual.

WHILE LONG PREPARED TO READ the first UMIB, Richard Burgess's crew was tapping on the hull of the overturned *Heather Lynne II* and listening for a response. Monitoring the VHF radios in the communications center, Barone heard the tug *Houma* call Coast Guard Station Gloucester and ask if the Coast Guard helicopter would be bringing divers; he was told it would not. *Houma* replied that the *Heather Lynne II* was capsized and that there might be survivors in the hull. Then Barone heard the *Scotia Boat Too* call Gloucester and ask if a helicopter was on the way. A Coast Guardsman at 5:36 A.M. told Burgess a helicopter was en route from Cape Cod. That's when Burgess told the Coast Guard, "Yeah, I got you. We're touching it here. It's right upside down, bow's in the water, stern's coming up here. I—there's not much we can do." To this, Coast Guard Station Gloucester replied, "Be advised, we're gonna call some divers."

Hearing this, Barone picked up the phone at 5:37 A.M. and called Angerstein. The Coast Guard had no rescue dive team of its own—and never had—so he would have to find one willing to assist. He asked Angerstein, "Hey, what you got for divers up there, man, anything at all?"

"I got Beverly [Fire Department] Dive Team," Angerstein said. "I'm calling them right now."

"OK," Barone said. "So I don't need to call them from down here. If you don't get them, give me a call."

Barone could hear Angerstein asking Petty Officer Dick Bourassa, "Are you talking to the dive team right now? If you are, get them out there. All right. How many divers? How many divers?"

"I'm talking to Beverly right now," Angerstein told Barone.

Barone listened as Angerstein told Bourassa to tell the dive team that Coast Guard Station Gloucester could give them a ride out to the capsized boat. Angerstein returned to the phone and asked, "Did you find a cutter, dude?"

"No," Barone said. "I'm still working on it." Once Barone learned that the nearest available cutter was at Group Portland Maine and not under his command, he had consulted with the District One SAR controller, who said he'd place the call to Maine for Barone.

"All right," Angerstein said.

"If you [can't] get a dive team, I was going to try to get one down here," Barone said. But Angerstein was again talking to Bourassa.

"I can get ten divers out there?" Angerstein asked Bourassa. "I don't need ten. I need as many divers as I can get right now, not tomorrow morning, like right now."

Barone said he'd call Angerstein back later.

"Now is it fair to say, sir," attorney Peter Black asked Barone, "at that point you ceased attempting to locate divers, you personally and the people in your immediate command?" The 5:37 A.M. phone call with Angerstein was included in a forty-page transcript of telephone conversations that Department of Justice attorney Stephen Campbell had faxed to Black the night before. The Coast Guard had prepared a transcript shortly after the accident but had never made it available to the plaintiffs' attorneys until Barone met with Campbell on the evening before he was scheduled to testify. Campbell said even he hadn't known the transcript existed until Barone handed him a copy.

Barone acknowledged that once he learned Angerstein was calling a dive team, he abandoned his own intention to do so. He said, "Our list wasn't quite as good as Gloucester for that area. It was obvious they would do a better job to get a local dive team, so I did stop at that point."

Black asked Barone to look at a list of divers, filed under the heading "D," that Barone had had available to him that morning. Barone said he had glanced through the list while he was on the phone with Angerstein.

"You were aware that there was a dive team available at Logan Airport, is that correct?" Black asked.

"I don't remember being aware of that, sir," Barone said. While he knew that Logan International Airport in Boston had rescue personnel available, including a fireboat, and that the state police had divers, he did not know what the state police specifically had for resources at Logan.

"Let me ask you sir," Black said. "Did you make any attempt to locate any dive team that would have been available sooner than the Beverly team?"

Barone said he did not because he assumed the Beverly Fire Department Dive Team would be able to respond the fastest. Even though he understood there could be a delay of twenty to thirty minutes before the helicopter would launch—despite his earlier assertion that he believed it would scramble and depart immediately—Barone did not try to locate a dive team on Cape Cod that could have boarded the helicopter before it departed. Nor did he make any attempt to locate a dive team somewhere between Cape Cod and Boston that the helicopter could pick up while en route to the scene.

"Can I ask you," Judge Saris interrupted. "Why didn't you see if there was a dive team in another location that the helicopter could pick up en route?"

"My list was very brief. Much more brief than this," Barone said. The list Black had handed him had been updated in October 1996, a month after the accident. "I didn't know of anyone that I could call. We didn't have any protocol for that. It would have been a matter of calling information to ask for dive teams. There's so many communities between the scene and Cape Cod that it was unrealistic at the time."

Judge Saris asked if Otis Air Force Base, where Air Station Cape Cod is located, had any divers.

"No, Your Honor, not that I know of," Barone said. "The Coast Guard certainly didn't."

"Well, you don't *know*, do you, sir?" Black asked.

"No, I don't know that," Barone said.

"By the way, one of the requirements in the SAR manuals . . . is to have a list of resources available to you, isn't that correct?" Black pressed.

"I suppose it is in there, yes," Barone said. He told Black that he didn't have a list of all the dive teams between New Hampshire and Plymouth, Massachusetts, but he did know the Coast Guard had stations between Cape Cod and Boston located on the Cape Cod Canal, in Scituate, and in Hull.

"And you didn't even bother picking up the phone and calling any of those stations and asking if they had dive teams available, is that right?"

"At the time, we weren't focusing on picking up dive teams," Barone said. "We wanted to get a helo on the scene as soon as possible."

Black, his voice raised, repeated his question.

"You didn't pick up the phone and call any of the Coast Guard units that you've named between Cape Cod and Boston and ask if they had dive teams that were readily available that could be picked up by helicopter en route, is that right?"

"No, I didn't," Barone said.

"And yet, in talking with Angerstein, you said, 'If you [can't] get a dive team, I was going to try to get one down here,' " Black began, reading from the transcript. He noted that while Barone was on the phone with Angerstein, he had heard Angerstein saying to someone in the background, "I don't need ten, I need as many divers as I can get right now. Not tomorrow morning, like right now."

"That was Angerstein's understanding of the urgency and need to get a diver," Black said. "Is that right?"

"Yes, sir."

"Did you share that urgency, sir?"

"Yes, sir, as soon as we could."

"Well, 'right now,' if possible, right?"

"Absolutely."

Black asked Barone when, exactly, he knew divers would be available in Gloucester. Barone said he didn't remember. He could only recall that although he had learned the Beverly Fire Department Dive Team was on the way, Angerstein had a hard time getting an estimated time of arrival.

AFTER COAST GUARD STATION GLOUCESTER had called the Beverly Fire Department Dive Team, Richard Burgess reported for the first time that they could hear yelling and banging coming from inside the *Heather Lynne II*. The tug *Houma* reported this to Coast Guard Station Gloucester at 5:41 A.M. Two minutes later, Angerstein called Barone.

"Did you hear the update?" Angerstein asked.

"Yeah, they're knocking on the hull?"

"Yeah. I got somebody on the inside knocking on the hull, so there's at least one. The guy was pulling the barge at the time," Angerstein added, correcting his earlier misimpression. "The position is the same. On scene weather is calm . . . I got maybe five knots out of the south, that's it. You guys got an ETA on the helo?"

"No," Barone said. "It's en route. Let me try to call."

"You want me to try to call them on [channel] 16, or they won't hear us?" Since VHF communications are line of sight—that is, limited to the horizon—calls from Gloucester to Cape Cod, even between powerful transmitters and well-located antennas, had uncertain chances of success.

"They'll call [us] as soon as they get in the area," Barone said. "There's only a half-mile visibility [on scene]. How you making out with divers?"

"Say again, buddy?"

"How you making out with the divers?"

"Waiting for a call from the divers right now [with] their ETA to the station."

"OK, all right, man, you gonna wait for them before you scramble the 47?" Barone asked. "Is that what the deal is?"

"Well, that's what it looks like right now," replied Angerstein, who was assuming he'd chauffeur the Beverly Fire Department Dive Team to the scene aboard the station's 47-foot motor lifeboat. The 47-footer at Coast Guard Station Gloucester was one of five prototypes sent to small boat stations around the country in the early 1990s for testing and evaluation; Angerstein had helped lead the analysis team at Gloucester. The new boats were designed to survive twenty-foot breaking waves, operate in hurricane-force winds, survive flipping end over end in large swells, and right themselves in eight seconds if they rolled over. Barone agreed that Angerstein should take the divers to the scene on board the station's 47-footer. Then Barone hung up and at 5:46 A.M. decided to check the status of the helicopter he had requested at least twenty minutes earlier and assumed was en route.

When he reached an Air Station officer at Otis AFB, Barone gave him the most recent information. He said the *Heather Lynne II* was capsized, her hull was floating, other fishing boats were responding, they could hear people knocking inside the hull, and Station Gloucester was trying to assemble a dive team. The Air Station officer noted that although there was a helicopter pad at Coast Guard Station Gloucester, it would be faster to take the divers to the scene by boat, especially since the helicopter was not yet airborne and, at this point, "should be getting ready to start the engines right now." He said he'd call Barone as soon as the helicopter was airborne.

At 5:48 A.M. Barone began updating one of the two SAR controllers at District One, but was interrupted by a cell phone call from Richard Burgess aboard the *Scotia Boat Too*. Barone told Burgess the helicopter was "in the air, en route to the position . . . it's probably midway here or a little less," when, in fact, he knew it hadn't yet launched. Burgess said he hoped it would be fast because he could hear men screaming from inside the boat. It was 5:51 A.M., at least thirty-six minutes after the collision.

As soon as Barone hung up the phone with Burgess, Angerstein called to report that he had already called the Coast Guard's Marine Safety Office, which would investigate the accident, and had told them to get a team to Gloucester. If the investigators arrived at the same time as the divers, Angerstein planned to take them with him aboard the 47-footer.

"Still don't have an ETA on the divers, though," Angerstein said. "You guys know you got three people supposedly trapped inside?"

"Now the 41's en route, right?" Barone asked.

"The 41 is en route," Angerstein said. "They'll probably be on scene in twenty minutes."

"OK," Barone said. "I don't think—I don't know if anybody mentioned this. I just walked in, obviously, but um, if we can get close enough, these guys are apparently knocking on the inside of the hull."

"Correct," Angerstein said.

"If somebody can tap on the outside," Barone said. "Just let them know that we're there."

"Yeah, they're being talked to by another boat," Angerstein said.

"OK," Barone said.

"All right."

"The boat's on scene—"

"Yep."

"—the *Scotia Boat Too*."

"Yep, it's a good guy," Angerstein said. "We've dealt with him before."

"Yeah. He said, first, the whole thing was on the surface."

"Yeah."

"He said the bow was starting to go down now, and they got the tug coming alongside the stern to try to secure the [boat] somehow."

"Just something to keep it afloat," Angerstein said, taking it in.

"Right, he's gonna try to do the same thing. I told him to see if he can try to get a buoy on it in case it goes down, so the divers have something to follow."

"OK."

"If they can go down that deep," Barone said.

"All right," Angerstein said. "So right now we're just dealing with the 41 and the helo, correct?"

"Helo's on the way," Barone said, even though the Air Station had not yet called him back to tell him the helicopter was airborne. Barone probably meant that its launch was imminent. "No ETA on the dive team?"

"Nope, they haven't called me back yet," Angerstein said.

"Are they gonna try to get them together?"

"Yeah," Angerstein said. "We talked to someone from the dive team, and he said he's gonna get a handful of divers together right now and they'll be en route."

"Good," Barone said. He heard Angerstein talking to someone else in the room, asking if the dive team was on the other line. He told Barone to hang on. Barone listened as Angerstein took the call.

"Hello. Yeah, how are we doing for divers?" Angerstein asked. "OK. I don't care if it's just one guy. I need them now. I need somebody now. So how soon can you guys get to the station? Fifteen, twenty minutes you'll be at the station? OK. That's all I need. I don't know. Fifty-five-foot boat possibly submerged on the surface and they hear people trapped inside. If you can get me two guys within fifteen minutes—all right. Thank you. 'Bye."

Angerstein returned to his conversation with Barone and said, "Fifteen to twenty minutes, at least two divers."

"Great," Barone said. "Just so you know, the nearest cutter is out of Portland. It's the *Wrangell*. It's scrambling. They're scrambling right now."

Barone told Angerstein he would take over the communications as soon as the divers arrived in Gloucester so that Angerstein could leave the station and drive the 47-footer to the scene. Although Barone had said earlier that he'd take over communications for the case, Angerstein had continued to handle calls from boats at the scene and from Station Gloucester's 41-footer.

"We'll both keep working it," Barone said. "I'm just trying to get some other things done."

"Yeah," Angerstein said. "I understand that."

"You know, it's working pretty good so far," Barone said.

"Anyway, two divers in fifteen minutes and I'm outta here," Angerstein said.

"Great."

"Like I said," Angerstein said, "I called MSO [the Marine Safety Office] and told them so we don't have to dick the dog later on. Get a team up here right now to investigate."

"Good idea," Barone said.

"All right," Angerstein said. "Hey, I'm pulling this out of my ass right now. But we have about sixty boats up there before, tuna boats."

"Yeah."

"So just a concern that I have right now," Angerstein said, "I've got a feeling this guy was on the hook"—meaning that he was anchored.

"Well, *[Scotia Boat Too]* said that," Barone said. "They said they see a ball around. They think he might [have] been on the hook."

"Yeah," Angerstein said. "I think he was on the hook, and this tug and barge, you're looking at a serious investigation on this guy."

"Oh, definitely," Barone said.

ATTORNEY PETER BLACK noted that in the phone log, Barone made numerous inquiries for more than thirty minutes to find out when the dive team would show up.

"And during that half-hour time period," Black said, "you made no attempt . . . to seek other available divers, is that correct?"

"That's correct."

"By the way," Black said, "there was no prohibition, is there, to seek multiple units and facilities to carry out the same task in a SAR mission, correct?"

"That's correct."

Judge Saris interrupted and asked Barone when he first learned, for certain, that the Beverly Fire Department divers were available.

"Your honor," Barone said, as he began to thumb through the telephone transcript, "I was never positive that we had a specific, manned, equipped team that was going to show up. It was never clear to me until they actually showed up. I had a fear that only one would show up or two would show up, and they were coming from different directions. . . . It was never clear to me until they actually showed up at the station that they were ready to go. Because of the time of day and the fact they were calling people from home or gathering people together, we didn't know how this dive team operated, whether they had people in a van that were going to head to the station ready to go immediately. I mean, that's not usually the way dive teams work. So it was really never clear to me that . . . there's three divers with gear en route to Station Gloucester. That kind of information was never absolutely clear to me until I heard that they were getting underway in the 47-footer, there was two of them, and heading out there."

Judge Saris wanted to know what time the divers left Gloucester on the 47-footer. After some discussion, Barone determined that he received that news about 6:33 A.M. By that time, the crew of the *Heather Lynne II* had been trapped under their hull in diesel-soaked water for at least 78 minutes.

"Essentially, it took almost an hour to know for sure you had divers, from the time you first requested it from Station Gloucester?" Saris asked.

"To be certain, yes," Barone said.

AT 6:05 A.M., Angerstein called Barone again and reported some new information. A commercial salvage boat with a diver on board was en route to the scene.

"Listen," Angerstein said, "I got, uh, Sea Tow Newburyport is departing the Merrimack River right now with one diver onboard."

"It has nothing to do with the others?" Barone asked.

"Right, it has nothing to do with the Beverly [rescue divers]."

"Good," Barone said.

"He has only one diver, though," Angerstein said. "I don't know how comfortable you feel with putting one diver in the water on his own, but he's 23 miles away, looking about an hour 'til he's on scene."

"OK."

"We can do two things here," Angerstein said. "I can have [Station] Merrimack tie up with his rig and run them out there. That'll be a long ride in that 21-footer."

Barone agreed. Coast Guard Station Merrimack River, in Newburyport, had a 21-foot rigid-hull inflatable with twin 135-horsepower outboards that was capable of speeds higher than 40 knots, or 46 miles per hour. It could travel 23 miles in about thirty-five minutes, which could get the diver to the *Heather Lynne II* by about 6:45 A.M., assuming it was ready to go and could depart within five minutes. Its readiness was apparently in question, however. The boat had been having engine problems and just ten days earlier had had one of its engines replaced. If still in its initial break-in period, the new engine might not respond well to a 23-mile full-throttle run. Further, both Angerstein and Barone may have felt the boat was too small for offshore rescue work. And seven years later, Angerstein would claim that the 21-footer had been performing a law enforcement mission miles up the Merrimack River that morning. Whatever the reason, neither Angerstein nor Barone pursued the idea of using the 21-footer, but Angerstein had an alternative suggestion: "Or I can go up the [Annisquam] river and meet [Sea Tow] and pick up the diver and get him on scene quicker," he said.

"How fast [is the Sea Tow boat]?" Barone asked.

"Twenty knots flat. He's got an hour to go, but he does have a diver on board. Hang on, let me give you an ETA from my boat if I was to launch right now," Angerstein said. He paused, listening either to the radio or to someone in the room with him, and then asked, "Did you hear that?"

"No," Barone said.

"If the helo can call in soon enough when the divers are getting here," Angerstein said, "then the helo can land and pick up the divers."

Barone agreed, but said he was concerned about lowering divers from the helicopter to the 41-footer, since that would be a maneuver that none of the rescue divers involved had ever trained to do. Angerstein ran through some time and distance calculations aloud and then added, "If the [Beverly] dive team were to get here right now I could probably be on scene [in the 47-footer] in about thirty-five to forty minutes."

"OK."

"But I'm waiting on the dive team," Angerstein said. "I've got Sea Tow still trucking out there. You're SMC [SAR mission coordinator], brother, what ya wanna do?"

"Sea Tow making about 20 knots, you're only going to beat them by about 6 or 7 [knots], right?" said Barone, trying to estimate how much time they could gain by meeting up with the Sea Tow boat. The 47-footer's top speed was about 27 knots.

"Right," Angerstein said.

"I don't think it's worth it," Barone said, later adding, "Let's let him keep trucking down there at 20 knots."

"Let Sea Tow continue with their divers?" Angerstein asked.

"Yep."

"We'll let Sea Tow Newburyport just continue," Angerstein confirmed, "and we'll wait on the Beverly team."

"I think that's the best way," Barone said. "Is the helo pad clear in case we decide to go that way?"

"Oh, yeah."

"OK. Great. I'm not sure if it would benefit. Brainstorm here with me, as far as getting the divers back to the water."

"Divers what?" Angerstein asked.

"Pick up the divers [with the helicopter] at the station, right?"

"Yep."

"Get them out there."

"Put them right down on the 41?" Angerstein asked.

"Yep," Barone said, adding that the divers could possibly be lowered in a basket. He concluded that idea could work, but for the moment he wanted to stick to the original plan: ferry the divers via the 47-footer while the helicopter arrived on scene and, Barone assumed, dropped its rescue swimmer into the water. Coast Guard rescue swimmers are certified as Emergency Medical Technicians and are trained to jump out of helicopters to assist people in the water, on a life raft, or on a sinking boat, often by helping them to be hoisted into the helicopter. A rescue swimmer is allowed to swim around a capsized vessel and reach under to assist any survivors, but not to dive below the surface and swim inside. Angerstein questioned what a rescue swimmer would be able to accomplish on the *Heather Lynne II*. He asked Barone, "Do you want him to [swim] up and under?"

"No, not really, but he can reach in," Barone said. "He can do a little better than our guys can."

"Obviously, my 41 has a swimmer," Angerstein said, meaning a surface swimmer, who was less trained than a rescue swimmer and subject to similar in-the-water restrictions. "But these guys are trapped all the way up inside like the galley, so it's nothing to reach around."

"I know," Barone said.

"You know what I'm saying?"

"To try to comfort them," Barone said.

"I hear you," Angerstein responded. "I hear you."

"I guess there's three people [on board], you know. That right?"

"That's what we know," Angerstein said. "Yeah. That's what we've been told, is three people and we have the information on the boat. Supposedly."

"OK."

"The *Heather Lynne II* out of Newburyport, Mass."

"Out of Newburyport, OK," Barone repeated.

"It's a 45-foot gillnetter."

"I guess he was on the hook or something," Barone said, returning to their speculation of ten minutes earlier.

"Well, that's what it sounds like, yeah."

"Gillnetters probably go tuna fishing once in a while," Barone said, incorrectly assuming that tuna were caught with gillnets. "They just set their nets."

"How 'bout, I got an owner here, Ted Rurak," said Angerstein, who may not have realized Rurak was already on scene and had been talking to Group Boston over the marine radio. "Anybody interested in giving his house a call to give him a heads up, or—Here's what I'm getting at. We worried about notifying family right now?"

"No, no," Barone said.

"No?" Angerstein asked.

"Not yet," Barone said.

ATTORNEY BLACK ASKED Barone what he knew about private divers from Newburyport who were making their own attempts to rush to the scene. Barone said he understood that two separate divers had responded, joined up, and continued on in one boat. (In fact, Barone did not learn that a second diver had joined with Sea Tow Newburyport until 6:17.)

"And you undertook no effort to assist those divers to get to the scene?" Black asked.

"Actually, no, that's not correct."

"What did you direct be done to get those divers on scene?" Black asked.

"Me and Petty Officer Angerstein discussed the advantages of doing what we could to get them there quicker, and we considered it. And we really didn't have any options except to meet them with the boat at that time. . . . So we did consider it, but the decision was made to proceed with our plan. . . . We already had Station Gloucester's 41-foot boat heading to the scene. And we had one boat at Gloucester waiting for the Beverly dive team, and as soon as they showed up they were going to go with them. So as far as assets go, to send [a boat] towards the Merrimack River away from the scene, the only one we really had available at that moment would be the 47-footer. And the 47-footer wouldn't do much faster than twenty knots. So for them to go up and pick up these divers—this is what we talked about—the advantage wasn't there. The boat was making twenty knots toward the scene, anyway. We didn't know who these people were. At first I thought it was one diver. One diver diving on a gillnetter with gill-nets sounds kind of dangerous to me. There really wasn't a good option to get them there quicker, so we decided to go with the Beverly dive team."

"In any case," Black said, "you did nothing to assist Sea Tow to get to the scene, correct?"

"We had better options," Barone said.

"That wasn't my question, sir," Black said. "You made the decision to do nothing to assist Sea Tow to get to the scene, correct?"

"Right, that's correct."

"By the way, at this time you still didn't know for sure whether you had the divers at Gloucester?"

"No, I didn't know. I knew they were on their way. That's all I knew."

"That's at 6:05?" Judge Saris asked.

"Yes, Your Honor."

"By the way, sir," Black said, "You knew, and you were trained, that SAR missions are time critical, correct?"

"Yes, sir."

"In fact, you had to assume that survivors have a very short life expectancy, correct?"

"Yes, sir."

"And for these survivors, the environment was an overturned vessel, correct?"

"At the time, I'm not sure if I knew there were people trapped in the hull, more than one, anyway. I knew there was one."

"You knew there was at least one, correct?"

"Yes, sir."

AT 6:16 A.M., SAR controller Lieutenant Tim Carton was on watch at District One headquarters together with assistant controller Petty Officer Eric Ashwell. He had been sleeping, as he was permitted to do, until Ashwell woke him soon after receiving Barone's first phone call. Carton called Barone to confirm that the 110-foot cutter *Wrangell,* which typically sailed with a crew of sixteen, would be en route from Portland and that the Marine Safety Office was sending a team to Gloucester as soon as possible for a ride out to the scene to begin their investigation. Carton asked for an update on the divers.

"The divers are, um, we got a diver coming down now out of the Merrimack River with Sea Tow Newburyport," Barone said. "It's only one, though, and he's making about twenty knots. He says his ETA's about an hour. And we still have the dive team [from] Cape Ann en route to the station. As soon as they get there, they're gonna jump on the 47 and head out there. We considered using the helo to get the divers out there, but it might be better to get their rescue swimmer in the area, too. I mean, the divers can probably get out there pretty quick with the 47."

"All right," Carton said.

"Then we got to worry about dropping them and stuff," Barone said.

"That was the concern?" Carton asked. "They have to jump out of the helo—OK, all right, that sounds pretty good."

A minute later, Angerstein called Barone with another update. It was 6:17 A.M. Angerstein said he had just received one hundred percent confirmation that there were three people on board and three people still trapped inside. Neither Angerstein nor Barone mentioned that this negated the need for a helicopter to fly over the scene and search for any adrift survivors, since they now knew all three men were trapped together and that the top priority was therefore to get divers to the scene as soon as possible. Instead, they discussed what VHF channels they were using to talk with the 41-footer—which had now been on scene for 7 minutes— and the helicopter. Then Barone again asked Angerstein if he wanted to hand over the communications with the 41-footer, leaving Angerstein free to leave in the 47-footer as soon as the divers arrived.

"Yeah, yeah, that's cool," Angerstein said. "We're just filling in the holes right now. That's all we're really doing from here."

"Sure," Barone said.

"You guys want it one hundred percent right now, say so and we'll stay out of it," Angerstein said, referring to who had control of the case.

"All right, we'll take it from here," Barone said.

"All right."

"Any word from the dive team?" Barone asked

"No," Angerstein said. "They're en route."

WHILE ANGERSTEIN and his crew at Station Gloucester were "just filling in the holes" as they waited for the dive team to arrive, more than an hour after the collision, the one or more men alive inside the *Heather Lynne II* were filling their lungs with hydrocarbon toxins. When the boat had turned turtle, the salt water that flooded in around them had mixed with diesel fuel, which spilled out of the air vents, and oily bilge water. It stung their eyes and coated their skin. It was nauseating. If they ingested a mouthful, the diesel would burn like fire. They'd wheeze and gasp. They'd be wide-eyed, with flared nostrils. Their breathing must have become increasingly distressed as the air pockets they found threatened to disappear. With each inhaled breath, the hydrocarbons of the diesel fuel would have slipped into their lungs and coated each membrane in the honeycomb of delicate alveoli, blocking the absorption of oxygen. Eventually these inhaled toxins would build up an impermeable wall against whatever remaining oxygen the men could find. Then, as their blood was starved for oxygen, their skin would become slate colored or bluish, their heartbeats would quicken, and their breathing would border on hyperventilation. By then the toxins would have clouded their thinking and given them nausea, convulsions, or feelings of dizziness or drowsiness. They needed cleaner air. They needed out.

And soon.

According to Commander Curt Murphy, a Navy salvage diver for twenty-five years, "If you think of a boat as a city, you could have diesel fuel, gasoline, and other solvents like ammonia or cleaning agents. There could be a number of things in the water. And it'd be dark—darker than the inside of a cow."

He said Hutchins, Foster, and Lowther, besides swimming in and inhaling vaporized diesel fuel and other toxins, faced a rising threat of asphyxia and hypothermia with every lost minute. Hypothermia occurs when one's body core temperature drops to an abnormal level. Because it slows down the central nervous system, normal muscular and cerebral functions are impaired. In the 64°F water that enveloped the three men, a person could lose consciousness—and even die—within two hours. In the first minute or two, the shock of the cold water would trigger involuntary gasps for air. In the minutes that followed, as a victim's core body temperature dropped, his muscles would become rigid and he would lose dexterity. His skin would sting and he would become confused. Ultimately, as hypothermia and lack of oxygen overwhelmed him, he would lose his ability to reason or to call for help. He might even deny help if it were offered.

"Being trapped in a small space," Murphy said, "would be absolutely terrifying."

Some people in that situation would panic and kill themselves trying to get out. Before the 41-footer's arrival, fear of encountering this level of panic, in addition to the darkness and the gillnets, had forestalled gathering bystanders from jumping into the water to attempt a rescue. Common sense, it seemed—the prudent course—was to tell Hutchins, Foster, and Lowther repeatedly to sit tight, try to conserve air, and hold on. The Coast Guard was coming.

"BY THE WAY, SIR," Attorney Peter Black asked Barone. "You never contacted the air station to inform them that the [Beverly] divers were going to Gloucester, did you?"

"I don't think we did," Barone said. He had told the Air Station at 5:46 of the effort to assemble a dive team, but he had never called back with confirmation.

"And just to back up, sir, at about 5:40, you had a conversation with the *Scotia Boat Too* . . . where they reported that people were inside, banging on the hull and yelling, is that right?"

"I remember that being stated numerous times, yes," Barone said.

"And certainly by 5:51 in the morning, you knew there were multiple people inside the vessel banging on the hull and yelling, is that correct?"

"I don't know if I knew there were multiple people," Barone said. "We knew there was at least one person. I'm not sure if I knew then that there were more than one."

Judge Saris interrupted Black to ask Barone, "Now, did you advise the helicopter of that situation?"

Barone said that he did not because he couldn't talk to the helicopter at this point—it was not in the air and not yet in VHF range. Black asked Barone if he had ever been trained to use a helicopter to deliver divers to the scene of a rescue situation. Barone said no; this was the first incident in which, as a SAR mission coordinator, he had needed to deploy divers to an accident by helicopter. He didn't know whether the helicopter crew had been trained to work with divers or if the divers had ever trained in a helicopter.

"By the way," Black said. "People being trapped in a capsized vessel is not an unexpected event as far as the Coast Guard is concerned, is it?"

Department of Justice attorney Campbell objected. Saris said she'd like to hear what Barone had to say.

Black rephrased the question: "Well, sir, people being trapped in a capsized vessel is something that you studied about as part of your . . . qualifications to become rated as a duty officer at Group Boston, isn't it?"

"Yes, sir."

Black asked Barone to refer to a paragraph in the National SAR Manual that stated, "Common casualties include entrapment in capsized, damaged or sunken vessels." He then asked Barone to look at chapter 6 of the Coast Guard Addendum to the National SAR Manual, which deals with "persons trapped in capsized vessels."

"So you'll agree with me that certainly this situation," Black said, "that is, persons trapped in a capsized vessel, was one that you, as a SAR mission coordinator, had contemplated before this event occurred, as part of your training."

"Yes, sir."

"And yet, it's your testimony that in your training, you never utilized a helicopter to transport divers to the scene in a simulated entrapment in a capsized vessel, is that correct?" Black asked.

"That's correct."

"The SAR manuals talk about training for the unusual, things that don't come up all the time. Are you familiar with that?"

"No, I'm not."

"Well, would you agree with me, sir, as the SAR mission coordinator, it would have been helpful to you to have trained in getting divers out to a situation where people were entrapped in a capsized vessel before the day of the incident?"

Campbell objected that Black was fishing for Barone's opinion. Saris overruled.

"I would agree with that," Barone said.

"By the way," Black asked later. "The helicopter wouldn't do any good if the vessel sank, would it?"

"Yes, in fact, if another survivor was adrift, it would have," Barone said. "[And with the vessel floating,] the rescue swimmer could have been dropped [to] communicate with people inside. So there was an advantage to send the helo to the scene based on the fact we didn't know . . . exactly when the divers were going to arrive at Gloucester."

"And those were the only divers you were considering getting to the scene?" Black asked.

"We considered those to be the quickest, yes."

"Well, those were the ones you, in your own mind, had decided you would use Coast Guard assets to get to the scene?"

"Right," Barone said, "because they were a team."

"By the way, sir, do you know Sea Tow's relationship to Station Merrimack?" Black asked.

"At the time?"

"Yes, sir."

"I knew that it was one of the commercial salvors out of the Merrimack River. Otherwise, I really didn't know."

"Were you aware that they were about 500 yards from Station Merrimack?"

"No."

"By the way, do you know Mr. Mike Goodridge?" Black asked, referring to a marine salvor who operated under the business names Marine Services and TowBoatU.S. and competed with Sea Tow.

"I do now," Barone said. Judge Saris looked at Barone and raised her eyebrows.

"Did you know him at the time?" Black asked.

"No, sir," Barone said. He paused before adding, "Now that I think about it, though, I did receive phone calls from him on occasion about other situations."

"Just so it's clear, you personally didn't call any of these divers, that is Sea Tow or TowBoatU.S.?" Black asked.

"No, sir, I didn't."

"And you don't believe Gloucester did, correct?"

"I really don't know."

"And you have no idea how any of these divers learned of the situation?"

"I don't know if they learned it from the UMIB," Barone said. "I really don't know."

"You *do* know they didn't learn it from any telephone calls that you placed?" Black asked.

"That's correct, sir."

DEPARTMENT OF JUSTICE ATTORNEY Stephen Campbell began his cross-examination by asking Barone to explain how the National SAR Manual and the Coast Guard Addendum to that manual were related. Barone said the National SAR Manual was broader in scope and the Addendum was a more specific internal document tailored for the Coast Guard. Campbell led Barone through passages in both the Manual and the Addendum describing search and rescue planning as an art as well as a science, "relying greatly on the creativity and experience of the personnel involved."

Campbell asked Barone to read aloud a paragraph of the Addendum:

> The provisions of this Addendum are intended as a guide
> for consistent and uniform execution of the Coast Guard
> Search and Rescue program. The Addendum does not cover
> occurrences best handled through experience and sound
> judgment. The Addendum is not intended to place undue
> restrictions on the use of sound judgment.

"So is it your understanding, Chief, that these manuals are primarily advisory in nature," Campbell asked, "[but] that in certain circumstances there may be a mandatory provision in them?"

"Yes, sir."

"Speaking of which," Judge Saris interrupted, "how many operations have you been involved with to search and rescue persons on a vessel which has either been submerged or, like this one, turtled?"

"I don't recall any. . . . It's very rare to have a vessel capsized and still be floating with people trapped," Barone said. "Usually, they sink. I may have been involved with a few, but none as dramatic as this, and I don't recall any specific instances."

"Had you ever been involved with any before this one?" Saris asked.

"I don't remember any, Your Honor."

"So this was a first for you, too?" Saris asked.

"For this type of incident, yes, Your Honor."

Campbell asked Barone to look at a nautical chart depicting the area where the accident took place. He asked Barone to point to Gloucester and to the Merrimack River. He asked Barone why he didn't have the 41-footer from Gloucester leave the scene of the collision and head northwest to meet the divers coming down from the Merrimack River.

Barone said that when he learned salvage divers were en route, at 6:05 A.M., he did not yet have a Coast Guard vessel on scene. In fact, the 41-footer did not arrive until 6:10. He explained, "I didn't know who was trapped on the vessel and who wasn't. And I was concerned with rescuing people at the scene. I didn't have any resources available to send to pick them up. The only resource would have been the 41 to proceed towards the Merrimack River, pick up the divers and make almost the same speed back to the scene. Knowing that [the commercial salvage] boat would also most likely continue to the scene anyway, it didn't serve any purpose to divert the 41 to them. It would have actually prevented us from getting on scene quicker."

"What does the 41-footer do for you when it's on scene?" Campbell asked.

"Well, the 41 would be my eyes and ears, and they have medical equipment on board, communications. They can start to control the situation and use the other vessels that show up effectively."

At Campbell's prompting, Barone again explained that he held the 47-footer back at the Gloucester station to wait for the Beverly Dive Team, which he expected to arrive at any minute, and rush them to the scene.

"We were looking at this from two different angles: that we needed to get people on the scene to rescue people who drifted free from the *Heather Lynne*, and also that the *Heather Lynne* is likely going to sink and, even if it doesn't, we need to get divers into it. So we needed to have two approaches to the situation. That's why the 47 is left at Station Gloucester."

Before concluding his cross-examination, Campbell asked Barone if he had—or would have—prevented any other divers in the area from responding to the incident. Barone said he couldn't think of any reason why he would do that, nor was he aware of any other divers responding.

Plaintiff's attorney Peter Black then stood up to ask Barone a few more questions. He first read aloud another paragraph from the National SAR Manual:

> The agency performing SAR may be subject to liability to a person needing assistance if physical harm results from a rescuer's failure to exercise reasonable care in carrying out a rescue or if harm results because a person reasonably relied on the rescue effort, foregoing other opportunities to obtain assistance.

Black asked Barone if he was aware of this on the morning of September 5, 1996. Barone said he was aware that any SAR case could have legal issues associated with it.

"And do you agree that nothing in these manuals should be construed as relieving SAR personnel of the need for initiative and sound judgment?"

"I would agree with that," Barone said.

Black noted that the National SAR Manual defines search and rescue as the "use of available resources to assist persons and property in potential or actual distress." Barone agreed that, as the SAR mission coordinator, his duty that morning was to effectively allocate and coordinate available resources toward the rescue operation, which he agreed was a "distress case"—one in which persons or property face imminent danger.

Black asked Barone to confirm that the 41-footer and the 47-footer were the only Coast Guard assets available to him to assist the Sea Tow divers out to the scene.

"Sea Tow had their own asset to get to the scene," Barone said. "There wasn't any need to use the 41 or the 47."

Black asked Barone if he had inquired at Station Merrimack River as to whether its 41-footer or its 21-foot rigid-hull inflatable could hurry the two divers to the scene faster. Barone said he did not because he assumed the Sea Tow boat was as fast as the 41-footer. (He did not mention that the 21-footer was breaking in a new engine and was, according to Angerstein's later assertion, far up the Merrimack River on a law-enforcement case. Neither did he suggest that, in their opinion, the boat was too small for a 23-mile ride to an offshore accident scene.)

"By the way, sir," Black said, "did the 41-footer do anything to attempt to stabilize the *Heather Lynne*?"

"I don't know," Barone said.

"Did the 41-footer direct others to move away from the *Heather Lynne*, to back off?"

"I don't know, sir."

"You expected the 41-footer to be your eyes and ears and keep you fully informed of the events that were occurring. That was one of the main reasons it was there, correct?"

"One of the reasons, sir, yes," Barone said. Slightly amending his earlier testimony, he explained that the main reason the 41-footer was on scene was to "recover survivors."

"By the way," Black said. "Nonmilitary units are considered SAR resources if they have abilities to assist and are willing to, correct?"

"Anything could be considered a SAR resource, sir."

"And that would include a diver sitting out on his boat?"

"As a last resort."

»Barbara and Gail
December 19, 1961

O NE OF THE MOST notable attempts to hold the government liable for a failed Coast Guard rescue—and one that would serve as a legal foundation for future civil cases like that of the *Heather Lynne II*—was based on events that took place on a stormy night a week before Christmas 1961. Early on the second morning of a scalloping trip to Georges Bank, forty-seven-year-old Captain Sheldon S. Kent discovered he had lost the rudder from his 90-foot wooden scalloper, *Barbara and Gail*. He had a crew of nine and 4,500 pounds of scallops on board. Adrift in calm seas 52 miles southeast of the Great Round Shoals channel buoy at the entrance to Nantucket Sound, Captain Kent called the Coast Guard and said that while he was in no immediate danger, he would need a tow home to New Bedford.

The Coast Guard rescue coordinators in Boston dispatched a 95-foot cutter with a crew of fourteen and one commanding officer, twenty-four-year-old Lieutenant Gerald McManus, who had graduated from the U.S. Coast Guard Academy less than three years earlier. The cutter's navigation equipment included a fathometer, or depth-finder, that the crew had described in the cutter's log as being "lousy"; they did not even turn it on. The magnetic compass was accurate, but the crew relied instead on an inaccurate gyrocompass. The loran (*LO*ng *RA*nge *N*avigation receiver, a then-new device for electronic navigation using precisely timed radio signals from shore-based transmitters) had been unreliable since the day it was installed in March of that same year, according to the crew. The radar worked as expected.

By four o'clock on the afternoon of December 18, 1961, the cutter had the *Barbara and Gail* in tow on a northwesterly course, bound for

New Bedford by way of Nantucket Sound. Two hours later, the 700-foot towline parted in worsening weather. Coast Guardsmen later variously recalled that the northeast wind ranged from 25 to 45 knots, with seas ranging from 6 to 18 feet. The cutter's log, however, recorded the seas as a 4-foot moderate swell.

For the next two and a half hours, unbeknownst to Coast Guard mission coordinators in Boston, McManus and his crew tried to reestablish the tow. At 8:30 P.M., a defeated McManus told Captain Kent that he had requested help from the cutter *Frederick Lee*, docked in New Bedford, and would stand by until the cutter arrived on scene. Captain Kent feared that in the meantime, his scalloper would drift and founder on the Nantucket Shoals to the west and south, so he asked McManus to try again to connect the tow. This time they succeeded. By 11 P.M. the weather had moderated somewhat, and McManus resumed his tow at a speed of 10 knots on a northwesterly course through the winter night, toward what he thought was Great Round Shoal Channel, at the eastern approach to Nantucket Sound.

Deceived by the unreliable loran, McManus believed he was farther north than he actually was. He had taken a few loran fixes to track his position that night, but had disregarded some of them because he doubted their reliability. Nevertheless, he was confident of his position when he set up on a course of 300 degrees, believing the Great Round Shoal Channel buoy was 18½ miles ahead. He selected this course to compensate for the strong currents that would sweep across his track, but he never consulted a chart to determine exactly what allowance he should make. He relied instead on the hope of accurate loran readings from which to make course corrections en route and on his limited local knowledge. He had been through these waters just once before.

At 11:24 P.M., Coast Guard headquarters in Boston received a message from McManus announcing that he no longer needed assistance from the cutter *Frederick Lee*. Officers at headquarters believed the men on scene were the best judge of their condition and capability, so they cancelled the *Frederick Lee*'s sailing orders. Meanwhile, McManus was trying to confirm his present location, but his loran could not get a fix. Following a seven-day trial during which the events of that night were scrutinized, Massachusetts District Court Judge Andrew A. Caffrey found McManus's next actions puzzling.

"Even though he knew that the *Barbara and Gail* had loran receivers, and despite the fact that he was steaming at ten knots toward some of the most treacherous coastline in the United States," Judge Caffrey wrote, "McManus, in an incredibly irresponsible act, shut down the loran without checking with the *Barbara and Gail,* from which he could have obtained a fix simply for the asking."

Sometime before midnight, McManus went to his bunk. He told a seaman that they should be near the Great Round Shoal Channel buoy by 1 A.M. and to wake him then. During the next hour, a seaman held the course according to the inaccurate gyrocompass. At about 1 A.M., a light appeared to port. Assuming it was the lighted buoy they were headed for, a crewman woke McManus. When McManus reached the bridge, he glanced out at the light and made the same assumption. He did not check the color, frequency, or pattern of the light against the published characteristics of the Great Round Shoal Channel buoy, nor did he check his position on the chart because, he would later say, the loran was in a small room off the bridge and he felt seasick when he went in there. A file cabinet had fallen over, strewing papers across the floor. It was just too rough, he said, to do any meticulous navigating. McManus did not consult with Captain Kent, who had thirty-three years of experience in these waters. He did not turn on his fathometer. Instead, he ordered the seaman to fetch him some fruit juice while he grabbed the helm and turned straight toward the light.

While McManus believed he was looking at the Great Round Shoal Channel lighted buoy, he was actually looking at Sankaty Head Lighthouse on Nantucket's eastern shoreline, about fifteen miles to the southwest of the buoy. Captain Kent on board the *Barbara and Gail* might have been alarmed had he been on watch, but he was asleep. He had designated two crew, brothers Clarence and Calvin Roberts, to stand watch, keep an eye on the fathometer, and wake him if they saw anything unusual. Since her engine was shut down and her wheel secured, the *Barbara and Gail* was under the navigational control of the Coast Guard cutter. When, near 1 A.M., one of the brothers saw a light to port, he reasonably was under what Judge Caffrey would call a "misguided impression that the crew of the CG-95321 were navigating a proper course to New Bedford."

Meanwhile, aboard the cutter, a seaman returned to the wheelhouse with fruit juice, cups, and ice cubes. A thirsty engineer followed. For about ten minutes they had unknowingly been steaming toward the Sankaty Head Light, about eleven miles away. When the engineer stepped out on deck and sipped his juice, he saw breakers off the port bow about two boat lengths ahead.

He asked McManus, "What is this white water out here?"

McManus replied, "That's what I'd like to know."

McManus tried to turn to port, but he could not. His 95-foot cutter—with a 6-foot draft—swept over the Rose and Crown Shoal, one of the Nantucket Shoals, at ten knots and back into deeper water. But the 90-foot *Barbara and Gail*—with a 10-foot draft—was not as lucky. She ran hard aground.

"I observed a great deal of white water ahead of us," McManus told investigators. "My exact words were, 'My God, I think it's a shoal.' We were right in the white water and I told the man at the wheel to straighten us out. I glanced back to see where the fishing vessel was and she had started in. She was in shoal water and I knew she had run aground. A seaman told me she was blowing her air horn. It seemed like we went through that white water broadside."

Captain Kent told McManus on the radio that he was taking on water in the bow and the stern. McManus cut the towline and maneuvered back around but could approach no closer than 150 feet from the grounded *Barbara and Gail*. As he did so, McManus tried to figure out where he was. He sent a frantic call to Coast Guard headquarters and first announced that the fishing vessel he had been towing was aground on Great Round Shoal. Thirty-five minutes later, he called back and said the *Barbara and Gail* was aground on Pollock Rip, five miles to the north of Great Round Shoal. In fact the grounding was six to seven miles south of the sea buoy for which McManus had thought he was headed.

Meanwhile, Captain Kent assembled his crew on the bow, told them to put on life jackets, and gave them instructions on how to abandon ship by using a keg and a line to which they would all be tethered. Kent dressed in a wetsuit that he had just bought in case he needed to free nets from the propeller, since at that time New England fishing boats were constantly getting hung up on Russian gillnets. Then he remembered a pair of swim fins he'd left in the pilothouse. He walked back to fetch them because he figured they'd help him swim with his men away from the boat in the frigid late-December waters. Upon retrieving them, he walked back toward the bow but stopped to put on his fins. That's when, he later said, "the boat went out from under me."

The *Barbara and Gail* slid off the shoal and sank seconds later at 2:01 A.M. on December 19, 1961.

"All hands had on life jackets and we were gathered around the foremast just before we came off the shoal . . . and then we were in the water," Kent told Coast Guard investigators. "I looked up and all I could see of the boat was the top of the mast. That was the last I saw of her."

Captain Kent's brother was the first to jump into the water. He clutched the keg and dragged the line with him as he swam toward the cutter; the rest of the crew struggled behind him. Within the hour, McManus and his crew would rescue five of the ten fishermen who had been aboard the *Barbara and Gail*: Captain Sheldon S. Kent; his brother, twenty-nine-year-old navy veteran Edgar Kent; his nephew, nineteen-year-old Ellis Kendal; forty-year-old Clarence Roberts; and Yves "Frenchie" Riendeau, a thirty-four-year-old native of France and veteran of the French Navy and merchant marine, who, upon returning to New Bedford, told assembled reporters, "I'm so happy to be here. It could happen to anyone."

Among McManus's crew was Boatswain's Mate second class James C. Jenkins, who was the officer on watch when the *Barbara and Gail* ran aground. The son of a Coast Guard veteran, he had been in the Coast Guard for three years and was the father of a week-old baby girl. Putting his own fears aside, he dove into the water without a life jacket to rescue Clarence Roberts and later hung from the cutter's boarding net in icy seas to pluck the four others from peril. The five survivors offered profuse praise and gratitude for Jenkins's act of heroism.

"As long as there are heroic men like these in the Coast Guard," a sobbing Captain Kent told Coast Guard investigators, "we can be proud of them and know they'll always help us."

McManus and his crew recovered three lifeless fishermen: thirty-nine-year-old Calvin Roberts; thirty-four-year-old Joseph Costa, a World War II veteran whose wife had begged him not to go, as they were expecting a baby in January; and Terrence "Mac" McCarthy, a forty-seven-year-old cook who hadn't wanted to take this trip but couldn't find anyone to replace him. Forty-four-year-old Walter Wicherski and Roger R. Desrochers, the twenty-eight-year-old engineer and Captain Kent's son-in-law, would remain lost at sea.

W HEN THE STORY of this stormy night was laid out before Massachusetts District Court Judge Andrew A. Caffrey, the Coast Guard sought to escape blame—and $1.4 million in liability claims—for the loss of the *Barbara and Gail* and five of her crew. In the case that would be known as *U.S. v. Sandra & Dennis Fishing Corp.*, government attorneys argued on behalf of the Coast Guard that it should be exonerated or at least limited from liability and, further, that the court should declare that the fishermen were at fault for the loss of their boat.

The case law of the time offered few legal precedents from which to draw. In the first twenty-five years following passage of the 1925 Public Vessels Act—which waives sovereign immunity and allows suits to be brought against the United States regarding conduct of government vessels—there had been no attempt to recover damages arising from failed Coast Guard rescue operations. Between 1950 and 1952 the question had faced courts in at least seven cases, albeit inconclusively. Then, in a June 1952 case, *P. Dougherty Company v. United States*, a shipping company sought compensation for damages done to its 267-foot barge *Harford* when it hit a Delaware breakwater while being towed by the Coast Guard cutter *Mohawk* in April 1947. A district court judge determined that the negligence of both vessels caused the accident and ordered the government to pay half the damages. The September 1953 decision was the first ruling to hold the Coast Guard liable for negligence during a rescue operation. The judge ruled that the Coast Guard was akin to a Good Samaritan, who is liable for injury if, and only if, his attempt to help renders the person in peril worse off than if no help had been offered.

The lower court ruling was overturned on appeal, however. The Third Circuit Court of Appeals agreed that the *Mohawk*'s crew did not use ordinary care when it navigated too close to the breakwater on which the barge foundered, but it stated that "the United States should not be liable for fault of the Coast Guard in the field of rescue operations at sea."

This appeals court ruling was the one the government relied on in its defense in the loss of the *Barbara and Gail*. Government attorneys argued that the Coast Guard's obligations in a rescue are no greater than those of a private salvager, in which risk of liability is kept purposely low so that there remains among salvagers a strong desire, uninhibited by fear of liability, to engage voluntarily in dangerous and selfless acts of valor in an attempt to save property or lives at sea. The Department of Justice insisted that the Coast Guard has no duty to provide mariners in distress with a seaworthy vessel with equipment in good working order and could not be held liable for failing to do so. Instead, distressed mariners are at the mercy of whatever assets the Coast Guard chooses—or does not choose—to send.

In 1966, the district court judge didn't see it that way. In his ruling, Judge Caffrey determined that the government "closes its eye to reality" when it asserts that its rescue response is similar to that of a private vessel. He believed the Coast Guard should be regarded as more than just a private salvager because it participates—and even orchestrates—immense search and rescue efforts using other government and military agencies that fall under the umbrella of the National Search and Rescue Plan. As such, Judge Caffrey determined, the government *can* be held liable for failed Coast Guard rescues—even when the errors made are not its own but those of entities operating under Coast Guard command.

He wrote:

> Today and for some years past, the United States Coast Guard
> has carried out a search and rescue operation on a grand scale,
> which it is authorized to do by statute, and which it is
> directed to do by the National Search and Rescue Plan. The
> nature and extent of these activities are widely publicized
> through the public relations offices of the Coast Guard
> and other participating branches of the military service. The
> availability, and the usual excellence, of the search and rescue
> service and the fact that many mariners have been saved over
> the years by the heroic action of the Coast Guard . . . are such
> matters of common knowledge as to be proper subject for
> judicial notice. As a result of the holding out of the availability
> of this search and rescue service and the extensive publicity
> which it has received over the years, mariners, commercial
> fishermen, yachtsmen and pleasure boaters, indeed all who go
> down to the sea in ships, have been induced to rely on this
> usually excellent search and rescue service rather than seek
> assistance from private sources. The instant case is but one

example of this reliance. Disabled because rudderless, but in no immediate danger, the *Barbara and Gail*, which merely needed a tow to land, turned to the Coast Guard for assistance rather than call upon a fellow fisherman. On the other side of the coin, those fishermen and mariners who, true to the tradition of seafarers would otherwise go to the aid of vessels in distress or in need of assistance, now rely on the Coast Guard to do so.

Judge Caffrey believed that the Coast Guard had breached its obligation either to send out a properly equipped vessel to assist the *Barbara and Gail* or to notify Captain Kent that it could not assist him. Judge Caffrey also rejected the government's assertion that the *Barbara and Gail* was not deprived of any other form of assistance—and her situation thus made worse off—when other vessels, upon learning the Coast Guard was responding and expecting the Coast Guard to be successful, abandoned their own efforts to assist her.

"The Coast Guard is liable for damages caused by its negligence to any mariners who in fact have relied on the availability of its search and rescue services," the judge wrote. "When . . . the Coast Guard has failed to use reasonable care in the course of attempting a rescue operation, [the Coast Guard] will not be heard to say that the unfortunate victims did not rely on the availability of its services."

Judge Caffrey found that Captain Kent clearly decided against seeking alternative assistance. He had a radio in good working order and had been a part of the New Bedford fleet for thirty-three years. The fishing grounds of Georges Bank afforded plenty of other fishing boats nearby who would have assisted him had he asked for their help, but he did not because he relied instead on the Coast Guard's response. Therefore, wrote Judge Caffrey, the government's contention that the Coast Guard was the only rescuer available—and that no other sources of aid were dissuaded from assisting—was "totally untenable."

The government also argued that the Coast Guard could not be held liable for making the *Barbara and Gail*'s situation worse because, it figured, had the Coast Guard not come to her aid, she would eventually have run aground on her own due to prevailing wind and sea conditions. Judge Caffrey disagreed. He believed that had the Coast Guard not attempted to tow the *Barbara and Gail*, she would have drifted out through the Great South Channel, clear of any shoals. Instead, the Coast Guard had towed her to a location where, when the hawser parted, she might have drifted onto shoal grounds. Even then, however, Captain Kent could have deployed one or more of his three 1,100-pound scallop dredges as anchors to hold his position in deeper water.

Finally, Judge Caffrey ruled that the sole cause of the sinking of the *Barbara and Gail* was the negligence of the Coast Guard. Its officers had the responsibility to supervise the rescue and make decisions based on sound judgment. Instead, officers at Coast Guard headquarters ignored this responsibility by "rubber-stamping the decisions of the inexperienced and immature McManus." In his ruling, Judge Caffrey denied all three of the government's requests to exonerate the Coast Guard of any blame for the loss of the *Barbara and Gail*.

The government appealed.

In part, the First Circuit Court of Appeals disagreed with Judge Caffrey. Chief Judge Bailey Aldrich believed neither that reliance on faulty navigational equipment caused the stranding nor that the towline parted due to Coast Guard negligence. He did agree, however, that there was evidence of inexcusable neglect by McManus and that the crew of the *Barbara and Gail* therefore could not be blamed for failing to watch out for their own safety. Judge Aldrich concluded that the government could not be exonerated from blame but that its liability as a volunteer rescue agency could be limited. He based his ruling on a few key facts of law, primarily that applicable statutes "do not amount to a general undertaking by the United States to provide rescue services on demand."

The judge stated that the government should not be held accountable for dispatching what some regarded as an improperly equipped cutter. How much equipment the Coast Guard has and how much money it spends, based on Congressional appropriations, must remain at its uncontrolled discretion. Therefore, the government cannot be legally obligated to have any particular resources available—nor can it be required by law to dispatch any particular resources—to assist the public. At the same time, the judge insisted the Coast Guard must not misrepresent its intentions or ability. Citing earlier cases, Judge Aldrich concluded that the Coast Guard must not make false promises by misleading those in peril—and those bystanders who could otherwise help—into believing that it is providing something it's not.

Judge Aldrich did find that the government could be held responsible for a Coast Guard officer's failure to use sound judgment.

"When the nature of the fault or faults is examined," he wrote, " . . . we consider this a clear case. The Coast Guard supplied McManus with a vessel capable of performing the intended mission if properly operated. . . . The [loss of the *Barbara and Gail*] resulted from his lack of care and failure to exercise judgment. For this the government is liable . . . "

The practical impact of the appeals court's limited-liability finding was to reduce the government's financial penalty. The final settlement amount was undisclosed.

THE LOSS OF THE *Barbara and Gail*, which was front-page, banner headline news in the historic Massachusetts seaport of New Bedford for several days in 1961, reminded the fishing community of past tragedies. It was considered the worst loss to hit New Bedford since 1955, when the scalloper *Doris Gertrude* and her eleven-man crew had disappeared without a trace despite a four-day search by the Coast Guard that covered 50,000 square miles. It also reminded them of the 69-foot dragger *R. W. Griffin*, which was run down seventy miles south of Martha's Vineyard by a 480-foot British freighter in July 1958, and a half-dozen other local boats whose losses were still fresh in the town's memory.

In the years that followed, little more was said about the *Barbara and Gail*. Then in 1987, the 50-foot fishing vessel *Lark* ran aground less than a quarter mile off Nantucket's Great Point one clear, cold October night. On board the dragger was twenty-nine-year-old skipper Rick Moniz, who had been fishing for eight of his last ten years. This was his fourth trip as skipper. A native of Acushnet, a small town near New Bedford, he came from a big family and had been president of his high school senior class. He had stopped fishing for two years to run *Chippy*, a barge that delivered freshwater to fishing boats preparing for long trips at sea, because he wanted more time to spend with his wife, Jacqueline, and their two young children, Ryan and Jamie. But, like most fishermen, he couldn't stay away from fishing long. He returned in the hope of making better money.

That's how he found himself and his deckhand on board *Lark* and aground in a spot notorious for rip currents where the sand bar drops quickly into deep water. Moniz called the Coast Guard at about 7:40 P.M.

to report that he had run aground in five-foot seas. A Coast Guard boat from nearby Station Brant Point arrived on scene and hitched up a towline to the *Lark*. But as the Coast Guard pulled the *Lark* off the ledge, her load shifted. She rolled over and sank in less than ten seconds at about 8:15 P.M. Using spotlights cast out over the dark stormy waters, the Coast Guard found and plucked forty-five-year-old deckhand Rich Silvia from the 53°F water eight minutes after *Lark* sank. Moniz had disappeared.

The Coast Guard launched a three-day search that would include four boats, two helicopters, and a jet to search 250 square miles for Moniz. All they found was a survival suit like the one Moniz had been wearing when last seen. When recovered about three miles from the sunken boat, the suit was partially inside out, as if Moniz had taken it off. Puzzled investigators theorized that the zipper might have jammed—a not uncommon problem in poorly maintained survival suits—and Moniz's suit filled with frigid seawater when he fell overboard. With a suit full of water, he would have found it extremely difficult to stay far enough above the surface to breathe. He might have torn the suit off in a panic, or he might have succumbed to drowning or hypothermia and wound up facedown in the water. Eventually his body and soaked clothing would have become heavier than the unzipped, loose-fitting suit, and his chest and head would sink downward, possibly pulling his arms out of the sleeves. Finally his feet might have followed, pulling the legs of the suit inside out as they went. The suit would remain on the surface, having expelled the drowned fisherman.

After the Coast Guard called off its search, family, friends, and the Nantucket Fire Department continued searching, but found only a pair of sneakers that belonged to Moniz along with gallon jugs of milk from a New Bedford dairy, oranges, and a propane tank from the boat. A diver, wondering if Moniz had been trapped inside when she rolled, searched unsuccessfully around the sunken boat.

Moniz remained lost at sea.

When news of what had happened to the *Lark* while the Coast Guard was trying to assist her spread along the New Bedford fleet, elder fishermen couldn't help but think back to what had happened twenty-six years earlier to their friends aboard the *Barbara and Gail*.

They were reminded, then, that history often repeats itself.

»The Officer of the Day

ABLARING SEARCH and rescue alarm woke Petty Officer Kevin Angerstein from a dead sleep at 5:20 on the morning of September 5, 1996. Angerstein would later remember the time more readily as "o-dark-thirty." Everyone at Coast Guard Station Gloucester was asleep except for one watch-stander. Within thirty seconds, Angerstein dressed, ran the length of the 120-foot-long brick station building, and entered the radio communications room. After the watch-stander told him about *Houma*'s Mayday call, Angerstein decided to sound the SAR alarm again and announced on the intercom that both boat crews should prepare to get underway. He told Christian Smith, coxswain of the station's 41-foot utility boat, to get underway first and he'd call him with more information in a few minutes. The 47-footer was the station's heavy-weather boat, but the 41-footer was the workhorse. This all-purpose rescue boat, designed in the late 1960s and put into service in the early 1970s, had the speed and maneuverability to perform a variety of Coast Guard missions; it typically got underway whenever the SAR alarm sounded. At 5:23 A.M.—five minutes after the *Houma*'s Mayday call had been received by Station Gloucester and monitored by Group Boston—Coast Guard vessel 41399 left a dock not far from the one Richard Burgess in his *Scotia Boat Too* and Billy Muniz in his *Scotia Boat* had departed a few hours earlier.

Coast Guard Station Gloucester sat on a grassy corner of a busy waterfront overlooking Gloucester Harbor. In addition to the three-story main building, there was a large boathouse used for maintenance of its rescue boats. On the lawn near a large paved parking lot was a helicopter pad. The station operated with a crew of thirty-five full-time Coast Guard men and women. It was also home to the Coast Guard cutter

Grand Isle at those infrequent times when it was not out on patrol.

At twenty-eight years old, Kevin Angerstein was a boatswain's mate second-class with almost eleven years' experience in the Coast Guard, as much as Barone. The son of German immigrants and a native of upstate New York, he had graduated from Colonie Central High School in Albany County, New York, with a hockey scholarship from Plattsburgh State University. He turned it down and instead enrolled in Hudson Valley Community College, planning to study accounting because he had a job waiting for him at an accounting firm owned by a family friend. But after six months he learned his two best friends were joining the Coast Guard, so he too signed on, though he knew nothing about the Coast Guard. He figured he would put in his four years, get his priorities straight, and then go back to school. That was in 1985. Four years later he was having so much fun that he stayed in, and, as he would later say, "It's been a nonstop, awesome ride ever since."

Following basic training, he had served aboard the Coast Guard cutters *Pendant* and *Cape Higgon*, as well as the *Escanaba*, a 270-foot cutter that had conducted illegal-immigrant interdiction patrols in the Caribbean. He had reported to Coast Guard Station Gloucester in 1993 as a coxswain of the station's rescue boats. He believed a coxswain was the undisputed captain of his vessel, responsible for himself (or herself), the crew, the boat, and the people and the property they were sent to assist. Even if the president of the United States or the Coast Guard's own commandant were aboard, Angerstein explained, the coxswain would still be in charge.

"Coxswain" is a qualification earned within what the Coast Guard calls a "rate," or declared specialty, such as boatswain's mate (or "boat driver"), machinery technician (or engineer), public affairs specialist, or food preparation specialist. An enlisted man or woman, after arriving at a Coast Guard station following boot camp, undergoes on-the-job training during which he or she selects a specialty and earns qualifications. Initially he or she has a third-class rating and is also regarded as a petty officer. Petty Officer Angerstein, as a boatswain's mate second class, was one step above the entry-level rating for that specialty. In addition to coxwain, he had earned other qualifications such as boarding officer and officer of the day.

During law-enforcement patrols Angerstein, as a boarding officer, would climb aboard fishing boats to check for safety equipment and compliance with fisheries regulations. He would sometimes serve as the officer of the day, overseeing the station's missions. By September 1996, his search and rescue expertise was founded on ten years of on-the-job training. He had read numerous commandant instructions, training manuals—including both the National SAR Manual and the accompanying Coast Guard Addendum—and Station Gloucester policies and procedures manuals. He had not received any formal training in search and rescue missions, however.

On the morning of September 5, 1996, Angerstein was standing watch as the officer of the day as well as the coxswain who would drive the 47-footer to the accident scene at Search and Rescue Mission Coordinator Richard Barone's request. At 5:30, after launching the 41-footer, Angerstein called Barone at Group Boston to ask if he wanted to take over the communications for the case, an unresolved issue that would appear to be important to both of them as time went on. Because Coast Guard Station Gloucester had responded to the first Mayday call, Angerstein believed he was the acting SAR mission coordinator until Barone was notified. Then Angerstein would confer with Barone as the rescue unfolded, advise him of Station Gloucester's activities, and recommend possible courses of action. Most group officers of the day, like Barone, understood that station officers of the day had the best grasp of their boat and crew capabilities. Angerstein's job was to give Barone a picture of what was going on at sea and brainstorm options with him.

During this first phone call, ten minutes after being awakened, Angerstein told Barone that he was, at this point, "doing this official plotting bullshit." The Coast Guard required him to plot the location of a reported event, particularly when sketchy information required a search to try to locate the vessel or people in peril. He called it "bullshit" this morning because he figured this rescue, like ninety percent of all distress cases handled by the Coast Guard, wouldn't need any searching, so the plotting he was doing was a formality and a distraction. Angerstein asked Barone if he had requested a helicopter, and was told that one was already on its way.

ANGERSTEIN SAT IN THE WITNESS CHAIR on the last Friday morning of April 2000, halfway through the trial, dressed in his blue Coast Guard uniform. A tall man with a deep, commanding voice, he had a military haircut and a thin, narrow face. He rocked back and forth in his seat as if on board a swaying ship and cocked his head to one side while carefully listening to the questions asked of him.

Plaintiffs' attorney Peter Black began by asking Angerstein about his 5:34 A.M. radio call to the tug *Houma*, in which he informed it that a helicopter was on its way from Air Station Cape Cod. Angerstein said he made this call because the Coast Guard considered the tug a SAR rescue unit (SRU) because it was involved and on scene, even though it wasn't under Coast Guard command or being told by the Coast Guard what to do.

"I understand that, sir," Black said. "But, in the manuals, they talk about private entities being involved as SAR rescue units, if they choose to, correct?"

"Correct."

"And the *Houma* had chosen to [be involved], implicitly, if not explicitly?"

"Correct."

"And it was important for you to keep everyone informed of the events—"

"Yes."

"—and information available?" Black asked.

"Yes."

Black noted that at 5:35 A.M., *Houma* asked Angerstein if the Coast Guard boat that was coming would have divers on board. Black asked, "This is the first time that mention of divers is made by any of the SAR units, correct?"

"I believe so," Angerstein said. "I mean, the decision to call divers was [made by] myself at the station immediately thereafter."

Black read aloud from a transcript of the *Houma*'s radio inquiry about divers. "And then, the *Scotia Boat Too* calls [and] asks, 'Did you say there's a helicopter on its way?'. . . And the response is 'Roger, Cap, one from Cape Cod, over.'. . . At 5:36, there's a transmission, '*Scotia Boat Too*, Station Gloucester . . . be advised we're going to call some divers.'"

"So you understood at that point," Black said, "that it was critical to get divers out to the scene as fast as possible?"

"Very much so," Angerstein said.

Black asked Angerstein to look at the list of divers Angerstein had on hand on the morning of September 5, 1996, while Black read the list aloud.

"There's Blackador, do you see that?" Black asked.

"Yes."

"Is that a diver?"

"I can't recall what his role is."

"All right. There's Joe Mullin. Is that a diver?"

"I'm going to assume so, if they're in this section."

"Then, there's Quincy Police?" referring to the Quincy, Massachusetts, department.

"Yes."

"Are they divers?"

"Yes."

"You didn't call them?"

"No."

"There is Beverly [Fire Department] Dive Team?"

"Yes."

"Is that the one you called?"

"Correct."

"There's the Salem [Police] Dive Team, did you call them?"

"No."

The Salem Police Dive Team, established more than ten years earlier, had a ten-man team available and trained for rapid response. These divers could have used the Salem Harbormaster's 60-knot, 31-foot boat to carry them to the scene, about twenty-five nautical miles away, a trip that would have taken them about twenty-five minutes. But this was not Angerstein's understanding of their capabilities at the time. In an interview five years after the accident, he said that despite the list of available divers, his only real options were Salem and Beverly, and he ruled out Salem.

"We didn't call Salem," he said, "because Salem was more of a volunteer dive team. I'm not saying that they're not capable, obviously they are capable, but they didn't have the immediate organization like the . . . Beverly team had or the state police team would have. . . . If I had to call Salem, they can get me a diver or two real quick, but it's not necessarily a thoroughly organized effort. Where I can call Beverly, they're nearby. I'm getting an organized dive team with a dive captain and two divers and an equipment guy, and these guys are *rescue* and recovery trained. You know any one of us could have put an oxygen tank on and gone under there, but that doesn't mean we would have accomplished anything."

Angerstein didn't have the chance to articulate this thought process on the witness stand because Black had moved on to the next name on the list.

"There's Marblehead Dive Team, did you call them?"

"No."

The Marblehead Fire Department Dive Team had a five-man team available that morning.

"Did you call Doug Parsons?"

"No."

Doug Parsons lived in Gloucester and was someone the Coast Guard would call to clear line tangled in their propellers. He, too, would have been available if called.

"Captain Inch?"

"No."

Captain Inch, also known as Anthony Gallo, lived a half mile from Coast Guard Station Gloucester and had been doing diving work for the station for thirty-two years. Though he felt comfortable enough to dive alone, that morning he had two other divers available, as well as a boat to carry them.

"And then there's commercial salvage," Black said. "Did you understand any of these entities to have diving capability?"

"No."

"You didn't?"

"No, not—"

"You didn't know whether Marine Services had diving capability?"

"Not *rescue* diving capability, no."

"Did you know whether Marine Services had diving capability?" Black asked again, his voice raised.

"No."

"Who runs Marine Services?"

"I don't know."

"You don't remember?" Black asked. "Does the name Mike Goodridge ring a bell?"

"Yes, yes," Angerstein said.

"Is he Marine Services?"

"He's affiliated somehow with commercial salvage."

"And he's a diver?"

"If he is, I wouldn't argue that," Angerstein said, "if you say he is in charge of Marine Services."

"He's a diver?"

"Oh, I don't know."

"What about Sea Tow?"

"No."

"You don't know?"

"No."

"You had no knowledge of civilian salvage divers that might be available to respond to this incident, is that correct?" Black asked.

"That's correct," Angerstein said.

"Now, by the way," Black said, "you understood, as the OD [Officer of the Day], that it was the responsibility of Gloucester to keep a list of resources external to . . . the Coast Guard, that could provide services that the Coast Guard wasn't able to provide—specifically, divers, correct?"

"Yes."

"And just so I'm perfectly clear on this, sir, after you called the Beverly Dive Team, you attempted to call no other divers?"

"No."

"Sir, wouldn't it have been better to call as many divers as possible," Black said, "given that it was extremely critical to get a diver out to the scene as soon as possible and take the first one that arrived?"

"No, I wasn't looking for any diver," Angerstein said. "I was looking for a trained *rescue* diver."

"Well, sir, was Beverly the only one on this list that were trained rescue divers?"

"No, but they were the closest."

"They may have been the closest," Black said, "but they may not have been the fastest to get there, correct?"

"Could be," Angerstein said, shrugging.

"But you chose not to call anyone else?"

"Correct."

"And you'll agree with me, in the SAR manual, it talks about people trapped in capsized vessels?"

"Yes, it does."

"It talks about finding facilities, in the plural, when trying to find divers, correct?"

"Yes."

"But you didn't do that?"

"No."

Angerstein confirmed that he and Barone did not discuss trying to find divers between Cape Cod and Gloucester for the helicopter to pick up en route to the scene.

"By the way, sir," Black said, his voice raised as he looked straight at Angerstein, "there was absolutely nothing that would have prevented your assistant to continue calling the rest of the divers that are listed . . . correct?"

"Correct."

"Sir, did you ever make an all-points bulletin, as they say in 'Car 54' or whatever, asking for any divers that are in the vicinity to proceed to the location and render assistance if able?"

"No."

"That's something you could have done?"

"Usually Group handles broadcasts like that," Angerstein said.

"Sir, you were doing a lot of the communications, weren't you?"

"Yes."

"And there certainly would have been nothing to have prevented you [from] using good judgment and initiative, which is expected of you, to get on the radio and say, 'hey, guys, if you're a diver and you're out there in the vicinity of this wreck, please proceed to the scene as quickly as possible, your assistance may be needed'?"

"OK," Angerstein shrugged.

"But you didn't do that?"

"No."

Angerstein said he had heard the Urgent Marine Information Broadcast that Group Boston issued six times that morning, between 5:37 and 6:50 A.M. Black asked him if he ever suggested that the broadcast be changed to include new information, like the fact that divers were needed right away. Angerstein said he did not, even though he agreed that he knew by 5:40 A.M. that people could be heard trapped inside and knocking on the hull. He knew this was important information, critical to the SAR mission, so he called the SAR mission coordinator, Barone, three minutes later to make sure he was aware of this fact.

"But, yet, you made no effort to let the rest of the world know," Black said. "You didn't get on the radio yourself and say, 'Attention all vessels, be advised there are people trapped inside the capsized vessel.' Or something to that effect?"

"No."

During their 5:43 A.M. telephone conversation, Angerstein had asked Barone if he had an ETA for the helicopter at the accident scene, and Barone said it was on its way. Angerstein said he was waiting for an ETA for the Beverly divers at Station Gloucester. During a phone call eleven minutes later, Angerstein again told Barone that he did not yet have an ETA for the Beverly divers.

As Black began his next question, Judge Saris interrupted to ask Angerstein if he had personally spoken to the dispatcher at the Beverly fire station.

"On the second phone call, Your Honor," Angerstein said. "I believe there were a total of three phone calls made." He explained the first phone call was by Petty Officer Bourassa, that morning's break-in officer of the day, someone who had not yet qualified for the position but was undergoing on-the-job training. "That happened relatively immediately after the first call. When it became aware to us that the hull was visible and his boat was capsized, but intact, that's when the decision was made to call the dive team right away."

Judge Saris asked if he knew what time that call was made because she was confused by the multiple phone calls. Angerstein said this first call made by Bourassa had taken place while Angerstein was on the telephone with Barone at 5:37 A.M., 19 minutes after *Houma*'s Mayday call. Angerstein said he'd been able to overhear Bourassa's conversation while he was talking with Barone. He believed at that time Bourassa had been told the Beverly divers would be in Gloucester in 30 minutes.

Judge Saris asked Angerstein about the second phone call.

"The second phone call happened, I'd say, probably within two minutes after the first phone call," Angerstein said. "I completed my conversation with Petty Officer Barone. I got the dive team [dispatcher] back on the phone and made it very clear to him that 30 minutes isn't a good time here. You know, they have protocol to follow, and I understood that. But, listen, if you have a ten-man team that always has to dive together, I don't need ten people right now. Just send me two divers here as fast as you can so I can get them out there."

Black turned to Angerstein's 5:54 A.M. telephone conversation with Barone, during which Angerstein again overheard a conversation with the dive team. He paused and took the call as Barone waited on the other line. Black read aloud from the transcript of this telephone call in which Angerstein said, " 'Hello? Yeah. How are we doing for divers? OK. I don't care if it's just one guy. I need them now. I need somebody now, so how soon can you guys get to the station? Fifteen, twenty minutes you'll be at the station? OK, that's all I need. I don't know. Fifty-five-foot boat possibly submerged on the surface and they can hear people trapped inside. If you can get me two guys within fifteen minutes. All right. Thank you.' "

"So this is the first time you've been given an ETA when you can expect the divers at the station, is that right?" Black asked.

"I'd say no," Angerstein said. "The very first phone call by Petty Officer Bourassa, I believe he was given an ETA. I then immediately called back afterwards and said, 'That's not good enough. Can you make it sooner? I'm not worried about your official protocol,' if you will, and to deviate from it, to that effect. That's when he made—the individual I talked to at dispatch, the Beverly Fire Department dispatch—it's not a dive team that's sitting in an office ready to go. These individuals are at home, and my understanding, they volunteer for this duty, and he needs to get in touch with each one individually."

Angerstein said his expected ETA for the dive team's arrival was based on his conversation with the dispatcher during his third call to the station. Then he hung up and resumed his phone conversation with Barone, saying, "Two divers in fifteen minutes and I'm outta here."

"Now, that's because you were going to be driving the 47-footer?" Black asked.

"Correct."

"And you were expecting to take divers on board the 47-footer, is that right?"

"Whoever got there first. The helo got there first or the dive team got there and I was their—"

"Well," Black said, cutting him off. "There's been no discussion between you and Barone up to this point about getting the helicopter."

Black couldn't resist asking Angerstein another question about his 5:54 A.M. phone call with Barone. Halfway through the call, Barone said that he was just trying to get some other things done while they waited for the divers and that everything was "working pretty good so far." Angerstein said he had called the Marine Safety Office and asked them to send a team of investigators to Gloucester.

"And you say," Black said, reading the transcript aloud, " 'I told them so we don't have to dick the dog later on.' " Black removed his reading glasses and looked at Angerstein. After a calculated pause, he asked, "Is that a term of art, sir, in the Coast Guard?"

"A term of art?" Angerstein asked, blushing.

"Yes," Black said, stone-faced. "Does that have special meaning in the Coast Guard?"

"Um, no," Angerstein said. "I made that one up myself."

Black asked Angerstein to look at the transcript of his 6:05 A.M. telephone call in which he informed Barone that Sea Tow Newburyport, a commercial salvage company, was responding to the scene with one diver on board. To Peter Black, the Coast Guard's dismissive treatment of the commercial divers responding that morning was negligent, and this was a matter to cover in detail with Angerstein as well as Barone. Angerstein had figured that Sea Tow had 23 miles to travel and would be on scene in one hour. Brainstorming with Barone in that 6:05 call, he said they had two options. One was to have Coast Guard Station Merrimack River's 21-foot rigid-hull inflatable pick up the Sea Tow diver. Angerstein had figured the rigid inflatable could go about thirty-four knots and, in theory, could get the diver to the scene in about forty minutes, or by about 6:45 A.M. But the two men dismissed this option, perhaps because they considered the inflatable too small a platform for offshore rescue and dive work. Angerstein said in court that he believed it may have been "in maintenance status," and a memorandum from Station Gloucester to Group Boston ten days before the accident did note that one of the boat's two outboard engines had been replaced. Several years later Angerstein remembered the boat as having been up the Merrimack River on law-enforcement duty that morning.

The second option, as Angerstein had figured it, would be to take a boat from Coast Guard Station Gloucester and travel up the Annisquam

River to meet the Sea Tow boat as it crossed Ipswich Bay, en route to the scene.

"Are we talking about [using] the 47-footer?" Black asked.

"No, we'd be talking about Station Gloucester's 24-foot [rigid-hull inflatable]," Angerstein said.

Black paused, stared at Angerstein, and asked, "Oh, OK, so you also had a rigid-hull inflatable?"

This was the first time Black—or any of the plaintiffs' attorneys—had heard that Station Gloucester had this smaller boat. Richard Barone had testified under questioning by Black that the *only* boats available at Station Gloucester to assist the salvage divers were the 41-footer and the 47-footer. Now Black had to consider the possibility that Barone had either consciously lied or had simply been unaware of the 24-footer. If the latter, perhaps Barone had misunderstood Angerstein to mean using the 47-footer when in fact Angerstein meant the rigid inflatable. Without revealing that this boat was news to him, Black offhandedly guessed at its speed. He asked Angerstein if it could go, say, 50 knots.

"Actually, a little quicker," Angerstein said. "We clocked about 58 knots, so just under 70 miles an hour."

"And that boat's status was," Black asked, "it could be used?"

"Yes," Angerstein said. He paused and then added, "I don't remember exactly."

"Sure," Black said. "Well, you wouldn't have been talking about it—"

"Right, right."

"—at Station Gloucester if it weren't available?"

"Right, correct."

"And you knew what was available?"

"Correct."

"But you elected not to do that, right? You—by the way, you had the personnel to run that boat, correct, without, let's say, losing use of the 47-footer?"

"I don't know," Angerstein said. "I know we had myself and Petty Officer Smith as coxswains there. I don't know of anyone else who was on duty that was coxswain qualified."

"Smith could have taken that [instead of the 41-footer] and you could have taken the 47-footer?"

"Sure."

"And so," Black said, looking down at the telephone transcript, "in here, when you're talking about you could 'blow his doors off,' you're talking about the relative speeds of the two vessels, Sea Tow and your boat that can go 70 miles an hour."

"Correct, in regards to speed."

"But you elected to let Sea Tow keep trucking?"

"Yes."

"At 20 knots?"

"Yes."

"Get there in about an hour?"

"Yeah. I don't remember what the distance was from Merrimack to the scene."

"And not use your 70-mile-an-hour-plus boat—"

"Correct."

"—to pick him up, to rendezvous with him, and get him out there?"

"Correct."

Black noted that during this same telephone call, after dismissing the option of a rendezvous with Sea Tow, Angerstein and Barone turned their attention to whether or not the helicopter should pick up divers and take them to the scene. Angerstein explained to the court that he never told the helicopter to proceed directly to Coast Guard Station Gloucester because he didn't have the authority to do so. It was a call Barone would have to have made. Black noted that, according to the radio log, the helicopter called Group Boston just after 6 A.M. and reported a 15-minute ETA to the scene. Angerstein was not aware of any effort made at that time to have the helicopter travel straight to the Gloucester Coast Guard Station.

To Black, Angerstein's phone calls with Barone held the key to what information the two men had at any given time that morning, and what decisions they had made based on that information. At 6:17 A.M., Black noted, Angerstein had called Barone and reported that he had "100 percent" confirmed that there were three people trapped inside the boat. He'd asked Barone if he wanted to take over the communication with the 41-footer that was by then on scene. Black read aloud from the telephone transcript.

"And then you say, 'Yeah, yeah, that's cool. We're just filling in the holes right now. That's all we're really doing from here.' And he says, 'Sure.' And then you say, 'You guys want it a hundred percent right now, say so and we'll stay out of it.'" Black put the transcript down and looked at Angerstein. "You're telling Barone, 'I really don't have much to do right now, but . . . do you want to take control of all the communications?' Isn't that what you're saying?"

"No, not at all," Angerstein said. "There were numerous things going on and numerous avenues being pursued. It was easier for me, as the OD at Station Gloucester, to stay in touch with the 41."

"Well—"

"And, at this point in time," Angerstein continued, "there was—you know, things had quieted down a little bit, the avenue that was chosen was chosen. It was a matter of waiting now . . ."

"OK. Let's read what it says," Black said and continued reading aloud. "Then he asked you: 'Any word from the dive team?' And you say: 'No. They're—it should be they are en route.' And then you say: 'Uh, I just got another word . . . What did [you] say? Towboat?' And you say, 'Hang on, TowBoatU.S. has a diver on board. They are going to rendezvous with Sea Tow Newburyport and pick up their diver and head out, ETA is 40 minutes, 40 minutes, four zero.' And Barone says: 'And you're still waiting for your guys, right?' And you say: 'Plus I'm waiting for my guys.'" Black looked at Angerstein. "Now, TowBoatU.S., who's that?"

"It's a commercial salvage company," Angerstein said.

"Is that Mr. Goodridge?"

"It could be," Angerstein shrugged.

"You didn't call Mr. Goodridge?"

"No."

"And was it your understanding that the boat that was rendezvousing with Sea Tow was faster than Sea Tow?"

"I don't know," Angerstein snapped. "What boat was it?"

"You just knew that . . . TowBoatU.S. was going to rendezvous with Sea Tow," Black said, "and pick up Sea Tow's diver and head out?"

"Right," Angerstein said.

As he reached the end of his questioning, Black asked, "Now, sir, wouldn't it have been more prudent to have sent your 70-mile-an-hour-plus boat to rendezvous with the diver that was going out there on Sea Tow to try to get him out there quicker?"

"No, not at all."

"Wouldn't it have been prudent to call all available divers as you were trying to find a diver to get to the scene as quickly as possible?"

"No, not in my mind, no."

"Wouldn't it have been prudent to have diverted the helicopter to Station Gloucester, instead of going out to the scene, in order to ensure you would get divers out there as soon as possible?"

"No."

"It was OK to just let Sea Tow keep on trucking, is that right?"

"Yes," Angerstein said. He explained that there were no restrictions on the size of seas that the 24-foot rigid inflatable boat could operate in. The only restriction Station Gloucester's commander had placed on the boat was that it not be used in breaking surf. Certainly the boat could have been driven out to the imperiled *Heather Lynne II*, about twenty miles from Coast Guard Station Gloucester, but Angerstein elected not to use it. Full speed, it would have taken Angerstein about twenty minutes, but he told Black that he would not have gone full speed.

"Well, you wouldn't have idled out there, would you have?" Black asked.

"That's up to the seas," Angerstein said. "That's up to Mother Nature."

"Yeah. Well, the sea conditions were reported to be essentially calm," Black said. "You could have gone full speed in that boat that day?"

"No, no," Angerstein said, explaining that he probably would have gone about three-quarters throttle, or about 50 miles an hour.

"And you could have pushed it a little more and seen how it did?" Black asked. "In other words, you would have pushed it as fast as you could under the conditions and see how it would handle?"

"Obviously," Angerstein said, "yes."

BLACK SAT DOWN and Campbell stood to begin his cross-examination. Campbell wanted Angerstein to explain why he wanted "rescue divers" and why it was that he chose the Beverly dive team. Angerstein said the Beverly team was the closest to Gloucester and that they had received specialized training in search and rescue and underwater recovery.

"With regard to the use of the [rigid-hull inflatable boats]," Campbell said. "Was there any mandatory directive or any requirement that you send those vessels out on this mission?"

"No."

"Can I ask you," Judge Saris interjected, thinking both of Station Merrimack's 21-footer and Station Gloucester's 24-footer, "why didn't you use them?"

"The RHI [rigid-hull inflatable], in either case," Angerstein said, "the 21 or the 24, they have a poor command platform. Yes, it's a fast boat, but it's limited in what it can actually perform on scene. It may sound simple, like somebody can hop in and out of the boat very easily. But no, that's not the case. That's actually one of the harder boats to get people into. Yes, it's fast, but I'm limited in what I can carry, and who I can carry. I'm limited in how long I can remain on scene. I've only got one radio and so I'm very limited in communications. And, in this case, we were roughly ten, eleven miles offshore. Granted, that's not that far, but the Group Boston area of responsibility is notorious for a communication problem. . . . So it's a fast boat, but it's not always the best resource. In this case, it wasn't the best resource. And if I had left on that, I had nobody else to drive the 47."

"I'll cross that question off, Your Honor," Campbell said, smiling.

Angerstein explained that he and Smith were the only coxswains on duty, and that Smith had already left aboard the 41-footer. If Angerstein were to take the 24-footer, no one would be left at the station to drive the 47-footer unless they called in off-duty crew, which they could have done. Angerstein said the 47 was a better platform because it had more room to carry the divers and all their gear.

Campbell then turned his attention to the phone call in which Angerstein told Barone that he'd confirmed there were three people on board and still trapped inside.

"What did you mean by 'trapped inside'?" Campbell asked.

"Trapped inside the boat. No way out."

"What was your understanding of that? Were they alive or dead?"

"My understanding was there were three people on the boat, and I knew at least one of them was alive."

Recognizing that Angerstein did eventually arrive on scene aboard the 47-footer, Campbell asked him if, while he was out there, he saw any scallopers, draggers, or shrimpers who may have offered their assistance. Angerstein said he did not.

"Just to make it clear," Campbell repeated, "while you were on scene, did you ever see any boat that was sufficiently big and had the type of gear that could have hooked onto the *Heather Lynne* and dragged it up the stern ramp?"

"No, not at all."

"Now, during the time of the accident, when you first got your report, let's say, until you got on scene, during that time did you tell anyone that extra lines or cables should not be put on the *Heather Lynne II*?"

"No. I was encouraging them to secure the boat as best as possible."

"During this same time, did you ever tell anyone that a scalloper, a shrimper or a dragger should not assist the *Heather Lynne II*?"

"No."

"And during that time, did anyone ever tell you that a scalloper or shrimper or dragger offered to assist the *Heather Lynne II*?"

"No. I mean, they were helping, looking for people in the water possibly, any other type of debris. There were a lot of boats out there helping out."

"Did anyone ever tell you there was a boat in the vicinity that wanted to take the *Heather Lynne II* and drag it up a stern ramp?"

"No, not at all."

Campbell sat down. Black had a few more questions.

"The 41-footer was on scene, correct?" Black asked as he walked up to a lectern facing Angerstein.

"Yes."

"OK," Black said. "So you certainly knew you had that nice big platform out there if you took your 70-mile-an-hour speedboat out, correct?"

"Yes."

"And you do agree with me, sir, and you knew, that time was of the essence. It was critical?"

"Yes," Angerstein said. He also agreed that if he had taken divers to the scene in the rigid-hull inflatable, they would have been able to enter the water directly from the boat, without first transferring to the 41-footer or any other vessel at the scene. Black sat down and Campbell asked Angerstein, again, why he didn't take the smaller boat that traveled twice as fast as the 47-footer.

"It wouldn't have been a comfortable ride," Angerstein said. "The RHI, again, it's a fiberglass hull boat. It has an air pontoon all the way around it, just for fendering purposes. It has nothing to do with actually making the boat float. There's a pair of outboard engines on the stern, again, capable of 70 miles an hour, extremely maneuverable. It has three snowmobile seats in a triangle set up on the stern, a relatively small working area up on the bow. There's no windshield. There is no cabin. All people on board are exposed to the elements. Only three people actually have a secured place to sit. Everybody else is hanging on. As far as gear, there aren't specific compartments that you can stow gear in, other than what comes with the boat for normal boat outfit. So any gear that would have been on board would have just been lying on the deck. [It's also] very easy for the boat to become airborne. I understand the weather says it was calm out. Yes. To me, a 3-foot ground swell is calm. To most people, no. A lot of people get seasick in that. A 3-foot ground swell, roughly the size of this table right here, that's one swell after another, after another, does not stop, you know, roughly fifty feet apart. At least every third one of those, at full throttle, the RHI would have been six, seven feet out of the water. So, no, I could not have run full speed."

What Angerstein did not say was that the Coast Guard routinely operates RHIs at high speeds in heavy seas. Many of them are deployed from cutters far offshore working law-enforcement patrols, like the one that was reported speeding at 40 miles per hour through 4- to 6-foot seas to approach a Gloucester fishing boat 120 miles offshore during a boarding one late January day in 2002. When asked during a later interview to explain again why he didn't use the 24-footer, Angerstein said, "The fast one that everybody's cryin' about? Can I do 70 miles an hour in the boat? Yes. Can I do 70 miles in the boat in 10-foot seas? Yes. But that's with me and only my qualified crew on the boat and no extra gear, number one, because they can handle the ride. [Transporting a dive team] would be like a SWAT team showing up on a motorcycle. It's not feasible. It doesn't make sense. And then, you know, trying to get the judge to understand that—you know, you drive over a speed bump in your car, you slow down a little bit. At 70 miles an hour, picture me doing a speed bump like that every 20 feet. And at 70 mph, there are points in time where I'm completely leaving the water. There's no part of the boat touching the water. I'm totally airborne. Just because it could do 70 mph doesn't automatically mean, 'Hey, take that boat and go.' I can do 70 mph under ideal conditions, but that doesn't mean under any conditions."

In court, when Judge Saris asked Angerstein at what speed he would have driven the RHI on the morning of September 5, 1996, he said, "Maybe half [throttle] is a safe, comfortable ride. But the first bump and there goes a regulator and an oxygen tank. Second bump, there goes one of my divers in the water. It just wasn't a good—"

"At half-throttle," Saris interrupted him, "when would you have gotten there?"

"At half throttle? It was still 20 miles. Even at half throttle, I'm only doing 40 miles an hour. You're still looking at thirty minutes to get there. Plus, I don't have the privilege of a chart table. I don't have the privilege of all the electronics I have in the 41 or the 47. I don't have the shelter."

"If you had gone there in 30 minutes," Judge Saris said, "would you have been able to get your divers there more quickly than a helicopter?"

"If I could have gotten there in 30 minutes, and it took the helicopter 31, yes, obviously, they could have been in the water sooner."

"So within a minute or two—a couple of minutes of savings if you had gone that way?" Saris asked.

"If I could have gotten them there at that speed, yes."

Campbell sat down and Black stood up.

"And, of course, if it was flat calm, you could have gotten out there at 70 miles an hour?" Black asked.

"Oh, definitely, yeah."

Black sat down and court adjourned for the week. Angerstein was free to begin his fifteen-hour drive back to his current duty station in Belle Isle, Michigan. By that afternoon, halfway through the trial, with the sun peeking through the rain clouds for the first time all week, it was hard to know what Judge Saris would decide. That Sunday, plaintiffs' attorney Brad Henry was feeling cautiously optimistic as he reflected on the previous week and looked toward the next morning's testimony of Tow-BoatU.S., Marine Services salvage diver Michael Goodridge.

"This is the buildup we want," Henry said in a phone interview. "The judge has been primed on Mike Goodridge. Everyone's going to remember the name Mike Goodridge, and that's what we want."

»The Salvor

Michael Goodridge was as elusive as he was predictable. On his own since age fifteen, by 1996 he had spent almost thirty years in a focused orbit between home and adventure. He was bound to his family as if by gravity, yet spun away on his own each day, as much apart from as a part of the community around him. He shielded himself in an armor of individualism, never fearing danger but always assessing risk, always asking what will I gain, what will I lose, and what will it be worth?

That's what the best marine salvors do.

Goodridge was of average height, with strong shoulders, clean, scarred hands, tanned arms, and a physique slim enough to slip through narrow openings in imperiled boats. His eyes were his most striking feature. Like a changeable New England summer sky, they were sometimes silver, sometimes pale blue. He spoke with a deep, calm, confident voice and could make anyone around him feel safe. He was a good storyteller and had plenty of good stories to tell.

He was first a scuba diver. At twelve years old in the summer of 1966, he tagged along with his father, uncles, and cousins, all of whom had jumped into the emerging sport of scuba diving in the early 1960s. As a young diver he would do favors for local fishermen, like retrieving keys and outboard engines that had been dropped overboard. He'd find lost moorings sucked into the sandy bottom of the Merrimack River, which became as much a home to him as his town of Salisbury, Massachusetts, which bordered it on the north.

As early as the eighteenth century there were Goodridges settled in Salisbury. Michael's great-grandparents—he was the postmaster and she was of Swedish descent—had raised nine kids in town. One son, Goodridge's grandfather, became the town's police chief. Another, Michael's great-uncle, brought the family nationwide fame when, as the harbormaster in Rockport, Maine, he adopted a two-day-old harbor seal in 1961 and named him Andre. The story of Andre, who spent his winters in the New England Aquarium in Boston and swam home to Rockport each summer for nearly twenty-five years, made Harry Goodridge one of Maine's most famous residents. Andre's story was turned into a movie in 1994. Michael Goodridge remembers visiting Andre as a kid, though to him it wasn't anything special, since he often had seal pups around his own house. They'd wash up on Salisbury Beach and he'd bring them home to a tub filled with water in the garage, play with them on the front lawn for a little while, then let them go.

Goodridge, the eldest son of an ironworker and one of five kids, had grown up on a rural Salisbury road not far from where he now lived, less than a mile from Bridge Marina, where he kept his towboats docked a stone's throw from the *Heather Lynne II*. As a kid he had spent summers tuna fishing with his father and grandfather. They'd follow the fish off the coast and down to Cape Cod Bay, where they'd sleep on the boat in postage-stamp harbors while waiting for sunrise to call them back to sea.

When he was thirteen, his parents divorced and his mother packed up the kids and moved to a town near Pensacola, Florida, where she married a Navy submariner with two kids of his own. They had another child together, giving Michael seven siblings, a new family, and a new school in a new part of the country. The new life didn't suit him, so he left, hitchhiking his way here and there. He'd think nothing of waking up in the morning and leaving a note on the dresser that said, "I'm going to Massachusetts for the holidays." He would go, but he always came back. And then he would go again, sometimes as far as Canada, sometimes as near as a different part of Florida.

In 1969, at fifteen years old, he decided to leave home for good and found a job hauling telephone cables through the Louisiana swamps. It was tedious, backbreaking work. They'd lug cables for about four miles before returning to the back of the line to coil them. Then they'd go to the head of the line and stretch them. His coworkers were all drifters like him, most of them seventeen-year-old hippies. While humping cables through the swamps, they had to watch out for water moccasins, alligators, and rattlesnakes. But they didn't care. It was something to do. It was a game, and he was good at it.

The Vietnam War draft ended the year he turned eighteen, and he was promoted to foreman at his swamp job. Instead of hauling cables, he worked from a computer truck. One day the truck wouldn't start, so he crawled under it to fix it. The truck started and another guy drove forward, right over his leg. Realizing Goodridge was still under the truck, he backed up and inadvertently ran over him again. Soaking up morphine, lying in a southern Mississippi hospital bed, Goodridge decided that since he wouldn't be able to walk—or work—for a while, he ought to return to Florida and finish high school.

At twenty years old he returned home to New England, where his father helped him join an ironworkers union. He didn't realize right away that, during the next twelve years spent hanging his butt off bridges and high-rises, he was learning skills he'd rely on to forge himself a reputation as one of the best—if not the best—salvors in the Northeast. He was learning the principles of mechanical advantage, about rigging lines to move heavy equipment, about risk, about balance, about getting a job done in the most efficient and safest way possible. One of his first jobs was to help build the drawbridge that spans the Merrimack River and connects Salisbury to Newburyport and points south. He would travel over and under that bridge countless times as the years passed. It was a constant reminder of where he'd been as he contemplated where he was headed.

He married his wife, Gerry, in 1978, and a son, Jake, was born a little more than a year later. By then, ironworking had started to lose its charm, as had New England winters. He took advantage of an opportunity to spend several winter months working as an internationally certified diving instructor on Grand Cayman Island, even though it felt as if he was doing things a little backwards—starting a family and then packing up and traveling abroad. After Christmas, he and Gerry would rent out their Salisbury farmhouse, take their son out of school, and move to Grand Cayman Island for a few months. Jake went to grade school with the island kids while Goodridge dove with vacationers, including author Peter Benchley and astronaut "Buzz" Aldrin. When he briefed Aldrin before a dive, he'd end it by saying, "This is what we want you to do and we don't care if you've been to the moon twice." Aldrin always got a kick out of that.

IN 1983, COAST GUARD COMMANDANT Admiral James Gracey endorsed the Coast Guard's new Marine Assistance Policy, the result of a Congressional directive to cease responding to nonemergency cases. At the time, as through most of its history, the Coast Guard was grappling with an increase in its responsibilities—most notably the "war on drugs"—without a commensurate increase in budget. Meanwhile, the recreational boating industry was booming, and with that came a growing number of amateur boaters who found themselves aground or adrift with engine failure, empty fuel tanks, or dead batteries. They waited, sometimes several hours, for a too-busy Coast Guard boat to come to their aid. Some Coast Guardsmen called themselves Uncle Sam's Towing Service; there was little time left in the day for training or for other missions, like law enforcement.

Something had to give.

When Goodridge read in a *Notice to Mariners* bulletin that the Coast Guard would no longer be responding to nonemergency cases, he saw an opportunity. In New England the Coast Guard invited interested mariners to contact the agency and be placed on its salvor list. This list would become part of a more comprehensive program in which the agency identified outside resources that it could call upon to assist with search and rescue. A friend of Goodridge suggested he would be perfect for the job, so Goodridge bought a used 31-foot JC, a lobster-style fiberglass boat named *Unity*. He liked the name, so he kept it. He installed a tall aluminum mast according to Coast Guard towboat regulations and mounted towing lights and navigation antennas on it. He bought portable pumps, rubber lift bags that could be inflated to raise a boat or keep it afloat, inflatable inner tubes, skeins of spare nylon line of various diameters and lengths, extra scuba tanks, spare jerricans for fuel, jumper cables, wooden plugs to stop leaks in boats, and anything else he could think of that might come in handy. He painted "Marine Services" in large blue letters on the outside of his white-hulled *Unity*. He waited for his first call.

It didn't take long.

He'd already met with the officer in charge of Coast Guard Station Merrimack River, and they had sparked a good, cooperative relationship. That first summer, anytime the Coast Guard knew of a boater in a nonemergency situation, it would call Goodridge. This amicable transfer of workload from the Coast Guard to Goodridge, who was well known to local boaters, helped him build his weekends-only marine assistance business into a full-time summer enterprise. In 1987 he stopped ironworking and took up towing and salvage full-time. Mostly, he worked alone and ran his *Unity* single-handed with grace and skill, as if she had become an extension of his own self. He didn't mind diving alone; he actually preferred it, most of the time, because that way he could focus on what he had to do and not worry about anyone else. For larger, more extensive salvage jobs, he'd call on a network of friends to help, including Dave Stillman, a dive buddy he trusted not to panic when the going got tough.

But his cordial relationship with the Coast Guard didn't last long.

Always concerned with its public image, the Coast Guard had been reluctant to advertise what it would no longer do. Instead, it stopped sending boats on demand and started asking questions to determine whether a boater *really* needed Coast Guard assistance or whether, perhaps, some other form of assistance would suffice. In areas of the country where no commercial assistance companies operated, the Coast Guard continued performing nonemergency services at no charge. As a result, depending on where a boater was, he might have to pay for services that would be offered courtesy of Uncle Sam in a harbor down the coast.

The recreational boating public did not respond well to this new Coast Guard. For nearly two centuries, mariners had expected the Coast Guard, with its *semper paratus*—"always ready"—motto, to rescue them anytime, regardless of the nature of their distress. The old Coast Guard—if not out on patrol already—would launch a boat first and ask questions later. The new Coast Guard would ask questions first and maybe not launch at all.

Instead, boaters found themselves at the mercy of Good Samaritans and commercial towboat operators like Goodridge. Now, when they ran out of gas, help was at hand, but they'd usually have to pay for it. Most towers charged around $100 an hour; the clock started when the towboat left the dock and didn't stop until its return. Most assistance calls lasted between two and three hours. Nighttime operations and rough weather calls often justified a higher rate. This compensation went into maintaining these new towing businesses. Entrepreneurs like Goodridge on the Massachusetts coast, John Andrews in Rhode Island's Narragansett Bay (he would form Safe/Sea), and Joe Frohnhoefer on the tip of Long Island (a former high school industrial arts teacher who used his savings to found Sea Tow) invested their own time and money in boats and equipment. They outfitted their homes, trucks, and offices with marine radios that they monitored twenty-four hours a day, seven days a week, for any signs of a mariner in distress. Harkening back to the days of the old volunteer lifesaving service, these men were locals who cared about the boating community, but they also cared about being fairly compensated for their time and capital investment.

What these towboat captains didn't care for was unfair government competition. The Coast Guard and its Auxiliary volunteers in pockets of the coastline held onto their seafaring traditions and continued to assist boaters in nonemergency situations. Some station chiefs figured the Marine Assistance Policy wouldn't stick, so they ignored it. Though stations that were swamped with a boater-oriented workload welcomed help on the water and forged amicable working relations with the towboat captains, stations facing loss of staff and budget in the face of light caseloads felt differently.

When the caseload at Coast Guard Station Merrimack River dropped—in part because Goodridge was doing much of the work on the river—so did its annual operating budget. In 1996 the station was among several across the country that was downsized as part of a national streamlining campaign. Its staff dropped from twenty-four in 1994 to thirteen in July 1996, most of them in their twenties; the chief in command at the station was the oldest of its crew at thirty-five years old. By 1996 the station was conducting about 200 search and rescue cases and 200 law-enforcement boardings each year. By comparison, Goodridge in 1996 responded to about 500 calls for assistance in and around the Merrimack River.

Some officers at Station Merrimack got along well with Goodridge and others despised him. They would tow boats in nonemergency situations and, when questioned by Goodridge as to why they were going against the spirit of the Marine Assistance Policy, would say they were training or that their young coxswain hadn't known any better.

"Fine," Goodridge would say. "Just hand me $100 for every boat you tow and I'll be happy, because every boat you tow is $100 out of my pocket."

They didn't like that. They didn't like that Goodridge would stand up to them, would question them, would go above them in the chain of command to resolve conflicts, and would often prove to be right. While all commercial towers nationwide questioned the Coast Guard from time to time, Goodridge was considered by the Coast Guard to be a little more assertive than most.

When Bob Albert, supervisor of Station Merrimack from 1994 to 1998, was asked by a local newspaper reporter about the Coast Guard's role on the river versus the private towers, he replied, "They are commercial and we are not." The reporter noted that Albert was hesitant to describe their working relationship but quick to separate them. Albert's answer was, "We will respond to all maritime distress cases. We have control of every single case while it is in distress. . . . The message here is that the Coast Guard maintains control of all distress cases."

As a downsized station, Albert and his crew were forced to operate under the command of Coast Guard Station Gloucester. This stung stalwart Coast Guard aficionados, because Newburyport had been the birthplace of the U.S. Coast Guard. The first revenue cutter, *Massachusetts*, was built on the shore of the Merrimack River in 1791. Coast Guard Station Merrimack River took pride in its reputation as the pearl of the East Coast, with the greenest lawn and the sharpest boats and crew, always ready to burst through the sometimes breaking surf at the mouth of the Merrimack—one of the most dangerous river entrances on the East Coast—to aid a boater in distress. But by the late 1980s and early 1990s its boats were often tied to the dock while Goodridge did the work of helping boaters, a job most Coast Guard men and women had enlisted in the service to do. As the crew and officers in charge rotated year after year, Goodridge found relations in some years more amicable than others. Sometimes the best he could do was earn the Coast Guard's respect the hard way, like the time a tug lost power off the coast and its full oil barge threatened to ground on Salisbury Beach. Alone in his *Unity*, he pounded his way out into the rough seas. When he arrived on scene, the tug captain wanted his help. The Coast Guard told Goodridge not to give it.

"The Coast Guard boat on scene said they had it under control," he later remembered. "They were just going to let the barge wash up on the beach. I called Group Boston and asked them, 'Do you really want me to do that? So when the newspaper reports there's oil spilled all over the beach, I can say the Coast Guard told me *not* to do all I could to help?' "

The Coast Guard told Goodridge that if he decided to help, he was on his own and would have to do so at his own risk. He kept the barge off the beach.

There were times he'd engage in arguments—on the water, over the cell phone, and at the Coast Guard station—with Coast Guardsmen about unfair competition and improper implementation of policy. For a while he was banned from Coast Guard property. One Coast Guard officer who threatened to put him out of business ended up writing him a letter of apology. After several years of the same arguments with different officers in charge, Goodridge realized that when he encountered a particularly tough commander, he would just have to wait it out until that person inevitably transferred elsewhere. That's what most of the other enterprising salvors across the country did, too.

IN EARLY 1986, a young Washington, D.C., lobbyist named Jeff Smith caught the eye of the nation's handful of professional towers when he wrote an article about industries, like these small towboat companies, that faced unfair competition from the government. Later that year, the towboat captains met with Smith over a few beers at the Hawk and Dove Tavern in Washington, just a few blocks from the Capitol, and created C-PORT: the Committee for Private Offshore Rescue Towing. Smith, they hoped, would help the towing industry stay afloat amid legislative initiatives aimed at sinking it. Goodridge's dues check was among the first to arrive.

Smith's first task was to counter the heavy lobbying by boating interest groups like the 500,000-member Boat Owners Association of the United States (BoatU.S.) and persuade Congress not to overturn Admiral Gracey's Marine Assistance Policy. In a *Wall Street Journal* editorial, Smith noted that the Coast Guard's effort to reverse the Marine Assistance Policy was in the same legislative package that sought emergency funding to redress budget cuts that had led to reduced drug patrols and the closing of 8 percent of the Coast Guard's search and rescue stations. He called this Washington Monument Syndrome, in which the services the Coast Guard had chosen to cut were "designed deliberately to create a public outcry, leaving intact areas that could sensibly be cut or turned over to the private sector." He suggested the Coast Guard had ignored the recommendations in studies by the General Accounting Office, the Grace Commission, and the National Advisory Committee on Oceans and Atmosphere that, to save public money, the private sector handle up to 80 percent of the Coast Guard's search and rescue caseload, which comprised mostly nonemergency cases. Smith noted that private towing firms were allowed in 1988 to respond to just 10 percent of the Coast Guard's SAR caseload because of "severe and persistent competition from the Coast Guard and the federally subsidized Coast Guard Auxiliary."

The Coast Guard Auxiliary vigorously disputed this position. Established by Congress in 1939, the Auxiliary comprised some 35,000 volunteers nationwide who patrolled local waters in their own boats and promoted boating safety. Many also underwent training to augment other non-law-enforcement Coast Guard duties such as radio watch-standing, checking safety equipment on recreational boats, and teaching boating safety classes, as well as responding to distress calls. Assisting boaters in all situations, including nonemergency ones, was its core mission. If not allowed to perform search and rescue, one longtime auxiliarist told a reporter in 1998, "We'd be a shadow of our former selves."

Smith responded that C-PORT and the marine assistance industry didn't feel responsible for keeping the Coast Guard Auxiliary happy. He asserted that the industry saved the Coast Guard money. In one year, he said, the Coast Guard spent $300 million on nonemergency SAR at a time when it was scrounging for every dollar it could find to meet budget cuts.

Despite Smith's arguments, both the Senate and the House unanimously passed a bill in 1988 to return to pre-1983 policy and authorize the Coast Guard to respond to nonemergency cases. By then, a growing number of commercial salvors had bought boats and invested considerable money in towing businesses. Suddenly it was an industry on the brink of being shut down. Then President Reagan vetoed the bill.

"It was a total David and Goliath thing," Smith remembered. "We were a small group that couldn't possibly compete against big boating organizations. . . . We had only about seventy members [in 1988] and I could barely get three or four to write letters to Congress, and Congress isn't going to pay attention to three or four letters. . . . The evidence of the argument is what carried us [with the Reagan Administration]."

Smith believed that within the marine-assistance industry were some towboat captains whose skills outshone the others. Competition among them forced each to sink or swim—in each pocket of the coastline, one good, capable provider would emerge. Off the northeast coast of Massachusetts, Michael Goodridge proved himself over time to be that one provider. Towers who were unethical or inexperienced or who damaged boats in their care did not survive long, especially once a boater or two had dubbed them "pirates." Once one earned a reputation along the waterfront—good or bad—it stuck and spread to other ports. Goodridge made sure he built up a good reputation over the years, even if that meant confronting Coast Guard conflicts for just as long. Of course, not every case brought with it a confrontation, and by the mid-1990s the Coast Guard had little to do with the bulk of the cases he handled, as more and more boaters called Goodridge directly. The trouble was that the toughest battles happened on the cases that mattered most, cases where lives or boats of significant value were lost.

"Of all of C-PORT's 175 members, one in thirty has severe relations with the Coast Guard," Smith said in 1998. "Some of these cases are based on the personality of the tower. In some cases where the tower has irritated the Coast Guard, [the Coast Guard] goes out of their way to irritate him the next time. In 85 percent of those severe cases, it's a personality issue, not a policy issue, because the policy is clear. The conflict happens almost always when the tower and Coast Guard have some personal issue.

"Mike Goodridge is one of the best examples. He's a rabble-rouser and a troublemaker, but he's also one of the most professional towers in the industry. The Coast Guard is conflicted about people like Mike. He's extremely professional, but he'll give them heartburn."

By 1996, GOODRIDGE HAD OWNED and operated his independent towing and salvage business, Marine Services, for thirteen years. Other towers signed on as franchisees under Joe Frohnhoefer's Long Island–based Sea Tow, which created a membership program like the American Automobile Association's. Sea Tow operators painted their towboats a patented Sea Tow yellow. For an annual fee, members could receive free towing within certain parameters. In Rhode Island, John Andrews founded a similar membership program called Safe/Sea, whose red boats could be seen plying the waters of Narragansett Bay. On the West Coast, David La Montagne founded Vessel Assist. Upon realizing its members nationwide would be at the mercy of these towing companies, BoatU.S. decided to abandon its efforts to dismantle the industry and instead to create its own towboat fleet and, as part of its membership program, offer a towing package. These towboats were run by largely independent operators who agreed to sign on with BoatU.S. and become TowBoatU.S. marine assistance operators. Goodridge was one of them. Now, in addition to responding to calls for help as Marine Services, he would also answer to calls coming in for TowBoatU.S. Newburyport, Beverly, or Boston.

Assisting recreational boaters was Goodridge's day-to-day work while he waited for a major salvage job to come along. The big jobs tested his skills and gave him both a pile of hair-raising sea stories and a healthy reputation as the leading small-boat salvor on the coast of Massachusetts. By 1996, he had responded to at least 5,600 calls for help from stranded boaters and had salvaged at least 350 sunk, capsized, or grounded boats from rocky shorelines, crowded harbors, and ocean waters as deep as 200 feet.

The business consumed his life and crowded its way into family obligations, pulling him away from his son's little-league games, family cookouts, and intended days off. He never strayed far from a marine radio and always tried to monitor VHF channel 16. He had radios in his garage, in his living room, and by his bed. He had a radio in his truck and when working in the yard, would leave the truck door open or the windows rolled down so he could hear what was going on. He developed a sixth sense for boaters in need. In the middle of dinner, when the volume on the radio was low, he would get up from the table, saying, "I think something's going on," or, "I think someone's calling," and usually, he was right.

Goodridge regarded his job as similar to that of a doctor who was always on call, except there was no one to cover for him. He rarely took a summer vacation, and then only with anxiety about what he was missing on his home waters. He couldn't have a beer or two with dinner, because any minute he could be behind the wheel of his *Unity* headed ten or twenty miles offshore to help out a fisherman who had caught a net or a line in his propeller, or maybe to deliver gas to a boater who was trying to get home from an overnight at the Isles of Shoals. If he was lucky, the call would come in the evening, but the most bothersome calls came at midnight or later. He rarely refused to get underway at any hour of the day in any kind of weather because he knew someone was stranded and needed him.

"I don't walk away from many jobs, but I should start doing that," he once said. "But I feel an obligation to people, like doing mooring work. Because I've done everything for everyone, they count on me to do it for them. . . . The trouble is when you've been up all night, but you say you will do it, and I always try to do what I say. Sometimes that becomes quite a burden because my hours run into days. Something else comes up and what you thought you had for spare time, you don't. . . . But if I don't go and get [a stranded mariner], who will?"

He viewed the spontaneity of the towing and salvage business as the hardest and yet the most exciting part.

"Who knows what we're going to do tonight?" he once said. "We could be salvaging a big sailboat. And people will look at me and say, 'no, that won't happen.' But it is going to happen at some point. That's what I count on."

Sometimes he worked under the centuries-old salvage tradition of "no cure, no pay"—if he didn't complete the job, he wouldn't earn any money no matter how much time, effort, and expense he put into it. When successful, he could claim a healthy reward based on the value of what it was he had saved, like a large Hinckley yacht on the rocks. Other jobs were work-for-hire in which he agreed on a price before the work began. And his jobs weren't just limited to boats. All kinds of people called him for help in all kinds of unpleasant situations.

Sometimes he was asked to find drowning victims, like the time family members called him on the morning of August 5, 1993, to see if he could help them find a man who had fallen off the back of a boat while pulling into a dock at a local marina near 9 P.M. the night before. Goodridge had heard the initial distress call and raced upriver to help. When he arrived, the Coast Guard and local police had begun their search and ordered him not to go into the water. Frustrated, he stood by and, after a while, went home. The next day, at the family's request, Goodridge dove underwater and found the drowned man within ten minutes. He was right where Goodridge thought he would be.

On Thanksgiving that same year, an insurance company asked Goodridge to help find a lost helicopter. An AirMed Skycare helicopter ambulance had crashed into the icy waters of Maine's Casco Bay while transporting an elderly man burned by a brush fire in his backyard. The pilot—a former Coast Guard helicopter rescue pilot—had swum free from the sinking wreckage and survived. The burn patient and two flight crew had not. Now the helicopter and three victims were missing.

The Coast Guard, Maine Marine Patrol, and numerous commercial and private vessels had scoured the bay in four- to six-foot seas to search, unsuccessfully, for the downed helicopter. Desperate for answers, the insurance company hired Goodridge to find and recover the lost helicopter and three missing people. Goodridge called his friend Gary Kozak. A side-scan sonar guru, Kozak was an expert at interpreting the rusty-brown images etched onto paper by a stylus in a machine connected by cables to a small, torpedo-shaped sensor towed behind a boat. Kozak had traveled all over the world with his side-scan sonar and had helped locate the *Titanic* and *Atocha* (a Spanish treasure ship sunk in 1622 and discovered in 1985), as well as wreckage of the space shuttle *Challenger*, TWA Flight 800, Swiss Air Flight 111, and Egypt Air Flight 990. If Goodridge was going to get the job done, he knew he'd need two things—a side-scan sonar looking in the right location and a man like Kozak who knew what the missing object would look like when the sonar found it. They found the helicopter within minutes. Goodridge then dove 85 feet underwater to the upside-down helicopter, where he found the burn patient and a nurse still strapped in their seats; the third victim was missing.

A short while later, he and Kozak located a small airplane that had crashed into the water off New Haven, Connecticut. The Coast Guard and others had been searching for the plane for three weeks without any luck. Four people were believed to be still on board. Kozak and Goodridge found the plane in about a hundred feet of water on the bottom of Long Island Sound.

Goodridge, his longtime friend and dive buddy Dave Stillman, their team of two other divers (Jim Mazur and Steve Smith), and a dive team from the New Haven, Connecticut, police department planned to recover the victims, who were still strapped to their seats. It was a grim task that would take two days of deep diving in poor visibility. One of the police divers, after recovering the first body—bloated and disfigured from three weeks underwater—refused to go back down. They recovered a second body and planned to go back for the third the next day (the fourth passenger was missing and never found). But the next day the New Haven police called to say that their dive team was unable to get air for their tanks and could not join Goodridge. The Coast Guard asked if he wanted to wait a day, but there was a storm coming. Goodridge said he could either dive down and pull the victim out then, or the tug and crane he'd hired for the day would raise the plane and the police could extract the body at the surface. The authorities let him dive to recover the body, which, he said later, was stuck inside the plane and difficult to pull free.

It was the kind of job that could brew up nightmares, but Goodridge didn't let it bother him. He never looked at the faces of trapped people he pulled from submerged wreckage. Working in dark, cold waters, he could distance himself from the human reality of what he was doing, especially when trying to extricate someone long dead from a confined space. Practicing disciplined control, he focused on the job at hand, knowing some family member would appreciate what he was doing.

But most of his salvage work dealt with boats whose passengers had already been rescued—if not by him, by the Coast Guard or a Good Samaritan. While Goodridge's job was to rescue boats—aground, sinking, or sunk—for grateful owners, sometimes boatowners didn't want their sunken boats found.

Suspicious circumstances once induced Goodridge to dig a tunnel in the sand and wriggle his way up and under a capsized 75-foot Western-rigged steel dragger (one that hauls its nets up a stern ramp and is also known as a stern trawler) that was sitting on the ocean bottom in 115 feet of water off Provincetown. The owner said the rudder had broken and dropped out. Water had filled the lazarette and overflowed into the fishhold, which was damaged and not watertight. This accumulated flooding had caused her to capsize and sink, the captain explained. Wanting to know if this scenario was true, the insurance company called Goodridge.

On a sunny fall day amid November swells, Goodridge and his dive buddy, Dave Stillman, set up over the wrecked boat and prepared to inspect her fishhold with a video camera. They suited up, descended, and discovered the boat was, as they'd been told, completely upside down with its rails buried in the sea floor. Because of the water depth, they had 18 minutes to work on the bottom; they had to work quickly. With a garden hoe they dug through the gravelly sand in ten feet of visibility. They pushed aside sand dollars and small codfish to open a hole three feet deep and as wide as Goodridge's shoulders. Taking the yellow air tanks off their backs, they pushed the tanks ahead through the tunnel, then squeezed in after. Looking up they saw that they were, as planned, inside the fishhold. It was perfectly intact. The only holes they found were in the captain's story.

Goodridge looked behind him at Stillman, who held the video camera. They surveyed the fishhold, and Goodridge ran his hands across the four walls. He did not think about the fact that he was more than a hundred feet underwater in total darkness inside a 5-by-5-foot fiberglass room encased in a heavy steel boat, which could shift and trap them. He instead focused on breathing. As long as he could breathe, he could deal with the unexpected. They wrapped up the video shoot and swam back through the tunnel, back to the blueness of the sea floor, and carefully ascended. Once on the surface, they stood on the deck of their dive boat, took a few deep breaths, and prepared to review their footage. They saw nothing. The camera had not worked. So they did it all over again.

Goodridge handled many more routine salvage jobs over the years, though there was nothing routine about any salvage, really. It was exhausting, grubby work. There was constant lugging of long hoses and heavy pumps and dirty lines and yellow, taupe, gray, and blue lift bags—rubber, balloonlike buoyancy aids that can be inflated underwater to lift a boat off the bottom or help keep it afloat. By the end of the job, most of the gear would be soaked in diesel fuel and oils, mud, sand, silt, and maybe a little blood from a skinned knuckle or two. The hours were tedious and laborious and always punctuated by trepidation, with moments of sheer anxiety when a boat rigged up in a cradle of lift bags on the bottom began her rise back toward the surface. Goodridge was always planning, calculating, and reconfiguring. He didn't believe in doing something just for the sake of doing it. If he didn't know what was going to happen when he untied a line or filled a lift bag, he wouldn't do it. There was too much at stake.

When all went well, Goodridge made it look easy. But it would take so little to sabotage success whenever a boat was being pumped out and hung perilously on—or just below—the surface. At such moments Goodridge might yell to, or at, his crew, but they learned not to take it personally. One mate said he hadn't truly been initiated in the salvage business until Goodridge had torn him a new asshole, but for that he was grateful, because he knew Goodridge was only looking out for his safety in a situation he was naive about. Safety remained Goodridge's top priority no matter how perilous the task at hand. And, after working all day in soggy wetsuits and beat-up boats, after bringing the boat back to a marina or boat ramp and hauling her out of the water, after working on an empty stomach with breakfast a distant memory and no time to stop for lunch for fear of missing a favorable tide, Goodridge would buy his crew a good hot dinner.

After these jobs, he'd return to his workshop and clean all the gear, repair it, and get it ready for the next job. Several lift bags hung along a cool concrete wall of his shop, which was no larger than one bay of a typical household garage. It had a dirty concrete floor littered with sand, multicolored wire shavings, and grease drippings. Fluorescent lights hung from the ceiling and lit the silver parts of diving gear, black and gray pumps, an empty boat trailer, half an outboard engine, socket sets and wrenches askew from jobs half done, jobs interrupted by a call for help from a boater in need. He bought two of almost everything, because he knew that when habitually immersed in salt water, half the gear wouldn't work when needed. Fighting corrosion was a constant, costly necessity.

What frustrated him most was when people—particularly the Coast Guard—passed judgment on his ability and tried to determine what he could and couldn't do, especially people who didn't really know anything about him. He had a problem with novice Coast Guard crews—usually enlisted men and women who operated the small rescue boats and had just a few years, some even just a few months, of experience under their belts—arriving on a scene of boaters in distress and ordering him around. The Coast Guard stations had a revolving door through which new people rotated every two years or less. Goodridge was constantly dodging new egos and other obstacles, trying to win acceptance of what he could—and would—do.

"Who do you want to come and get you," Goodridge once asked, "me, or someone who's just learning how to drive a boat? Do you think a kid at the [Coast Guard] station is capable of telling me I'm not qualified to do something?"

While many local mariners had come to respect and rely on Goodridge, often vowing to call him before they called the Coast Guard,

Goodridge knew there were some people who were just waiting for him to fail and shatter his reputation. Bystanders watching him raise a derelict Gloucester fishing boat mused aloud among themselves about all the things that could go wrong. When told later of those murmurs, directed more at the salvage and less at him personally, Goodridge smiled and sighed.

"Yeah, I know it," he said. "Everybody loves a good disaster."

But it wasn't disaster that Goodridge liked; it was the cleaning up afterward. It was finding imperiled boats and bringing them to safe harbor where they could be hauled out, repaired, and returned to sea. It was finding people trapped in helicopters, planes, and boats—alive if possible—and at least bringing some comfort to loved ones left ashore. It was using his unique skills to bring peace of mind to others. Certainly not all the jobs were pleasant. Some were downright horrific.

But, like Richard Burgess, in all his years at sea he'd never seen anything that affected him as profoundly as what he saw on the morning of September 5, 1996.

GOODRIDGE ARRIVED at the courthouse on the first Monday morning of May 2000 accompanied by his wife, Gerry, his dive buddy Dave Stillman, and Stillman's wife, Mary. Usually dressed in a pair of jeans or shorts and a Marine Services gray T-shirt, on this morning he wore a pressed pair of khakis, a blue striped shirt, and a tie with a red jeep on it, a reminder of the recent surfing trip he had taken in Costa Rica with his son. Gathered on benches next to and behind his wife and friends were Captain Jeffrey Hutchins's sisters, mother, father, and aunt; six members of the Lowther family, including John Michael's grandfather; the Coast Guard's expert witness; the plaintiffs' expert witness and his wife; a handful of uniformed Coast Guard men and women; two reporters; and a lawyer working on another case against the Coast Guard in which Goodridge would become involved.

Goodridge drew the largest crowd of the eight-day trial.

He offered an abridged version of his diving and salvage background to plaintiffs' attorney Brad Henry. He explained to the court that as an internationally certified diving instructor, he was qualified to teach anyone—or any developing rescue dive team—how to dive. He had received training in all aspects of recreational and support diving, including underwater rescue and recovery.

Goodridge said that by 1996 he had owned five boats and employed ten captains covering the northeastern Massachusetts waters from the Merrimack River to Salem and Beverly and down through Boston Harbor. Due to the nature of this work, he would talk to officers at Coast Guard Stations Merrimack River and Gloucester almost daily. He had even done diving work for the Coast Guard, like the time he dove on the 41-footer at Station Merrimack to free it from underwater cables. He'd assisted their aids to navigation work by hooking onto buoys that were off station so the buoy tenders could retrieve them. He'd done underwater video inspections of the Coast Guard's larger cutters, like the cutter *Grand Isle*, which was losing bottom paint just after it was commissioned. And he had worked with the Coast Guard when they were on the scene of his salvage work or recovery of drowning victims.

Goodridge explained how, at Coast Guard Group Boston's request, he often sent them a letter listing all his salvage and diving services and equipment. He always added a footnote explaining that he could acquire larger equipment on short notice. He never wanted the Coast Guard to overlook him for certain jobs because of what it might think his capabilities were.

"So, in other words," Henry said, "you don't want to be limited by what you state on the equipment list?"

"Right," Goodridge said, "and their interpretation of what we may be able to do with it."

Judge Saris interrupted to ask, "When did you begin sending out this literature?"

"I think it's been almost ten years," Goodridge said. "It's not done on a regular basis. They just kind of call you up once in a while."

"You've been providing equipment lists back to about 1990?" Henry asked.

"Right," Goodridge said. He explained that when he first entered the towing and salvage business in 1983, the Coast Guard would do an onboard inspection and ask him to demonstrate his proficiency by towing other boats, usually another Coast Guard boat.

Henry asked Goodridge what kind of search and rescue work he had done since 1983.

"Basically, on every call we get underway," Goodridge said. "If you want to call it like the Coast Guard does, we respond to every call and have to go locate the vessel and assist them in any way that they need help. So we're pretty much responding to every case as a search and rescue."

"Whether or not they're life-threatening, correct?"

"Right."

Goodridge estimated for Henry that from 1983 to 1985, he had probably responded to about 100 cases. From 1986 to 1996, he figured he did about 550 cases each year. On top of that, his company did about 30 salvages annually. Since 1996, he had done about 850 cases a year. Henry asked Goodridge if, as part of doing so many cases, he had had an opportunity to know the Coast Guard's officers of the day back in 1996.

"Yes," Goodridge said. "I mean, I don't know them by sight. I've usually talked to most of them. We have to call in any cases that go through them [and provide information on] who we assisted. . . . And I also have to, you know, once in awhile we'll call them on policy issues or that type of thing. We'll find out why a case is being handled a certain way and why we're not responding."

"And how frequently would you have occasion to talk to the officer of the day at either Station Merrimack or Station Gloucester?"

"On a regular basis, but it would also depend on what the caseload was doing at that particular time."

"What about your busiest time, the height of the season?"

"There's different cases," Goodridge said. "We're called directly by some vessels, and then there's cases that call into the Coast Guard saying they need assistance. And those cases are always handled through the Coast Guard. They'll take all of the information [and] put out a Marine Assistance Request Broadcast, which we generally answer."

"Are there occasions when you go out to assist a vessel and the Coast Guard is on scene, waiting?" Henry asked.

"Yes."

"Why are they waiting, do you know?"

"There's times where they'll get on scene and they'll determine that it should be handled by commercial assistance," Goodridge explained. "They'll sit by until we arrive on scene. That's in nonemergency cases."

"Do you know if the Coast Guard logs those as search and rescue cases?"

"Sometimes they do. I know they do case folders, and usually if I have to report back to them, usually there is a case folder being filled out."

Henry asked Goodridge about his familiarity with the Coast Guard's equipment and vessels. Goodridge explained that Coast Guard Station Merrimack in 1996 had a 44-foot motor lifeboat as well as a 41-foot utility boat and a rigid-hull inflatable. Goodridge explained that once the Merrimack station had given him a ride to the scene of a drowning accident on board its inflatable.

"I was contacted by the West Newbury Chief of Police by my pager and requested to respond to a possible drowning up in his area," Goodridge said. "I was down off the Coast Guard station in my larger boat. I informed the Coast Guard that there was a possible drowning upriver. I would like to use their rigid hull. There were two guys underway in the rigid hull. I asked if I could tie my boat up at their dock and they could put my [dive] gear on their rigid hull and give me a ride upriver, which they did."

"And how fast did they get to the scene, or how fast were they going to the scene?"

"I don't know, exactly, but it was probably thirty-plus knots."

"Which is approximately how many miles per hour?" Saris asked.

"Thirty-six."

"And was that the rigid hull out of Merrimack?" Henry asked.

"Yes."

"And were you able to suit up on that ride?"

"Yes."

"Have you ever been on a rigid-hull inflatable going full out, as fast as it could go?"

"I believe we were probably going as fast as that particular one could go."

Goodridge added that this case was sometime after the *Heather Lynne II* accident, maybe 1997. There were numerous cases in which he had worked alongside the Coast Guard, he said, the exact dates of which he couldn't recite from memory.

"Have you ever been contacted by the government to serve as an authority regarding diving?" Henry asked.

"Yes."

"Can you tell me about that?"

Campbell objected, saying, "Your Honor, I wish you'd hear my objection. I think we are getting outside the fact testimony of this witness. I think they are attempting to qualify him as an expert witness."

Judge Saris overruled and nodded toward Henry, inviting him to continue.

"I was involved in the search and recovery of a downed plane in Long Island Sound," Goodridge said, "and the Justice Department has called me on numerous occasions to give my opinion on what the situation was."

"That's a consulting opinion as opposed to a testifying opinion?"

"Right."

"Turning to the incident we're here for today, September 5th, 1996, can you tell me how you first learned that there had been an accident?"

For the first time all morning, Goodridge paused. His mind had begun to travel back in time to the dark, oily waters he found inside the *Heather Lynne II*. Now, three and a half years later, he still had skin rashes from swimming so long in diesel fuel as he wrestled with the inverted boat. The day haunted him—mostly, he figured, because the whole event didn't have to have a tragic end.

"I was called by Bob Yeomans," Goodridge said quietly.

"Do you know about what time that was?"

Goodridge did not answer. His face reddened. He raised his left hand and shielded the welling emotions on his face from those who watched him.

"That's OK," Henry said in a soothing voice as he sought to change tack. "Did you ever sign a statement in this case, do you remember?"

"Yup," Goodridge said, his eyes welling.

"Do you want to take a break?" Henry asked. "Do you want some water?"

"Yeah," Goodridge said, as he reached to a pitcher set on the desk before him.

"Do you want to take a few minutes?" Judge Saris asked.

"Yeah," Goodridge said, "I need one minute."

He walked out of the full courtroom and into the expansive open gallery. He looked out over the waters of Boston Harbor through the enormous windows designed to hide nothing. And cried.

»The Race Against Time

ICHAEL GOODRIDGE spent the first week of September 1996 working all hours of the day salvaging boats caught in the wake of Hurricane Edouard. By Wednesday night he was looking forward to a quiet Thursday, a day to clean up and organize his salvage gear in time for Hurricane Fran, which was barreling up the coast. He had wanted to go tuna fishing Thursday morning, but, exhausted, he was now looking forward to catching an extra hour of sleep and maybe treating himself to the first hot breakfast he'd had in weeks.

Instead, his ringing telephone woke him at 6:05 A.M. on Thursday, September 5. When he picked up the receiver he heard a boat's diesel engine growling in the background. Then Bob Yeomans shouted into the phone and asked if he'd heard what was going on.

"The *Heather Lynne*'s been hit and it's upside down," Yeomans said. "They can hear people banging inside. You better hurry."

Goodridge dropped the phone, dressed, and ran out of the house. As he sped toward Bridge Marina, he called Yeomans from the VHF radio in his truck and asked, "Are they still inside?"

"Yeah, everybody is still inside," Yeomans told him at 6:08 A.M. "The boat is still upside down . . . and I guess the Coast Guard is trying to get a team together, there, and they're going to drop them off by helicopter, but I don't know any more than that."

"OK," Goodridge said. "How far offshore are they?"

"Ten miles east of Thachers. The [loran coordinates] are 680 and 740, about somewhere around there. I don't know the exact number, but we're headed in that direction. I think you're going to be close to it."

Goodridge pulled into the marina and parked near Jeffrey Hutchins's blue-and-white Ford truck. He ran down to the dock, grabbed his wetsuit and some dive gear, and started up his 24-foot towboat, which was faster than his *Unity*. Four minutes after waking from a dead sleep in his home a mile away, he sped away from the dock not far from the *Heather Lynne II*'s empty slip. He continued his conversation with Yeomans via the VHF radio in his towboat. He asked, "How far does that put them out?"

"About 22 miles from the river, Mike," Yeomans said.

Meanwhile, Station Gloucester's 41-footer was arriving on scene. Someone on board the tug *Houma* asked, "Hey, Cap, you have a diver on board?"

"Negative, sir," the 41-footer's coxswain, Christian Smith, said. "Station already contacted an underwater recovery team. We got [a helicopter coming from] Cape Cod, and we're gonna go from there."

"Yeah, OK," *Houma* said. "There's banging on the hull, Cap, and we're gonna need someone here as soon as possible."

"Roger that," Smith said.

Seconds later, at 6:11 A.M., the helicopter reported to Coast Guard Group Boston that they were about 15 minutes from the scene. Group Boston told the helicopter pilot that its 41-footer was on scene, that they could hear people in the water banging on the underside of the hull, and that they were trying to stabilize the hull. The helicopter said it would try to hail the 41-footer directly.

At about the same time, David Swiss of Sea Tow Newburyport called Coast Guard Station Gloucester and reported that he was en route with one diver on board. Swiss asked if the Coast Guard would send a boat out to meet him and help his diver get on scene faster. A Station Gloucester watch-stander said the Coast Guard couldn't assist him and instead asked him just to get there as fast as he could. Overhearing this, Goodridge called Swiss and said, "Dave, if I pass you, have Jay ready."

Normally, Goodridge and Sea Tow's David Swiss were business rivals. As he raced out the Merrimack River and saw Swiss ahead of him, Goodridge did not know that Swiss had been awake for awhile. Swiss, a certified diver, was just starting to plan his day when, over the VHF radio in his bedroom, he heard the tug *Houma*'s Mayday call to the Coast Guard at 5:18 A.M. Swiss paged Jay Lesynski, his business partner, ran out of the house, and sped down the street to his towboat, *Say Ah*, which he also used to haul several hundred lobster traps. Swiss, the son of a doctor, at forty-one years old had been boating since childhood and had started his towing and salvage business in 1990 at Lesynski's suggestion. Lesynski's family owned and operated Merri-Mar Marina; his father, Wally, had been a Seabee in World War II and, as of 2003, had fifty-three years of service in the Coast Guard Auxiliary, earning him the distinction of having the longest active-duty Auxiliary career in the country. Jay Lesynski, aside from being a boat construction and maintenance guru, was a certified dive master and had done a number of salvage and diving jobs along the northeastern coast of Massachusetts during the past twenty-five years.

Lesynski ran half-dressed from his home across the marina parking lot toward the *Say Ah*, whose engine Swiss was already warming up. Lesynski grabbed extra air tanks and regulators from his salvage barge, *Salvage I*, and loaded them onto the boat. Swiss paused before getting underway to be sure they took extra salvage and diving gear. Swiss didn't want to arrive on scene unprepared.

They tore away from the dock and steamed at 20 knots through the mooring field. A hundred yards or so downstream, by 5:45 A.M., Swiss called Coast Guard Station Merrimack River and asked if they'd give Lesynski a ride to the scene in its faster 21-foot rigid-hull inflatable. The station officer said they couldn't assist him because the boat was unavailable. Meanwhile, Lesynski ducked below, grabbed extra scuba tanks, and piled them on the back deck. He also grabbed extra regulators and a roll of duct tape and began connecting a regulator to each of three tanks. Then he taped the hose to the side of the tank. He figured if he could build a compact setup of tank and regulator, when he got to the *Heather Lynne II* he could pass the whole thing underwater to whomever was trapped. There would be enough air inside each tank, in Lesynski's estimation, for a panicked man to breathe for at least ten minutes—enough time, hopefully, to begin calming his nerves.

"All I could think of was to sustain life, those boys needed air," Lesynski later remembered. "My primary concern was they needed air."

As they raced toward the scene, they could see Goodridge closing in on them, so Lesynski got ready to start heaving gear into Goodridge's boat when he pulled alongside. At 6:21 A.M., Goodridge told Swiss that if he had any underwater lights, Lesynski should bring them along. Then Goodridge called Yeomans and said, "We're coming as quick as we can."

As Goodridge pulled alongside Swiss, neither stopped his boat; they kept running forward slowly as Lesynski threw gear into Goodridge's boat. Then they sped off. Goodridge kept driving while Lesynski dressed, kicking himself for grabbing a drysuit by mistake. Lesynski would have preferred a wetsuit because it's easier to move around in and cooler to work in, but the only thing that mattered was getting there in time.

After he had dressed, pulled his gear together, and finished making up spare tank and regulator setups to pass to the trapped fishermen, Lesynski took the helm so Goodridge could suit up. They listened to the helicopter trying to contact the Coast Guard 41-footer for an update. At 6:22 A.M., they heard the 41-footer report that the tug had the *Heather Lynne II* alongside and that the bow of the fishing boat seemed to be sitting pretty high in the water, an opinion that directly contradicted the consensus of the gathered fishermen, all of whom thought that the bow, where the men were trapped, was sinking.

"The only thing we can do now," Christian Smith on the 41-footer said, "is to have divers get the people out." The fishermen had been trapped at least 68 minutes, and the 41-footer had been on scene 12 minutes.

As the helicopter approached, the pilot asked if they should search the area for any survivors who might have been cast adrift. Smith reported that the owner of the *Heather Lynne II* had told him there were only three people on board, all trapped inside; Kevin Angerstein at 6:17 A.M. had reported this to Richard Barone. The helicopter called Group Boston at 6:23 A.M. and asked where the divers were. "Have the divers left shore already? It would probably be quicker for us to go into Gloucester and pick them up."

Group Boston told the helicopter to stand by. While waiting, the helicopter called the 41-footer and asked what the weather was like in Gloucester. Smith said the weather was fine when they'd left; the weather on scene was approximately a one-foot roll with 1½ miles of visibility. *Houma* broke into the radio conversation at 6:25 and asked Smith on the 41-footer, "How long before you get a boat out here with the divers on it?"

"We're working on that right now," Smith said. "We have a helicopter trying to go to Station Gloucester to bring divers out here."

Barone at Group Boston then broke into the radio communications to tell the helicopter that he could make arrangements for it to pick up the divers, but he was concerned about how to drop them off from the helicopter, a maneuver neither the helicopter crew nor the divers had trained for.

"I guess we would have to drop them off on the 41 with a basket," Barone said. "How do you feel about that?"

"How long would it take them to get out here with the boat?" the helicopter asked at 6:26 A.M.

"Approximately forty minutes."

"We need them out here," the helicopter said. "It'd probably be fine to drop them onto the 41-footer."

Barone asked Station Gloucester, "Have you got an updated ETA on the divers?"

"Roger," Station Gloucester replied, "Be advised, [the] 47 is getting underway with the dive team from Beverly right now."

"I want to make sure I understand," Barone said, hearing this news for the first time. "They're on the boat and getting underway at this time?"

"Roger."

Barone called the helicopter and asked if the pilots wanted him to tell the 47 to wait. Did the pilots think that they could save a lot of time, considering the time it would take to lower the divers onto the 41?

Meanwhile, on another VHF frequency, Goodridge was talking to other fishermen and learning more about the situation at the accident scene. As the helicopter circled overhead, its rotors rending the air with an authoritative, percussive tattoo, fishermen on scene were relieved. They believed help had arrived and the trapped men would be rescued in a matter of minutes. They didn't hear the helicopter talking with Group Boston, telling Barone that if the divers were already underway in the boat, it would probably be faster to let them keep going due to the delay involved in transferring divers to the 41-footer in a basket. That seemed to be the plan until, seconds later, Smith on board the 41-footer broke into the conversation and said, "I don't know if the people in this vessel have forty minutes left of air inside the vessel."

Barone called the helicopter pilot back and asked what his ETA would be if he flew from the accident scene to Gloucester, picked up the divers, flew back to the scene and then dropped the divers off onto the 41-footer. Would that take less than forty minutes?

"It will probably be less than forty minutes," the helicopter said at 6:28 A.M. "We can have one guy in the water—at least one guy in the water—in less than probably thirty minutes. It'll take me five minutes to get to Gloucester."

One of the pilots told Group Boston that it would be faster to pick up the divers after landing on the helicopter pad in Gloucester, rather than try to pick them up off the 47-footer, which was already underway. Group Boston called Station Gloucester and told it to clear the helo pad. The helicopter would be there in five minutes.

The fishermen on scene by now had spent an hour or more drifting alongside the *Heather Lynne II*, waiting for the Coast Guard to fulfill its promise to bring divers to the scene. Every now and then, one would holler to the men on the tug's deck. Someone would give a thumbs-up and yell back to the fishermen that yes, they could still hear knocking and, "They're still alive." The sun cleared the eastern horizon, reddish through the haze. The still morning was already warm. The first press helicopter—smaller than the Coast Guard Jayhawk—arrived high overhead. Out of the way and almost unnoticed, it started broadcasting video of the accident scene into homes across New England. Richard Burgess fielded calls from reporters on his cell phone while he waited for a rescue to progress. To the fishermen locked into this static tableau with three trapped and possibly dying men at its epicenter, time was acquiring a surreal dimension.

At about 6:30 A.M., these fishermen watched with horror-filled eyes as the Coast Guard helicopter hovered overhead and then flew away. Expecting that the divers were already on board, they couldn't understand why the side door hadn't opened and divers hadn't jumped out. They believed help had arrived—and then it left. Dean Holt on board the *Jan Ann* later said this part of the morning remains his worst memory.

"The helicopter circled around and sped off," Holt remembered, "and we all just stared. We wanted to start waving our arms and shouting 'Hey, you're in the right place!' "

His deckhand, Joe Cyr, remembered how sad it was when the helicopter left.

"When the helicopter first arrived, we were all kind of relieved and thought they were going to get things going. I believe it made two passes, fairly high above us, two circles around the scene and flew back to the west."

Still without divers on scene, the fishermen didn't know what else to do.

"You know, you're waiting, the anticipation of this happening, and knowing, you know, here they come and you could see them all. And all of a sudden, they're going in the other direction," Cyr said. "It was just a, you know—we didn't do anything other than gasp. You just don't understand what's going on, because you don't know. Not being aware of who's on the helicopter, it was easy to assume that the divers were here and they left."

On board the *Scotia Boat Too*, Richard Burgess looked up at the departing helicopter and screamed, "Where are the divers?"

AT 6:32 A.M., while the helicopter was arriving in Gloucester to pick up two of the Beverly Dive Team members, Goodridge called Yeomans on the marine radio and said, "OK, about forty-four minutes and I'll be there. Just let them know I'm going as fast as I can." He also called Coast Guard Station Gloucester and reported that, including himself, he was en route with two divers. He and Lesynski were all suited up, so all they could do was race to the scene and try to follow what was happening from the radio traffic. He didn't try to engage the Coast Guard in further conversation because he knew that "the first thing they'd tell me is they don't want to talk to me."

Goodridge expected that everyone—the Coast Guard, the tug crew, the fishermen standing by, and especially Jeffrey Hutchins, John Michael Lowther, and Kevin Foster—needed his help. This was a salvage situation with people trapped inside, what is known as "life salvage," and he was uniquely qualified to offer assistance. What he didn't know was what the scene looked like. He only knew he had to get there fast.

At 6:39, Goodridge heard the *Houma* call the Coast Guard and ask for an update on when the divers would be on scene. *Houma* was concerned because it looked like "the fishing boat has taken a little bit of a list on one side [and] has rolled a bit." Smith, on board the 41-footer and about a quarter mile from the *Heather Lynne II*, said the helicopter was at Coast Guard Station Gloucester at that moment, picking up divers.

Fishermen on other radio channels continued brainstorming and talking about putting cables under the boat. Some later recalled that a scalloper had offered to help, but its offer was lost among the many offers being made that morning. Time was running out and the would-be Good Samaritans on scene were growing increasingly desperate. Hearing pieces of this radio traffic, Goodridge feared the fishermen were considering rolling the boat, which he believed was a bad idea because it would upset the trapped men's air pocket. What the boat needed was to be stabilized, to be held as still as possible.

"Don't let them roll the boat," Goodridge directed on the radio. "Don't let them roll the boat."

A fisherman answered him but was stepped on by communications between the 41-footer and the helicopter, which was now en route with the Beverly divers. They were discussing how to lower the divers to the Coast Guard boat.

"Is the [capsized] boat just sitting there?" Goodridge asked a fisherman.

"The tug's got a line lashed around it, Mike."

"OK," Goodridge said, his voice full of concern. "I'm coming. I'm coming."

ON BOARD THE *Jan Ann,* Dean Holt could see the helicopter returning to the scene. It hovered a few hundred yards away and began lowering divers onto the 41-footer, but it didn't seem fast enough. He remembered, "It didn't look like an emergency—maybe like some training mission. . . . There was just no urgency."

Captain Breen on board the *Houma* must have felt the same lack of urgency. At 6:47 A.M. he called Coast Guard Group Boston.

"I see a helicopter approaching our position now," *Houma* said. "The boat is still upside down, but there's air in it, keeping it still buoyant. She is taking a little bit of a list. I do have a doubled-up line around the skeg. The Coast Guard is on scene. The helicopter is over there with the divers . . . [but] we need to get these men out. We do hear tapping. They're still tapping on the hull."

Coast Guard Group Boston told *Houma* that there were two divers on board the helicopter and three more en route on board the 47-footer. While the Coast Guard lowered divers to the 41-footer at

6:49 A.M., and Goodridge was still twenty minutes away, the crew on board the *Houma* watched the *Heather Lynne II* threaten to roll. Air seeped out and bubbles burst on the surface. The sun was sharper now. A faint breeze ruffled the sea. It was a beautiful day to be on the water. The assembled fishermen watched from behind salt-speckled sunglasses, grateful for each breath, yet trapped in a sense of their own futility.

At 6:53 A.M., the *Heather Lynne II's* crew had been trapped at least ninety-nine minutes. *Houma* called Coast Guard Group Boston again.

"Their nose is starting to go down. I'd like to get them out of here immediately," *Houma* said. "Whatever we have to do to expedite it. [The divers are] out there with the Coast Guard helicopter, but they have to get here. It's going down! It's going over!"

"They are in the process of getting those divers out of the helo at this time," Barone at Coast Guard Group Boston answered him. "In your estimation, how much time does this boat have? Are we talking one minute? Five minutes?"

"We're talking it's going over now!" *Houma* shouted. "It's going on its side. We're talking right now!"

The fleet of assembled fishermen watched, horrified, at 6:53 A.M. as the boat rolled some forty-five degrees to port, then stopped, straining against the single line that now held a few inches of its port stern quarter tight against the tug. Now, from the *Houma*, the brown-tinted port-side pilothouse windows were clearly visible. They heard air whoosh out of the *Heather Lynne II's* port side.

"And then it got quiet," Dean Holt recalled. "And we knew it didn't look too good."

GOODRIDGE CALLED THE Coast Guard at 6:54 A.M. and said, "We have [two] divers on board and we still have six miles to go, fifteen minutes. If the draggers are there, put the cables under the boat. If you got two back-to-back, tie them together and just try to hold her for a minute."

A dragger needs strong steel cables and heavy-duty winches to tow and retrieve its trawl, and Goodridge knew these cables could be rigged like a cradle under the inverted boat. But no one answered him.

Instead, Group Boston called *Houma* and asked if he were concerned about the stability of his own boat should the *Heather Lynne II* start to sink. Captain Breen said that the *Heather Lynne II* had just taken a severe list, but the *Houma* should be OK for the moment. After a pause he added, "We haven't heard the men knocking for a while. We've taken a pole over to the cabin, because it's gone over on its side more. It doesn't look like it's gonna stay afloat much longer. I just hope they can get out here." It had been eight minutes since he'd last reported the trapped men tapping.

At 6:57 A.M., *Houma* reported to Group Boston that the 41-footer had the divers on board, adding, for emphasis, "There's no need to do anything other than let them go in the water and see if they can retrieve them."

Richard Burgess noticed that the tug crew was trying to tie another line to the *Heather Lynne II*. He called the *Houma*. "You guys can't, with a long gaff, can't see a bow line dangling off that bow cleat, can you? It's probably just about visible. . . . You should be able to reach something there."

"Uh, no, we don't see it," *Houma* said. "The Coast Guard, they're here now, anyway, so it's best to let them go in and get them out as quick as possible."

"OK," Burgess said. "I just thought you might be able to grab something. But all right. I'll be standing by."

At 6:59, ten minutes after the helicopter had begun lowering divers to the 41-footer, Christian Smith reported to Group Boston that he had the divers on board and was headed toward the tug.

At 7 A.M., Goodridge called Yeomans and said he was four miles away and couldn't see anybody. Yeomans told him the loran numbers and said he'd shoot off a flare for him. The helicopter was right overhead. He told Goodridge to head right for it. At 7:03 A.M., the helicopter dropped its rescue swimmer, Fred Fijn, into the water so that he could assist the divers. At 7:04 A.M., Goodridge asked Yeomans if the Coast Guard had any divers in the water yet.

"I don't know, Mike. I tell you right now, I don't know," Yeomans said somberly. "It's been a lot of time here. They just got another line down there, but they need someone in the water there, quick, or they don't have it."

Goodridge said he could see the helicopter and would be right there.

He asked if the *Retriever*, with *Heather Lynne II*'s owner Ted Rurak, was right on scene. Yeomans said it was.

"OK, anybody there we have to take off we'll be putting right through the [*Retriever's*] tuna door," Goodridge said.

"Uh, no, we got the Coast Guard here, too" Yeomans said. "You'll see it."

"We don't want to fight with getting people up over the side of the 40-foot boat," Goodridge said. "They can pick them up off [the *Retriever*]. Just ask Teddy to get close."

At 7:06 A.M., almost two hours after the collision, one Beverly Fire Department diver entered the water. The other followed.

At 7:09, Goodridge called Coast Guard Group Boston and said he was approaching the scene. He asked if any divers had pulled anyone out yet. No one answered him. He again asked if any divers had entered the water yet.

"If you're getting ready to get close to the area," the Coast Guard answered, "request you contact the Coast Guard vessel on scene, over."

"Who's on scene, here?" Goodridge asked, urgently.

"We are, we have the fishing boat secured to our side," *Houma* answered Goodridge. "[The divers are] going down now. They're inside the [*Heather Lynne II*] now."

"We're coming up to give them a hand," Goodridge said. "Which side is the boat tied to?"

"The boat is on my starboard side. . . . You can come in on my port side if you have to," *Houma* said.

"I want to go where the capsized boat is," Goodridge said. "Where is it?"

Houma said, "It's on my starboard side."

Goodridge called Yeomans and said he would be approaching to pick up Yeomans's son, Rob. Goodridge wanted Rob to drive his towboat out of the way once he and Lesynski were in the water alongside the *Heather Lynne II*.

"Marine Services," the Coast Guard 41-footer called to Goodridge. "Say again your intentions?"

"I'm gonna come right up here. I wanted the fishing boat to put someone on board," Goodridge said. "We got two divers on board here. We'll be going in as soon as we get there."

Goodridge pulled up alongside the *Erica Lee* at 7:11 A.M. Rob Yeomans jumped on board. Goodridge drove over to the *Heather Lynne II*. Lesynski sat all suited up on the stern, ready to roll into the water. As he pulled alongside, Goodridge yelled to Lesynski, "Go! Go! Go!" Lesynski could hear men on the tug and the Coast Guard boat shouting "No! No! No! Stay out of the water!" At that instant Lesynski had to decide whether he was going to help or hurt the situation. He couldn't for the life of him see how he would hinder it, so with Goodridge yelling in one ear and the Coast Guard yelling in the other, Lesynski rolled into the calm, clear green sea.

Goodridge jumped in and swam past him, straight for the *Heather Lynne II*.

IN THE GALLERY outside Courtroom Thirteen, Goodridge collected his thoughts. Then he returned to the witness chair. Attorney Brad Henry asked him to walk up to a large navigational chart and mark on it the location of his home, his boat, and Coast Guard Station Merrimack River. Goodridge then began answering the first of several questions about what could have happened had the Coast Guard worked with him. Henry hoped to prove that the Coast Guard, once it had decided it needed divers, should have placed a call to Goodridge. At the very least, once the Coast Guard learned he was responding on his own accord, the Coast Guard should have made an attempt to help him arrive on scene faster.

With Angerstein's testimony revealing the availability of a 70-mile-per-hour rigid-hull inflatable at Station Gloucester fresh in the court's mind, Goodridge explained that if the Coast Guard had elected to meet up with him as he raced to the scene, the most prudent route for the Coast Guard vessel would have been to travel up the Annisquam River, a canal-like shortcut through Cape Ann, just as Angerstein and Barone had discussed. Goodridge believed the Coast Guard's 24-foot rigid inflatable, in the early-morning hours of September 5, could have traveled up the river at near top speed, making the trip in ten minutes or less.

Henry asked Goodridge how long it would have taken the Coast Guard to then travel from the mouth of the Annisquam River to meet up with him as he was crossing Ipswich Bay at his top speed of 28 knots. Goodridge said that would depend on when the Coast Guardsmen left their dock and when he left his dock. If they were to have joined forces, they would have coordinated their times and speeds and figured out the fastest point at which to rendezvous. He explained for the court that the distance from the Annisquam River to the mouth of the Merrimack River is about 11 nautical miles. If the Coast Guard's 24-foot rigid inflatable were to travel at a speed of 60 knots, it could have run from the mouth of the Annisquam to the mouth of the Merrimack River in 11 minutes. Therefore, if the Coast Guard had called him at 5:36 and departed Gloucester within, say, 4 minutes to meet him, it would have reached the mouth of the Merrimack by about 6 A.M. From there, it could have traveled the 21 miles to the scene in 21 minutes, or by 6:21 A.M. If the Coast Guard's 24-foot RHI had met up with Goodridge a few miles east of the Merrimack River, the time to get him on scene might have been even less. Further, if the Coast Guard had rendezvoused with him once it learned he was responding on his own, he might, at the very least, have reached the trapped fishermen by 6:45 A.M., 8 minutes before the *Heather Lynne II* rolled onto her side.

After determining that, in any scenario, had the Coast Guard picked Goodridge up in its faster 24-foot rigid-hull inflatable, he would have reached the trapped fishermen before the boat rolled and that the sea that morning was "glassy calm," Henry paused.

"Now, you had seen the rigid-hull inflatable traveling very fast before, correct?" Henry asked.

"Right."

"Based on your knowledge and experience and the conditions of the sea at that time, would that rigid-hull inflatable have been able to go at that same speed, very fast?"

"Yes."

Campbell objected and asked to strike Goodridge's answer. "They're asking for an expert witness opinion from a witness who has not been properly disclosed as an expert."

Saris overruled. "He's a lay witness who has experience on the sea. He's allowed to base it on his observations, rather than a hypothetical. So, based on his observations. You've seen that boat in action?" she asked Goodridge.

"Yes."

"All right," Saris said. "I'm allowing that answer."

Henry asked Goodridge how long it would have taken him to get on scene, on his own, had the Coast Guard called him at 5:35 A.M.

"Less than an hour," Goodridge said. "You have to understand, I transferred gear from Sea Tow's vessel. If I had gone directly with my own gear, I would not have stopped to pick up someone else and I would not have had to transfer gear. . . . Even though it was done as quickly as possible, it took a few minutes."

Goodridge figured he could have been on scene sometime between 6:20 and 6:30 A.M. if called at 5:35—assuming Sea Tow's diver was ready at that early hour. Goodridge believed Lesynski wasn't ready to go, since it had taken Sea Tow 45 minutes to get underway from its dock.

"They had a 45-minute jump on me," Goodridge said, "and they were still only passing my dock when I got down to my boat. . . . So, had I been called, I wouldn't have waited for them because I would have gone immediately to my boat, like I did, and got underway in 3 minutes."

"If you had left at 5:35—if you had been called at 5:35, could one of those vessels [at Station Merrimack] have transported you to the scene faster than your own vessel?"

"Yes," Goodridge said. "Taking the [21-foot] rigid-hull inflatable, they do upper thirties, I believe. So they would have been quicker. But even the 41 does the same or better than I do, and it could have been quicker because I wouldn't have had to operate my own boat as I was getting gear ready."

"So someone else could worry about navigation while you were getting suited?"

"Right."

Henry told Goodridge that he could return to the witness chair.

"Now, Captain Goodridge," Henry began, "if you had arrived on the scene and were the only diver, would you have gone in?"

"Yes, at some point," Goodridge said. He explained that he would have looked at the situation and stabilized the boat before swimming inside her. If the Coast Guard had driven him to the scene, he could have spent that travel time monitoring what was happening on scene, forming a clear picture in his mind of what to expect, and offering advice.

"I would have asked them questions of how it was sitting, what it looked like, what was going on," Goodridge said, "and told them what to do until I got there."

Henry showed Goodridge photos taken at the scene before the boat rolled. He asked Goodridge what he would have told people at the scene to do to stabilize the boat. He hoped to show that, had the Coast Guard *not* taken control of the scene, Goodridge could have guided the gathered and willing fishermen through the steps needed to stabilize the boat in preparation for his arrival.

"Arriving at this point, where it was still upright?" Goodridge asked. "We would have looked to stabilize the boat. . . . I would have moved a line to the bow. The bow is the more critical point. From my reports, I was unaware that it was in this position, you know, [as I was] coming out. But once I got on scene and saw that, I would have just stabilized the boat, added a line to the bow, brought in a couple of fishing boats and—I probably at one point would have been conversing with the tug operator to find out what equipment he had on board. At this point here, his air compressor could have been—"

Campbell interrupted Goodridge to object. Saris sustained. Henry rephrased the question. He asked, "Had anyone on the scene described for you, while you were en route, that circumstance, would you have told them to tie up the bow?"

Campbell objected. Saris overruled.

"Yes," Goodridge said.

"Would you have—"

Judge Saris interrupted Henry and asked Goodridge, "Did you actually see the boat at some point, the bow piece of the boat?"

"Oh, yeah," Goodridge said. "Have I seen the boat? I mean—"

"At that point, was the bow secured against the tug?" Judge Saris asked. "When you—"

"I wouldn't say secured against the tug. I think a line had been added at that point," Goodridge said. "There's a big difference between just tying a line that holds it to the side and taking the weight off the bow."

"I'm just trying to understand," Saris said. "What would you have done differently?"

"I would have put lines under it, and on either side of it, to keep it from rolling. The critical point was don't let the boat roll. I relayed that to Mr. Yeomans numerous times on my way out. Do whatever has to be done to keep it from rolling. Because, at one point, there was conversation that somebody was going to try to roll it over and I told him: Don't let them roll it."

Henry directed Goodridge to the exhibit book, where he found the Station Gloucester case file. Included was a typed telephone list of commercial salvage and divers available. "It says 'Marine Services.' Is that you?" Henry asked.

"Yes."

"Is that your telephone number?"

"Yes."

"Did you receive any commendation from the Coast Guard for your actions that day?"

"Yes."

"And what was the commendation for?"

"Participating in the recovery," Goodridge said softly.

On September 27, 1996, the Commandant of the U.S. Coast Guard had bestowed on Goodridge a Meritorious Public Service Award. It cited his "exceptional courage and initiative," his "deliberately placing himself at extreme risk in order to come to the aid of the three trapped crewmembers," and his "swift response and valiant efforts." The Coast Guard concluded that, "Mr. Goodridge's heroic actions and unwavering commitment to aiding those in peril are most heartily commended and are in keeping with the highest traditions of public service."

DEPARTMENT OF JUSTICE ATTORNEY Stephen J. Campbell stood up to begin his cross-examination, in which he would try to poke holes in Goodridge's testimony. He believed Judge Saris considered Goodridge as more of an expert than a lay witness, and Campbell wanted to suggest that Goodridge didn't know as much as he appeared to know. After introducing himself, he said, with annoyance in his voice, "Try to concentrate on the actual rescue time and where we were in the incident of September 5, 1996. The Coast Guard never told you, to your knowledge, not to assist in this case, did they?"

Goodridge paused. Henry objected. Saris overruled.

"What was your answer, sir?" Campbell asked.

"Not to my knowledge," Goodridge said.

"Other than some kind of question we had as you—once you arrived on the scene, did the Coast Guard ever direct you not to go to the scene from the time you left your house until you arrived on scene?"

"Not that I know of."

"You mentioned the vessels that were at Station Merrimack. Do you know, as you sit here today, that those vessels were actually at Station Merrimack on the day of this accident?"

"No," Goodridge said. "I didn't bother to look."

"Did you request the use of any of those [Coast Guard] vessels as you were transiting out to the scene?"

"I put out a call on channel 16 requesting anybody that could get us there quicker, anybody with a faster boat."

"Did you ask the Coast Guard that?"

"I put out a general call requesting any vessel that is faster than us to respond."

"The question to you sir: Did you ask the Coast Guard that?"

"No. I didn't direct it to the Coast Guard, no." What Goodridge did not say was that he had already heard the Coast Guard refuse David Swiss's request for a faster boat.

Campbell referenced the calculations that Goodridge had done earlier. "You said you were at the mouth and transferred [gear and picked up Lesynski] at 6:25 A.M.?"

"That was based on the times that everyone just told me," Goodridge said.

"So, you don't know what time you actually did it? You extrapolated using various distances and speeds, right?"

"Right," Goodridge said. "I wasn't keeping track of the time."

"And with regard to your departure from the dock, you didn't log that anywhere, did you?"

"No."

"How about your arrival time at the *Heather Lynne*, did you log that anywhere?"

"No."

"Don't you normally charge for those times when you're doing commercial assistance?"

Henry objected to the implication of the question as Goodridge said indignantly, "I was *not* responding as a commercial provider."

Campbell referred Goodridge to the spot on the chart that he had marked "HL." He asked Goodridge if he remembered the precise loran coordinates of the accident scene. Goodridge said that he did not and instead had made his best guess in testimony based on the facts provided.

"So, as you sit here today, you don't know what the loran lines were where the *Heather Lynne* was?" Campbell asked.

"No," Goodridge said. "But I did find the *Heather Lynne*."

"Your boat that you took is faster than a 41-footer or about the same speed, is that correct?" Campbell asked.

"Yes, just about," Goodridge said. "It all depends. I'm not sure what their top-end operating [speed] and what mine is, depending on fuel and how much weight I'm carrying, but they're pretty close."

"So the 41-footer would not have helped you very much in getting on scene, is that correct?"

"I believe it would have," Goodridge said.

"It would have gotten you there not that much faster, would it?" Campbell asked.

"About the same amount of time, but I could have . . . dressed and been following the conversation while it was going on."

"But if you took the 41-footer, instead of your boat, at the time you left, you would have gotten to the scene after the other divers were already in, anyway, right?"

"From the time that I was called, apparently."

Campbell paused for a minute to review his notes. Judge Saris asked Goodridge, "That Marine Services phone number that was [on the telephone list], would that have come into your home?"

"Yes," Goodridge said, "it rings at my home."

"When you got on scene," Campbell asked a few minutes later, "if I recall what you told the Court, you would have first assessed the scene, before you dove?"

"Yes."

"And you would have probably had them tie up the boat better?"

"Depending on what the situation was."

"Well, we're talking about the scene at this time."

"When I arrived on scene and it was already rolled?"

"Yeah."

"No."

"You would just jump right in?"

"Yeah," Goodridge said. "That's what I did."

Attorney Brad Henry, questioning Goodridge again, asked who most mariners—recreational boaters, commercial fishermen, or sailors—understand to be in charge when the Coast Guard is on scene. Campbell objected to the question, and after much back and forth between the lawyers and Judge Saris, Goodridge interrupted and said he could clear it all up.

"On a regular basis this is not anything that's new or unheard of," Goodridge told Judge Saris. "I cannot assist a boat until they give me authorization. It's in policy. It's in SAR policy. . . . They routinely tell us we cannot interrupt communications [and] we cannot assist a boat until they determine that we can. That's always the case."

"OK," Henry said. "Captain Goodridge, on this day, in this circumstance, were you responding to the scene as a salvager?"

"No, I was responding as trying to help."

"As a rescuer?"

"As a Good Samaritan or whatever."

"So you were trying to rescue the people trapped in that boat?"

"Right."

As Goodridge stepped down from the witness stand and headed for the courtroom door, an attorney sitting in the back row pulled him aside and introduced himself. He wanted to talk about another pending negligence case against the Coast Guard in which Goodridge could figure prominently, the loss of the fishing vessel *Northern Voyager*. Goodridge sighed. The emotions and failures of September 5, 1996, had still been fresh on his mind a year later when he had again raced to the waters off Gloucester in the hope of working with the Coast Guard to save a boat in peril. But the end of that story was just as puzzling.

» Northern Voyager
November 2, 1997

N UNSTEADY voice booming through Michael Goodridge's living room caught his attention at 8:54 A.M., November 2, 1997. He was on his way out the door to trailer a towboat up to Rye, New Hampshire, where he planned to spend the morning raising a small boat that had sunk at its mooring during an overnight nor'easter. As he stepped closer to the VHF radio in his living room closet, he heard David Haggerty, captain of the *Northern Voyager*, calling Coast Guard Station Gloucester.

"Yes, ma'am," an out-of-breath Haggerty said. "We're, ah, our position is, ah, 42-33, 70-36. We've got water coming in our lazarette fast, entering our boat fast. I was wondering if I could get a pump out here, please?"

"Roger, skipper, can I have the number of people on board?"

"We have thirteen."

Goodridge turned up the volume. Watch-stander Julia Tiernan, a Coast Guard Auxiliarist, confirmed the position, asked for the name of the boat, and asked the captain if he had his pumps going.

"We do," Haggerty said. "We have all our pumps going. Yes, we can't keep up with it."

Haggerty and his crew aboard the 144-foot Western-rigged freezer-processing trawler had been rolling through two- to five-foot swells three miles southeast of Gloucester Harbor, where they had been headed. Standing at the helm, one of Haggerty's mates had noticed that the boat, which had been steering on autopilot, had started to circle. When he turned the wheel hard to the left, she continued turning to the right. When the engineer was sent to investigate, he found flooding in the

lazarette, the compartment at the stern. The captain immediately suspected—correctly, as it turned out—that one of the ship's two rudders
had dropped from the hull. Later the crew would discover that a part of
the lost rudder's linkage had jammed the remaining rudder hard over to
one side, and the flooding prevented a repair.

Watch-stander Tiernan instructed Haggerty to have his crew put on
life jackets and have their survival suits handy. She reminded him to make
sure his life raft would float free, and if they had to abandon ship, to activate the EPIRB and take it with them. A few minutes later, she asked if he
could head toward Gloucester Harbor. Haggerty said he could not.

"I have no steering," he said. "I cannot move."

Goodridge looked at his watch. He was expected in Rye Harbor
within the hour.

He called Station Gloucester on the telephone at 9:03 A.M. During
this 29-second phone call, he said he was available to respond with dive
gear and extra pumps and wanted to know if they would need his assistance. A Coast Guardsman told him they were busy and that they were
going to handle it. Goodridge hung up the telephone and continued to
listen to the radio communications. He heard a Coast Guardsman who
was headed out to the scene ask, "How much water are you taking on,
and do you know where it's coming in?"

"Yeah, it's coming in through the lazarette," said Haggerty. "I think
it's coming up through our rudderpost. We . . . dropped the rudder. We
have water in our machinery space. What's gonna happen is the water is
gonna rise so high it's gonna go into our engine room."

Station Gloucester's 41-foot utility boat and its 47-foot motor
lifeboat raced to assist the foundering *Northern Voyager.* Also responding
was the Coast Guard's 110-foot Island Class patrol boat *Adak,* which had
just been leaving Boston Harbor. The *Adak* was one of forty-nine Coast
Guard vessels in the country used primarily for law-enforcement activities
like drug and illegal alien interdiction. She was usually equipped with one
25-millimeter and two M-2.50 machine guns and had a crew of sixteen:
two officers and fourteen enlisted personnel.

Goodridge, who had been summoned miles offshore plenty of times
to dive under fishing boats and clear propellers, knew that a missing rudder left a grapefruit-sized hole in the bottom of the boat. He reasoned,
correctly as it turned out, that Haggerty's greatest need was for a diver to

plug the hole if possible. The effort would take a matter of minutes and could slow or even stop the flooding. Even if only partially successful, it could allow the pumps to keep ahead of the flooding long enough to tow the boat to shore where she might be hauled out or, at the very least, grounded in shallow water. For a good half-hour he paced his living room, listening as Haggerty told the Coast Guard that there was about three feet of water in the machinery space and the flooding was not slowing down. Goodridge decided to help if he could, despite the Coast Guard having told him it was handling the situation.

He drove to his shop and started up his mobile unit, a former ambulance he had transformed into a truck capable of holding much of his salvage gear. After tossing six pumps onto their shelves, Goodridge loaded his diving gear, two scuba tanks, and several gray-and-yellow lift bags into the back of the vehicle now used to save injured boats instead of injured people. He slammed the rear doors shut and drove toward Gloucester. On the way, he confirmed via cell phone that his friend Dave Stillman's dive boat—similar to his own *Unity*—was ready and waiting there.

Goodridge figured that a boat of *Northern Voyager*'s size would have to be in top-notch condition to withstand weeks at sea. He did not know, as he drove his mobile salvage unit toward Gloucester that fall morning, that she typically fished up to 200 miles offshore, from the Hague Line dividing U.S. and Canadian waters in the Gulf of Maine to as far south as Virginia. The steel-hulled *Northern Voyager* had been built in 1981 in Panama City, Florida, to serve as an offshore supply vessel. In 1990 she was converted to a brilliant-blue fishing trawler with a white raised pilothouse forward. Two large A-frames held two net reels, and her fishhold was capable of processing, freezing, and storing a half-million pounds of herring. She could carry 48,000 gallons of diesel fuel to serve two engines that spun four-bladed stainless steel propellers. Goodridge did not know that the *Northern Voyager* had just spent three months at the Thames River Shipyard in New London, Connecticut, undergoing extensive renovations and repairs, which included rebuilding her two engines and refurbishing the rudder system. Each rudder, about 6 feet tall and 4½ feet wide, was attached to a steel rudder stock that extended down through the hull via a 5½-inch hole. One nut welded at the top of each assembly held the rudders in place. While at the shipyard, she had also undergone a voluntary three-hour commercial fishing vessel safety inspection and a marine survey that found her to be in "very good condition." The surveyor placed her value at $6 million.

Common sense and experience told Goodridge a boat the size of the 144-foot *Northern Voyager* would need a lot of things to go wrong in order to sink. One dropped rudder shouldn't cause such rapid flooding that the boat couldn't be saved. Boats as large as the *Northern Voyager* have discrete watertight compartments in their hulls. If the bow were to hit a submerged object and water flooded in, the damaged area could be sealed off from the rest of the ship. If one compartment flooded, the remaining sealed compartments would still keep the ship afloat. In fact, when a ship is too light it will bob around on a rough sea like an empty soda can in a sputtering home spa. To steady a vessel and make her heavier, some captains will purposely pump water—ballast water—*into* the boat in rough seas so she rides smoother. If the *Northern Voyager* had flooding only in the lazarette and it could be sealed off from the rest of the boat, she shouldn't have trouble staying afloat. If Goodridge could slow the flooding, provide more pumps, or both, it should be possible to avert a sinking.

He also knew what this could mean for him: a "save."

FOR MORE THAN three thousand years, maritime law has recognized that a marine salvor is entitled to a reward for saving imperiled marine property. This reward is not regarded as simple payment for services rendered. The amount typically takes into consideration the degree of danger from which the vessel is rescued; the postcasualty value of the property saved; the salvor's risk; the promptness, skill, and energy displayed; the effort expended to prevent or minimize environmental damage; and the value, readiness, and efficiency of the salvor's equipment and the danger to which it is exposed.

In addition, the salvor's credentials influence the reward paid by an insurance underwriter, which in the *Northern Voyager*'s case was Lloyd's of London. A Good Samaritan would receive less than a professional salvor who has devoted significant time, money, and energy to the round-the-clock services he or she provides. While the Coast Guard counts saving property as one of its top missions, Coast Guard personnel, for the most part, are not trained in and do not engage in the art of salvage. Therefore, professional salvors are entitled to claim top dollar so as to encourage them to maintain their equipment and expertise.

Goodridge was a professional. His fourteen-year-old business in 1997 oversaw six boats and ten captains; maintained a dozen dewatering pumps, hundreds of feet of hose, and piles of lift bags; and had gathered decades of sea experience and salvage expertise. The day's post-nor'easter sea conditions offered plenty of promise for placing his equipment and himself in peril. Though the Coast Guard had told him his help was not needed, he was volunteering to assist anyway. He did not know that the insured value of the boat hung around $6 million, but Goodridge knew he could claim a sizable reward if he could save her from sinking.

En route to Gloucester, he thought about his options. He figured if the seas were not too rough (he later discovered they weren't), he could dive under the boat, confirm whether the flooding was due to a lost rudder, and attempt to plug the hole. Though he had done it before, this would be a risky, exposed dive under the heaving stern of a large trawler. One false move and he could be battered or perhaps knocked unconscious. But if it were just a lost rudder, he could shove a lobster buoy (or a life jacket, sweat shirt, or even a blanket) into the hole. That ought to be enough to slow the leak and enable the pumps to keep up with the flooding. Goodridge did not know that Chief Warrant Officer Wesley Dittes, the Coast Guard on-scene commander and the man who had taken charge of Coast Guard Station Gloucester after the *Heather Lynne II* tragedy, was not planning to allow Goodridge to dive under the boat even if he arrived in time. Dittes, on the 47-footer, had already mentally dismissed any benefits of working with Goodridge.

Aside from offering his services as a diver, Goodridge was also carrying six pumps, which were exactly what Haggerty was looking for. Haggerty later remembered that he was, at the time, "requesting more pumps [and] just hoping somebody is going to bring us more pumps." Goodridge knew he couldn't single-handedly save the boat. He was counting on the crew of the *Northern Voyager* to help him carry pumps to the necessary compartments, direct the hoses so the water could be pumped overboard, and brief him on the particulars of her predicament. He also knew there were three Coast Guard boats on scene and that they had pumps of their own. With enough pumps and cooperative hands, they ought to be able to save her.

At the very least, it couldn't hurt to try.

At 9:33 A.M. Goodridge called the Coast Guard from the cellular phone in his truck. He told them he was on his way and would be there in one hour with his dive gear. Brian Dishong, the officer of the day at Station Gloucester, called Chris Borkowski, the group duty officer and SAR mission coordinator at Group Boston, to report that Goodridge was responding.

"I just got a call from Newburyport divers up there, Mike Goodridge, commercial salvage. He says he can come down, he's about an hour out," Dishong said. "He said he could come down and plug that rudderpost. Ah, I really don't like the idea, but I'm gonna run it by—"

"Nope, I don't want him," Borkowski said. "I don't want him doing that now until I get that thing stabilized."

"OK, that's all I needed to know."

"The thing is, tell him, thank him very much for his assistance but until I can get that vessel stabilized, I'm not putting a person in there."

"Right, I—"

"You just wanted me to concur with you, didn't you?"

"What's that?"

"You just wanted me to concur with you, didn't you?" Borkowski asked.

"Yeah," Dishong laughed.

"I concur!"

"OK, all right."

"Tell him if he wants, he can start making [his] way down there."

"Right."

"But if, yeah, if this is going to be a charge for him," Borkowski said.

"Right."

"You know, he can take that up with the owner. Also, if we can get the owner's name, so we can contact the owner."

"All right, so I'll ask Mike Goodridge if this is gonna be a charge, if it is?"

"Yeah, well, tell him that we're not gonna put anybody on board that, inside that vessel until we get it stabilized."

"Correct."

"You know, anyway, I'm not going to take the risk."

The Coast Guard didn't appear to understand that Goodridge intended to dive under the boat and plug the hole from the outside, not the inside. Stopping the source of the flooding would be one giant step toward stabilizing the boat, which is what Borkowski wanted. Further, Goodridge was responding as a volunteer salvager, and in accordance with the 1989 International Salvage Convention the Coast Guard could not order him away from the scene.

After telling Dishong to inform Goodridge his help was not needed, Borkowski began calling around the coast to find a boatyard capable of hauling a 144-foot boat of 490 gross tons. Not many boatyards were equipped to handle a boat that big, especially one filled with 430,000 pounds of frozen herring and taking on water, and especially not on short notice on an off-season Sunday morning.

Haggerty, meanwhile, asked the Coast Guard if they could locate a tugboat or salvager, someone to make a house call, someone who would help remedy the situation on the spot or get him to shallower water, where, if all else failed, the *Northern Voyager* would at least sink in a depth from which salvage would be feasible. But the Coast Guard did not tell Haggerty of Goodridge's efforts to get to the scene. Instead it told Haggerty only that it was trying to locate salvage assistance.

As Goodridge drove toward Gloucester, crew from the Coast Guard's 41-footer, which had arrived on scene at 9:12 A.M., reported that three pumps—two of the five did not work—were on board the *Northern Voyager* and seemed to be keeping up with the flooding. The cutter *Adak* arrived at 9:47 A.M. and offered to lend a larger pump if necessary. While the *Adak* was supposed to serve as the on-scene command vessel, her officers decided to defer to Dittes, aboard the 47-footer, because they believed his judgment and ability to assess what was going on would be better. The *Northern Voyager* still rode high atop the two- to four-foot swells, barely revealing her flooding. From a distance, she did not appear to be in peril.

Goodridge drove into the parking lot at the Cape Ann Marina at 10:02 A.M. while a young Coast Guardsman on board the *Northern Voyager* stood in the dark bowels of a ship he didn't know and watched thirty inches of water flood past his ankles and toward his thighs. Adam Sirois gave the impression that he didn't want to be in charge of pumping out the boat. Meanwhile Coast Guard Petty Officer Sean Connors walked around on deck, talked to the captain and remaining four crew—the other eight having been removed to safety—and relayed information to Dittes aboard the 47-footer.

"[Sirois] didn't think that we were going to get the boat pumped out, and he really wasn't enthusiastic about pumping the boat out," Peter Flaherty, the *Northern Voyager's* mate, said later. "He was leading me to believe that we were all going to get off the boat. It didn't seem like he was there very long before he was saying we'd have to stop this pumping and get everybody off."

Flaherty was right. As time went on, Sirois, an engineer, didn't feel that the pumps were keeping up with the flooding. He later recalled, "It seemed that no matter what I did, it wasn't doing any good." Sirois was trained not to succumb to tunnel vision, not to let the impulse to save a boat override levelheaded risk assessment. He remembered being taught that when water is flooding out of control, no one's life is worth risking. Besides, they'd be able to save the lives of thirteen men. As Lieutenant Matthew Seebald, chief of operations for Coast Guard Group Boston, said a few weeks later, "That's thirteen men who will be home for Thanksgiving and Christmas."

One Coast Guardsman aboard the *Adak* and one aboard the 41-footer documented the scene with video cameras. There were as many Coast Guardsmen filming the foundering vessel as were on board trying to save her. The remaining twenty on-scene Coast Guard personnel—some of them officers with far more experience than the young engineer sent to help pump her out—stood by with eight of the *Northern Voyager's* thirteen-man crew and watched while a fleet of gulls napped in the nearby swells.

FROM THE VHF RADIO in his truck, Goodridge heard that Haggerty was still asking for more pumps and that he wanted to use his onboard crane to hoist a heavier pump off the *Adak*. He believed the flooding was still manageable and that his trawler could be saved. Goodridge called the Coast Guard on VHF channel 16 at 10:03 A.M. He tried to get the Coast Guard to switch to channel 22, the radio channel on which it was working the case, so that Haggerty might overhear him and learn of his efforts, but the Coast Guard switched him to an alternate channel. Goodridge knew that if he attempted to contact the *Northern Voyager* directly, the

Coast Guard might accuse him of interfering with a SAR case and might even charge him with an FCC violation.

"Just to inform you, we're just getting to Cape Ann Marina and boarding a vessel," Goodridge said. "We're wondering if we should take time to load pumps, if they need extra pumps out there, or just diving to make repairs is their best bet? We've been listening and we're not sure what the pump situation is. We have six pumps with us, a couple of 3-inch and four 2-inch gas[-powered] pumps."

There was a pause followed by a short reply.

"We're not sure at this time, until the situation is stabilized," Coast Guard Auxiliarist Tiernan told Goodridge. "I need to keep this frequency clear." (In fact, she would later admit that she hadn't needed to keep the frequency clear and that actually Goodridge had called at a bad time. Station Gloucester was too busy trying to follow what was happening on scene to answer his question.)

"Roger," Goodridge sighed. "We'll be out there in a little bit."

He decided to take everything he had. He loaded all six pumps and his scuba gear onto Stillman's 31-foot dive boat. He grabbed a friend who happened to be standing on the pier to ride with him and help. He did not hear the Coast Guard conversing over the next ten minutes while he loaded gear. He did not hear that seven seconds after his call, the senior officer aboard the cutter *Adak* was questioning the situation, too.

"Are we keeping up with the water that's coming in, or what are we trying to do here? Are we trying to get enough water out so we can tow the guy in or what?" he asked. "What are we looking at?"

Goodridge did not hear Dittes say that they would try to transfer the larger-capacity pump from the *Adak*, as Haggerty had been requesting, and then minutes later change plans and discuss abandoning the *Northern Voyager*. He did not hear that four minutes after his call, the Coast Guard crew reported the flooding had not slowed, contrary to what they had believed earlier.

"That's progressive flooding," Dittes, on the 47-footer, told his men on board the *Northern Voyager*. He had learned just a few minutes earlier that the Coast Guard could not locate anybody who was willing to haul the boat out. "Let's remove everyone. We're not going to slow that down."

To Dittes it appeared that the *Northern Voyager*, since his arrival, had taken on a greater list. Knowing that his engineer, Adam Sirois, was unable to keep up with the flooding, he feared she might capsize and take the five crew and two Coast Guard personnel on board down with her. The prudent course of action, he believed, was to abandon her.

His orders were echoed by the *Adak* officer, who said, "Let's get everybody off and quit screwing around with this thing."

Haggerty, who had fished aboard the *Northern Voyager* for eight years, did not agree with the decision to abandon ship. He believed that if he could just get some more pumps going, that would buy time to get a diver on scene. As he prepared to operate the crane to transfer the larger pump from the *Adak*, he looked down on deck and saw that the Coast Guard was packing up their pumps and preparing to depart. Angry and unwilling to give up, Haggerty asked Petty Officer Sean Connors again about any salvagers who might be able to help them.

Connors told him that he could discuss that with his commanding officer, Dittes, aboard the 47-footer, but that they weren't going to stay on board the *Northern Voyager* and debate it. Haggerty later recalled that Connors essentially ordered him off his boat, threatening to use force against him if he refused to abandon ship. Haggerty did not know—and at that instant had no way to verify—whether the Coast Guard had the authority to order him off his boat; he only knew that he was "not prepared to risk falling or being dropped into the water at a time when my hands were shackled. With this threat against me, I reluctantly followed the order of the Coast Guard to leave the *Northern Voyager*."

As Haggerty left, he did not agree with Dittes's fear that the boat might capsize at any second. He believed that with more pumps, it would have been a long time before she reached the point of capsizing. In fact, his boat always carried a small list even under routine circumstances. This was intentional, allowing liquids on the factory deck to drain to the port side and be pumped overboard. On this day her slight list to port exposed her starboard side to the wind, which increased the list somewhat, but this was something Haggerty and his crew were used to and had experienced in the past. The situation, as Haggerty saw it, was far from hopeless.

"It is part of my training and responsibility to be in a position to make serious decisions about the safety of my crew and ship at a time when we have no one to look to but ourselves," Haggerty wrote in a statement four years later, noting that they usually fished far offshore in waters where Coast Guard assistance was likely to be several hours away. "As of the time that the Coast Guard forced us to leave, the level of risk involved in staying aboard was not significantly more than the risks involved in off-shore fishing."

But it was too late now. Haggerty climbed on board the 47-footer. Someone asked him, "Cap, you want to stay and watch the boat go down?"

Haggerty didn't look up. He shook his head no. He stared down in disbelief. He had just stepped off his boat for the last time.

At 10:12 A.M. Dittes asked Station Gloucester if they had found a tug that could tow the *Northern Voyager*. Station Gloucester told him that the owner would have to be the one to arrange any further salvage efforts.

Meanwhile, Goodridge was still heading to the scene, unsure if Haggerty knew of his impending arrival. He only knew he couldn't call Haggerty directly because the Coast Guard would tell him to keep the radio channel clear and not interfere with a Coast Guard search and rescue case. Besides, he didn't technically need the captain's permission to attempt to save the foundering trawler. Under maritime law it isn't necessary for a vessel master or owner to consent to the rendering of salvage services if, under the circumstances, a prudent mariner would have accepted. Goodridge correctly assumed Haggerty would welcome his help.

While Goodridge dressed in his wetsuit and his friend drove the boat, he overheard talk on the radio of abandoning the *Northern Voyager*. At 10:27 he heard a Coast Guardsman aboard the 47-footer report that all crew had been taken off. Ten minutes later, he saw both Station Gloucester boats pass him on their way back to the station, and at 10:44, he called to find out why. He again tried to get the Coast Guard to switch from VHF channel 16 to 22, so that Haggerty on the 47-footer might overhear that he was on his way. Instead, the Coast Guard made him switch to VHF channel 12. Haggerty still did not know of Goodridge's impending arrival or intentions.

"We're just about on scene. We saw the 41 and the 47 going in," Goodridge asked. "Did they evacuate everybody?"

After a short pause, the Coast Guard replied, "Call us landline."

The Coast Guard told him by cell phone that he could speak to Haggerty back at the Coast Guard station, but Goodridge believed it would take too much time to drive back to Gloucester Harbor, chat, and then return to the scene. By then it would be too late. He couldn't believe he had been so close when the ship was abandoned. It must be pretty bad, he thought. He knew he'd have a hard time accomplishing much with none of her crew there to help. He turned around and headed in. He did not go see for himself.

The Search and Rescue Plan for Group Boston in effect in 1997 included a chapter titled Maritime Assistance Policy. It read, in part, "Commercial providers should not be instructed to stand down from proceeding to the location and rendering assistance to a vessel in distress. All mariners, including commercial providers, are encouraged to respond to mariners in distress, and if they arrive on scene first may render assistance without receiving authorization from the Coast Guard. However, if the Coast Guard arrives on scene first, the commercial provider may be told to 'stand off' until the situation has been evaluated by on-scene personnel."

Goodridge had made his first call to the Coast Guard at 9:03 A.M. The 41-footer, the first Coast Guard boat to arrive on scene, did not reach the *Northern Voyager*'s position until 9:12. Coast Guardsmen told Goodridge they did not need his assistance before they had arrived alongside the *Northern Voyager* and seen the situation for themselves.

THE COAST GUARD CUTTER *Adak*, left alone with the abandoned *Northern Voyager*, circled the boat and waited for her to sink. At 11:22 A.M. the trawler rolled over onto its side and began to submerge. Gloucester fisherman John Schwind watched the two boats from shore. He had been at sea that morning and had come back to port at about the same time Goodridge was headed out. From the beach, Schwind monitored his handheld VHF radio and heard the *Adak* call Coast Guard Group Boston at 11:29. The *Adak* said visibility was dropping, and the half-sunk boat was becoming a navigation hazard. It wanted to shoot a hole into the bow of the boat and burst the air pocket that held her high in the water.

"Recommend we go ahead and sink this thing as a hazard to navigation at this point," *Adak* said. SAR Mission Coordinator Chris Borkowski in Boston spent the next half hour trying to get permission to do that. It was a complex request, rendered more so because the *Northern Voyager* was a pollution problem with all the fuel on board. Eventually the Coast Guard reached *Northern Voyager*'s owner, James Odlin, and asked if he would give them permission to shoot his boat, to which he replied, "Obviously, I'm not going to give you permission to do that."

Before Borkowski could secure an overriding permission—which would have to come from the Coast Guard commandant—to sink the *Northern Voyager* with a shot through her bow, which was sticking thirty feet above the surface, the boat sank at 12:34 P.M. It was two full hours after the Coast Guard had abandoned her for fear she would capsize and sink at any moment. She had drifted two miles from her position at the time of Haggerty's first call to the Coast Guard near 9 A.M. to request more pumps.

It made Schwind sick.

"None of it's making any sense," he said while standing on a Gloucester pier a few days later. "It goes beyond what you'd expect a normal vessel to do. A boat that size can't sink with just a lost rudder. . . . You have to wonder, what really happened? It was the most understated sinking I've ever seen. There was no concern. It was like nobody cared."

THE NEXT MORNING Goodridge answered a phone call from Marine Safety Consultants, marine surveyors hired by the *Northern Voyager's* insurance company. The Coast Guard was concerned. The boat had sunk in 165 feet of water, taking with her 10,000 gallons of diesel fuel, roughly the equivalent of two large tanker-truck loads. She also had 200 gallons of engine oil and 430,000 pounds of packaged frozen herring on board. The fuel could spill, so it could not be left in the ocean, especially so close to the shoreline. Though the boat was abandoned, her owners were still responsible for her. Someone had to pump the fuel out of there, the Coast Guard said, and soon. After calling owner James Odlin to request permission to shoot his *Northern Voyager* that morning, the Coast Guard had called him back, reported that she had sunk, and asked, "What are you going to do about it?"

Marine Safety Consultants considered Goodridge their top pick for salvage jobs north of Boston and would give him any job he was willing to do. They wanted Goodridge to find the sunken *Northern Voyager*. The Coast Guard had taken approximate latitude and longitude coordinates where she had sunk but did not put any marker on her beforehand, so her precise location was unknown. Once located, someone—

they hoped Goodridge—would have to dive with a video camera and film the presumed-to-be-absent rudder to document why she had sunk. During their conversation, Goodridge learned of the boat's insured value and realized that had he been successful, he could have been awarded close to a half million dollars: a professional salvor's percentage of the insured value, plus a claim for having prevented a possible oil spill, plus the value of the cargo. Instead, he hadn't earned a cent. Instead the multimillion-dollar boat was sunk on lobster fishing grounds, no use to anybody, a potential environmental hazard. Although the crew had been saved, their boat was lost, and with her all the jobs, both shoreside and at sea, that she had supported.

"Did you know I was only a mile away when the Coast Guard ordered everybody off?" Goodridge asked the marine surveyor.

"Oh, don't tell me that," the surveyor sighed.

Goodridge spent the rest of that day working in Rye, New Hampshire, to raise the sunken boat he'd had to put off the day before while trying to assist the *Northern Voyager*. He struggled with air hoses, rubber lift bags, storm surge, and zero visibility, knowing he could have been sitting on Easy Street. Instead he was underwater in the dark, his back crammed against the side of a 25-foot boat that was wedged into the mud and refusing to budge.

GOODRIDGE HEADED BACK to Gloucester the next morning with a half-hearted desire to find the *Northern Voyager*. The terms of this job were "no cure, no pay." If he were unsuccessful in locating her, he would receive no pay, regardless of the time he spent trying. A part of him wanted no involvement in the ensuing effort to deal with the sunken vessel. He had already expended considerable time and effort on this boat and received nothing in return, not even the satisfaction of helping a mariner in distress. Now he was to be part of a cooperative effort among the shipowner, the marine surveyors, the insurance company, and others to find federal- and state-mandated solutions to the myriad of problems posed by the lost trawler. The greatest fear was that the boat was leaking fuel, though only a slight sheen had appeared on the sea surface the day before. Where was the rest of the fuel? Goodridge believed the boat had probably rolled and sunk upside down, trapping the fuel inside her hull. That's why there was no spill.

Yet.

He returned to the scene, this time alone in one of his 25-foot tow-boats. A stiff wind stirred the sea, and he could see whitecaps as he edged away from the dock. Aloud, Goodridge reviewed his terms for the search. If it's too rough, I'm not going to bother. If it's too foggy, I'm not going to bother. It's just not worth it. He couldn't help but wonder what the outcome might have been had the Coast Guard been willing to work with him. The *Northern Voyager* might not have been lost, in which case he would not now be in his little boat in a pounding sea looking for what was, though a substantial vessel, still a small object compared with the deep and vast expanse that hid it. He plunged onward as his boat slammed into large swells. It was far from a pleasant fall day. The confused sea offered no hints of the *Northern Voyager*'s whereabouts. The mile-long sheen of diesel fuel that had been seen on the afternoon she sank had disappeared. There were no tiny bubbles bleeding to the surface. There was nothing but a churning ocean.

Goodridge arrived at the Coast Guard's last recorded longitude and latitude coordinates and dropped a rusty 50-pound angle iron into the water. He attached a white fender to the line to mark where the Coast Guard had thought the *Northern Voyager* had sunk. It offered a starting point. He spent the next three hours in a circular search pattern through the wallowing sea around the marker while staring at his color sonar for any sign of the lost boat.

One hour into his search, a small boat approached the area and slowed down. Goodridge was suspicious. He didn't know that this man, John Schwind, had witnessed Goodridge's Sunday morning attempt to save the *Northern Voyager*. Goodridge wondered who Schwind was and what he was doing. Was he looking for the wreck, too? Was he a treasure hunter, hoping to locate the wreck and lay a salvage claim to her? That wouldn't be possible, because the boat still belonged to the owners, and Goodridge had been hired to search for her. Maybe he was a lobsterman interested in knowing where the wreck was so he'd know where not to put his lobstering gear. Goodridge drove over to find out.

"How are you this morning, Cap?" he yelled into the wind.

Schwind was dressed in orange rubber foul-weather overalls with red straps that could inflate in an emergency. His short gray hair framed a round, weather-beaten face. He nodded and yelled, "This is where the *Adak* said the boat sunk, right?"

"Yeah," Goodridge said, "we're looking for it now."

"Yeah. I'm going to give a look, too."

Goodridge looked at Schwind. "Why? You got gear in the area? Or are you just looking for yourself?"

"Yeah, more or less," Schwind said. Once a salvor himself, he wanted to see if he still had a knack for finding lost ships. He wanted to satisfy his own curiosity.

"Yeah," Goodridge said, unhappy with a vague answer but deciding not to press it. "Well, I'm searching this side of the ball. If you want to search that side, that'd be fine."

"Yeah, OK," Schwind said and eased off in the direction Goodridge suggested.

For the next two hours, the two boats passed each other as they made laps near the marker. Goodridge stopped on what looked on his sonar like a possible spot and decided to take a closer look. He made tighter circles, trying to decide if it was the wreck or just a pile of rocks on the bottom. The presence of lobster buoys hinted that it was a pile of rocks—good lobster habitat. Goodridge looked up from the sonar screen and saw Schwind's boat approaching.

"You got somethin', Cap?" Goodridge yelled.

"Look at my screen," Schwind said and jockeyed his boat into position to reveal an image saved on his sonar. The outline of a red object rose up over the bottom and then sank again in a rectangular shape. It looked like the overturned bottom of a sunken ship.

Goodridge nodded. He asked, "Where'd you find that?"

"A ways from here. Follow me."

Goodridge followed Schwind a half mile to the east, where he saw the structure on his own sonar screen. The absence of any peripheral marks around it hinted that Goodridge had been right. The *Northern Voyager* had rolled and was upside down in 171 feet of water. Fuel was still trapped inside the hull. Goodridge called the surveyor from his boat's cell phone to tell him the *Northern Voyager* had been found. But Goodridge knew the job was far from over.

As he sped back to shore, he called Dave Stillman and began making arrangements to dive the next day with a video camera to document the overturned boat, still holding her fuel and the secret of why she had sunk. They planned to dive at low tide, shaving close to nine feet off the depth of the descent and giving them a little more bottom time to work. They planned to take a third diver and a lot of spare air. They planned to pray for good weather.

"I hope the sun is out tomorrow," Goodridge told himself as he secured his towboat on its trailer for the ride home. "That way it won't be so dark and scary down there."

He shook his head with a wry smile and laughed.

"It'll be dark and scary anyway."

Scuba diving at such a depth requires intense mental preparation. Deep underwater, a diver has no contact with the surface, no surface-fed air supply. No room for mistakes. Goodridge gave little thought to performing deep dives in the warm waters off Grand Cayman, but the cold Gulf of Maine was a different story. Diving down to 150 feet wouldn't be too bad, but the last 15 to 20 feet would be tough going. Every 33 feet of depth is the equivalent of another atmosphere of pressure on the body, or almost 15 pounds per square inch. At 171 feet, he would feel close to six additional atmospheres of pressure squeezing his body and equipment. Since the volume of a gas varies inversely with pressure, Goodridge's air supply would be compressed to one-sixth of its original size, at which point it would be thick, almost soupy, and would be used up six times as fast. He'd have to take in a lot more molecules of air, then, to fill his lungs, since the molecules were so tightly compressed. He'd be breathing from tanks filled with air, which is composed mostly of nitrogen. When nitrogen enters the bloodstream under pressure in high concentrations, it can become a narcotic. Like an anesthetic, it can dull a diver's senses, making him unable to think clearly, understand his actions, or make sound decisions. Only a skilled diver can recognize the approach of nitrogen narcosis and avert its effects.

It would be cold at that depth, too. Goodridge would wear a drysuit over an insulated snowmobile suit and two pairs of wool socks. Stillman, as a matter of personal preference, would wear a wetsuit, which would trap a thin layer of body-warmed water between the neoprene and his skin. The sea floor would be dark. It would be a long way from the surface.

Most of all, they had to race the clock. They could spend no more than 3 minutes descending to the bottom and no more than 5 minutes examining the *Northern Voyager*. Their remaining 20 minutes would be spent on a slow ascent. The risk of decompression sickness—known as "the bends"—dictated this timing, as did their available air supply. Goodridge and Stillman would each carry one air tank on their backs. The third diver—their "safety diver"—would wait at 120 feet with a spare tank of air in case it was needed. Another spare tank would be tied to their anchor line 30 feet below the surface.

Cooperation among the three divers would be critical. One error, one malfunctioning air supply, one panicked or disoriented diver, one mistake that cost time could prove fatal.

Goodridge ran through the motions on his way to Gloucester the next morning. He speculated on what could go wrong and decided how he would handle every imaginable problem. He told himself that if at any point it seemed too dangerous, he would abort the dive. If the sea were too rough, he'd abort. If there was too much current, he'd abort. If they could not locate the hole left by the lost rudder in less than a minute, he'd abort. He would rely on his instincts. If at any time it looked bad, he'd abort.

"If we can't do it quickly and safely," he told himself, "it's not worth it."

He hoped the seas would be calm. He hoped the sun would stay high in a cloudless sky, because that would make the dive before them more palatable, the dark depths less foreboding. He hoped they'd be able to anchor right above the stern of the sunken *Northern Voyager*, make a 2-minute descent down the anchor line, land on top of the stern, film the assumed-to-be-absent rudder and its vacated hole, and then get the hell out of there.

He met his crew at the dive shop: Dave Stillman, the safety diver, and a fourth to stay with the boat. They filled twelve air tanks: one for each of the three divers, two spares in the water, and five spares on board, just in case there'd be a need to do a second dive, though Goodridge had no plans to do so. One attempt was enough. The two remaining tanks were left in his truck, just in case he got another call for help on the way home.

Goodridge borrowed a rebuilt regulator, since his own was sticking. They considered consulting the sport diving tables, but those diving tables do not cover depths over 120 feet. They glanced at the Navy tables and laughed. The tables were meant for use by athletic young Navy trainees, not men in their forties. They also remembered hearing that a percentage of young Navy divers died after following the tables. They left the tables behind and decided to rely on their own bottom-time calculations.

Forty-five minutes later, Stillman's dive boat prepared to set up directly over what Goodridge assumed was the stern of the sunken *Northern Voyager*. Goodridge had put two markers on it the day before, but the one attached to the angle iron had disappeared. For the next hour the boat circled the remaining marker. After repeated passes, Goodridge chose what he hoped was the perfect spot to set the anchor. It was time to put fears aside and skills to the test. It was time to go for it.

The sun shone brightly as they slipped into their dive gear and Goodridge reminded his crew of the plan.

"If it's too dark, we're outta there. If we're not on the stern, we're outta there, because 144 feet both ways [bow to stern and back again] is a long ways to swim. And if the current is too strong, forget it. Everyone got that?"

Heads nodded.

No one smiled.

Stillman leapt into the choppy, early November, 50°F sea. The safety diver jumped in. Goodridge leapt in last. The divers swam over to the anchor line, formed a circle, and looked at each other. They decided it was time. Goodridge and Stillman aimed their heads at the ocean floor, flipped their fins to the sunny sky, and swam as fast as they could down the anchor line. Goodridge popped his ears to relieve the pressure as they passed through two, three, four atmospheres into the depths below. The safety diver followed behind with a spare air supply.

The remaining crew waited on the boat and watched for the telltale bubbles that marked exhaled breaths, but they were hard to follow in the chop stirred by a stiff northwest wind. Sometimes minutes passed between bubble sightings.

They were long minutes.

Goodridge noticed that more bubbles than usual were escaping his regulator. He had a leak and was losing air, but he could not think of that now. He had to focus on the job. There was virtually no current, and they had close to twenty feet of visibility. With his lips he felt the water temperature drop to 40°F degrees. He concentrated on his descent. Two minutes after leaving the surface he saw the chain attached to their anchor. They had reached the bottom.

He started to follow the anchor chain, then felt his chest tightening. The enormous pressure was closing in. He felt his drysuit squeeze, pinching his skin and leaving tiny bruises all over his body. He needed to put some air into his suit to relieve some of the pressure, but he'd lost a lot of air already and had none to spare. He ignored the discomfort. Hearing only the sound of his own breathing, he looked up.

Shiny, silver, brick-shaped objects were suspended over him. He fought back the dawning effects of nitrogen narcosis and realized they were dead herring, stuck in the nets of the boat. With a swoop of his right hand he stopped Stillman from swimming past him. They had been about to swim under the overturned boat and into a wall of fishing nets. They backed up. The water column had absorbed all color and left behind a dark gray seascape. Only the fluorescent light from the video camera brought the ship back to life, revealing the *Northern Voyager*'s brilliant-blue hull. No barnacles, sea stars, or marine life had yet claimed her. Relief washed over Goodridge. They were right at the stern where they wanted to be, right near where a rudder should be.

A few kicks of his swim fins put him in front of a large propeller and over a small hole, the hole that once held a starboard rudder as tall as Goodridge. The hole was about six inches in diameter. Stillman used a video camera to film Goodridge as he reached inside the rudder hole as far as his elbow. It was wide enough to have been plugged with a lobster buoy.

Just as Goodridge had thought.

THE *NORTHERN VOYAGER* STILL LIES RUSTING on the bottom of the sea just a few miles outside Gloucester Harbor. Her owners and her insurance company in October 1999 filed a lawsuit against the Thames Shipyard and Repair Company, who had repaired the rudder, and against the U.S. Coast Guard, who prevented the crew of the *Northern Voyager* from keeping their vessel afloat. Central to the plaintiffs' argument was that a salvor, Michael Goodridge, was "instructed and/or induced by the Coast Guard to turn back" when he was a mile away, which under the Good Samaritan doctrine worsened the condition of the *Northern Voyager*. The plaintiffs are seeking $9,663,874.41 for loss of the boat, profit the boat would have made from the 430,000 pounds of processed frozen herring on board, loss of fuel, and lost gear. On June 2, 2000, Water Quality Insurance Syndicate joined the suit and is seeking $354,350.98, the amount of money it spent removing the several thousand gallons of fuel trapped on board.

In July 2001, the Department of Justice, on behalf of the Coast Guard, requested a summary judgment based on written pleadings in advance of the trial testimony scheduled later in the year. The government argued that the sinking of the *Northern Voyager* was caused by the crew's own negligence. The audible high-water alarms had been deactivated, and fittings missing from a door between the engine room and the auxiliary machinery space rendered it no longer watertight, which meant that once flooding progressed from the lazarette to the auxiliary machinery space it could not be sealed out of the engine room where the electric bilge pumps were located. In this manner, the Coast Guard believed, progressive flooding would have filled the boat's compartments and eventually sunk her, which is probably what happened.

The government further argued that the Coast Guard retained total discretion in how it handled SAR cases and that the court should not second-guess actions taken by rescuers at sea.

Judge Rya Zobel, in a written decision granting that request, believed the Coast Guard's response to the *Northern Voyager*'s distress was in accordance with the discretion allowed it by law in all search and rescue cases. She wrote, "It is axiomatic that the Coast Guard has complete discretion over all search and rescue procedures. . . . Policy judgments that concern the safety of individuals must be protected from the 'armchair admiralty' of judicial second-guessing."

Lawyers for the *Northern Voyager* requested that she reconsider.

"Plaintiffs have *not* claimed that they were owed a successful rescue at the hands of the Coast Guard," Attorney Michael Rauworth wrote. "Plaintiffs have *not* claimed that they were entitled to have the Coast Guard respond at all to the distress of the *Northern Voyager*. Nevertheless, the government characterized this case as one of simply an unsuccessful effort to prevent a sinking. The Ruling seemingly adopted this characterization and thus concluded that the Coast Guard acted within protected discretion."

Rauworth argued that the plaintiffs alleged a different set of facts: that the Coast Guard acted beyond its power by forcibly removing the crew from the vessel against their will, that the Coast Guard did not tell Captain David Haggerty that Michael Goodridge was en route or allow Goodridge to speak to Haggerty, and, further, that the Coast Guard dissuaded Goodridge from assisting by telling him it was handling the situation. In so doing, the Coast Guard delayed Goodridge's own response by about thirty minutes, which clearly contributed to worsening the condition of the foundering *Northern Voyager.*

As Captain Haggerty wrote in a statement prepared for the case, "We had more than enough time and resources available to us to have saved the *Northern Voyager*, without putting our safety at serious risk, if the Coast Guard had simply let us do our jobs, as we insisted."

Rauworth, who before becoming a lawyer had had twelve years of sea experience both as a Coast Guard officer and as a master of merchant ships and then continued his Coast Guard career as a captain in the Coast Guard reserves, consulted with Rear Admiral John Linnon. Linnon was commander of the Coast Guard's First District during the *Heather Lynne II* incident and the TWA Flight 800 tragedy. He had retired just three months before the *Northern Voyager* sank, appearing as an analyst on CNN after the crash of John F. Kennedy Jr.'s plane and after the Egypt Air disaster. Linnon had spent more than forty years in the Coast Guard, a career that included commanding a multiagency drug task force, serving as second in command of the Coast Guard's Seventh District in Miami, and overseeing the operations of all Coast Guard missions on the Atlantic Coast, Gulf of Mexico, and America's western rivers. He had also overseen search and rescue operations in the Central and Western Pacific Oceans from a base in Honolulu and had served aboard various cutters. His whole career had been centered on Coast Guard operational missions, particularly search and rescue.

In the case of the *Northern Voyager*, Linnon believed the Coast Guard had acted improperly.

"The decision to compel the master, mate and engineer to leave the *Northern Voyager* against their will was a decision that none of the Coast Guard people involved had any discretion to make," he wrote in a report prepared for the plaintiffs. "It was beyond their authority to do this." He further believed, "With the fate of the vessel hanging in the balance, there was no good reason to force experienced and professional mariners off the vessel against their will."

Linnon identified several shortfalls in the Coast Guard's actions that November morning. He determined, among other things, that it demonstrated "an anxiety to be done with the case." He believed the Coast Guard had overestimated the magnitude and immediacy of the vessel's peril and thereby erroneously concluded that the "incident would probably be too much for its resources"; had failed to use its most experienced on-hand personnel to evaluate the situation; had failed to assess sources of flooding, which would have led them to "recognize the value of having the services of a diver"; and had failed to seek any damage-control advice, "including but not limited to Michael Goodridge."

As for Goodridge, Linnon had met with him after the *Heather Lynne II* morning and was familiar with his expertise. Linnon believed that the Coast Guard at no time was in a position to conclude that the *Northern Voyager* would not need salvage help. He noted that the Coast Guard has a policy intended to "maximize the availability of commercial salvage services to the maritime public, and to permit commercial salvors to optimize their opportunities to continue in business . . . by generating revenue in serving the needs of the maritime public. In fact, the service relies upon such commercial entities to provide capabilities, such as divers, that the Coast Guard does not, itself, possess. Anything that stands in the way of commercial salvors making contact and reaching an agreement with mariners in need is at odds . . . with the Coast Guard's commercial assistance policy. The Coast Guard knew or should have known that the *Northern Voyager* needed significant help beyond what Coast Guard forces on scene could provide. It also knew (or should have known) that Mike Goodridge was in a position to provide the needed help."

Linnon believed that if the Coast Guard was unclear about what benefits Goodridge could provide, it should have asked. Linnon noted that Goodridge had a history with the Coast Guard and that he and his business "were well known to the decision-makers at both Station Gloucester and Group Boston," in part because of semiannual meetings the Coast Guard held with area salvors and in part because of Goodridge having called from time to time to complain that a case he thought should have been turned over to commercial assistance was not. Linnon believed the

Coast Guard, in its actions, should not have given Goodridge the impression that it "was likely to make it difficult for him to negotiate and to conduct business of marine salvage with the *Northern Voyager*. This had a natural and foreseeable tendency to discourage the response on the part of a reasonable commercial salvor such as Goodridge." Instead of blocking Goodridge's efforts to contact Haggerty, Linnon believed, the Coast Guard should have facilitated the exchange of cell phone numbers so that the salvor and captain or owner could discuss salvage arrangements.

"[T]he actions of the Coast Guard," Linnon wrote, "in impeding the flow of information between the *Northern Voyager* and Mike Goodridge were improper and at odds with the fundamental purpose of the Coast Guard's commercial salvage policy."

During a deposition, Chief Warrant Officer Wesley Dittes told Rauworth and other assembled attorneys that he had told Haggerty of Goodridge's efforts to respond; Haggerty said he had not.

"At no time before I was put ashore in Gloucester did I ever learn that there was a salvor approaching with pumps and dive gear," Haggerty wrote. "The Coast Guard had already made it abundantly clear that they were prepared to use force to remove me from the one place where I obviously could do the most good for the vessel that I was in charge of, and I understood this to mean that I would be prevented from ever setting foot aboard the *Northern Voyager* again. The Coast Guard people never gave me any reason to believe that anything could or would happen to give the *Northern Voyager* any hope of surviving. . . . My entire approach during our time on board was to maximize pumping capacity to reduce the rate of accumulation of water in the vessel in order to buy time while other resources could get to the scene. . . . I certainly would have remembered if I had been told anything about anyone with dive gear close enough to help, since this was the whole point of my thinking in trying to save the vessel, and there was nothing of the kind ever said to me."

Haggerty, had he known of Goodridge's efforts or been given any reason to believe he would be allowed back on the *Northern Voyager*, said he would have deployed a Jacob's ladder—a rope ladder—before he departed so that it would be easy to climb on board. If he could have talked to Goodridge before being forced off the boat, Haggerty said he would have learned what Goodridge needed to assist the *Northern Voyager* and would have made every effort to accommodate him. He could have given him whatever he needed to plug the rudder hole and used the *Northern Voyager*'s crane to lift Goodridge's six pumps on board in a hurry.

But this was not to be.

Haggerty said that, once aboard the 47-footer, he saw returning to Gloucester as his only option because, since he didn't know about Goodridge, he believed, "Neither I nor anyone else could do anything at that point to save the vessel."

In the summer of 2002, the plaintiffs took the case to the First Circuit Court of Appeals. Plaintiffs feared—and, in a friend of the court brief on behalf of the marine assistance industry, C-PORT agreed—that if Judge Zobel's judgment were allowed to stand, the Coast Guard would have dangerously autonomous discretion over how it handled all future SAR cases. Rauworth wrote, "There will be no future remedy against the government for death, personal injury, or property damage in distress-response no matter how grievously the conduct of the Coast Guard may violate the principles of the Good Samaritan doctrine . . . "

As of mid-2003, the First Circuit Court of Appeals was still reviewing the case.

»A Good Samaritan

I N THE PREDAWN darkness of September 5, 1996, eight miles northeast of where the *Northern Voyager* would sink a year later, the 86-foot scalloper *Kathy & Jackie* was making slow, thirty-minute passes over southern Jeffreys Ledge. She and her seven-man crew dragged for scallops toward the east, and then, 2½ miles or so later, she'd haul her dredges up over the side with two large Number 7 Pullmaster winches. She'd make a slow turn, then drop the emptied dredges into the sea and drag them across the bottom back toward the west. She had been fishing there all night.

In the wheelhouse her forty-eight-year-old Croatian-born captain, Branimir "Bronko" Viducic, was listening to the marine radio while watching the sonar and keeping an eye on both of his radars. They were set at different ranges so he could see what was headed toward him from up to 12 miles away as well as what was within a 3-mile radius. A tug and a barge were approaching from the north; he'd been watching them since they'd entered his 12-mile range. He saw smaller targets flying around like gnats across the radar screen. As the tug and barge drew closer to him, he saw what he figured was a fast-moving tuna boat heading toward the tug and barge. He watched the three targets draw close to each other.

And then there were just two.

He heard tug *Houma*'s Mayday call at 5:18. At 5:41 he heard the *Houma* report that *Scotia Boat Too* could hear voices from inside the hull. Viducic knew it would be dark underwater as the trapped fishermen struggled to escape. At about five minutes before six o'clock, he picked up his VHF microphone and called out to anyone on scene. John Frawley aboard the *Blue Heron* answered him.

"Yeah, you wanna shine some lights out there for these guys," Viducic said. "Shine lights in the water so they know where to swim out. [It] might help them out."

Viducic also recommended that Frawley tie some weights to an underwater flashlight and drop it near the boat. Frawley said he'd look for some underwater lights and give it a try.

"It's dark and they only have three to four inches of breathing room and their heads are banging and they can't see the way out," Viducic said five years later. "So you have to give them light. . . . These guys needed to know where the light is."

As Viducic, like several other fishermen, listened to the radio traffic that morning, he considered what he could do to help. He had once salvaged a large fishing boat off the coast of Delaware. He had a salvor's way of thinking, a problem-solving set of wheels turning in his head. He calculated that he was 3 miles southwest of the *Heather Lynne II* and could be alongside in 18 minutes. Fisherman Michael Leary, who had guessed in his testimony that the unidentified scalloper was 4 miles away and would take about 26 minutes to arrive on scene, had been pretty close.

Viducic said he called home to New Bedford and spoke to the owner of the *Kathy & Jackie*, who gave him permission to assist. He talked with his crew, and they weighed the odds of success. If they failed, they'd waste time and lose money to accomplish nothing. They were catching eight or nine hundred pounds of scallops an hour, and at seven dollars a pound, it was something to consider. But then, how much is a man's life worth?

Viducic raised the scallop dredge and traveled toward the accident scene. When he arrived, someone—he later thought it was someone on the tug, but he couldn't be sure—waved him off and told him to go away. They said he'd only make the situation worse. He watched a small green dragger from Gloucester speed over and offer to help, but its offer was also turned down. It resumed its course and headed offshore. Frustrated, Viducic knew he could help.

The *Kathy & Jackie* was a wide, steel boat built in 1973 in Brazoria, Texas. She was equipped with an 850-horsepower Caterpillar diesel engine and could reach about ten knots. Her two big winches were capable of lifting ten tons each. He figured he could lift the bow of the *Heather Lynne II*, where the men were tapping, right out of the water. Unlike the *Houma*'s captain, Viducic didn't worry that the *Heather Lynne II* could sink and take his boat down with her because, he said,

"Once the boat was up in the air, it wouldn't sink, and so it wouldn't take you with it." He also figured he could put a cradle of cables under her to keep her from sinking. This would stabilize her, which was a more immediate priority than getting divers to the scene. Once she was stabilized and the air pocket in which the men were banging was secured, he figured, the men might have been able to wait all day for divers to arrive.

He thought about rolling the boat over. He thought about cutting a six-by-six-foot hole in the hull with the circular saw he had on board. He had torches and welding equipment, air compressors, and air hoses. Of course, he thought, you don't know exactly what you're going to do until you do it, but he had plenty of gear and ingenuity at hand.

At 6:33 he heard the Coast Guard reissue its urgent marine information broadcast, requesting all vessels to assist if possible. A few seconds later, Viducic sent a general broadcast over the marine radio.

"Yeah, break, break, this is the *Kathy & Jackie*," he said. "I'm a trawler here. . . . You guys need me to come haul the boat, call me up. I'm on 16 and 13."

No one answered him. He said he tried to call the Coast Guard on the radio. Still no one answered him.

Four minutes later he heard another fishing boat—the *Robyn Ann* from Newburyport—talking to the *Houma* and passing along word that a scalloper had offered to help.

"Yeah, this is the *Houma*, who's calling?" Captain Al Breen said.

"I don't know," the fisherman said. "He offered to put cables under the boat and lift them out."

"What did he say he'd do?" Breen asked.

"The other fishing boat is a dragger," the fisherman said. "He said he was standing by on 16."

"At this point in time, I'm not sure if that would be good," Breen said. "Right now the best thing to do is just hope that the helicopter gets here."

Viducic lingered a while longer.

"I wanted to grab the bow with hydraulic tackle and raise it up as high as I can so the guys can get air," Viducic said later. "But nobody would let me get close." He paused, trying to assemble his memories into a pattern that made sense. "I think maybe the tug person called his insurance company and his boss, and he did not want to do anything."

As precious minutes passed, he began to lose confidence that the Coast Guard would be successful.

"I'd been listening to the Coast Guard for [over an hour] and they had excuses for everything," Viducic said. "They got caught off guard."

After awhile, Viducic realized he needed to get back to work. He'd already lost almost $5,000 in uncaught scallops. He traveled back to where he'd been fishing, his potential influence on the events of that morning and its aftermath fading with his wake. The *Kathy & Jackie* was not a local boat, and later none of the gathered fishermen could remember her name. Nor was Viducic's offer of help recorded in the Coast Guard's transcript of radio communications for the plaintiffs' attorneys to find. He never testified at the trial and would have no impact on its outcome.

There was no doubt in Viducic's mind that morning that he could have helped rescue those men, but no one would let him. Why? He would never know.

As he dropped his scallop dredge back into the water, a Coast Guard helicopter passed overhead.

»The Helicopter Pilot

AT AIR STATION CAPE COD, on the Massachusetts Military Reservation in Falmouth, Lieutenant Craig Lindsey's thirty-fifth birthday kicked off with a memorable 5:26 A.M. wake-up call. It was Thursday, September 5, 1996. The operations duty officer banged on his door and shouted that the helicopter crew had to respond to a fishing boat that had capsized. Lindsey and his crew—copilot Bill Bellatty, flight mechanic Anthony Edwards, and rescue swimmer Fred Fijn—dressed and ran out of their sleeping quarters. As they jogged across the dark and foggy parking lot toward the hangar, the pilots wondered what lay ahead. Bellatty, who had spent eighteen years in the Coast Guard, wondered how far offshore they'd have to travel, which alternate airports they could land at once they were airborne, and whether the fishermen were wearing survival suits or had made it into a life raft. He considered what questions to ask his Coast Guard colleagues on this SAR case to form a mental picture of the scene. And he wondered what the helicopter crew would be expected to do.

Once inside the hangar, the flight crew ran upstairs. Someone handed them a sheet of paper with notes scribbled on it, including the latitude and longitude coordinates for the accident scene. They checked the Cape Cod weather: winds out of the south at three knots with fog covering the runway. Ground-level visibility was only an eighth- to a quarter-mile—a matter of concern. It would take them about two minutes to rise through the fog, above which was a cloud ceiling starting at 800 feet. They ran downstairs to the white-and-orange Jayhawk helicopter. It flew with a crew of four—a pilot, copilot, flight mechanic, and rescue swimmer—and could seat six people in its approximately 8-by-12-foot cabin. Before launching, they had to consider numerous variables and run through preflight safety checklists printed on 4-by-6-inch laminated cards. It wasn't like getting into a car, turning the key, and going. But they all felt the urgency.

"A boat flipped over gets people going around here," Bellatty said later. "It gets people pretty spooled up."

While they prepared to launch and considered what to do about the fog, they also thought about what they would be able to do on scene. They didn't know what they'd find. They didn't know that the fishing boat was tied up next to a tug, that people were trapped inside and begging for help, or that divers had been called from Beverly.

At 5:58 A.M., 32 minutes after being awakened, the flight mechanic sitting in the back of the helicopter noted on his time sheet that the helicopter was airborne. They had been tasked by Richard Barone, the SAR mission coordinator at Group Boston, to go directly to the scene, so they headed to the given coordinates. It wasn't until they were closer, about fifteen minutes later, that they overheard radio conversations about a need for divers. That's when the thought occurred to them that maybe it would be faster to divert from the scene to pick up the divers in Gloucester.

"I remember getting there and saying, 'Wow, it's tied off,' " Bellatty said. "I remember green—was it green? I remember seeing a big green belly and saying, 'Wow. Let's go get some divers.' "

By noon on September 5, 1996, the Coast Guard was already under fire for its helicopter response that morning. The public wanted to know what had taken the helicopter so long to launch and why it hadn't gone straight to Gloucester to pick up divers. Why did it first show up on scene without any divers on board, when the Coast Guard knew as early as 5:40—almost twenty minutes before the helicopter departed—that divers were vital to the rescue's success?

Almost four years later, plaintiffs' attorney Peter Black opted not to pursue the issue of a delayed launch. The Coast Guard in its defense said that the weather over Air Station Cape Cod had been questionable and that it had followed the usual guideline of launching within thirty minutes, though that's not a mandatory requirement. In ideal conditions, the helicopter could be airborne in about twelve minutes. Black instead focused on the more troubling decision to send the helicopter to the scene without divers on board. He hoped to prove that, had the helicopter gone straight to Gloucester to pick up the divers, crucial minutes could have been saved.

Black looked forward to questioning Craig Lindsey, who had been promoted from lieutenant to lieutenant commander since 1996. As a former naval aviator himself who had flown 150 combat missions in Vietnam, Black respected the helicopter pilot. He hoped Lindsey's testimony would show that he, the senior Coast Guardsman on scene, was not kept informed about pertinent facts as the case unfolded. Lindsey's helicopter was one of the most important rescue assets, but—not unlike divers Billy Muniz, Charlie Rine, Mike Goodridge, and Jay Lesynski—Lindsey was continually kept out of the loop of essential evolving information.

Lindsey, with a crew cut, had a deep voice and spoke so softly that Judge Saris had trouble hearing him. At Black's request he raised his voice while explaining that he had been born and raised in St. Genevieve, a small town outside St. Louis, Missouri, near the Mississippi River. In January 1980, he had joined the Army, attended flight school, and flown Blackhawk helicopters (similar to the Coast Guard's Jayhawks) from Fort Campbell in Kentucky. In 1985 he had attended evening aviation classes to earn a Bachelor of Science degree from Embry-Riddle University. He left the Army in 1986 after being accepted to the Coast Guard's Officer Candidate School. During his subsequent career he had served as a commander of aircraft in Detroit, Michigan, and Kodiak, Alaska, before arriving at Air Station Cape Cod. (He would retire as a lieutenant commander in January 2001, nine months after the trial, after twenty years of much-decorated military service.)

On the morning of September 5, 1996, serving as the aviation safety officer at Air Station Cape Cod, Lindsey was responsible for overseeing the safety of the station's operations in the air and on the ground. He also served both as an operations duty officer—someone who is specifically assigned to conduct search and rescue and training missions—and as the pilot-in-command of the Coast Guard's Jayhawk helicopter. The Jayhawk, a medium-range helicopter, can travel at a maximum speed of 180 knots, cover 700 nautical miles without refueling, and has a maximum endurance, or flight time, of seven hours. It's a big bird, 65 feet long and 17 feet high with a 54-foot rotor diameter.

From his seat on the witness stand, Lindsey watched as Black reached into his briefcase and pulled out a ruler. Black walked across the courtroom floor and handed the ruler to Lindsey. He said, "I'm not going to rap your knuckles. Don't worry."

Black reminded Lindsey that, during a deposition given in preparation for trial, Lindsey could not recall the maximum sustainable air speed for the Jayhawk helicopter in the conditions existing on the morning of September 5, 1996. While his flight plan for this mission had indicated a true air speed—speed over the ground—of 130 knots, or about 150 miles per hour, Lindsey believed he had actually flown faster than that during the mission. During the deposition Black had shown Lindsey a printout from a Coast Guard website citing the maximum speed of the Jayhawk helicopter as 180 knots. Now he asked if that was accurate. Lindsey replied that the true maximum speed would depend on prevailing conditions such as wind speed and direction and aircraft weight. One hundred eighty knots, Lindsey said, was at best a fair estimate.

Black asked Lindsey if he knew how far the scene of the *Heather Lynne II* accident had been from Air Station Cape Cod. Lindsey said he did not have the coordinates, so Black handed him an aviation chart and asked him to measure the distance. The courtroom fell silent as Lindsey maneuvered the ruler, finally agreeing that 62.5 nautical miles was a fair estimate. Black reached into his briefcase again and pulled out a small black device that looked like a handheld calculator. He handed it to Lindsey.

"Would it help you, sir, if I give you an ER-1 computer?" Black asked. "Are you familiar with computers like these?"

"E-6Bs, yes, sir," Lindsey said, smiling.

Black stood next to Lindsey and showed him the computer. He said, "This gives a nice little handy-dandy conversion from nautical to statute [miles], is that correct?"

"Yes, sir."

"OK. Now, I take it your helicopter, because it had sophisticated navigational gear, had a means of putting in the location you were going to and getting an instant readout on your estimated time of arrival?"

"Yes, sir," Lindsey said, agreeing that he had used his navigational instruments that morning to arrive on scene.

"So you knew, as you were flying in your helicopter, to within a matter of seconds, when you would actually arrive on scene?" Black asked.

"Correct, sir."

"And that equipment also told you what your true air speed was?"

"Yes, sir," Lindsey said. "It provides a lot of information. Whether or not you get the chance to look at it is another question."

"Sure," Black said. "You could get ground speed?"

"Sometimes, yes, sir."

"In fact, it uses ground speed to calculate the time of arrival, whether or not you had the ground speed function selected so you could see it?"

"Yes, sir."

"So, you would agree with me, sir, that at 130 knots, it would have taken about 28½ minutes to get to the scene?" Black asked. Lindsey silently looked through him. "Do you want to use the computer?"

"Well, I could compute it," Lindsey said. "I don't remember exactly the time."

Black noted that in preparation for his deposition, Lindsey had determined that it took him 25 minutes to get to the scene at a speed of about 150 knots, which was the normal speed they would try to fly in a search and rescue mission when the location of the vessel in distress was known.

"Sure," Black said, "And just so it's clear and fair, the endurance of your helicopter would be directly related to the speed you were asking from it. The faster you flew, the more fuel you would burn and the less time you could stay aloft in the helicopter, right?"

"Yes, sir."

"But endurance in this case certainly wasn't an issue?"

"At this point, no, sir."

"No," Black repeated. "You knew where the wreckage was, you knew it was about 62½ miles away, and you knew you could fly the helicopter as fast as it would go and you'd still have a ton of time on the scene, correct?"

"Well, you never know, I guess, until you get there," Lindsey said. "You make your decisions as you go along."

"Sure," Black said, looking at a printout of a web page. "Well, this handy-dandy little publication that the Coast Guard put out for the HH-60 Jayhawk says its endurance is 7 hours. I take it that's the maximum endurance?"

"That's way out there, yes, sir."

"Yeah, and I'm sure you'll agree with me that flying at full speed out to this location and then going into max endurance, you'd have 6½ hours?"

Lindsey agreed that flying just 62½ miles at the helicopter's top safe speed would not have seriously impaired its endurance. Black hoped to suggest to Judge Saris that Lindsey could have saved time by flying to the scene faster.

Black paused and switched gears. He asked Lindsey if, as the operations duty officer, he was expected to be familiar with the SAR resources available to the Coast Guard on Cape Cod. Lindsey said that was generally true, but he didn't remember any specific requirement that he be familiar with available dive teams. Black reminded Lindsey that the National SAR Manual and its Coast Guard Addendum both require SAR units to be aware of resources available outside the Coast Guard itself, especially those resources that provide capabilities the Coast Guard doesn't have—like divers.

"So, whether or not you have specific recollection of any particular list of divers being kept at Coast Guard Air Station [Cape Cod]," Black asked, "there's no doubt in your mind there was such a list?"

"I don't remember such a list, sir."

"All right. So, is it your testimony that you believe that there was no such list available to operation personnel at the Coast Guard Air Station Cape Cod?"

"Well, let me explain that there was a large binder with a lot of information in it. I don't specifically remember a list of divers. I do remember, however, a list of hyperbaric chambers, multiple lists of hospitals . . . fire departments, landing pads. You name it, it was in there."

"But you're unsure whether that list included divers?"

"I don't remember the diver list, yes, sir."

"Now, you, sir, took no steps on the day in question to locate divers to go to the scene, correct?"

"No, sir."

"And you did not expect that divers would be needed at the scene until you were virtually on scene, is that correct?"

"Just before arrival to scene, we observed the vessel *Heather Lynne* capsized, tied off to the tug. At that point . . . we learned that [divers] had been requested. Our job, at that point, was to compute how long it would take to get the divers out there and [determine] if we could help, if we could actually speed up the process, which is exactly what we did."

"That's not what I asked, is it, sir?"

"Well," Lindsey said. "Ask the question again."

"You did not expect that divers would be needed at the scene until shortly before you arrived on scene?"

"I don't remember considering that. My job at the time was to focus on getting to the scene, that was my task."

Black asked Lindsey to look at the radio log in which the *Scotia Boat Too* at 5:40 said they could hear tapping on the hull. Lindsey agreed that this was about fifteen minutes before he departed in the helicopter from Air Station Cape Cod. Black asked, "And you weren't informed prior to departing Cape Cod that it was known that people were knocking inside the hull, correct?"

"That's correct, sir."

"And it wasn't reported to you en route to the scene that people who were trapped in the hull [were] knocking?"

"No, sir."

"In fact, you queried the air station and Group Boston several times to get updates on the situation, isn't that true?"

"Yes, sir."

"And, until you were within five minutes of the scene, the information you received remained the same, that the vessel was capsized [with people possibly on board]?"

"Yes, sir."

"You didn't contemplate the need for divers, did you?"

"No, sir."

"And you didn't learn that anyone was contemplating divers until you overheard, as you approached the scene, the talk about getting divers out from Gloucester to the scene, correct?"

"Yes, sir."

"Now, as part of your SAR training, sir, you knew that communication of information up and down the SAR chain was critical to a successful SAR mission, isn't that true?"

"With any mission, yes, sir."

"And no one ever told you why you weren't informed that there were people alive in the hull prior to overhearing it as you approached the scene?"

"I didn't receive any information," Lindsey said, "but [the VHF radio ranges] were not very good that morning."

"Sir, you queried Cape Cod. You queried Group Boston. After the fact, no one ever told you why they didn't bother telling you that there were people trapped in the hull, correct?"

"No, sir."

"You were never told that people were alive on the vessel?"

"No, sir."

"And you were never told divers were being sought to get to the scene?"

"Not until just prior to arriving."

"And you got to the scene around what time, around 6:25 or so?"

"That's approximate, yes, sir."

"All right," Black said. "So roughly an hour, a little less than an hour after you were awoken and given the initial information, you overheard radio discussion about people being trapped on the boat and the need for divers?"

"Yes, sir.

"No one ever told you after the fact, 'Oh, we forgot about you, that's why we didn't bother telling you.' Or, something to that effect, right?"

"Yes. No one ever said, either way, sir."

Black asked Lindsey if, once arriving on scene, they hovered in the air for about 4 minutes.

"A very short 4 minutes," Lindsey said, "yes, sir."

"So, on your own initiative, you and your copilot's, as you approached the scene and learned that people were trapped and alive inside and that divers were needed and that the 47-footer was being contemplated as being used, on your own initiative and that of your copilot," Black said, "you did the calculations that told you you could get a diver out there quicker than they could using the 47-footer, isn't that true?"

"Yes, sir."

Lindsey agreed that it had taken him about 12 minutes to travel from the scene to Coast Guard Station Gloucester, though he couldn't be sure what the distance was. Black suggested it was about 16½ miles. Lindsey looked down at the aviation map on the table in front of him, picked up Black's ruler and measured a distance of 12 miles. He had thought it had been a little farther.

"Now, I take it some . . . of that 12 minutes was when you were landing?" Black asked. "In other words, you're not going full speed and then you lock up the brakes and screech to a halt on the helo pad, correct?"

Lindsey agreed, explaining that he had to slow down at some point to make a transition to a hover. This took a minute or two, and so he spent about 10 minutes actually flying to Gloucester. When he departed, he could accelerate his speed much faster.

"So you were on the deck roughly 8 minutes, loading?" Black asked.

"Six minutes, I believe," Lindsey said, noting he was at Gloucester from 6:36 to 6:42 A.M.

"It's a good thing you're on your toes, sir," Black said, smiling. Lindsey was back on scene over the green belly of the *Heather Lynne II* 5 minutes later. Black calculated that to cover 12 miles in 5 minutes, the helicopter was flying at about 150 knots.

Black then calculated, and Lindsey double-checked, that the distance from Air Station Cape Cod to Coast Guard Station Gloucester was about 57 miles.

"There would have been nothing to prevent you, had you wished, from going directly to Gloucester, correct?"

"Other than our tasking was to proceed to the scene."

"Oh, right. No, I understand. You were told to go to the scene, you were going to the scene. And no one told you to do anything else?"

"Yes, sir."

"If you had been told before you took off to go to Gloucester, you would have had to have flown approximately 57 miles?"

"Yes, sir."

"And at the speed you're going, 150 knots, that would have been about 17 minutes?" Black asked.

"Approximately, yes, sir." In this scenario, the helicopter would have been at Station Gloucester by about 6:15 A.M.

"Would you agree with me, sir, if you had proceeded directly to Gloucester, and the divers were there, and you boarded the divers in the same 6 minutes and then proceeded to the scene—the same speed that you did when you actually had the divers on board—you could have gotten to the scene at least 15 minutes earlier with the divers than you did?"

Steven Campbell objected. Judge Saris overruled.

"That's a fair estimate," Lindsey said. "I would say it would be on the lower side. Maybe not 15 minutes."

"Maybe even faster?" Black asked.

"No, I think we wouldn't have saved that much."

Black began running through a series of time, speed, and distance calculations. Had Lindsey gone straight to Gloucester—a distance shorter by about 5 miles than from Cape Cod to the accident scene—he would have saved the time that he took to fly directly to the accident scene, 4 minutes of hovering, and 12 minutes of traveling back to Gloucester.

"Now, again, you weren't told to go to Gloucester and I'm not suggesting that you were, sir. But if you had been told to go to Gloucester from Cape Cod, you'll agree with me you could have had divers, assuming they were at Gloucester when you got there, to the scene about 20 minutes sooner?" Black asked.

"That's reasonable," Lindsey said. "Yes, sir."

"Now, you knew, from your training, that time was critical in a survival situation?"

"Yes, sir."

"Minutes counted?"

"Yes, sir."

"Seconds count?"

"Sometimes, yes, sir."

"If they're my seconds, they might count. If they're your seconds, I'm sure they would count, isn't that true?"

"Yes, sir."

DEPARTMENT OF JUSTICE attorney Campbell began his cross-examination by asking Lindsey if he knew what time he had launched. Lindsey said he didn't remember. Upon reviewing the SAR incident report folder, Lindsey agreed he had taken off at 5:55 A.M., about 29 minutes after he was directed to launch.

"What was happening during those 29 minutes?" Campbell asked.

"We were awakened in our green rooms. Got dressed, hurried up to the operation center. En route, we could see that the weather was bad. It was fogged in pretty thick, so much that we couldn't see the hangar from the duty room. We got to the operation center, started checking weather, because we knew that would be a factor, both on scene and where we were departing from. At that point, we looked at the reported weather conditions and determined that it was about a quarter-mile visibility. And I don't remember the ceilings, but it's in this document, exactly," Lindsey said. "After takeoff, we realized that [visibility] was less than what they reported. So we actually—we were allowed to reduce our visibility to. . . . A quarter of a mile, that's our minimum takeoff requirements by the regulation, [but] we're allowed to reduce that by half in SAR cases, and this certainly fit within that sleeve, so we were operating at the very minimum that we possibly could have."

Judge Saris asked Lindsey how the weather factored into the launch.

"If it had been a clear day, Your Honor, we would have went right to the helicopter and got in and took off. But, because of the weather, we have to determine what our risk factor is for takeoff and for en route and arrival on scene."

Lindsey added that he didn't know how fast he was going that morning as he flew to the scene.

"In your mind," Campbell said, "were you going as quickly and safely as possible with the aircraft conditions as they existed?"

"Yes, sir, we always do that in SAR cases."

"Your orders were to proceed to the scene, correct?"

"Yes, sir."

"Did you believe that to be a prudent action?"

"Yes, sir."

"And with regard to that—let me ask you a question. The Jayhawk helicopter, has it got the capacity of landing on water?" Campbell asked.

"Only one time, sir," Lindsey said, filling the courtroom with laughter.

"You stole my joke," Campbell said. "OK. So it's not an amphibious helicopter?"

"No."

"If you had known that one or more of the persons in the water, you were originally informed of, were actually trapped inside the *Heather Lynne*, even earlier than you did learn, would you have changed your actions in any way?"

Black objected. Saris overruled.

"No, sir."

"You still would have proceeded to the scene?"

"Yes, sir."

Saris asked him to explain why.

"We're . . . equipped with a rescue swimmer. If one or more people had been in the water in the area and needed to be rescued, we could have effectively gotten that swimmer down immediately if they had been injured or in the water. We're also the best platform for searches if somebody had drifted away from the vessel."

"If at some point you found out the best information was that everyone was trapped inside," Judge Saris asked, "would that affect your decision making?"

"Only if we had access to other assets," Lindsey said. "At that point, I didn't have any information, Your Honor, on what other assets were available. I wouldn't have processed it quite that way, anyway. My tasking was to go to the scene, you know, and try to assist the [fishermen]."

Campbell asked Lindsey if there was any discussion inside the helicopter once they found out there were people trapped alive in the *Heather Lynne II.*

"It was between the copilot and myself and the crew in back," Lindsey said. "I don't remember if the flight rescue swimmer was involved. . . . But we all discussed: 'Well, the thing's rolled over. Why can't they swim out?' We wondered what was underneath, and we didn't know what type of fishing vessel at the time, what type of rigging it had. So we were trying to decipher why they couldn't get out on their own. At that point, we couldn't attempt a rescue, to help them with a rescue swimmer. Rescue swimmers are not allowed to go beneath the surface of the water for rescues. So they're not allowed to enter a wreck or an overturned vessel."

"Do you have any information as to what time the Beverly dive team was available [in Gloucester] for pickup?" Campbell asked.

"All I know is that when we arrived, they were just getting there. They weren't quite ready. Some of their gear was unloaded, but they were still— they were not ready to jump into the helicopter as we got there. I don't remember the exact time."

"So when you went through this whole discussion about 20-minute delay, 15-minute delay, how much delay it was, was it critical in your thinking that you get there by the time the divers were ready to go?"

Black objected. Saris overruled.

"In my—it would not have—the time that we arrived was the time the divers were available. I don't believe that they were there any earlier. We couldn't have taken off [from Station Gloucester] any quicker, I don't think, if we had gotten there 20 minutes earlier."

"How do you feel you and your crew performed during the rescue?" Campbell asked.

Black objected. Saris overruled.

"I can say with all sureness that that was one of the most intense cases I've had and the best use of facilities and resources from start to finish. I had a great crew and my copilot [Bill Bellatty] was invaluable. He was ready and waiting and took care of a lot of things, actually a lot of thinking a little faster than me. It's kind of embarrassing to admit, but he was certainly on the ball."

Campbell asked him what was going on during the 6 minutes the helicopter was on deck at Coast Guard Station Gloucester.

"We had to load gear aboard," Lindsey said. "Again, like I said, some of the divers were still arriving; they weren't all standing right by the helicopter. Some were either in the station or behind one of the vehicles. We had to get them in, strap them in, distribute their gear within the cabin, which is a pretty confined space, and then [do] takeoff checks before we depart."

Lindsey said the trip to the scene from Gloucester was faster than the trip in from the scene because they had a tailwind.

"Were you also pushing the aircraft?" Campbell asked.

"Yes, considerably."

Campbell asked what happened after he picked up four Beverly Fire Department rescue team members and traveled to the scene.

"While en route to the scene, we communicated with the 41-footer and asked them to, again, you know, move a safe distance away from the vessel. We were concerned with the stability of the *Heather Lynne* and our rotor wash, which is quite substantial in 150 knots of wind. We didn't want to upset the situation and make it worse. So we instructed the 41-footer to get it away [from the *Heather Lynne II*], on a heading just 30 to 45 degrees out of the wind line so we could hoist and drop our divers into the 41-footer, so they could, in turn, be a little closer in delivering divers to the scene."

Lindsey said lowering a basket down to a 41-footer is an operation that they trained for several times a week, and that on this day it went very well.

"It was pretty quick," he said, "considering everything that was going on."

Once the divers were aboard the 41-footer, the helicopter crew discussed whether or not their rescue swimmer could assist. They moved about 100 to 250 yards away from the scene and dropped rescue swimmer Fred Fijn into the water, a 20- to 25-foot free fall wearing a snorkel, mask, and fins, and from there he swam over to the scene. After the rescue swimmer was deployed, Lindsey started talking with Group Boston about which hospital to take the fishermen to.

Campbell asked Lindsey if he would have diverted to pick up civilian divers from a vessel that he had not worked with before.

"Only if I was tasked to do so."

"If someone had asked whether you should or shouldn't, what would you have said?"

"I would have taken a look at the distance," Lindsey said. "But, generally, a civilian diver off a civilian platform, they're unfamiliar with our procedure. It would have taken a lot longer, depending on where they were, to get in close to the scene. If they were right next door, we wouldn't have need[ed] to transport. A lot depends on the distance we're talking about and the risk factors associated with the civilian divers."

"Now, when you were in the helicopter during this entire evolution, did you ever tell anyone not to come to the scene or not to send divers to the scene?" Campbell asked.

"No, sir."

Did you ever tell anyone not to tie up to the *Heather Lynne* or not to assist the *Heather Lynne*?"

"No, sir."

BLACK HAD A FEW MORE QUESTIONS. He reminded Lindsey that he had told Campbell about speculation among the flight crew as to why the men didn't swim out from under the *Heather Lynne II*.

"Now, as a trained professional, who was knowledgeable of the National Search and Rescue Manual, you *were* aware, weren't you, sir,"

Black said in a loud, deep voice, "that it should be assumed—quote, 'it should be *assumed*'—and this is Urgency of Response Section 443 paragraph C sub 2: 'It should be assumed that all survivors are incapacitated, capable of surviving only a short time, under great stress, experiencing shock and requiring emergency medical care. Normally able-bodied, logical-thinking persons may be, as survivors, unable to accomplish simple tasks or to assist in their own rescue.' "

Black looked up at Lindsey.

"It's in the manual," Lindsey said.

"Now, you knew that?"

"Yes, sir, it's in the manual."

"And when you said you were speculating about why people didn't swim out of the boat, you weren't suggesting to this Court that that should have been attempted by the survivors?"

Campbell objected. Saris overruled. Lindsey asked Black to restate the question.

"You're not suggesting . . . that your speculation as to why people didn't swim out of the boat was in any way a suggestion that they should have tried, is it?"

"The discussion was merely curiosity as to why they haven't come out yet, why they would not swim out."

"Now, the fact of the matter is, sir, you didn't have all the pertinent information as you went out to the scene and you didn't even get the pertinent information that people were trapped inside the vessel and divers were needed until you were virtually on scene, isn't that true?"

"About two to five minutes before we got there," Lindsey said, "is when we received information about the divers."

"So all this speculation about what you might have done if you had been provided that information is just that, isn't it? Because, on the scene, when your decisions might have made a difference with life and death, they certainly could have been different, right?"

"Would you put that in the form of a question?" Lindsey asked.

"I think that was in the form of a question, sir, and there was no objection. Can you answer it?"

"Well, can you restate that, please?"

"Sir, your counsel asked you to speculate about what you would have done had you been told that people were trapped inside the vessel, begging for help, that divers were urgently needed. And your testimony was 'I wouldn't have done anything different.' "

Campbell objected. Saris sustained.

"Wasn't it your testimony, sir . . . that if you had been aware that people were trapped in the vessel and divers were urgently needed, at the time you took off from Cape Cod, you wouldn't have done anything different?"

"That isn't what was said," Lindsey said.

"Well, sir, would you have done something differently if you had known that before you took off from Cape Cod?"

"If I was tasked to go to Station Gloucester to pick up divers," Lindsey said, "I would have gone to Station Gloucester to pick up divers."

»Morning Dew
December 29, 1997

ICHAEL CORNETT could not have known on Christmas Day 1997 that the voyage he would begin in two days would make national headlines and subject the Coast Guard to intense public scrutiny. Cornett, with his two sons and a nephew, planned to depart Little River, South Carolina, aboard his recently purchased 24-foot 1978 Cal sloop *Morning Dew*. He intended to follow the Intracoastal Waterway (ICW) all the way to Orange Park, Florida, during the boys' winter break from school.

The young sailors called themselves "the three amigos." The eldest, sixteen-year-old Michael Paul, had been born while his parents, having quit their teaching jobs, were living on a sailboat and cruising the waters of Florida and the Bahamas. He and his younger brother, thirteen-year-old Daniel, had spent most of their lives learning about sailing, boats, and the sea. Their mother, Libby, home-schooled her boys, and in preparation for this weeklong, 300-mile trip had taught them about boating safety and navigation. Their cousin, fourteen-year-old Bobby Lee Hurd Jr., had never been sailing, so he didn't want to miss this adventure. The teenage boys had called each other several times in recent weeks to make plans about what to take, particularly which CDs to pack.

The day after Christmas, Libby Cornett kissed her family good-bye in Hiltons, Virginia, and traveled to Florida to await their arrival. Later that day, Michael Cornett and the three amigos arrived at the boat in Little River and stowed life jackets and other items—bags of Christmas candy, CDs, and new foul-weather gear—aboard the *Morning Dew*. By ten o'clock that evening the boys were asleep in sleeping bags in the forward V-berth. Early on the morning of Saturday, December 27, they shopped at a marine supply store for signal flares and about $150 worth of charts, on which Cornett penciled his intended route along the ICW to Florida. They departed around lunchtime.

Good weather was predicted for Saturday, although a storm was on the horizon for late the next day. A bridge tender saw the *Morning Dew* pass through the Little River swing bridge at North Myrtle Beach and enter the ICW at 1:10 P.M. The landlocked waterway carried them south and into the Waccamaw River. Georgetown's Winyah Bay, Cornett's first opportunity to head out to sea, was still 27 miles away.

At 8:30 P.M., *Morning Dew* stopped at a marina and Cornett called family members in Jacksonville, Florida. He was frustrated that they'd gotten a late start and that he hadn't made as much progress as planned. He didn't mention any problems with the boat. After he hung up, the sailors traveled another 12 miles south and anchored for the night by the Boat Shed Marina, which had closed for the season. At about noon on Sunday, December 28, TowBoatU.S. captain Ronnie Campbell spotted the moored *Morning Dew* while en route to a salvage job. Headed home later that afternoon, Campbell saw the *Morning Dew* cruise past him, bound for sea. The boys, all dressed in windbreakers and at least one wearing shorts, stood on the bow of the boat. They were playing with lines and getting a big kick out of *Morning Dew* splashing through Campbell's boat wake. Cornett, wearing foul-weather gear, stood at the helm. The sails were down and the boat was traveling on engine power, as planned.

Campbell suspected that Cornett had missed a turn and believed he was still in the ICW when instead he was headed out to sea through Winyah Bay, from where Nelson Beideman's fishing vessel *Terri Lei* had departed on her fateful trip four years earlier. He tried to alert Cornett via the marine radio but was unsuccessful. He expected that once Cornett found himself closer to the open sea, still 8 miles and sixteen channel markers away, he, like most boaters, would realize the error and turn around. It was a common mistake.

But Cornett did not turn around.

The weather worsened as afternoon turned to evening. The air temperature felt colder than the recorded 50°F. The wind kicked up to about 25 knots, and the seas hit four, five, then seven feet. It began raining and turned squally. Maybe Cornett planned to put into Charleston Harbor, a long 43 miles away, and proceed to Florida via the ICW. As night fell, the boys probably stripped off layers of clothing and crawled into their sleeping bags below. Alone in the wet, cold cockpit of *Morning Dew*, Cornett pressed on down the coast.

AT ELEVEN O'CLOCK the next morning, a couple walking the outer beach of South Carolina's Sullivan's Island at the entrance to Charleston Harbor found the dead, partially clad teenage bodies of Daniel Cornett and Bobby Lee Hurd in the surf. A National Park Service officer arrived, found no pulse and called 911. One boy wore boxer shorts; the other wore a pair of jeans. Stenciled letters on a nearby horseshoe buoy read *Morning Dew*.

The local fire chief asked the police to request that the Coast Guard search for the *Morning Dew*. At about 11:30 A.M. a pilot boat accompanying the outbound car carrier *Pearl Ace* spotted a sunken sailboat inside the north jetty, which extends three miles seaward from Sullivan's Island to protect the dredged Charleston Harbor approach channel. At 12:56 P.M., one mile northeast of the sunken sailboat, a Coast Guard helicopter crew spotted the floating teenage body of Michael Paul Cornett, dressed in boxer shorts, a pullover, and a life jacket. His father's body would wash ashore weeks later, dressed in a nylon jacket, a windbreaker, two T-shirts, a sport shirt, a pair of nylon foul-weather pants, blue jeans, dress socks, and boat shoes.

A bereaved Libby Cornett begged to know if her family had cried out for help. The Coast Guard told her it was not aware of any distress calls from the *Morning Dew*. For months she was led to believe that her family had died at sea amid tragic circumstances that made rescue impossible. Then came a visit from the Coast Guard.

At five o'clock on Tuesday evening, March 17, 1998, Commander Manson Brown of Coast Guard Group Charleston met with Libby Cornett and Bobby Lee Hurd's parents. Brown had initiated the meeting by telling the families he had evidence that might be connected to the accident. Libby Cornett asked him to bring the evidence along. Inside the Hurds' living room, he first expressed his condolences before reporting that the Coast Guard had discovered an audio recording of a three-second transmission from an unidentified source. He pulled a small tape recorder out of his pocket and pressed play. An agitated boy's voice cried out, "Mayday! U.S. Coast Guard! Come in!" Brown played the recording twice, but once was all Libby Cornett needed to recognize the distressed voice of her younger son, Daniel.

"My God, they didn't have to die," she wept. "They could have been saved."

Desperate to know what had happened to her family, she had searched for months and met dead ends. Now she had evidence that her son—if not her whole family—had cried out to the Coast Guard for help. She believed that her boys, who probably could see the lights of the city of Charleston, expected they would be rescued. At the very least, she knew there was more to the story of what had happened to her family in the dark, stormy December waters off Charleston. She had a gut feeling that the facts weren't adding up.

She was right.

AFTER MIDNIGHT on December 29, 1997, Petty Officer Eric J. Shelley was the lone watch-stander in the communications center at Coast Guard Group Charleston, located a few miles inside the entrance to Charleston Harbor. At twenty-three years old, he had been qualified to stand this watch for four months. He had enlisted in the Coast Guard in April 1996 and reported to Group Charleston in July 1997, where he worked as an apprentice under a qualified watch-stander. He completed a Group and Stations Specialist Qualifications Guide in about three to four weeks and passed a thirty-minute review by a qualifications board. By late August 1997, he was qualified to stand watch alone.

In the first hours of December 30, his commanding officer was asleep in a room nearby. The past summer, Coast Guard Group Charleston had undergone a 75 percent personnel turnover; this caused many ripple effects, including a policy change that allowed the officer of the day (OD) to sleep at night. Before the summer of 1997, the OD would stay awake with the watch-stander through the night. Although Shelley was alone, he knew that he could wake up the OD if he needed a hand.

At 2:17 A.M. Shelley was pouring himself a cup of coffee seventeen feet from a console of numerous marine radios when, in the background, he thought he might have heard someone say, amidst static,

"Coast Guard, come in." He walked over and attempted to answer the call, saying, "Vessel calling U.S. Coast Guard, this is Group Charleston, over." He heard no reply. Four minutes later, he heard a burst of static with the words "day" and "guard." Shelley tried to reply twice but did not receive an answer. Shelley figured whoever had called probably didn't need his help any longer. Either that or it was a hoax.

HOAX DISTRESS CALLS had plagued the Coast Guard for years, but the agency had little legal recourse until 1990, following the loss of a father and son on board the fishing vessel *Sol E Mar*. The 70-footer was under the command of forty-four-year-old William Hokanson, who was accompanied by his nineteen-year-old son Billy and Billy's new Rottweiler puppy, Max, on a fishing trip about ten miles south of Martha's Vineyard in March of that year. When she was three days overdue, the family alerted the Coast Guard; it launched a 27,000-square-mile search that turned up nothing. On a tip from a local mariner who thought he might have heard a distress call from the vessel, the Coast Guard reviewed their tapes. Sure enough, they heard the younger Hokanson cry out.

"This is the fishing vessel *Sol E Mar*," Billy Hokanson, his voice rising in pitch, shouted over the marine radio. "We are sinking! We need help now!"

Coast Guard Station Brandt Point on Nantucket had received the call and found the message garbled and hard to understand. It had tried to call the vessel back but heard no response. Family and friends were outraged when they learned of Hokanson's plea. They accused the Coast Guard of ignoring the distress call and not launching a search until the boat was reported overdue a few days later.

How could they have missed it?

The Coast Guard said the name of the boat was unclear in the radio transmission, which also did not give a location. Nor, at the time, had the vessel been reported missing. Upon listening to the tapes, the Coast Guard presumed *Sol E Mar* had faced a catastrophic situation and sunk. The Coast Guard said it was being unfairly criticized for missing the weak and barely four-second-long distress call. Repeated attempts to reach the vessel had gone unanswered.

Massachusetts Congressman Gerry Studds, a former Coast Guards-man and chair of the House Merchant Marine and Fisheries Committee, believed there must be more to the story. Congressional investigators soon discovered that less than a minute after Billy Hokanson's panicked call, a second call had come into the Coast Guard Station: "SOS. I'm sinking!" came the voice.

And then there was a laugh.

Based on this second call, the Coast Guard said it had assumed Hokanson's call and the second, laughter-filled SOS call were from the same source and therefore were probably both hoaxes. That's why, a Coast Guard officer said, they hadn't launched a search. No one had bothered to play back the call to confirm it was a hoax. Coast Guard stations on Menemsha and Nantucket asked superiors at Group Woods Hole if they had heard the distress call. Group Woods Hole concurred that it was probably a hoax since the calls were received within minutes of each other.

On April 5, 1990, the Coast Guard issued a new policy for dealing with potential hoax callers. It required Coast Guard personnel to investigate and respond to all emergency calls unless a superior officer called off the search. The policy insisted that no call would be declared a hoax unless a perpetrator was found. Congressman Studds, meanwhile, introduced legislation increasing the fines and penalties for hoax calls. He would tell reporters in July 1990 that outdated Coast Guard radio equipment, overworked young watch-standers, understaffed radio rooms, and public abuse of VHF channel 16 had all led to the death of the father and son.

The Studds Act, passed in November 1990, established a maximum sentence of six years in prison and a $250,000 fine for people found guilty of issuing false distress calls. Convicted perpetrators would also have to reimburse the Coast Guard for the cost of the search. Yet the problem did not go away. During the year 2000, the Coast Guard received 6,838 hoax calls, which cost taxpayers an estimated $18 million and risked the lives of Coast Guard men and women, who must treat every call as a legitimate distress case. The Coast Guard estimated in 2001 that it cost taxpayers $5,000 an hour for a helicopter response and about $1,500 an hour for a 41-footer. One of the Coast Guard's challenges in prosecuting these cases is that 50 percent of hoax callers are kids, and in cases where juveniles break federal laws, the cases are usually sent back to the states, which do not have a comparable law with a stiff penalty; offenders are usually required to perform community service. The Coast Guard has encouraged states to consider new laws to crack down on pranksters.

ON THIS RAINY late December morning in 1997 at Group Charleston, Petty Officer Eric Shelley figured that a kid, bored during school vacation, might be playing with the radio. The excited voice, the dead-of-night hour, and the wretched weather did not set off any alarms in his appraisal of the call. He did not believe the call warranted replaying the tape, which he knew to be a cumbersome task on the station's aged equipment. It was like trying to find a scene on a videotape. He dismissed the call from his thoughts. He neither noted it in the log nor alerted his sleeping officer of the day.

Four hours later, at 6:28 A.M., Shelley answered a telephone call from the dispatcher for the Charleston Branch Pilots' Association. The dispatcher told Shelley that they had put a pilot on board the car carrier *Pearl Ace* to guide it into Charleston and that a boatswain on deck had called the bridge to say he had heard someone yelling for help near buoy 22, well inside the north jetty and a half mile off the Sullivan's Island beach. The pilot asked the pilot boat, which had just returned to the dock from dropping him off, to go back out and look around. Then he asked his dispatcher to call the Coast Guard, who he expected would go out to help.

"The pilot wanted me to call you to let you know what was going on," dispatcher John Henning told Shelley. "Like I said, we've got the pilot boat out there looking for somebody now."

"They weren't able to talk to them any?"

"Well, no, it was somebody in the water."

"Oh, it was somebody in the water," Shelley said.

"Yeah, that's what they think."

"Oh, I see."

The dispatcher said he'd call back and let Shelley know if his pilot boat found anything. Shelley thought that was a good idea. At 6:30 A.M., with his watch duty over, he headed out the door but paused to tell his officer of the day, thirty-seven-year-old Petty Officer Michael J. Sass, about the call. Sass, who had been in the Coast Guard seventeen years, decided not to launch a Coast Guard boat to assist the pilot boat, nor did he tell any of his commanding officers of that decision. Sass expected that if there were something to find, the pilot boat would find it.

Meanwhile, apprentice pilot John Stuhr had gone back out alone to search in the miserable early morning weather. It was still dark, and it was raining. The northeast winds blew at about thirty knots and the seas topped five feet. He assumed someone might be drowning, so he went straight to buoy 22, finding nothing. He drove his boat forward about fifty feet, stopped, and walked outside on deck in the rain to listen. Then he walked back to the wheelhouse and moved ahead another fifty feet, then walked back on deck. He kept this up for at least a half hour, expecting—and hoping—that the Coast Guard would launch its own search with trained personnel.

At 6:46 A.M., Stuhr called the pilot to report that he hadn't found anyone in trouble. The pilot asked him to look a little more, or at least until first light. Still he found nothing. Two minutes later, the pilot's dispatcher called the Coast Guard back to say that the pilot boat hadn't found anything and was returning to the dock. Sass looked at the chart of the harbor and looked at buoy 22. He didn't launch a search because, again, he assumed if there had been something to find, the pilot boat would have found it.

About four hours later—and nine hours after the distress call—the police reported that two bodies had washed up on the beach. Later that afternoon, Sass called Shelley at home, told him about the three drowned boys and sunken sailboat, and asked for more details of his conversation with the pilot's dispatcher. About ten minutes later, Shelley called Sass back.

"I remember that last night—I guess it was a couple of hours before that happened," Shelley said, "I remember hearing a call, I think, calling 'Coast Guard,' and I called out and called out and called out and never got another answer. . . . It just said, 'Coast Guard, Coast Guard.' I think it was about an hour and a half or about two hours before that pilot office called . . . it should be on the recordings. [You] guys want to check it out or not?"

According to the National Transportation Safety Board, when the tape was played for Coast Guard Group Charleston Commander Manson Brown, he immediately suspended Shelley's qualifications and ordered an administrative investigation into the matter. Shelley requalified to stand watch in about two weeks, but a notation was placed in his personnel file documenting his failure to notify his operations duty officer when he could not confirm the nature of the 2:17 A.M. call.

Though this early morning distress call and the subsequent call from the pilot dispatcher shook up Coast Guard Group Charleston internally, no one outside the Coast Guard—neither the Cornett and Hurd families nor the North Carolina Department of Natural Resources officers who were conducting their own investigation into the boys' deaths—was informed of the calls. The DNR officers learned about the pilot's phone call only by reading about it in a local newspaper. As for the 2:17 A.M. distress call, the Coast Guard would later say it was a part of their ongoing investigation and therefore was not releasable, in response to which the NTSB determined that the Coast Guard had no such policy of withholding information. News of this distress call finally surfaced following a Freedom of Information Act request filed by *Boating News* seeking all pertinent facts from the Coast Guard related to the loss of the *Morning Dew*. While the Coast Guard suspected the 2:17 A.M. call might have been from one of the boys, it could not be sure. It also didn't want news of the tape reaching the families via the press. That's why Commander Brown paid the families a visit on March 17—he needed to know if they recognized the voice. A tearful Libby Cornett gave him his answer.

"So many wrong things happened," Cornett told television show *20/20* reporter Cynthia McFadden in March 1999. "There was more than one opportunity for them to have been saved. They just missed them all."

IN EARLY 1999, Libby Cornett and Bobby Hurd's mother, Deirdre Lynn Hurd, sued the government for $35 million. They alleged that the Coast Guard's negligence led to the deaths of the three boys and Michael Cornett. As the lawsuit preparations began, the NTSB launched its own investigation. In its report issued in October 1999, the NTSB determined that the cause of the sinking of the *Morning Dew* was Cornett's failure to "adequately assess, prepare for, and respond to the known risks of the journey into the open ocean that culminated in the vessel's [collision] with the jetty at the entrance to Charleston Harbor. Contributing to the loss of life in this accident was the substandard performance of U.S. Coast Guard

Group Charleston in initiating a search and rescue response to the accident." The NTSB report also concluded that, "Under the Coast Guard's Search and Rescue Communications System, the evaluation [of distress calls] is performed by individuals making decisions and judgments more or less autonomously. . . . Unfortunately, as shown by the accident involving the *Morning Dew* and several other accidents the Safety Board has investigated, the Coast Guard does not always exercise effective oversight of its operations and communications experts."

In August 2000, on the day Judge Saris would release her ruling in the *Heather Lynne II* trial, a two-day trial concerning the loss of the *Morning Dew* began in Charleston. Lawyers representing the families argued that the Coast Guard did not do enough to rescue the *Morning Dew* crew. They might have been saved, Attorney Gedney Howe argued, if the Coast Guard had not acted like "stumbling, bumbling fools." Testimony indicated that the *Morning Dew* hit the Charleston Harbor jetty at about 2:17 A.M. Seas pinned her there at dead low water until the tide rose and washed her up and over the jetty—which was partially submerged at high water—leaving a trail of debris—a bell, a stove, rubber carpeting, and pieces of the fiberglass hull. *Morning Dew* eventually sank sometime between 5:30 and 7:30 A.M. The NTSB figured the boys probably stayed with the boat until it sank out from under them. Then they must have tried to swim more than a mile to the Sullivan's Island shore in 55°F water. The young boys might have been alive until 8 A.M. or later.

The Justice Department, on behalf of the Coast Guard, denied all blame and argued that because the Coast Guard never attempted to rescue the crew, it could not be found liable for a failed or even negligent rescue. The case was not about what the Coast Guard should have done, Department of Justice attorneys argued, but what it did do.

"This case unfortunately is nothing more than an explicit reminder to the would-be seafarer," Department of Justice Attorney Debra Kossow was quoted in the press as saying, "that he should not venture blindly into unfamiliar waters armed with the simple faith that the Coast Guard will extricate him from his self-made dilemmas, whenever and wherever they occur."

The government called no witnesses.

In March 2001, South Carolina District Court Judge David C. Norton issued a $19 million ruling in favor of Libby Cornett and the Hurd family. He determined that the U.S. Coast Guard *did* engage in a search and rescue mission by relying on the harbor pilots to search the Charleston Harbor entrance. Judge Norton disagreed with Department of Justice attorneys, who argued that since the Coast Guard is not required by law to perform search and rescue operations, it could not be held liable for a rescue effort it claims not to have commenced. Norton cited testimony from one search and rescue expert who said the Coast Guard should not have allowed the search to terminate before sunrise. "The search and rescue could not terminate," Norton concluded, "if it never began."

"While [Petty Officer] Sass had no affirmative legal duty to do so, Sass did, in fact, decide to render aid and assistance," Judge Norton ruled. "Once Sass made the decision to render aid, his actions were not discretionary because Coast Guard policy specifically prescribes a course of action for him to follow." Just as in *U.S. v. Sandra & Dennis* (regarding the loss of the *Barbara and Gail*), Norton noted that once the Coast Guard has agreed to rescue a person in distress, it must do so with due care. While he acknowledged other courts' warnings not to serve as "armchair admiral and second-guess the decisions of rescuers," Judge Norton said his evaluation of this case was on different terms.

"This court's decision is not premised on hindsight," Norton wrote, "rather it's based on the circumstances facing the Coast Guard at 6:27 A.M. on December 29, 1997. The Charleston Group's communications with the Pilots' Association initiated a search and rescue mission that the Coast Guard clearly failed to execute properly. The Pilots' Association reasonably expected the Coast Guard to send a boat and helicopter to look for the persons whose screams had engendered the pilot boat's search near and around buoy 22 in the Charleston Harbor. As a result of the Coast Guard's reckless suspension of the search for the passengers of the S/V *Morning Dew*, these children suffered horrific deaths in the cold waters of the Atlantic Ocean."

Judge Norton believed the Coast Guard had recklessly breached the standard of care owed to the imperiled sailors by compelling the pilots to stop searching because they believed the Coast Guard had the situation under control.

"This tragedy was avoidable," Norton concluded. "It was not an angry sea or cruel weather that impeded the Coast Guard's ability to rescue the *Morning Dew*'s passengers. It was human error, the impetuous termination of a search and rescue mission."

In its May 2001 appeal of the *Morning Dew* verdict, the government argued that if Judge Norton's ruling were upheld, the Coast Guard would be forced to immediately "respond to all reports of distress, or, perhaps before sufficient information has been gathered, state that it is NOT launching assets. Otherwise, the Coast Guard may be subject to liability every time it learns that some other persons or entity has conducted any sort of search activity. Instead . . . the Coast Guard has and must retain discretion to decide when and how to respond to reported distress situations."

Despite this argument, the U.S. Court of Appeals for the Fourth Circuit in April 2002 affirmed Judge Norton's decision and awarded the families $21 million.

WHEN NEWS SPREAD in the spring of 1999 of the NTSB's investigation into the *Morning Dew* tragedy, the commandant of the Coast Guard, Admiral James Loy, seized the opportunity to turn a black eye into a battle scar by spreading word of his agency's troubles. In a message that went against much of what had been churned out by the Coast Guard's public relations machine over the previous several decades, Loy announced that his agency had more than a few internal and performance shortfalls. It was struggling with an inadequate budget, he said, as well as poor communications and distress response management system, novice watch-standers and boat crews, and what he called "unreasonable expectations" from the American boating public.

Loy called the loss of the *Morning Dew* "a horrible accident, and one made more horrible by the possibility that the Coast Guard missed the opportunity to rescue one or more sailors." He noted the agency's high public praise over the years for numerous successful rescues, such as its response during what became known as the Perfect Storm in 1991 and during the January 1998 sinking of the Alaskan fishing boat *La Conte*. A story by Associated Press writer Todd LeWan ran for several days in the *Washington Post* and in other national papers about the amazing helicopter rescue of three of *La Conte*'s crew in hurricane-force winds and eighty-foot seas. Then Loy issued the first of several warnings to mariners that would follow during the remainder of his four-year tenure.

"We must carefully guard against the possibility that video footage of our dramatic rescues may lull some boaters into a false sense of security," Loy said, "[and] may give rise to a misplaced confidence that the Coast Guard can bail them out of whatever peril comes their way. We can't guarantee that we'll be there."

The Coast Guard's motto of *semper paratus*, "always ready," was under internal scrutiny by Loy and others who feared the nation's oldest maritime service, even older than the Navy, was no longer all that ready to rescue a seafarer in peril, despite its continual promises to the contrary. Not all Coast Guardsmen shared Sebastian Junger's confidence when he asserted in his book *The Perfect Storm* that, "Any weekend boater knows the Coast Guard will pluck him out of whatever idiocy he gets himself into."

FOR TWO CENTURIES, the Coast Guard had saluted smartly and said little whenever Congress heaped another maritime task on it without raising its budget accordingly. In 1790 Congress authorized then President George Washington to have ten revenue cutters built to prevent smuggling. The first cutter was a two-masted, 60-foot schooner named *Massachusetts*, built in Newburyport and launched in 1791. Until the Revenue Cutter Service was formally established in the 1890s, cutter crews were simply customs officers, and were at first charged only with protecting revenues by enforcing tariffs. More tasks soon accrued, however. In 1797, the cutter crews were charged with protecting the coastline and defending commerce. Two years later, the cutters enforced coastal blockades to quarantine ships that were believed to be carrying contagious diseases like cholera and yellow fever. Then came enforcement of slave trading laws, which was followed in 1832 by the first recognized obligation to patrol and assist vessels in distress. This humanitarian role soon expanded into patrols of Alaskan and Arctic waters, and the importance of this duty over the years eclipsed in the public's eye the service's obligations to high-seas law enforcement.

Meanwhile, along the New England coast as early as 1786, small organizations such as the Massachusetts Humane Society, often funded by insurance underwriters, set up beach stations with lifesaving boats manned by volunteer crews of local men who performed shore-based rescues. This became the U.S. Life-Saving Service in 1878, and Congress appropriated $200,000 to build 189 lifesaving stations along the nation's coastline. In 1915, Congress merged the Revenue Cutter Service with the U.S. Life-Saving Service, giving birth to the U.S. Coast Guard. It would serve under the Department of the Treasury in peacetime and under the Navy in time of war.

In the following years, Congress heaped more and more missions on the Coast Guard. The service chased rumrunners during Prohibition and assisted in all major wars and conflicts. On the occasion of its 210th anniversary on August 4, 2000, the Coast Guard described itself as a multimission military maritime service that, despite being one of the nation's five armed services, fell under the Department of Transportation, where it was moved on April 1, 1967, and thereafter competed for funding with Amtrak and the Federal Aviation Administration. Its Congressional mandate was to protect the public, the environment, and U.S. economic and security interests in the nation's ports and waterways, which included 95,000 miles of coastline, as well as in U.S. territorial seas and overseas. In 1999 alone, according to the Coast Guard, its personnel saved 3,800 lives, conducted 141,000 courtesy marine inspections on pleasure boats, taught boating safety to 211,000 boaters, and inspected 50,000 merchant vessels. It stopped 111,689 pounds of cocaine, 28,873 pounds of marijuana, 32,634 pounds of hashish, and 4,333 illegal immigrants from entering the United States. Further, the Coast Guard boarded 14,000 fishing vessels that year to check for compliance with safety and environmental laws, inspected 900 offshore drilling units, responded to 12,500 reports of hazardous spills, insured safe passage of 1 million merchant ships through the nation's ports, and managed 50,000 aids to navigation. It accomplished these national and international missions with about 34,000 personnel, a force smaller than the New York City Police Department.

In the early 1990s, the Coast Guard asserted, "No other government investment can match the reward and unique value delivered by us." The agency promptly stepped up to the plate in 1993 when the Clinton Administration called for government-wide streamlining. By 1996, the agency had shrunk by 12 percent, cutting 4,000 people to save $400 million annually, making it smaller than it had been since 1963. Despite the trimming, the Coast Guard insisted its search and rescue mission would not be compromised if Congress allowed it to save another $6 million by closing 23 and downgrading 17 of its 185 small-boat search and rescue stations, including Station Merrimack River. Although search and rescue remains the agency's most visible mission, in 1996 SAR comprised only about 14 percent of the Coast Guard's total operating budget. Law-enforcement missions took up 37 percent, and the rest was allocated to maintaining aids to navigation, marine safety, environmental protection, ice operations, and defense readiness. The 1996 budget for SAR was $346 million; for fiscal year 1998, the Coast Guard would request $354 million for drug interdiction alone as part of its total law-enforcement budget.

In the spring of 1996 Vice Admiral Arthur Henn, chair of the Coast Guard Senior Advisory Group, noted that downsizing had led to stiff competition among Coast Guard personnel and that a long career in the Coast Guard was no longer guaranteed. One downside of the competition was the tendency for people to avoid potentially rewarding but risky career moves.

"Some people are saying, 'Why should I stick my neck out and be innovative when I might fail and be passed over?' Some, particularly junior officers, are backing away from potentially high-reward positions," Henn said. "We want to encourage people to be innovators and take calculated risks. This doesn't mean that we should condone negligence or shortcut standing operational procedures, but innovation and creativity are vital. We must reward calculated risk taking, and we must accept some failures. These failures should not be career-ending but instead should be experience-building."

The Coast Guard's failure to rescue the teenage boys aboard the *Morning Dew* was a wake-up call for the agency. It realized that in trying to trim fat it might have cut muscle. In 1999, Admiral Loy used the story of the *Morning Dew* to draw a line in the sand against further streamlining. He noted that the Coast Guard's search and rescue system needed to be rebuilt and that recreational boaters during the summer of 1999 had good reason to wonder if the Coast Guard would still be there for them. Loy said the *Morning Dew* tragedy forced the Coast Guard to realize that 1990s streamlining had cut a thousand people too many.

In his 2000 State of the Coast Guard Address, Loy announced that he had too many people in positions for which they were not qualified, and deferred maintenance had taken its toll and led to parts shortages and more accidents. The following year, in his 2001 State of the Coast Guard Address, he said, "We may have to recognize a gap between the amount of

Coast Guard we think America needs and the amount of Coast Guard that the taxpayers have actually paid for. If such a gap becomes apparent, I will stand firm in refusing to bridge it by overworking either Coast Guard people or their equipment."

Meanwhile, Inspector General Kenneth Mead of the Department of Transportation supported many of Loy's assertions in a written audit of small-boat rescue stations released three days after September 11, 2001. Mead examined the Coast Guard's 188 small-boat search and rescue stations, staffed by 4,049 personnel and 554 rescue boats. He noted that more than 90 percent of all offshore SAR missions occur within 10 miles of the coast and that the SAR mission in fiscal year 2001 took up 12.3 percent of the total operating budget, down from 15.4 percent ten years earlier. Meanwhile, the number of registered recreational boats had more than doubled from 5.9 million in 1972 to 12.1 million in 1996. During 1998, 78 million Americans went boating; by 2020, the number is expected to hit 129 million.

Mead found that SAR station readiness had continued to deteriorate. Since 1989, Coast Guard studies had identified serious staffing, training, and equipment problems in the SAR program, but the Coast Guard had yet to implement many of the studies' solutions. Specific readiness problems he found included staff shortages that required crew at 90 percent of the SAR stations to work an average of 84 hours each week. Eighty-four percent of the rescue boat fleet inspected by the Coast Guard in 2000 was found not ready for sea, though many of the identified problems were minor ones, corrected within about two days.

Mead noted that since fiscal year 1998, Coast Guard rescue boat accidents had increased by 225 percent. Coast Guard analysis showed that 56 percent of the 130 accidents in 2000 were caused by poor judgment, poor navigation, or operator error. The Coast Guard relied on experienced personnel to conduct on-the-job-training, but since January 1996 the senior level personnel at SAR stations had decreased by 21 percent, while inexperienced crew rose by 194 percent. A high turnover and transfer rate further eroded its experience base. This created a dangerous situation, Mead said, because many stations deal with unique weather, sea, and geographic conditions.

"Conducting SAR missions in these areas requires a high level of expertise and local knowledge that can take boat crews a year or more to acquire," he wrote. "Because the Coast Guard relies on on-the-job training to pass on basic skills, local knowledge, and SAR expertise to its junior personnel, a high turnover rate among the more experienced station personnel can seriously disrupt the continuity and quality of SAR training."

Mead was particularly alarmed to learn that there was no formal training for those recruits who wished to be boatswain's mates, the ratings who interact most frequently with the public at small-boat search and rescue stations. Boot camp graduates, who fill 70 percent of the positions at SAR stations, received little prior training in seamanship and water survival and no training in small-boat handling, SAR techniques, or piloting and navigation. These boot camp graduates instead qualified as boatswain's mates after eight to eighteen months of on-the-job training.

Mead concluded in his September 2001 report that "the SAR small-boat stations' problems with staffing, training, and equipment have been identified in Congressional testimony and Coast Guard studies for at least two decades. The Coast Guard has not taken adequate action to correct the problems but has instead conducted additional studies, which reached similar conclusions."

This was the state of the Coast Guard when it found itself enmeshed in the *Morning Dew* tragedy, the sinking of the *Northern Voyager*, and the attempted rescue of the trapped crew of the *Heather Lynne II*. It was a time when the average experience of a small-boat search and rescue crew—the ones charged with the authority to make life-or-death on-scene decisions affecting mariners in peril—was less than one year. It was a time when the Coast Guard knew that many of its personnel were unqualified to fill the billets to which they had been assigned. It was a time when public faith in the Coast Guard surpassed the Coast Guard's own faith in itself.

"The American public *knows* the Coast Guard will be there to save him if he can just hang on," Admiral Loy said in December 1999. "Unfortunately, his knowing doesn't make it so."

None of the people gathered around the capsized *Heather Lynne II* in the growing dawn of September 5, 1996, knew about the Coast Guard's personnel deficiencies. They knew only that they were close to shore and rescuers should be only a matter of minutes away. In response to the urgent pleas for help rising through the thick inverted fiberglass hull, Mike Simpson and others yelled back the most reassuring words they could think of: "Just hold on. The Coast Guard is coming."

» The On-Scene Commander

WHEN THE SAR ALARM SOUNDED at Coast Guard Station Gloucester at 5:20 A.M. on September 5, 1996, Christian Smith woke up and ran to the telecommunications center. His 41-foot rescue boat would be the first Coast Guard asset to respond to the scene. Along with performing any possible rescues, he believed his primary responsibility would be to serve as the eyes and ears of the Coast Guard. Richard Barone and Kevin Angerstein would base many of their decisions on the information Smith reported back to them.

Christian Smith—known as "Smitty" to Angerstein and others—was a twenty-seven-year-old boatswain's mate third-class who had been in the Coast Guard for about eight years. In 1986 he had graduated from high school in Haverhill, a small city a few miles up the Merrimack River from Newburyport. In January 1987, Smith had started eight weeks of basic training in Cape May, New Jersey, and then was stationed at the Coast Guard Academy in New London, Connecticut, where, for two years, he served on the yard forces doing tasks nobody else was assigned to do, like setting up for functions. After leaving the yard forces he changed his rating and became a cook. Following about two months of formal food service training, he served as a cook for two years on board the 270-foot Boston-based cutter *Escanaba*.

"Smitty and I were together on the *Escanaba*," Angerstein said later. "He enjoyed watching what I did when I was on the ship with him—doing the [search and rescue and law enforcement], driving the boat, working with the helicopters."

After four years and nine months, Smith left the Coast Guard and the

Escanaba and worked at Home Depot for about eighteen months. In 1993 he reenlisted in the Coast Guard, saying he wanted to be a coxswain rather than a cook—"changed his rate and went boatswain's mate," as Angerstein described it—and was assigned to Coast Guard Station Gloucester. There, his first job was to serve as a duty boat crewman. He would set up the deck for towing other boats, handle lines, and operate dewatering pumps.

"He was an excellent, excellent crewman," Angerstein said, "[an] excellent coxswain, a great stand-up guy."

He was a crewman for about two years before being certified as a coxswain in July 1995. The way he saw it, a coxswain was akin to a ship captain whose job was to supervise any mission he was dispatched to do and to be responsible for the safety of his boat and crew. In a deposition prepared for trial, he told attorneys that he believed that as coxswain he must "ensure the proper execution of the mission that the boat is going out for."

On this September morning, when Smith reached the communications center, Angerstein ordered him to get underway to respond to a boat accident off Thacher Island. Angerstein would call him in a short while with more details. Smith ran to the 41-footer and found that an engineer already had the engines running. With two deckhands—a seaman apprentice and the engineer—Smith left the dock at 5:23 A.M. and within seconds brought both engines up to full speed and departed Gloucester Harbor. A few minutes later, Angerstein called to tell him the accident involved a tug and barge. Angerstein gave him latitude and longitude coordinates and a compass course to steer. On board, Smith's two crew were also qualified as surface swimmers. Angerstein expected a swimmer would be needed, so he wanted to remind Smith of the proper use of a surface swimmer—to tether the swimmer to the Coast Guard boat at all times, and not to let him go below the surface of the water.

"I'm just making sure that we all know his surface swimmer is probably going to get used," Angerstein would say later. "But just a reminder to be careful of the situation that you're getting into because they're not allowed to do certain things and, again, we're looking at an inverted boat here. We knew the cabintop was obviously crushed or else the people would have gotten out if they could."

While Angerstein was correct in assuming a surface swimmer could have been an effective rescue tool, his assessment of the *Heather Lynne II*'s condition and his speculation as to why her crew remained trapped were not.

Following Angerstein's orders, Smith headed to the scene, monitoring the marine radio along the way. He overheard talk about voices being heard from inside the capsized fishing boat. Angerstein called Smith again and told him they were trying to find a dive team and get a helicopter on scene. Smith turned over the wheel to one of his deckhands and plotted his course on a chart. The lights of Gloucester faded behind them as the wheelhouse filled with concerned voices booming in over the marine radio.

A DARK-HAIRED, tall man with broad shoulders, Smith lumbered heavy-footed to the witness stand and began answering questions posed to him by attorney Annette Gonthier Kiely. A tall, thin woman who wore tailored suits and a string of pearls, she had represented Jeffrey Hutchins in a lawsuit surrounding his 1995 motorcycle accident and now, along with Brad Henry and Peter Black, represented his estate. After being asked about his Coast Guard background, Smith agreed with Kiely that within 8 minutes of his departure from Gloucester he was aware that there were men trapped in the hull of an overturned vessel.

"That they were banging?" Kiely asked.

"Yes, ma'am."

"That they were yelling 'Help! Help! Help!'?"

"Yes, ma'am."

"And that someone had discussed a call for divers?"

"Yes, ma'am."

Smith agreed with Kiely that he had another 38 minutes of travel time before reaching the scene, but during that time had not done any rescue planning as required by Coast Guard procedures. He had not asked Barone or Angerstein for any advice on what he might be able to accomplish once on scene.

"Did you discuss with your crew what equipment you had that you might utilize, given the fact that you now knew," Kiely said, "38 minutes before arrival, that there were men trapped inside the hull who were alive and banging?"

"No, ma'am."

"Did you feel prepared, sir, to deal with the need for immediate rescue action when arriving on scene," Kiely asked, "when you learned about ten minutes into this that there were men trapped inside the hull of an overturned vessel?"

"The only thing, I was just going to go to the scene to stabilize the scene," Smith said. "Just to report. Be the eyes and ears of the Coast Guard up there."

Kiely asked if he recalled overhearing that Mike Goodridge was responding on his own accord. Smith said he did not, nor did he suggest that Goodridge be called.

"I didn't know what Mike Goodridge's capabilities were," Smith said. Earlier, he had told Kiely that he'd heard Goodridge's name tossed around the station from time to time as a commercial salvage operator around Newburyport and the Merrimack River. He said Angerstein and other petty officers above him in the chain of command knew of Goodridge, but Smith did not know him.

Kiely asked Smith what the weather had been when he arrived on scene at 6:10 A.M. Smith said there was a 3-foot swell, but it was calm. Kiely referenced the radio transcript in which, at 6:15 A.M., he had reported to Group Boston that the weather was calm to approximately 1-foot rollers, with winds at approximately 5 knots.

"And, sir, calm to 1-foot rollers on the ocean is about as good as it gets, is that correct?" Kiely asked.

"No, ma'am, it can get calmer than that."

Kiely noted that other fishermen had reported the morning's sea conditions as dead calm. She asked Smith if the wind conditions were about as favorable as it can get. Smith disagreed, saying, "No, 5 knots is a little bit of wind."

Smith said that when he arrived on scene, he took control of the situation on behalf of the Coast Guard by establishing a security zone. He did this by placing himself between the *Heather Lynne II* and any other onlookers who might drift too close and make the situation worse. While sitting on his boat and maintaining a security zone as they waited for the divers to arrive, Smith considered himself, and therefore the Coast Guard, to be in control of the scene. From time to time, he spoke to Ted Rurak, the owner of the *Heather Lynne II*, on scene aboard the *Retriever*. There was little to do, Smith figured, other than watch the *Heather Lynne II* and wait for divers to arrive. He didn't instruct any of his crew or the assembled fishing boats or tug crew on what to do or not do. Smith didn't conduct any search for people adrift in the water—what Barone had feared and believed necessitated sending the helicopter directly to the scene—because, after arriving on scene and covering about a half-mile area around the *Heather Lynne II* without spotting any debris, he assumed all three men were inside the turtled boat. He said an extensive surface search was not necessary based on the scene as he saw it. Kiely asked if, from the time he arrived on scene at 6:10 A.M. until 6:47 A.M., when he left the scene to meet the helicopter, he followed orders not to allow anyone not authorized by the Coast Guard to enter the security zone. Smith said that was not true because, "Nobody attempted to enter the security zone." Kiely reminded Smith that during a deposition he had given before the trial, he had mentioned that he told an unspecified fishing boat to back off and not enter the security zone.

Judge Saris interrupted and asked, "Is that a boat that was on the scene?"

"Yes, ma'am. It was one of the boats that was spectating."

"Did you ask the boat, sir, what their intentions were?" asked Kiely.

"No, ma'am."

"So you have no idea what they were attempting to do at that time, correct?"

"I didn't ask them what they were going to do, but I could tell by looking at them they weren't intending to do anything."

"How do you know that, sir?" Kiely asked.

"For the previous hour, they were sitting about 50 feet off with their hands in their pockets, looking at the boat, upside down. So, I mean, by them moving a little too close, I could tell they weren't attempting to do anything."

Smith acknowledged that while he had spent at least 36 minutes maintaining a security zone 40 to 50 feet away from the *Heather Lynne II*, he determined the trapped men's status by hollering to the crew of the *Houma*, who continued to bang on the bottom of the *Heather Lynne II*. Smith said he did not hear the voices himself.

"Did you think that that might be of some importance, that you or your crew members be on the *Houma* to hear, to be directly the eyes and ears and report, based on your own personal observation, to the command center?" Kiely asked.

"No, ma'am."

"Isn't it a basic principle of search and rescues that men trapped in a hull have a limited air pocket and, therefore, with the passage of time the likelihood of their surviving is diminishing as time passes? Is that correct?"

"Yes, ma'am."

"And it was clear to you," Kiely asked, "that the more time passed without getting them out of that hull, the greater the likelihood of death, is that correct?"

"Yes, ma'am."

Judge Saris interrupted and asked, "Did you ever get any closer to the boat than 40 to 50 feet away?"

"No, ma'am."

"Why not?"

"Because the 41 will throw—as soon as you engage the engines, it will actually throw a good amount of water underneath the boat through the prop wash, and I didn't want to take a chance of my prop wash tilting the *Heather Lynne* and losing air."

"Did you ever ask another vessel to go up alongside it to try to secure it?" Saris asked.

"No, ma'am," Smith said. "There was a line already on it when I arrived on the scene."

"Did you think that was sufficient?" Saris asked.

"Yes, ma'am. It was a 3-inch-circumference line, it appeared to me, and the line itself was a pretty strong line. I don't think, even if there was no air in the vessel, I don't think the boat would have went down with the strain on the line. It's a very heavy line."

"And why did you think [the line] was enough to keep up the whole boat?" Saris asked

"Because the lines we use . . . to tow boats with . . . the line itself could take an awfully heavy strain before it would break," Smith said. "And by looking at the boat itself, seeing the way the line was run through the bottom of the boat and brought back to the tugboat, I thought, just looking at that, it was very secure."

"Was anything securing the bow?" Saris asked.

"Not that I'm aware of, ma'am."

"Did that worry you?"

"No, Your Honor, because I didn't want to take the chance of someone tying a line to it and pulling too much and affecting the stability of the boat. As far as I was concerned, it was tied off and then the boat would stabilize itself. And I didn't want to jeopardize it at the time, Your Honor."

Kiely asked if he knew that voices were heard begging for help from the bow area. Smith said he didn't know of any particular location, just that there were voices. He paused and then said he might have, at some point, heard something about the bow. Kiely asked if tying a line on the skeg forced the bow deeper into the water. Smith said he wasn't sure how the line was affecting the boat and that he didn't consider attaching a line to the bow or sending in a surface swimmer to investigate the perimeter of the boat. Kiely wondered if he realized that once the Beverly Fire Department divers entered the water, they had to take time to tie a line to the bow and stabilize the boat before they could begin their rescue attempt. Smith said he was aware of that.

"And, at that point, sir, you had been on scene for almost an hour, is that correct?"

"Yes, ma'am."

"And either your men directly, and/or someone in the immediate vicinity, or through getting assistance, could have fastened that bow in that hour that you were waiting for the divers, correct?"

"Yes, ma'am."

"And, sir, did you learn that there was a bow line floating free, attached [at one end] to the capsized *Heather Lynne*?"

"I learned it later."

Smith agreed that a surface swimmer could have swum around the perimeter of the boat so long as his head didn't go beneath the water. Smith did not direct any of his crew to do so, however, nor did he send a swimmer in with a boathook to try to grab a suspended bow line. Kiely pointed out that Ted Rurak was on scene, knew his boat well, and could have directed a swimmer toward the boat's bow line. Smith never explored this option, either.

"Did you have discussions about securing the bow area with Mr. Rurak?" Judge Saris asked.

"No, Your Honor."

"With anybody?"

"No, Your Honor."

"Let me ask you this," Judge Saris said. "Did you stop anyone from coming close to tie up to the bow area?"

"No, Your Honor," answered Smith, despite his earlier admission of having turned aside a boat whose intentions he did not know.

Kiely returned to the issue of a rescue plan. She noted that, as the assumed on-scene commander until Angerstein arrived in the 47-footer after 7 A.M., Smith was required to complete a rescue plan if it was not already complete. He was further required to shape and revise the plan if it was not appropriate for the situation he found on scene. Smith told Kiely he wouldn't assert the authority to revise a plan that had been handed down to him from the search and rescue mission coordinator at Group Boston. Kiely countered that the SAR manual not only permitted but instructed the on-scene commander to complete a rescue plan, because he or she was in the best position to assess what was needed. Smith said the manual was a guide and not "a hundred percent telling me what to do." He agreed, however, that part of a rescue plan included dispatching or diverting rescue units such as helicopters, 24-foot rigid-hull inflatable boats, or any other available resource. Kiely pointed out that the manual also said the on-scene commander should effect a rescue if possible.

"Were you able to [effect a] rescue at the time you arrived on scene?" Kiely asked.

"No, ma'am."

"And that's because you didn't have divers?"

"Yes, ma'am."

"And you knew the need for divers 10 minutes en route to the accident, correct?"

"Yes, ma'am."

"And that need for divers was the solution to the problem presented on that day, correct?"

"Yes, ma'am."

Kiely reminded Smith that if he could not perform the rescue, the Coast Guard expected him to develop a plan. The first task would be to evaluate survivability. She asked Smith if he did that.

"No, because Group [Boston] is the SMC, and they already had a plan," Smith said. "So I didn't need to change it."

"And, sir, the plan was what?" Kiely pressed.

"The plan was to maintain the stability of the vessel while they were getting divers out to the scene."

"And when were they going to get divers to the scene?"

"As soon as possible."

"So, just so I'm clear, what was your assessment as on-scene commander of survivability of the men trapped in this vessel?" Kiely asked.

"We were just hoping we could get divers there in time."

"Did you make an assessment of their survivability in terms of time, sir?"

"No, I didn't."

"It's true, sir, that you took no affirmative action to stabilize the vessel?"

"True."

Smith agreed that the SAR manual offers guidelines for taking action when something needs to be corrected on scene.

"So if the rear was lifted, [which put] more weight on the bow where the voices were coming from, remedial action would have included lifting that bow so as to maintain the air pocket or even increase the air pocket, correct?"

Campbell objected. Saris overruled.

"I don't know. I'd have to—I mean, I don't remember seeing anything in this book that tells me to adjust the boat for the air pocket," Smith said, flipping through the SAR manual on the desk in front of him.

"Based on all your years in the Coast Guard, you knew that, basically, buoyancy is a function of air displacing water, correct?" Kiely asked.

"Yes."

"So to the extent that there was more air in the vessel—the more the air, the longer the men could breathe, correct?"

"Yes."

"And so to the extent that you lowered the water level, you would increase the air, correct?"

"Yes, that would happen."

"And the hull was already one-third above water, correct?"

"Yes, ma'am."

"And so it would have been a reasonably prudent action to raise that hull more than one third above water to increase the air pocket?"

Campbell objected. Saris overruled.

"No, it wouldn't have," Smith said, "Because if you would have tilted that boat in the slightest way port or starboard, left or right, you would have probably lost what air was in there, and the boat would be sitting on the bottom right then."

"Well, sir, as I understand it . . . a line was attached [to the skeg], and there was still an air pocket maintained, correct?"

"Yes."

"So that established that the boat could be stabilized successfully by careful maneuvering of the vessel, correct?"

"The boat was stable as it was," Smith said. "I wasn't going to turn the boat any way to jeopardize it."

Kiely turned Smith's attention to the radio transcript. Smith agreed that from the moment he learned at 5:40 A.M. that men were trapped, alive, and shouting and banging on the hull, that information never changed. He did not report any change to Barone or Angerstein. Further, Smith agreed it would have been prudent to make sure the helicopter and anyone with access to Station Gloucester's 24-foot rigid-hull inflatable had that information. Kiely reminded Smith of a radio conversation between Group Boston and the helicopter in which the helicopter was updated on conditions at the scene. Smith said, contradicting pilot Craig Lindsey's testimony, that there had been no communication problems with the helicopter.

"And so to the extent that there were men adrift requiring a helicopter to fly overhead, that was not the situation as you observed it on scene. Is that true?"

"No, that's not the situation as I observed it."

Smith said he did not tell Barone that the helicopter should go straight to Gloucester. They looked at the radio logs again and established that while the helicopter was on scene without divers, the divers had arrived at Station Gloucester. But Smith told the court he had not thought it his responsibility to divert the helicopter straight to Gloucester because its operations were being directed by Barone, who was the SAR mission coordinator. Smith would only have diverted the helicopter if it weren't already being done by Barone.

"Well, did the SMC at the 6:12 radio transmission divert the helicopter at this critical point in time to Station Gloucester where the log shows the divers had arrived by 6:20?"

"No, ma'am."

Judge Saris asked Smith if he knew how much time would have been saved if the helicopter had flown straight to Gloucester. Smith said it would have been about 20 minutes. He agreed that Coast Guard Station Gloucester's fast 24-footer could have traveled to the scene in about 23 minutes, and that weather conditions that morning were appropriate for the high-speed boat.

Before concluding her questioning, Kiely again turned to a section in the SAR manual that addressed what to do for people trapped in capsized vessels. She read five out of a list of six recommended procedures. The first item was: "Keep in contact with person(s)." Smith agreed that neither he nor any of his crew did that. Instead, Smith, as the on-scene commander, relied on the crew of the *Houma* to keep in contact with the trapped fishermen. Next, the manual advised: "Estimate the volume of air remaining."

"Did you do that, sir?" Kiely asked.

"No, ma'am."

" 'Surface swimmers may attempt to direct trapped persons out, but shall not dive under the vessel.' Did you or any of your crew attempt to direct trapped persons out?"

"No ma'am."

" 'Inject clean air if possible' . . . Did you attempt that, sir?"

"No, ma'am."

Finally, the manual advised, "Stabilize the hull." "Now," Kiely said, "neither you nor your crew made any efforts to stabilize the hull, is that correct?"

"Yeah, we couldn't make any efforts," Smith said, later adding, "To me, stabilization wasn't needed. The divers are the ones that requested the stabilization."

DURING HIS CROSS-EXAMINATION, Department of Justice attorney Stephen Campbell asked Smith to describe what a security zone is and why he would establish one.

"All it is, is just basically getting between a group of people and an object or an area to prevent a situation from worsening," Smith said. He explained that he stayed about 40 feet away from the *Heather Lynne II* "to prevent anybody from going up to the vessel itself. I mean, I didn't want anybody bumping it or anything. Because, just looking at it, you could tell if someone bumped it, I mean, the thing would go right over. So I didn't want to take a chance on that. So I just sat between the four or five boats in the area that were just observing what was happening and the tug *Houma*, just to prevent any further unstabilization of the vessel."

Campbell asked Smith about the boat that he had told to move away from the scene.

"It was there the whole time I was there, from the time I arrived on the scene. And, I mean, the people on the boat, they were just standing on the boat, so, I mean, to me, it didn't look like they intended on doing anything. So I just told them to move back."

"Did they ever tell you they wanted to do anything?" Campbell asked.

"No, sir."

"At any time . . . did they ever tell you that they really wanted to approach to do something?"

"No, sir."

"Prior to the arrival of the Beverly Fire Department [divers] in the water, did you ever tell anyone *not* to come to the aid of the *Heather Lynne?*"

"No, sir."

"Did you ever tell any scalloper, dragger, shrimper, or some other large vessel such as that that he couldn't come tie lines on the *Heather Lynne?*"

"No, sir."

"Did you ever tell any of those types of vessels they couldn't come to drag the *Heather Lynne* up a stern ramp?"

"No, sir."

"Did you ever overhear any request of any such vessel wanting to do something like that?"

"No, sir."

Returning to the security zone issue, Campbell asked if there had still been voices coming from inside the *Heather Lynne II* up until the time Smith moved a quarter to a half mile away from the scene to meet the helicopter. Smith said that was true, adding, "The boat was fine when I left to go get divers."

Before concluding, Campbell had just a few last questions.

"As you sit here today, Petty Officer, do you believe you or any one of your crew failed to take any mandatory actions in this rescue?"

"No, sir."

"As you sit here today, do you believe that the actions of yourself and your crew were prudent under the circumstances?"

"Yes, sir."

"Did you feel that the instructions and the guidance and the information given to you in this case were reasonable and what you would have expected to have gotten?"

"Yes, sir."

"Did you want to rescue these people?"

"Yes, sir."

»The Experts

ALTHOUGH RICHARD BARONE, Kevin Angerstein, Craig Lindsey, and Christian Smith believed that every decision and action they had taken in the early morning of September 5 was prudent and that they had not failed to do anything required of them, retired Coast Guard Captain Adrian Lonsdale, the plaintiffs' expert witness, thought otherwise. Lonsdale had been attending the trial nearly every day, sitting with his wife in the front row. A slender man with distinguished-looking white hair, he often wore a white shirt, blue sport coat, and blue tie. He listened to the testimony in a contemplative way, seeming to weigh what he heard against common sense. What he was hearing, he concluded, wasn't representative of the Coast Guard he had known.

Lonsdale had enlisted in the Coast Guard in 1945, graduated from the U.S. Coast Guard Academy in 1950, and retired with the rank of captain in 1979. He had attended the Coast Guard's SAR school in 1966 and in 1975 and had served on ocean station vessels in the Atlantic and Pacific and at Loran Station Naktu Island. During the Vietnam War he commanded Coast Guard and Navy forces on the Vietnamese coast while also serving as the senior adviser to the commander of the Vietnamese Navy. Lonsdale had served aboard the cutters *Winona* and *Sebago* and the Gloucester-based *General Greene*. Ashore, he had served as a First District deputy group commander. For two and a half years he was the group commander in Portland, Maine, where his duties included reviewing SAR mission performance. In his thirty-four-year Coast Guard career he had handled more than 1,500 SAR cases, although none involved a capsized boat with people trapped inside. After retirement, he'd attained an unlimited master's license and worked as a captain of coastal tankers and container ships and as a relief captain on the research vessel *Endeavor*. In 1987 he founded Northeast Maritime Institute in Fairhaven, Massachusetts, to train mariners seeking Coast Guard licenses. Before the trial, Lonsdale had submitted a report in which he offered three primary opinions on the Coast Guard's performance during its rescue attempt.

"Several opportunities were missed," he wrote, "through misleading communications and failure of the Coast Guard to take advantage of immediately available diver resources."

According to Coast Guard policy, Lonsdale noted, if a commanding officer is faced with a life-threatening situation and has no highly trained military or municipal dive team available, that officer can use anyone with recreational diver qualifications—in this case, Michael Goodridge, Jay Lesynski, or Charlie Rine, any of whom might have been able to respond as much as thirty minutes faster than the Beverly Fire Department Dive Team.

Lonsdale believed the *Heather Lynne II* might have been kept from sinking further had Smith, as the Coast Guard's on-scene commander, utilized the services of a nearby scalloper. Instead, he believed that Smith had rejected offers of assistance and had set about establishing a perimeter around the *Heather Lynne II* to keep all vessels away from her, despite a Coast Guard policy that said stabilizing the hull was a top priority. Lonsdale believed that, at the very least, tying a scalloper or dragger alongside the *Heather Lynne II* and passing cables under her to create a cradle—as Goodridge had suggested over the marine radio while traveling to the scene—might have prevented her from sinking further and might have bought more time.

In addition—and no less essential to the trapped men's survival—Lonsdale believed Smith should have made an attempt to supply Kevin Foster, Jeffrey Hutchins, and John Michael Lowther with fresh air, despite the fact that *Houma* Captain Allen Breen "apparently abandoned the idea because he was led to believe the divers would be there by 6:30."

During the trial, attorney Peter Black asked Captain Lonsdale if he had formed an opinion of the Coast Guard's performance. Lonsdale replied that the Coast Guard personnel had done everything they were supposed to do during the initial phase of the rescue. They gathered information, dispatched a boat and helicopter and, on realizing divers were needed, made efforts to get a dive team.

"And then," Lonsdale said, "they kind of quit."

Black asked Lonsdale what he meant by "kind of quit."

"Well," Lonsdale said, "I think they had checked off the things in their list, and they had everything moving, and they figured that was sufficient."

Black asked Lonsdale if the Coast Guard, in its response, compelled would-be rescuers not to help and thereby worsened the peril of the trapped crew of the *Heather Lynne II*.

"I think that they left people with the expectation that the helicopter was to arrive momentarily with divers on board," Lonsdale said, "which led people to let down on their guard and say: 'Well, everything's under control and there's going to be a favorable outcome.' "

Black asked Lonsdale if this was an adequately conducted Coast Guard SAR mission.

"Only in the initial phases. Once they had the initial check-offs done, they fell down on the job."

ATTORNEY STEPHEN CAMPBELL began his cross-examination by noting that Lonsdale's last SAR job for the Coast Guard had been more than twenty years before.

"Now, you made a couple of opinions, Captain, about what the Coast Guard *should* have done. And I'm going to ask you . . . what they *had* to do," Campbell said. "Now, Captain, is there any requirement in the Coast Guard manuals . . . that says the Coast Guard is *required* to attempt to pass lines under a vessel?"

Lonsdale said there was not.

"And is there anything in any of the manuals . . . that says that the Coast Guard even has to undertake the rescue?"

"It's my assumption that once the call comes in, you'd be legally bound in this case," Lonsdale said. "You certainly would be in big trouble if you didn't."

"It's your belief that the Coast Guard has to respond to every rescue?" Campbell asked. "Where does it say that, sir?"

"I can't tell you offhand. I just know the Coast Guard slogans."

"OK," Campbell sighed and stepped back. "I guess when you were there, was there a saying going around the Coast Guard that 'You have to go out, but you don't have to come back'?"

"That's true."

"Are you aware of what the Coast Guard standards are for responses, such as in this case, with regard to safety of their own personnel or the safety of the personnel they are trying to save?"

"I can't say that I'm aware that there's any change," Lonsdale said.

AMONG THE MANY CHANGES in the Coast Guard since Lonsdale had retired was the abandonment of its unofficial motto, which had belonged previously to its predecessor, the U.S. Life-Saving Service. According to the Coast Guard historian's office, the quote is attributed to Patrick Etheridge, who was stationed at the Cape Hatteras Life-Saving Station in the late 1800s. His crew was called to assist a ship that was stranded on dangerous shoals. When Etheridge ordered the lifeboat to put to sea, one of the sailors remarked that they might make it to the wreck, but they'd never make it back. Etheridge looked at the man behind the oars and said, "The Blue Book says we've got to go out, and it doesn't say a damn thing about having to come back."

Etheridge was right. According to the *Regulations of the Life-Saving Service of 1899*: "[A station keeper] will not desist from his efforts until by actual trial the impossibility of effecting a rescue is demonstrated. The statement of the keeper that he did not try to use the boat because the sea or surf was too heavy will not be accepted unless attempts to launch it were actually made and failed." This rule existed in the Coast Guard at least through the 1930s. For every life lost, the station keeper would have to explain why and write a detailed report in the service's annual report to Congress.

But although Congress, when it created the Coast Guard in 1915, intended that the obligations of the Life-Saving Service be absorbed in letter and spirit by the new service, the policy regarding risk had changed in recent years. The First District's Search and Rescue plan in 1996 stated: "No mission is important enough to unduly hazard boat and crew. . . . The commanding officer/officer in charge has the responsibility and the authority to recall or to not dispatch a boat when the mission is deemed too risky to the crew or boat."

Today, Coast Guard men and women are trained in risk assessment. Today they are told, "You *don't* have to go out, but you *do* have to come back." This attitude was summed up in the words of the coxswain of a 44-

foot Coast Guard boat that had failed to save a sailboat from foundering on the rocks near California's Monterey Harbor; the coxswain told the judge in a subsequent trial that his priorities boiled down to: "Us. Ours. Them. Theirs."

CAMPBELL ASKED LONSDALE if injecting air into the hull of a capsized boat was a mandatory Coast Guard requirement.

"Well, I don't think any of this is really mandatory," Lonsdale said. "I mean, it depends on your ingenuity."

Campbell wondered aloud where this clean air could have come from. The 41-footer did not have an air compressor on board. The tug had decided its engine room air was not clean enough. Lonsdale said there were numerous fishing boats in the area and at least one of them must have had a compressor on board.

"Now, as you sit here today, are you aware of any other sources of clean air at the scene of the accident?" Campbell asked.

"We'll never know because the Coast Guard never broadcast the need for it."

"Is there a requirement that the Coast Guard broadcast a need for fresh air?"

"No."

Campbell asked Lonsdale if he knew what would have happened to the *Heather Lynne II* if *Houma's* Captain Breen had poked a hole into the hull to feed an air hose inside the boat.

"Before it was stabilized, it would not have been a wise move because it would have let out all the remaining air, which was leaking out slowly anyway. After it was stabilized, it wouldn't make any difference."

Campbell asked Lonsdale if he believed the 41-footer's actions to create "a little buffer zone" around the *Heather Lynne II* to keep spectators away were prudent. Lonsdale said the 41-footer should have gone alongside the *Heather Lynne II* and tried to stabilize it.

"So, as you sit here today, is it your opinion that no effort should have been undertaken by the Coast Guard to keep . . . vessels away from the *Heather Lynne*?"

"The Coast Guard boat could have broadcast a warning to vessels in the vicinity."

"Is that the same as creating a buffer zone around the vessel when you're on scene?"

"No, it isn't. I think they had more important things to do."

"Captain . . . did you see any mandatory requirements that the Coast Guard violated in this rescue attempt?"

"No, I didn't."

"And is it your understanding, at least when you were in the Coast Guard doing search and rescue cases, that a great deal of discretion is given to the individual Coast Guard members . . . in what procedures to use in any particular vessels, is that correct?"

"Yes."

Peter Black followed up with a few more questions.

"Now, sir," he said, "we'll never know, will we, whether there were other divers available to respond because the Coast Guard never asked them to respond, isn't that true?"

"That is true," Lonsdale said. "Yes."

Black turned to Campbell's questions about injecting air into the hull and his suggestion that engine room air was not clean air.

"Do people breathe in the engine room?" Black asked.

"Yes, they do. They're in there all of the time."

"Once the vessel was stabilized, sir, other than poking a hole to put air in, what other holes could have been put in the hull?

"You could have done whatever was necessary to open it up and get the people out of there."

Black asked Lonsdale why he believed it was not prudent to keep people away from the *Heather Lynne II*.

"If there is someone else that could contribute to the rescue, get them in there. A vessel with an A-frame on its stern . . . could get a hold of a bow line or whatever and hoist the [bow] right up."

Black sat down. Campbell stood and asked Lonsdale who he would have sent into the *Heather Lynne II*, once stabilized, to get the crew out.

"Whoever could help," Lonsdale said. "I'm sure there were plenty of willing hands in the area."

"So, you would let just anybody try to enter the vessel to get these people out?"

"I would supervise it," Lonsdale said. "I certainly would supervise it.

. . . I'm talking about chopping holes in the hull, whatever we have to do to open it up."

"You would have started taking axes to the hull to chop it up?"

"Whatever I had to do to get it open, get them out."

"Don't you think that chopping a hole in an overturned hull might exacerbate the situation for those inside?"

"I looked at the tug's mooring lines, and they're 5½-inch nylon, breaking strength of around 40,000 pounds," Lonsdale said. "They had oodles of them. And you get those under the boat and, supported by that, you could do anything you want to."

THE GOVERNMENT HAD ITS own expert witness. Coast Guard Commander Robert S. Walters, a short man with an emotionless face and blue uniform decorated with colorful ribbons and three gold stripes, stepped up to the witness chair. He had observed a few days of testimony while sitting quietly in the front row of benches beside Lonsdale and behind Campbell. From time to time, Campbell would walk over to Walters and whisper in his ear, then they'd smile and converse below audible level. He said little to anyone, never looked around the room, never made eye contact, and offered no indication of who he was or why he was there—until Campbell called him to the witness stand.

Walters at the time of the trial was serving as the chief of the National Search and Rescue School in Yorktown, Virginia, where he was responsible for the school's curriculum and administrative activities. He also served as acting adviser to the managers of the Coast Guard's search and rescue program. His school trained SAR controllers from 114 countries, as well as the Coast Guard's own on-scene commanders and SAR supervisors. Lessons taught at the school were drawn from the National SAR Manual and the Coast Guard's Addendum to that manual. Coursework also included reviewing case studies, commandant instruction manuals, and any other pertinent publications. Walters often offered his opinion to Coast Guard unit commanders on the review of SAR cases.

He told the court that he had enlisted in the Coast Guard in 1976 and had trained as a search and rescue medic on helicopters at Air Station New Orleans. In 1983, he completed officer candidate school, where he would later return as a SAR instructor. In his Coast Guard career, he had done search and rescue at Air Station Miami, had been a deputy commander in Monterey, California, and had served as the commander of Group Hampton Roads, Virginia. He recited his résumé in rapid fire. Judge Saris noted that they were in a rush to get him out, but that he could slow it down a little. Walters apologized, saying he tended to talk quickly. Campbell asked him if he had received any SAR awards. Walters said he had received a Coast Guard medal for heroism in 1979 while serving at Loran Station St. Paul, Alaska. A Japanese fishing vessel had run aground and the Coast Guard had rescued eighty-one people.

Walters had recently written a paper titled, "Training the Lifesavers: A Discussion of the Split Between the Scientific Side and the Art." As Campbell began to ask about this paper, Judge Saris interrupted and asked Walters if he had ever personally dealt with a capsized boat with people trapped inside. He said he had not.

At Campbell's request, Walters explained his interpretation of the difference between the National SAR Manual and its Coast Guard Addendum. He said the manual is a basic overview of search operations. Various government agencies are encouraged to adopt their own addenda to offer their rescue personnel more specific guidance.

"Now, Commander, you used the word 'guidance' as opposed to 'requirement,' " Campbell said. "Is it your understanding that both [of] the manuals are mandatory?"

"The manual is pretty clear," Walters said. "If you look in the front of the manual, it pretty much tells you what is required as a mandatory item and what is, you know, in the wording of 'shall,' 'should,' 'will,' 'may.' And that particular wording kind of gives you an idea of where you are at a particular time. . . . It's certainly not a mandatory manual in every sense of the word. There are some areas that are more mandatory than others."

Walters said he had evaluated the *Heather Lynne II* case in terms of what Coast Guardsmen are trained to do and what the Coast Guard expects of its crew. A SAR case has various stages, he explained, starting with awareness, which is the initial notification of the case. This is followed by initial actions, those things you do upon notification, and then the planning stage: you decide what actions to take, such as calculating search patterns. This is followed by the operation stage: the execution of the search and rescue plan. In this case, Walters believed that the Coast Guard acted appropriately by classifying the case as a distress situation. He found no fault with the Coast Guard's response in the awareness stage.

Campbell asked Walters to discuss the next stage, the initial action stage. Walters said this was where they get the ball rolling—you have a distress case, now what are you going to do about it? In this case, the Coast Guard had launched a boat, requested a helicopter, contacted a local dive team, and briefed the next level in the chain of command, all of which were appropriate and prudent actions. He explained that program goals—not requirements—are that a SAR response be initiated within five minutes of awareness and that a search and rescue unit should be moving within thirty minutes and arrive on scene within ninety minutes. In this case, the Coast Guard met all program goals.

Campbell asked if Group Boston's actions on the morning of September 5, 1996, were appropriate.

"Yes. Definitely, they were appropriate," Walters said. "They did exactly what they were supposed to do [and] they did it very quickly."

Walters said it was appropriate that Group Boston requested a helicopter and issued an Urgent Marine Information Broadcast. He believed Barone was wise to devise a plan for using the 47-footer in case the weather prohibited the helicopter's launch, and it was wise to send the helicopter directly to the scene to search for any survivors who may have been cast adrift or who, fueled by a basic desire to stay alive, might break free of the boat. Walters noted that there had been a lot of concern on the part of the Coast Guard that the fishermen who assembled on scene were too focused on the overturned *Heather Lynne II* to do any real looking around for adrift survivors. How terrible it would be if the *Heather Lynne II*'s crew had drowned, Walters said, because nobody was looking for them.

Campbell asked Walters for his assessment of the planning stage.

"Well, I looked at a couple of things. Number one . . . they knew exactly where the accident happened. They did not have to go into detailed search planning. . . . They had a good plan. They had divers that they were in the process of contacting. . . . They felt good about that. . . . It was a sure thing; they knew they had them. They were confident in knowing that they had those divers. And so they had a plan of attack, and they were pushing forward."

Campbell asked if it was appropriate to call the Beverly Fire Depatment Dive Team.

"Well, it was a known entity, number one. It was a dive team that they knew about, that they were comfortable with. It was a dive *team* . . . a group of folks who were used to working together and used to working in those types of conditions, which, again, gives you a greater level of confidence about their ability to take care of the case. . . . It's always better to work with folks who are very focused, specifically on that task, if they are available, rather than, you know, to try to piece something together."

Walters said contacting the Beverly team, then, was reasonable and not in violation of any SAR manuals. Campbell asked Walters for his assessment of the Coast Guard's actions in the operation stage.

"Well, the operation stage at that point was the actual carrying out of the plan that the SAR mission coordinator had developed. In this case, it was getting the Beverly Fire Department team to Station Gloucester, making a decision on whether to use the 47 or the helo. They used a combination of both when they found that they could utilize the helo and make it a little bit faster. That was a good decision. The timing was real critical there, obviously. The Beverly Fire Department arrived on scene . . . but their equipment was a little bit lagging behind. So, even though they were at the station, they weren't really ready to go. And so the helo arrived—I mean . . . it was a pretty quick turnaround."

"In view of all the stages that you mentioned, was it your opinion that the Coast Guard personnel involved in this case acted reasonably and prudent under the circumstances?" Campbell asked.

"Yes, sir."

"Did any of them at any time violate any of the requirements or policies and procedures in the [National] Search and Rescue Manual or the Coast Guard Addendum to the Search and Rescue Manual?"

"None that I found, sir."

BLACK BEGAN HIS CROSS-EXAMINATION by confirming that Walters had achieved the rank of commander on July 1, 1999. He asked, "And I take it then, 'commander' is your terminal rank?"

"Yes, it is."

"Kind of harsh," Campbell interjected.

"You have no expectation of being selected to captain?" Black asked.

"Sir, twenty-four years, I've had a blessed career," Walters said, "and I'm at the point where there's not much excitement left on the horizon."

"That's even bleaker," Judge Saris said. Laughter broke the silence in the courtroom.

Black noted that Walters had attended SAR school twice, the first time in 1991. In his prior seventeen years in the Coast Guard, his SAR training was mostly from correspondence courses. Besides being qualified to serve as an EMT, he was a qualified SAR crewman on helicopters. Walters had returned to SAR school in 1998 in preparation for becoming chief of the school. In response to a question from Black, Walters said he was very familiar with the search and rescue manuals.

"Now, use of the word 'must,' that makes something mandatory, is that correct?" Black asked.

"It depends upon what the definition is in the manual, sir," Walters said as he reached for the manual.

"Well, sir, I'm not asking you to look in the manual," Black said. He raised his voice as Walters opened the cover of the manual. "I'm asking you to look at me. Sir, please don't look in the manual."

Walters looked at Black. After a barbed interchange about the manual's use of "shall," "must," "may," and "should," Black asked if the word "must" were used in the National Search and Rescue Manual, would Walters understand that to be a mandatory direction. Walters didn't recall the word appearing anywhere in the manual. Black moved on.

He asked, "Now, sir, in this manual, I believe it says SAR is both an art and a science. Does that sound familiar?"

"Yes, sir."

"Did you write a book about that?" Black asked.

Walters said he had written a three- or four-page article about the art and science of search and rescue, which was published for a seminar he delivered at a conference. It was his only published writing.

"Is it fair to say, sir, that the 'science' portion, as dealt with in that article, has to do mostly with the method of conducting searches, taking into consideration the tides and the currents and the weather and the winds, that kind of thing?"

"Yes."

"All right. And the 'art' portion of search and rescue is the cognitive analysis that's used, isn't that correct?"

"Yes, sir."

"And it's, in fact, a critical part of the search and rescue mission," Black said. "That is, the ability of the people performing the mission to utilize their intellect, not just plug numbers into a computer or follow checklists where boxes are checked off. Isn't that true?"

"It goes deeper than that, sir."

"At least that deep?"

"Yes, sir."

"If not deeper?"

"Yes, sir."

"In fact, in your opinion, science is the easy part?"

"Absolutely."

"It's the art that's difficult?"

"Art is the most difficult," Walters agreed.

"Do you remember saying in the article that being an artist means that you have the ability to imagine yourself in all kinds of otherness, [and in] doing that, you can rearrange perspectives on things, which can provide a revelation?"

"I remember that. . . . It may have been a quote that I pulled for that particular part, but I can't remember exactly."

"And the purpose of that was to inform those people attending this seminar that you have to think, you have to go beyond the routine, go beyond the dictates, the words in the manual and use your intellect to come up with the best possible solution to the situation you face, correct?"

"When appropriate," Walters said. "Yes, sir."

"Now," Black said, pacing the carpet with his head down. "I think you said in that article, that the art of search and rescue means interweaving of data, the experience and intuition to change one's perspective in such a way that you can decipher and transform into notions of potentiality, and thus allowing the mind to create, process and accept alternative resolution. By changing the perspective, you expand the possibilities of seeing what was hidden before." He looked up at Walters. "Do you remember saying that?"

"Sure do."

"And, sir, by that you were saying that it's critical for the SAR personnel to take consideration of all the facts and draw them out and use all of the information so that they can constantly update what their plans are and how they intend to bring about the best possible solution available, correct?"

"Yes, sir."

"Now, finding and employing often-overlooked SAR resources tucked away in small communities," Black said, "that's one of the things you talked about in that article. That's something the SAR commander ought to have done before the SAR mission comes up, correct?"

"Uh-hum," Walters said, watching Black.

"Yes?"

"Yes."

"And, certainly, that would include . . . having a list of potential divers, correct?"

"It would."

"Isn't that, in fact, a requirement?" Black asked. "Isn't there a requirement that the SAR controller locate and search out and familiarize himself for the benefit of his command the assets that are available outside the Coast Guard command?"

"Oh, yes, sir," Walters said. "Yes, sir."

"Which would include diving capabilities?"

"Yes, sir."

"And that would include the Beverly team?"

"Yes, sir."

"That would include commercial divers [who] are recognized as being trained, capable people?"

"Yes, sir."

"Now one of the things you talked about in the article was critical thinking. It's important to think critically: 'What have I done? Was it the right thing to do? Is there something else I can do that will make it better?' . . . And you also said—well, what you're really saying, sir, is you expect people to use good judgment?"

"Yes, sir."

"Not just follow a particular recommendation in the manual, but use good judgment?"

"Yes, sir."

"In fact, the manual . . . tells us that nothing in the manual should be perceived as preventing you from using good judgment. In fact, you're expected to use good judgment."

"Yes, sir."

"And you'll agree with me that search and rescue is the use of available resources, as defined in the manual," Black said. "We can look it up if you need to look at it."

"I agree with you," Walters said. "Sir, I agree with you in the definition of use of available resources. But . . . you have the choice of which resources to be used in the circumstances, based on your experience and what you think the case requires."

"You'll agree with me that divers, very early on, were viewed as critical?"

"Yes, sir."

"And, knowing that," Black said, "is it your testimony, sir, that good judgment dictated calling one dive team and stopping there?"

"It is my testimony, sir, that [Barone] had chosen a dive team which he had considered to be reliable," Walters said, "[Barone] had chosen a dive team which he was confident would be able to respond, and he put a plan into effect which would use that team to his best advantage."

"And, in fact, sir, you are basing your opinion in part on the assumption that Mr. Barone chose the dive team?" Black asked.

"Well, Mr. Barone—"

"That's a 'yes' or 'no' question. Is that correct?

"No, sir."

"Well, sir, you'll agree with me that only one dive team was called, correct?"

"Yes, sir."

"Now, you're aware, aren't you, sir, that Mr. Barone testified that it was an extended period of time before he was even sure that the Beverly dive team would respond?"

Campbell objected. Saris overruled.

"Are you aware of that, sir?" Black asked.

"I'm not aware of that, sir."

"Sir, Mr. Barone . . . was uncertain at least until six o'clock in the morning that the Beverly Dive Team would, in fact, respond. Now, with that assumption, sir, would you consider it prudent just to have called the Beverly Dive Team?"

"If Petty Officer Barone . . . was confident . . . that that team was going to be able to respond within his comfort zone," Walters said, "then, yes, I think it was prudent."

"So, sir, we have divers that are absolutely critical, and we have the SAR mission coordinator who is expressing doubts and uncertainty about divers up until six o'clock in the morning, and you think it's still prudent to just call one dive team?"

Campbell objected. Saris overruled.

"Well, sir," Walters said. "I think that he was aware that it was a dive team that was on the alert status. I think he was given—and again, I hate to think—I can't speak of what he was thinking, because I don't know, but if I had to make an assumption, I would assume that his feeling was that it would take time for these folks to get together. He obviously was concerned about how long it would take to get together. But he was trusting that they were going to be able to do it."

"Sure, trust is a wonderful thing," Black said. "And the people in the boat were trusting the Coast Guard was going to be able to [rescue them]."

Campbell objected. Saris sustained the objection. Black sighed. "Well, sir," he continued. "You'll agree with me that the art of SAR includes making that one extra phone call?"

"It could, yes, sir."

"Did you put that in your article?"

"Yes, I did." Walters had written that the art of SAR includes, "responding to that nagging little voice that spurs you to make one more phone call."

"And, yet, you're sitting here saying that one call to the Beverly Dive Team was all that it took to do a good job in this case?" Black asked, voice raised.

"In his judgment," Walters said, "that's what he felt, yes, sir."

"And, sir, there certainly would have been no prohibition to have called every diver on that list to see who could get there first?"

"There was no requirement, either."

"I didn't ask if there was a requirement, sir," Black said. "I said there would be nothing inappropriate about that?"

"No, sir."

"And wouldn't you agree with me, sir, using the art of critical thinking and using the art, as you describe, of the SAR mission, where divers are critical, that you're going to take all reasonable steps to ensure that not only will you eventually get a diver, but you'll get a diver as soon as possible?"

"If Officer Barone felt that the team that had been contacted—"

"Sir, I'm asking you," Black said with clear anger in his voice. "I'm asking you, sir, wouldn't it have been prudent to keep calling divers in order to assure yourself that you're going to get the diver who's most able to respond when the diver's need is critical. Isn't that true?"

"It would be an option."

"Of course it would be an option. Isn't it true it would be the prudent thing to do?"

"No, sir."

"Are you worried about hurting the feelings of the first diver you call if you get a diver that can come sooner?" Black asked. "Is that the problem?"

"No, sir," Walters said.

" 'The SAR mission coordinator *must* use good judgment to modify, combine or bypass SAR stages and procedures to cope with unique, unusual or changing circumstances,' " Black read from the manual. "Isn't that true?"

"Yes, sir."

"And 'must' is a mandatory direction as that word is used, isn't that true?"

"Yes, sir."

"Nothing was done to change the attempt to get divers after the initial call to Beverly, isn't that true? No other calls were made to any other dive entity in order to see whether that diver would or would not be available and able to respond sooner?"

"No, sir."

"By the way," Black said, "a SAR rescue unit is a resource performing SAR operations?"

"Yes."

"That includes Coast Guard and non–Coast Guard entities that are involved in the rescue attempt, correct?"

"It could, yes, sir."

"There's no prohibition about having civilian entities involved in a SAR rescue, is there?"

"No, sir, not at all."

"Now, in the manual, it's very clear that communications are critical to a successful SAR rescue operation, isn't that true?"

"Yes, sir."

Black quoted from the manual: "SAR communications may be the most important and often the weakest link in the SAR system."

Walters agreed.

"Now, you're aware, sir, are you not, that the helicopter pilot, Commander Lindsey, made repeated requests to be . . . provided additional information as he proceeded to the scene. You are aware of that, aren't you?"

"I heard his testimony," Walters said. "I understand he called back to ask for more information, yes, sir."

"And, in fact, it was known at least 10 minutes before he took off that there were people alive, trapped inside the hull, correct?"

"Yes, sir."

"And it was Commander Lindsey, when he learned . . . that there were people trapped in the hull and there were divers available at Gloucester . . . he and his copilot are the ones who figured out it might be quicker for them to go from the scene to Gloucester, pick up the divers . . . bring them out and get them in the water [rather] than to send them all out in the 47-footer."

"Yes, sir, that was his testimony."

"Sir, don't you think he should have been fully informed of the facts as they became known," Black said, "which, in this case, meaning people trapped inside was known approximately 10 minutes before he was even airborne?"

Walters paused and said nothing.

"Are you having trouble with that question?" Black asked.

"It would have been good, yes, sir," Walters said.

"And it would have been simple to do, pick up the phone and call Air Station Cape Cod: 'Hey, latest word. People trapped inside the boat are alive. Pass it on to the helicopter.' "

"It would have been pretty easy, yes, sir," Walters said.

"Because the helicopter is in radio communication with people on the ground at Cape Cod, right? You were an air crewman."

"Yes, sir."

"So, there's no question it would have been prudent, and it would have been feasible, correct?"

"It could have been feasible. It's the SAR mission coordinator's decision as to whether or not the information was pertinent to the helicopter crew at that time."

"Sir—" Black said, sounding frustrated.

"He's asking your opinion," Judge Saris said. "Would it have been a wise thing to do to tell the helicopter pilot earlier about the people trapped inside?"

"Oh, yes."

"Sir, it is a fact that as approaching the scene, the crew of this helicopter, when learning . . . that people were alive and trapped in the hull and that divers were either at—or going to—Gloucester, they took it upon themselves to figure out they could get there sooner, that is, to Gloucester, pick up the divers, bring them out to the scene and get them in the water quicker than the 47-footer?" Black asked.

"Yes, sir."

"Isn't it just possible, sir, where the SAR communication may be the most important and often the weakest link in the SAR system, isn't it just possible, sir, that had the crew been informed of the true state before they took off, they might have suggested: 'Hey, we could get there sooner if we go right to Gloucester. We may be able to save 20 or 30 minutes.' "

"They could have done that, sir."

"And don't you think they would have?" Black asked.

"Not necessarily, sir, because there still was a concern of people in the water. [Barone's] concern was whether or not there were a potential for people to be in the water," Walters said. "So he wanted his fastest resource to get to the scene. That was a prudent decision [based] on the information."

"Absolutely, sir. Absolutely, sir. And I think you, in your opinion, state that Barone's choice . . . to hold the 47-footer for divers was prudent because he didn't know whether the helicopter could take off because of the weather conditions at Cape Cod."

"Yes, sir."

"Now, Mr. Barone testified that when he called Cape Cod, he was told, 'We're launching.' Do you know that?"

"No, sir, I do not."

When Black asked Walters if the Coast Guard's 41-footer could have searched for anyone in the water, Walters said a helicopter was more effective.

"Well, you know . . . that there were ten fishing vessels in the area and that a search had been made for people in the water?" Black asked.

"I didn't read that in the transcript, sir," Walters said. "I saw that there were fishing vessels in the area. I didn't see anything where it said they conducted a search."

"You know the tugboat looked and the barge looked and the *Scotia Boat Too* looked?"

"Looked and searched are two different things, sir," Walters said.

"Now, sir, alerting ships at sea . . . is often one of the most effective means of getting assistance to persons in distress the quickest. Isn't that true?"

"Yes, sir."

"And you'll agree with me the Coast Guard never in this case requested any available diver in the vicinity of this wreck: 'Please identify yourself and proceed to the scene if you're willing to assist,' or something to that effect? That was never done, was it?"

"No, sir."

"In fact, the urgent information broadcast never talked about people being trapped in the hull, correct?"

"No, sir."

"Never talked about a need for divers, correct?"

"No, sir."

"And, certainly, that would have been a prudent thing to do, wouldn't it?"

"Not necessarily, sir."

"Why not?" Judge Saris asked.

"Well, ma'am, the urgent marine broadcast is designed to get resources moving in that area to render assistance to people who are in the water, on the surface of the water," Walters said. "That's the primary context [in] which it's generally used. If I can make an analogy, ma'am, it's kind of like, you know, there's a fire alarm goes off, you've got a lot of people who run to the scene, but you don't necessarily want them all running into the burning building. It's the information to get the folks out there. . . . I have never seen a case where we have deviated much from the standard UMIB broadcast."

"I understand, sir," Black said. "And that goes right back to the art of search and rescue. You don't just do it because it's always done. You don't just send out an urgent marine information broadcast the same way they always go out. If you have a need, you make that need known to the people who may be out there that can help. Isn't that true?"

"Yes, sir."

"Now, sir, you're aware that there are specific provisions in the addendum regarding persons trapped in capsized vessels, correct?"

"Yes."

"And that is direct guidance to the on-scene commander, isn't it?"

"I'd have to look at it to see what the wording is, sir," Walters said.

"Sir, are you telling this Court that as you sit here, having prepared for this case, you're unable to tell us whether the provisions of Section 6.C.3 . . . are not intended to provide guidance to Coast Guard units responding to a situation?"

"You used different words, sir."

"Sir, you understand that that provision in the manual is intended to provide guidance and instruction to Coast Guard units that were on scene in a situation where persons were trapped in an overturned vessel?"

"Guidance, yes, sir," Walters said.

"Not instruction?" Black asked.

"Not instruction. Guidance, sir."

"What is the difference between guidance and instruction? You instruct people in your course," Black said. "Do you give them guidance or do you instruct them?"

"Sir, 'instruction' would be specific techniques to do something specific," Walters said. " 'Guidance' would be things that would be recommended that you might wish to consider."

Black asked Walters to look at the section in the Coast Guard Addendum to the National SAR Manual that lists procedures recommended for rescue of personnel trapped in a capsized vessel.

"Now, in utilizing good judgment," Black said, "you follow recommended procedures unless there's a specific cognizable reason not to, correct?"

"Yes, sir."

" 'Keep in contact.' Do you agree with that?"

"Yes, sir."

"And, as far as you know, that was being done by others . . . ?"

"By the tug, by the *Houma*, yes, sir."

" 'Stabilize the hull.' "

"Yes, sir."

"And you'll agree with me the only efforts to stabilize the hull in this case was to put a line around the skeg in the rear of the vessel?" Black asked.

"The on-site commander thought that was prudent."

"I didn't ask you if someone thought it was prudent," Black said. " 'Estimate the volume of air remaining.' That wasn't done, as far as you know, correct?"

"No, sir."

" 'Surface swimmers may attempt to direct trapped persons out but shall not dive under the vessel.' " Black read. "That wasn't tried, correct?"

"No."

"The surface swimmers didn't go into the water?"

"No, sir."

"And they certainly didn't go into the water to see whether there were lines readily available that could have been passed up to the tug to further stabilize the vessel, right?"

"No, sir."

" 'Inject clean air if possible.' That wasn't done?"

"No, sir."

"No attempt was made to tie off another vessel on the other side of the overturned *Heather Lynne* to help keep it from rolling?"

"No, sir."

"In fact, the on-scene commander got there and set up a security zone?"

"Yes, sir."

"He didn't follow any of these procedures, did he?"

"These recommended procedures," Walters said. "No, sir."

"Sir, I'd like you to assume that by not directing the helicopter to go to Gloucester that at least 20 minutes was lost not getting divers to the scene," Black said. "With that assumption, sir, was it prudent not to send the helicopter to Gloucester immediately?"

Campbell objected.

"I can't make that assumption, sir," Walters said.

"Well, yes, you can, sir, because I've asked you to do it," Black said.

Judge Saris interrupted and said, "If you assume some approximately 20 minutes could have been saved if the helicopter went directly from Cape Cod to Gloucester—"

"I can only make that assumption if I can also assume that the divers would have been there and been ready," Walters said. "In this case, the divers weren't there. They weren't ready. So I can't make that assumption. They weren't ready. They weren't there, and they weren't ready."

"Well, according to the log, they were there, sir," Black said, noting the divers had said they were ready to go at 6:20 A.M. "Now, you'll agree with me, sir, that the decision to call one or more divers isn't an either/or decision. In other words, calling one diver to ask for assistance does not rule out calling other divers."

"No, it does not."

"And, by the way, sir, you were aware that there were civilian divers, commercial divers, that were en route within 10 minutes of this accident?"

"I heard that, yes, sir."

"And no effort was made by the Coast Guard to get those divers on scene to assist the survivors, correct?"

"Yes, sir."

"Sir, you understand the significance of the meaning of time, don't you?"

"Absolutely, sir."

"In fact, the Coast Guard was nice enough to publish your change of command speech when you left Group Hampton Roads, and it was on the Internet?" Black asked.

"Yes, sir."

"And you said in that speech—and I take it you meant everything you said in that speech—?"

"Yes, sir."

"—and you said it because you believed it to be true?"

"Yes, sir."

"You said," Black began, reading a copy of Walters's speech, " 'So, as my last official counseling session with you, my direction is simple. Take my vision, use it, and pass it on. Remember: it's only just a minute, only sixty seconds in it. Forced upon me, can't refuse it, didn't seek it, didn't choose it. But it's up to me to use it. I must suffer if I lose it. Give account if I abuse it. It's only just a minute but eternity is in it.' "

Judge Saris smiled. Black looked up at Walters.

Walters paused and said, "Yes, sir."

"The eternity for these people trapped in that hull was two hours they sat there waiting for divers to get to that scene, isn't that true?"

"For them," the Coast Guard commander said. "Yes, sir."

» Kavkaz
January 30, 1999

ASIDE FROM THE CREW of the *Heather Lynne II*, no one had a better feel for minutes passing like an eternity than the two brothers who were trapped inside the turtled *Kavkaz*. Their iced-up, 37-foot fishing vessel was headed back to Homer, Alaska, on Saturday, January 30, 1999. At 4:30 P.M., a half hour before sunset, she made a course change in 12-foot seas and rolled over.

Vasily Kuzmin was the captain of the fishing vessel *Arizona*, the sister ship to *Kavkaz*, and had been traveling alongside her. He watched the *Kavkaz* capsize, called 911 in Homer, and asked the dispatcher to tell the Coast Guard that after the boat rolled, neither of the two men on board had surfaced. He was certain that his brother-in-law, Anton Sanarov, and Anton's brother Fred were trapped inside.

Air Station Kodiak launched a Jayhawk helicopter at 5:25 P.M. into snow squalls and wind gusts peaking at 90 miles an hour; the air temperature held steady at −17°F. The helicopter arrived on scene an hour later and searched in the darkness for two hours but found no sign of any adrift *Kavkaz* crew. At 8:15, two hours after being notified, the 110-foot Coast Guard cutter *Roanoke Island* arrived on scene, found the hull of the *Kavkaz* still floating on the surface, and searched for any adrift survivors until past 10 P.M. Icing spray and heavy seas prevented the *Roanoke Island* from going alongside the turtled *Kavkaz*, which would remain adrift overnight, so the cutter spent the rest of the night on anchor in Port Graham.

The next day, the *Roanoke Island* and a Coast Guard helicopter again searched for the floating *Kavkaz* and any adrift survivors. Port Graham resident and EMT Jeff McMullen, who had been following the rescue and overheard talk about the missing *Kavkaz* on the VHF radio in his home that morning, drove his truck along the coast. He spotted the red bottom of the blue-hulled *Kavkaz* about two hundred feet offshore, two miles north of the village. With his handheld VHF, he directed the Coast Guard to her, still upside down and afloat. McMullen launched his skiff and helped the crew of the *Arizona* tow the turtled *Kavkaz* to an old pier at an abandoned cannery.

At 11 A.M. on Sunday, nineteen hours after she'd capsized, McMullen, a few residents of Port Graham, and some Coast Guardsmen drove alongside *Kavkaz* in a skiff. They heard banging sounds from inside her hull and assumed it was debris floating around inside. Wally Burgess, a Coast Guard chief petty officer, wasn't convinced. He asked for a hammer and banged on the hull. Ice chipped away.

Then they heard a tap back.

Burgess tapped three more taps. They heard three taps back.

Burgess shouted, "If you can hear me, tap once!"

He heard one tap.

"Hang on!" Burgess shouted. "Divers are coming!"

Four pararescuers from the Air National Guard's 210th Rescue Squadron at Kulis Air National Guard Base in Anchorage, Alaska, arrived on scene about an hour later. These aircrew elite were trained to jump, rappel, or parachute into any combat or noncombat situation, with or without dive gear, to provide emergency rescue and treatment, but to the spectators who had gathered around the turtled boat, the divers appeared to take a long time donning their gear before dropping into the 39°F water. The divers swam beneath the surface and into the cabin of the *Kavkaz*, where they found Fred Sanarov blocking access to the tiny engine compartment. The divers could not see Anton Sanarov. They found no air pocket and could detect no pulse or signs of life in Fred Sanarov, so they assumed both trapped fishermen were dead. Feeling the effects of hypothermia, the divers left the water and Fred and Anton Sanarov behind; the *Roanoke Island* crew and the Port Graham public safety officer planned to remove the bodies at low tide. While the Coast Guard called the fishermen's wives and told them the men had died, the tide dropped around the now-grounded boat, and Wally Burgess and Coast Guard Chief John Beechwood gathered up their gear.

Then they heard moans and more taps.

At home, Jeff McMullen was putting on dry clothes when over his VHF he heard, "Jeff, the guy's alive!" He grabbed his coat and chain saw and ran out the door. Meanwhile, Beechwood tried to break a window in the *Kavkaz*'s wheelhouse, now exposed by the falling tide, with a fire ax, but it was built of Lexan and would not budge. So, with a cordless drill, they unscrewed the window and popped it out. Fellow Coast Guard petty officer Mark Davis slithered inside, where he reached Anton Sanarov. He tried to yank him out, but couldn't. Sanarov was wedged in the engine room against the fiberglass hull in a two-foot gap between a generator and a freshwater tank where, immersed in oily bilge water, he had found an air pocket.

"The only thing that crossed my mind is, 'what's the fastest way to get him out?' " Beechwood later remembered. "I made the decision to cut a hole in the hull because it was obvious that there was no way he was coming out the way he went in."

Davis drilled some guide holes and yelled to McMullen, who had arrived with his chain saw, to cut carefully because he would be one inch away from a man and a fuel tank. Everything was covered with diesel fuel. McMullen tried to hand the chain saw to Beechwood, but Beechwood could not start it so he handed it back and said, "It's your saw, so start it."

Using the chain saw as skillfully as a fillet knife, McMullen cut an 18-by-24-inch hole right down to the insulation that lined the hull inside. Beechwood started the final cut with an 18-volt cordless circular saw. As insulation began to fall, Davis tried to protect Sanarov with a blanket. Once they had cut the hole, McMullen reached in and, with the help of a fellow EMT, pulled the forty-one-year-old Sanarov out onto a stretcher lined with blankets. It was 4:13 P.M. on Sunday. Sanarov's core body temperature had fallen to 87°F, but he had survived being trapped in a capsized boat for almost twenty-four hours, despite being passed up for dead—twice.

The Coast Guard later suggested that Sanarov, with his prolonged exposure to cold water, had probably experienced the mammalian dive reflex, in which a person's core temperature drops sharply. While he was still alive, he may have appeared dead.

"Believe me," Sanarov said later. "It was cold."

But his brother, Fred, was dead; he left behind a wife and three sons.

Both men had survival suits on, but Fred's zipper had failed in a six-inch section, and near-freezing seawater had leaked into his suit. On Monday, Anton Sanarov was recovering in a hospital, talking with his family, and "thanking the Lord." Explaining what had happened to a reporter from the *Anchorage Daily News*, he said he and his brother had seen searchers' lights shining through windows and vents. They had spent the night waiting and talking.

"What else can we do, tell me?" Sanarov asked the reporter. "We didn't have much of a choice. All we did was ask each other, 'Are you OK?' and the answer was, 'OK.' "

But he had hope. He knew that his brother-in-law had watched the boat roll. In Port Graham, Sanarov could hear voices around the hull and someone banging.

"I felt that somebody was out there," he recalled, "and that we could get rescued."

Anton Sanarov, a certified diver, had been born in China, lived in Brazil, and moved to the United States in 1965. A Russian Old Believer—the conservative Russian Orthodox sect many of whose members emigrated from Russia in the twentieth century to escape Communist persecution—he lived with his wife and seven children in Voznesenka, Alaska, one of the villages on the Kenai Peninsula near the head of Kachemak Bay. He had fished year-round—salmon in the summer, gray cod the rest of the year—since 1977 and had bought *Kavkaz* in 1978.

In January 1999, while the rest of the nation mourned the string of tragic clam boat sinkings on the East Coast, he and his brother caught 11,000 pounds of gray cod during a ten-day longlining trip. Short on groceries and without a tender, Sanarov was heading home on Saturday afternoon, January 30, while his brother-in-law aboard the *Arizona* traveled alongside. They were trying to round Point Pogibshi at the southern tip of Kachemak Bay, about 18 nautical miles from Homer, when they ran into 12-foot seas and 30 knots of wind, which heaved freezing spray over the boat faster than they could chip it off. Kuzmin, aboard the *Arizona*, called and said he'd have to turn around and run with the swells to try to knock off more ice. Sanarov agreed that was a good idea—he had ice building up on his own mast, deckhouse, and scuppers—so he turned, too. After turning the *Arizona*, Kuzmin looked back at *Kavkaz* and watched with wide eyes as she rolled a little from side to side. *Kavkaz* had started taking on water in the stern. Roiling riptides came at the boat from every direction. As she turned, she took on a list that held her on her side.

"And poof," Sanarov told the newspaper reporter. "Upside down. It was just a matter of seconds."

As water flooded into the cabin, the men struggled to get into their cumbersome, orange neoprene survival suits and stay with the pocket of air. Floor hatches fell on them as the flotation of their survival suits forced them into the engine compartment. Sanarov shut off the engine. Wires to the battery sparked and caught fire, filling the air pocket with smoke. All around them, gear was banging and floating. They tried to calm each other down by saying that help was nearby. He recalled, "We kept waiting. We kept thinking that help should be coming." But sometime during the night, his thirty-five-year-old brother succumbed to hypothermia.

Sanarov credited McMullen with saving his life and figured the least he could do was give McMullen his boat. Sanarov later bought himself a 41-footer, a little wider, named *Cascade*, and continued fishing. McMullen, meanwhile, took the *Kavkaz* seining.

Haunted by the memories of that tragic weekend, Sanarov and his family were also angry at the Coast Guard, particularly because it had waited a whole day before trying to retrieve the trapped fishermen.

"If the Coast Guard had responded earlier, Fred would have been alive," Anton Sanarov said. "They anchored up in the bay and let us drift around all night. [The *Roanoke Island* crew] did nothing. Vasily asked them to put a blinking light or something on the boat to at least track it while it drifted, but they did nothing. . . . The Coast Guard—they're out there to rescue people. That's what our tax dollars are for."

In the Coast Guard's defense, John Beechwood said there was a strobelight on the life raft, still attached and floating near the *Kavkaz*. He said the cutter *Roanoke Island*, which was in "maintenance status" when it launched, did so without it's small boat, a rigid-hull inflatable that was on a trailer in the shop. The Coast Guard could not go alongside the *Kavkaz* without its small boat, nor could it tow the fishing vessel to shore, given the draft of the cutter. Therefore, it was forced to rely on the help offered by Port Graham residents like McMullen. "What some may see as lack of action, I understand, but that's because we had no options. There was nothing we could do that night without our small boat."

Anton Sanarov said the Air National Guard divers could not have checked on Fred or taken his pulse, because doing so was impossible through a thick neoprene survival suit. Instead, he figured, they swam inside the cabin, took a quick peek, and incorrectly assumed the men had died.

Sanarov had a message to send to the rescuers who had passed him up for dead.

"In the courts of this land, a person is innocent until proven guilty," he said. "In an overturned boat, the crew is alive until proven dead."

»The Rescue Divers

AT 5:40 A.M. on September 5, 1996, the Beverly Fire Department dispatcher, sitting on the second floor of a brick fire station at the corner of a tree-lined street, answered a call from the Coast Guard asking if the department's dive team could assist with a fishing boat that had capsized northeast of Cape Ann. The dispatcher asked the Coast Guardsman how the divers would get out to the scene. If the team could muster to Gloucester, the Coast Guard said, it would give them a ride out to the turtled boat. As the dispatcher noted this telephone call in his log, Richard Burgess and his crew were hearing the first cries for help from inside the *Heather Lynne II.*

The dispatcher alerted on-duty firefighters and divers Darryl Boardman and Steve White. They ran down to the apparatus floor and began preparing the dive van, dwarfed by a couple of bright red fire trucks, for a trip to Gloucester. Firefighter and diver Mike McCadden was also on duty, but there was talk that he'd stay behind because no one was sure how many divers would be needed. Most of the team would later remember the initial call from the Coast Guard as more an alert to the developing situation and a request that they be on standby for a *possible* dispatch. They would remember some initial confusion as to what response was called for. There was talk of an overturned vessel, something about people possibly trapped but maybe adrift in the water. It might be a surface rescue, but they also heard something about the boat being sunk in up to 240 feet of water. If the latter were true, the divers thought, you've got the wrong people. Call the Navy. This standby status confused them, they said, because the fire department didn't usually receive that kind of request—either they were needed immediately or they weren't needed at all.

The Coast Guard called back a few minutes before six o'clock. The dispatcher noted at 6:01 A.M.: "Coast Guard now advises three people trapped inside an air pocket," and it was this call that compelled the dispatcher to activate the entire team. He called four dive team members at their homes, told them the Coast Guard had a capsized vessel seven miles off the coast with victims trapped inside, and requested that team members muster at the fire station so they could drive to Gloucester together.

Darryl Boardman and Steve White, along with off-duty firefighter William Walsh, jumped into the red dive rescue van, a converted U.S. Air Force truck built in 1982. They turned onto Hale Street with the siren blaring. Inside the van were shelves filled with scuba diving gear, safety lines, medical equipment, an inflatable boat, and a small outboard motor. The van could hold everything the team needed, but it wasn't built for speed. It shook and wobbled as White pushed its top speed of 65 miles an hour up Route 128 toward Gloucester, 14 miles away. It didn't take long for other team members to pass them. Meanwhile, dive team leader Robert Atherton Jr., who had been at home when the dispatcher's call woke him up, bolted out of bed, dressed, jumped into his truck, and headed straight to Gloucester. On the way he called Beverly Fire Chief Kenneth Pelonzi, who said he was already en route. Atherton caught up with the chief on the highway and followed him to Gloucester.

Firefighter Jeff Sirois, who was also asleep at home, mustered at the fire station with McCadden. Sirois wanted to take a fire department car because he knew he could speed to Gloucester faster in a car equipped with a siren and flashing lights. Team member Frank Kavanaugh would join them but, when reached at home, said that he'd first have to go to the city's other station out by Beverly Farms to get his dive gear; this was the one morning he didn't happen to have his gear in his car. He drove about four miles to the other end of town and back again, and then all three—Sirois, McCadden, and Kavanaugh—sped toward Gloucester and caught up with the dive van along the way. All seven divers and the fire chief arrived at the Gloucester Coast Guard station within minutes of each other. It was about 6:20 A.M.

Kevin Angerstein met them in the parking lot and informed them that they'd be taken to the capsized boat aboard the Coast Guard's 47-footer. He offered little further information. He did not tell them about the cries for help heard from inside the *Heather Lynne II.* The divers put on their suits, grabbed their diving gear, and considered what extra rescue items to take and what to leave behind. The firefighters expected to assist the Coast Guard by serving as scuba divers and not as trained emergency medical technicians. They took extra ropes, but they left their medical equipment in the dive van.

As they began loading air tanks, weight belts, and other gear onto the 47-footer, a Coast Guardsman announced that there had been a change in plans. A Jayhawk helicopter was headed their way and would fly a few divers to the scene; the rest of the team would stick to the initial plan and travel aboard the 47-footer. The team needed to figure out fast who would travel aboard the helicopter. Steve White later remembered, "The Coast Guard did not want to wait."

Six divers huddled around Atherton. They knew Atherton and Sirois were the team's most experienced divers and had trained together, so it made sense that they should go. Joining them would be EMTs White and McCadden. McCadden was the most experienced medical person on the team, and worked off-duty for an ambulance company as an EMT. White, who had served in the Army, loved helicopters and had been in and out of them on several occasions. He agreed to go aboard the helicopter and serve as the dive team's tender and line handler, someone who would oversee the rescue from a boat. Since he expected to be responding to a capsized boat with fishermen possibly trapped inside—he would later recall hearing something about scratching, kicking, and clawing coming from inside the boat—he assumed his job would be to make sure the scene was safe before Sirois and Atherton dove in. Someone grabbed Atherton's dive gear off the 47-footer and hustled it back up to the helicopter pad, where the gear for Sirois and White had already been placed. McCadden waited with them for the helicopter to arrive. He later remembered the wait as "an extremely short five to ten minutes."

While the four waited for the helicopter, the rest of the team—divers Boardman, Walsh, and Kavanaugh, along with Fire Chief Pelonzi—loaded their gear onto the 47-footer and departed, with Angerstein at the helm. At 6:36 A.M., Craig Lindsey landed the helicopter and the crew made room for the four divers and their gear. After a safety briefing, the helicopter sped away 6 minutes later and headed back out to the waters off Cape Ann. En route, a myriad of thoughts went through the four divers' minds. They had never trained with the Coast Guard for a situation like this. Three of the four had never been aboard a helicopter or a fishing boat.

THE BEVERLY FIRE DEPARTMENT DIVE TEAM had formed following a tragic local drowning. One frigid December day in 1989, a twenty-year-old woman lost control of her car and drove off the Kernwood Bridge into the icy Danvers River twenty feet below. She was found clinging to a bridge piling about three hundred yards away. Her three young children and her fifty-six-year-old mother were still trapped inside the car. The neighboring Salem Police Dive Team struggled to free the hypothermic grandmother and kids, but all four died at Beverly Hospital the next day. The Beverly firefighters had responded to the scene, but without a dive team of their own could do nothing but watch. They decided to do something about it. In 1990, they began the years-long training needed to become public safety divers. In 1996 they had responded to a handful of calls, most of them in lakes and rivers. Notwithstanding the Coast Guard's apparent confidence in them, the morning of September 5, 1996, was their first open ocean call.

Since Atherton and Sirois would be the two divers to swim inside the turtled *Heather Lynne II*, they used the minutes flying out to the scene to try to glean more information from the helicopter crew. They ran through checklists and brainstormed options. They talked about giving one of the fishermen a secondary air source—either a spare regulator or an independent air source in what's known as a pony bottle—but they worried about finding them in a panic mode. Then they tried to imagine what they'd see underwater.

"Until we got there," Sirois said, "I had no idea what to expect."

With more than eighty collective years of firefighting experience, however, they had rescued plenty of people from peril ashore. As they sped toward the scene aboard the noisy helicopter, they remained focused and optimistic. They expected to save the trapped fishermen.

"My mindset [was], 'What's my job and what am I going to do when I get there?' " McCadden later said. "Our jobs were not clear right away. . . . But if you're going to say they're already gone, then you might as well not even go. We're not the judge and jury. We go and let someone else decide—God or whomever you believe—what happens."

DRESSED IN HIS FIREMAN BLUES, Robert Atherton sat in the witness chair one early morning of the trial and told attorney Peter Black that, before 1996, the team had not participated in any formal training initiated by the Coast Guard. Atherton recalled that twice the team had participated in drills alongside the Coast Guard and other municipal and federal agencies, although none of the dive training involved the use of Coast Guard helicopters. Atherton, as the dive team member in charge of the team's training, said he personally had had no interaction with the Coast Guard prior to this accident. In fact, Black reminded him, he had characterized his training with the Coast Guard before this incident as "half-assed."

Atherton offered an abridged version of how the team assembled that morning and how he came to be aboard the Coast Guard's helicopter. Black asked him what he was told once he was aboard.

"The pilot's aide, during transport, I had asked him if he had a better understanding of what . . . our team was expecting to find once we arrived," Atherton said. "He had told us on a clearer note that there was a capsized vessel, indeed, and that there was possibly victims trapped inside the vessel. And that we were required to extricate the victims as quickly as we could."

"Now, sir, you were told there were *possibly* victims inside, not that there *were* victims inside?" Black asked.

"There was no verification on whether or not the gentlemen in question were alive or not alive."

"You were just going under the assumption that they might be alive?"

"Correct."

"Were you ever told before you entered the water," Black said, "that sounds and voices had been heard coming from inside the vessel?"

"Yes, I was."

"When was that?" Black asked, knowing that after the divers were lowered to the 41-footer, they were transferred to the tug *Houma*. "When you were on the tugboat?"

Atherton said it was. As he and his two fellow divers arrived on board the tug, they heard yelling and chaotic screaming between the tug crew and Coast Guard personnel. He tried to pay little attention to them and instead focused on the task that lay ahead. His first priority was to make sure the boat was secure and safe enough for them to swim inside her. He looked at the way the *Heather Lynne II* was tied to the tug.

"Can you tell us," Black asked, "whether or not, when you did that, you felt the vessel was adequately secured and stabilized for you to enter it?"

Atherton paused and said nothing. He looked at Judge Saris and then at Black.

"No, it was not," he said. He paused as the courtroom fell silent. "The boat was not adequately tied off in order for us to perform our rescue immediately."

WHEN THE HELICOPTER reached the scene, the divers looked out of the wide door and saw the red *Houma* tied alongside the green belly of the *Heather Lynne II*. A cluster of fishing boats idled nearby. The helicopter crew discussed what would be the best way to lower Atherton, Sirois, White, and their gear to the 41-footer and settled on using a metal basket in which they'd be lowered one at a time. The final, fourth, basket drop would lower their gear. The 41-footer idled a quarter to a half mile away from the *Heather Lynne II*, far enough so that the helicopter's rotor wash, a wind estimated at up to 150 miles an hour that could flip a small car, would not endanger the overturned vessel's stability. As each diver climbed into the metal basket, the flight mechanic instructed him to hold on. Once they reached the deck of the 41-footer, the helicopter moved a little closer to the *Heather Lynne II* and Coast Guard rescue swimmer Fred Fjin jumped into the water and swam about a hundred yards to the scene.

McCadden, alone in the helicopter with the two pilots and the flight mechanic, looked out at the scene below and tried to prepare for the unexpected.

Aboard the 41-footer, Atherton walked into the wheelhouse to try to learn more about the situation they'd be facing. He discussed with Christian Smith, the coxswain, how the team should deploy into the water. They decided it would be best to work off the tug, a large and stable platform, and minutes later they tied up alongside it. White, Atherton, and Sirois passed their gear up to the tug crew and climbed aboard. Sirois was surprised to see the familiar face of *Houma*'s mate, Mike Simpson; they had attended the same high school. Simpson was just as surprised.

"The whole thing was so surreal," Simpson said later. "I was not embarrassed, really. Maybe it was a comfort. It was just so surreal. There's this whole big ocean, and then there's guys you went to school with [arriving to help]."

Simpson and the rest of the *Houma's* crew told Sirois and Atherton about voices and tapping coming from inside the boat. Until that point, Sirois and Atherton had been told that a boat had overturned with *possible* victims trapped inside; now the tug crew said there was no doubt there were men trapped inside. Captain Allen Breen said he thought he had briefly glimpsed a hand by the tinted wheelhouse window, so maybe they should start their search there. Breen said he was concerned about his own boat and his crew. He feared the *Heather Lynne II* would burp, sink, and take his tug down with it. He wanted the rescuers to hurry. It had been 10 to 12 minutes since the *Heather Lynne II* had rolled onto her side.

As Sirois donned his gear, all he could be sure of was that he was going into the water to do the best he could. He looked at Simpson and said, "No matter what, I'm makin' sure I get back out of this." His wife was about to have a baby. Sirois asked how deep the water was. Someone said it was 180 feet deep; they were trained and equipped to go only to about 130 feet. With their dive gear, he believed, 180 feet would have meant death for them.

"We weren't prepared to go that deep," Sirois said, "if the boat sank while we were in it."

As Atherton and Sirois made final preparations, the third diver, Steve White, looked at the *Heather Lynne II*. He looked at the line that had been tied to her stern. He looked at the bow. He didn't know that the *Heather Lynne II* had been edging away from the *Houma* all morning, but he did know that the scene didn't look very secure to him. White requested that another line be tied onto a steel staple at the *Heather Lynne II*'s midships, but the staple broke.

"It looked like it was trying to fight itself," White later remembered, "and I wondered why they didn't just back off and let it roll."

Atherton and Sirois jumped off the *Houma* and into the calm, cold water. Atherton found the bow line of the *Heather Lynne II* floating 8 feet beneath the surface. He handed it up to the tug and they attached another line to it. Now that the stern *and* the bow were tied off—something Bob Yeomans and other fishermen had wanted to do at least an hour earlier—the scene looked as safe as it was going to get. It was 7:06 A.M. It had been 19 minutes since the divers had arrived overhead in the helicopter and

Captain Breen had last reported hearing knocking in the hull, 13 minutes since the *Heather Lynne II* had rolled 45 degrees away from the tug, and 11 minutes since Breen had told Group Boston, "We haven't heard the men knocking for a while." Later it would be unclear whether the knocking had continued until the moment the boat rolled, expelling air.

Atherton and Sirois dropped a few feet beneath the surface and swam along the boat's port side. Through her tinted Lexan windows they could see into the flooded wheelhouse, where they found Captain Jeffrey Hutchins and John Michael Lowther suspended upright in the water, as motionless as lobster pot buoys. No air pocket remained. Looking inside the boat with their flashlights was like looking into a dark cave; upside down, the hull blocked the strengthening sunlight. Mike Simpson, who was chain smoking as he paced the deck of the *Houma*, remembered that when the divers surfaced, they said it was a "complete horror show" underwater and asked to borrow a hand saw that they could use to cut away a wooden beam and make it easier to remove the fishermen. Atherton later said that in the end they did not need the saw.

"We figured if we found someone that was conscious, we'd have to go into the boat a different way, but when they are unconscious the rescue is simple. You just pack and screw," Atherton said, meaning that if the men were unconscious, the priority would shift to getting them out as quickly as possible so they could receive medical attention.

The divers found a tear in the forward port corner of the wooden pilothouse roof. Sirois ripped away wood and debris to create a 32-by-36-inch hole, then wiggled into the hole up to his chest. From there he reached a little farther and grabbed Hutchins by the ankle. Hutchins didn't respond. Sirois pulled Hutchins from the wreckage and dragged him, dressed in dungarees, T-shirt, an unbuttoned flannel shirt, and socks, the few feet to the surface. The Coast Guard's rescue swimmer grabbed the captain's lifeless body and swam him over to the 41-footer. Its young crew pulled Hutchins out of the water and laid him on the gray steel deck, and a seaman apprentice prepared for CPR. It was 7:14 A.M., two hours after the collision, 21 minutes after the *Heather Lynne II* had rolled onto her side, and at least that long since the tapping had stopped.

Medical professionals describe a Golden Hour, in which the race to get a person who has been in a tragic accident to the nearest trauma center can make a life-or-death difference. Also regarded as the "critical hour," the phrase was coined in the early 1970s by former World War II Army surgeon Dr. R. Adams Cowley, a trauma expert in Maryland. He regarded shock trauma as the uncoupling of body functions, which is the process of dying. If that unraveling could be interrupted early enough—within the first hour—then survival was possible. If too much time passed, however, the damage would be irreparable and the victim would die. To rescue personnel like Atherton and Sirois, Cowley's Golden Hour has come to mean the period of time—not always exactly 60 minutes—in which, depending on the injuries, there remains a chance to intervene and stop the body's dying. If the Golden Hour for the crew of the *Heather Lynne II* had begun with the loss of their air pocket at 6:53, they needed to be at a trauma center within 40 minutes to have some hope of survival. Given the conditions they had suffered for more than 90 minutes prior to 6:53, perhaps 40 minutes wasn't soon enough.

At 7:16 A.M., Christian Smith called Barone at Group Boston.

"One crewman [is] on board," Smith reported. "He's not breathing, uh, [we're] trying to get the water out of his mouth [and] start CPR. Request directions—he still has a lot of color to him."

"Request you commence CPR as necessary," Barone said. "As the 47 arrives, they can assist with CPR. We'll try and get all three in the helo at once unless there's a severe delay."

Smith told Barone that he had also "advised Marine Services not to put divers in the water," but that they—Michael Goodridge and Jay Lesynski—had gone in anyway. Minutes earlier, while standing on board the *Houma* and watching for Sirois and Atherton, Steve White had seen a 24-foot boat with the names "Marine Services" and "TowBoatU.S." painted on its side race into the scene and drop its engine to an idle. Two divers jumped into the water. Smith and White yelled to them to turn back. White didn't know who they were and he didn't want them to get in the way of Atherton and Sirois. One diver remained on the surface. The other one headed straight for the *Heather Lynne II*.

After delivering Hutchins to the rescue swimmer, Atherton and Sirois had dropped back underwater and returned to the hole in the pilothouse roof. Atherton reached into the dark cabin but couldn't get hold of John Michael Lowther. Sirois pushed Atherton in up to his waist, and he was then able to grab Lowther, who was wearing only a pair of cut-off dungarees, by his bare feet. As he pulled Lowther out of the torn roof, he scraped Lowther's back on some protruding nails. Then Atherton headed for the surface. Suspended in the water over him was Goodridge, who looked down and saw Atherton bringing Lowther up. Goodridge yelled over to Ted Rurak on the *Retriever* and asked him to back up and open his tuna door, which exposed his fiberglass deck level with the sea. Goodridge helped as Rurak and his mate grabbed the limp body of John Michael Lowther, pulled him in through the tuna door and laid him on the deck. Lowther was not breathing but still had some color. It was 7:18 A.M.

Meanwhile, Atherton and Sirois had dropped beneath the surface again to look for Kevin Foster. They returned to the windows and scanned the flooded interior with their flashlights, but they couldn't see him. They swam along the port side toward the stern, then turned and swam under the roof and through the partially opened pilothouse door. A chain was stretched taut across the middle of the door, and they had to work their way around it and other fishing gear that choked the passages. It was a real mess. It's no wonder, the divers thought, that the men couldn't find their way out in the dark through all the debris.

But with daylight now and with the boat no longer directly upside down, the divers could see the surface of the water through the portside windows. They found Foster farther inside, near the helm. He had probably been just three feet or so from Hutchins and Lowther, as all three were found together in the flooded pilothouse, but because Foster was closer to the starboard side, the divers had not seen him right away when they reached in through the hole in the roof to port. The open hatch to the engine compartment was right below the helm, or, from where Foster was found, right above him. At first all they saw was a dark beard and a lot of hair. Then they could see that Foster was suspended in the water, hunched over, wearing jeans, a T-shirt, and one sock.

Atherton grabbed Foster and started swimming out of the boat. Sirois helped by grabbing one arm, and together they worked Foster out through the pilothouse door and started swimming him spread-eagled, with his back facing the sunlight, toward the surface about ten feet above them. Atherton looked up and saw a diver swimming down to them, so they handed Foster over and the lone diver took him up the rest of the way. Atherton figured the diver was one of his own team members. They were glad to see him because these fishermen were big, heavy men, and by then Atherton and Sirois were exhausted.

When they surfaced, they found out the diver wasn't one of their teammates.

"I asked him who he was," Atherton said later, "and he said, 'I'm Mike Goodridge and these are my friends.' And I told him to get out of the water, but he wouldn't listen to me."

At the surface, Goodridge rolled Foster over and started CPR while Lesynski, holding Foster's feet, helped Goodridge swim Foster over to a small center-console fishing boat that was nearby. Goodridge picked this boat because its low sides would make an easier lift for Foster. Besides, no one else was offering assistance. The fishing boat's crew pulled Foster up and laid him on deck. Goodridge climbed aboard and continued CPR as they raced over to the Coast Guard's 47-footer, which had just arrived on scene. The 47-footer crew lifted Foster aboard at 7:26 A.M., and Goodridge jumped on with them. With Foster laid out on the aft deck, Goodridge resumed CPR. He yelled for assistance and medical equipment, like a pocket mask (a plastic barrier that protects the rescuer from any diseases the victim might have), but the Coast Guardsmen offered neither. Goodridge would later remember that the Coast Guard crew watched him do CPR on his own until the helicopter hovered overhead and hoisted Foster up.

Meanwhile, Atherton and Sirois floated on the surface and caught their breaths. They were uncomfortable in this wide, deep ocean. Sirois saw a whale surface not far away and thought, as he later recalled, he might "get chumped." The Coast Guard wanted to confirm that there were definitely three people on board. John Frawley aboard the *Blue Heron* said he had seen the boat leave the dock and that there had been three people on board, but owner Ted Rurak wasn't so certain.

"I'm sure there was [at least] three," he said over the VHF radio, "but I'm not sure [whether] there was four. But I'm sure there was three aboard. I don't know if they took an extra guy with them."

Another fisherman called Rurak and said he was sure there had been just three on board, "Jeff, J'Mike, and Kevin." But Rurak feared Jimmy Bashaw, a close friend who often accompanied Hutchins, might also have been with them, so Atherton and Sirois dropped back underwater at 7:32 A.M. and again began to search the boat. They struggled to maneuver their way through the dark interior amidst debris and gear. Everything that floated—pillows, cushions, coolers, wooden boards, paper, and plastic debris—filled the flooded cabin. Dropping like curtains among the gear were lines, nets, and chains.

It was scary.

"Every step, I was going like this—" Sirois said later, stretching out his arms as if to ward off whatever might appear before him. "Know what I kept thinking of? *Jaws*, when they go into that dark place and that guy pops up."

Atherton was worried less about what he couldn't see than what he could see around him. He later said, "I didn't know how much fuel was there, and if there were electrical currents in the water. My biggest concern was getting tangled up." After searching the inside of the boat and finding no one else, they surfaced and climbed back on board the tug.

KEVIN ANGERSTEIN HAD ARRIVED in the 47-footer with the rest of the Beverly Dive Team at 7:13 A.M. On the way out to the scene, Angerstein later remembered, he had been feeling optimistic.

"If anything, this . . . really fit into what appeared to be a simple case," Angerstein said. "You know a bad tragedy happened, but we know somebody's alive. We got them in a trapped hull. It's secured as best we can. We got a dive team showing up. So everybody actually felt good about it. I remember heading out on the 47, talking to the fire chief and talking to my crew, saying, 'Hey, you know, despite what happened, something's going to be good for somebody here.' And . . . [then] I remember hearing a call from my 41 that was out there saying the knocking had stopped. And that's when it sank in that, wow, this might not be the case."

The dive team onboard the 47-footer had brought ropes and marking buoys with them. While they were en route, Coast Guardsmen told them the *Heather Lynne II* was tied up alongside the tug and people were possibly alive inside, because people on scene had heard tapping. These firefighters expected to be assisting as backup divers. Then word came that Atherton and Sirois had pulled three fishermen out of the capsized *Heather Lynne II* and that none of them were showing any vital signs. As firefighter and diver William Walsh arrived on scene, he tried to make sense of what was happening. His first impression was of the beauty of the whole thing. It was so peaceful. Whales and dolphins surfaced through gently rolling waves.

"It was a beautiful scenario," he said, "and then amongst that, there is something so horrible. It was really pretty out there, and it was hard to believe what had happened. There were the pretty fishing boats [gathered around]—they were beautiful boats—and then here's this boat with just the stern section stuck in the air."

Walsh, whose father had been the police chief and had been friends with the parents of Mike Simpson, had grown up around boats. His uncle's cousin had a fishing boat in Nova Scotia, and sometimes he went along. He'd been diving in Cape Ann waters, mostly searching for lobsters, since he was thirteen years old. The trouble was that he got seasick easily. So, on this morning, he wasn't feeling well by the time they arrived on scene. When they pulled up alongside the 41-footer sometime between 7:18 and 7:25, Walsh saw Hutchins and Lowther, who had been transferred from the *Retriever*, lying on the deck unattended, even though Barone had told Smith at 7:16 A.M., "Request you commence CPR as necessary." Maybe the crew of the 41-footer, which Smith had reported was trying to get the water out of Hutchins's mouth, no longer felt CPR was needed or useful, but it was instinct and training that compelled Walsh and Boardman to jump on board and begin CPR on both victims. The Coast Guardsmen had no pocket masks and it didn't look to Walsh as if they were quite sure what to do. Steve White could have been administering CPR in the previous minutes except that White was on the tug. Christian Smith, coxswain of the 41-footer, would later say he wasn't about to tell a trained dive team how to go about their business.

"It was a pretty somber situation," Walsh said. "I was ready to be [one of the] backup divers and the next thing I know, we're in a medical situation, an ill-equipped medical situation. . . . And they [had] probably just perished before we arrived."

Walsh and Boardman, wishing they had brought their own medical equipment with them instead of leaving it ashore in the dive rescue van, continued CPR despite Walsh's queasy stomach.

"I get seasick just looking at the water, and the exhaust from the 47 was right in our faces," Walsh said, "and the boats are going up and down. And we're doing mouth to mouth, and the guys are reeking of fuel."

BY THE TIME Walsh and Boardman reached them, Lowther and Hutchins had lost their color and were pretty blue. As the firefighters began CPR, white froth bubbled from the two fishermen's mouths. After a few minutes, word came that the fishermen would be hoisted up to the helicopter. The Coast Guardsmen ordered Walsh and Boardman to stop CPR because Coast Guard regulations forbade any unauthorized personnel from being on deck during helicopter hoisting operations. So they went down into the cabin of the 41-footer, where Walsh, dizzy and nauseous, vomited out the window.

At 7:26, while Hutchins was being hoisted up to the helicopter, Foster was hauled aboard the 47-footer, and Goodridge followed after to resume CPR. Beverly Fire Chief Pelonzi and Frank Kavanaugh had just been ordered below in preparation for Foster's helicopter hoisting. Kavanaugh remembered that the lack of onboard medical equipment made for an awkward situation. He later said, "The Coast Guard knew that the fire department was there . . . as divers but then we became, well, we were all geared up to go in the water, we had some guys in drysuits and it's cumbersome, and then we've got [a medical situation]."

BY THE TIME the hoisting operation began, diver McCadden, up in the helicopter, had lost touch with the operation on the water. Since he couldn't speak to his team members directly, he was unsure what was going on, but he did his best to pull some medical equipment together. He tried to get an update on the fishermen's status, and he asked the Coast Guard how many he'd be treating. At first he was told just one fisherman. The next thing he knew, three fishermen were being hoisted aboard, followed by the Coast Guard rescue swimmer.

"We got one guy and then another and I said to the crew chief, 'Are we getting another?' And he said, 'yeah,' and I thought, 'whoa, who made this plan?' " McCadden later recalled. "I was alone and I asked for help. I told them to get me firefighter Steve White. I was looking at the situation, and I needed someone who could hold his own."

When White arrived inside the noisy helicopter, he remembered, "that's when the fun really began." When the hoisting was completed at 7:57, there were two firefighters to attend to the three fishermen.

Throughout the 19-minute flight to Boston, McCadden gave the fishermen oxygen while White pushed on their chests. Facing the tail of the helicopter, Hutchins lay on the right, with Lowther in the middle and Foster on the outside. Right away, the pilots realized the helicopter was too heavy, so they started throwing gear out the door. Anything they didn't need, they tossed—litter hoist, pumps, and the metal basket. There were four Coast Guardsmen, two firefighters, and three big fishermen on board. At first the flight mechanic and Fred Fijn, the Coast Guard's rescue swimmer, let McCadden and White do their thing. Then Fijn, at McCadden's direction, joined in on the CPR.

"The scene inside the helicopter was an all-around clusterfuck, logistically, spacewise, equipmentwise, everything," McCadden said. "The rescue swimmer was [an] unbelievable [help]. It was a tough situation, and I put him to work right away. I was basically directing the operation. . . . The helicopter crew graciously let us have at it, which was unusual, because there are often interagency turf wars. 'Here,' the helo crew said, 'we'll keep you safe and get you there, and you take care of the victims.' The 'copter crew worked with us so well."

They still had hope for two of the three diesel-soaked fishermen—later, for reasons of patient confidentiality, they wouldn't say which two—though McCadden knew that ingesting all that toxic fuel hadn't helped—petroleum ingestion is poisonous, and it certainly didn't add to their chances of survival. In addition, ingesting salt water causes fluid buildup in the lungs. McCadden said later there wasn't a lot an EMT could do with petroleum ingestion once the hydrocarbons are in the lungs and have coated the membranes of the alveoli, blocking oxygen access to the bloodstream.

As the loaded helicopter sped toward Boston, the rescuers engaged in an intense race to induce signs of life from the three men, who were in cardiac arrest. McCadden, White, and Fijn worked from fisherman to fisherman to fisherman. They compressed chests, cleared vomit and diesel fuel from airways, and tried to get oxygen into lungs.

And prayed that at least one would pull through.

McCadden remembered that when they landed on a baseball field next door to a hospital, the helicopter door flew open and an ambulance crew grabbed the fishermen and pulled them out. Television cameras and reporters filmed their arrival. Lindsey shut the helicopter down. And then the scene around them turned eerily quiet. It was 8:19 A.M., three hours after Mike Simpson's Mayday call.

"It was like getting hit with a tornado," McCadden said, "and then the tornado goes by and you think, 'what happened?' "

Inside the helicopter it had been loud but not deafening. McCadden had been kneeling in the same position for so long that the ambulance crew had to carry him out of the helicopter. They set him on the grass, where he stayed until he could move his legs again. McCadden thought about the men; he still had hope for two of them. He knew he had done his best. It meant a lot to him when hospital staff later told him the men had clear airways. That was a big compliment.

White remembered the absolute silence once they landed, following what he knew he would always regard as the longest helicopter ride of his life.

"It was the strangest thing," he said. "The helicopter landed, the doors opened, the ambulance people scooped them up and grabbed them and started CPR. The last forty-five minutes had been completely chaotic, and then the pilots left and it was just Mike and I, just sitting there alone . . . with our legs up, and it went from instant mayhem to complete silence. Everybody was gone. . . . We sat there looking down and couldn't believe what had just happened."

»The Families

AT 6:40 A.M IN Jeffrey Hutchins's Byfield home—about five hours after Foster and Hutchins had left, forgotten their keys, locked themselves out, and Hutchins had kissed his girlfriend good-bye—the telephone began to ring. Then it stopped. Then it rang again, and stopped. Then it rang, kept ringing, finally waking up Hutchins's sister Jennifer. She was sleepy and confused and could not find the phone. She'd forgotten she'd left it in the living room for Foster, who had used it the night before to try to reach his girlfriend in Concord, New Hampshire. When Jennifer finally picked up, a friend was on the other end of the line. She said, "I think something's happened to the *Heather Lynne*."

Hysterically upset, Jennifer called her and Jeff's mother, Diane Fondow. Their stepfather, Bill, answered. Jennifer wasn't making much sense, but it sounded to Bill like something was wrong with the *Heather Lynne II*. They turned on the television and saw footage of the overturned boat broadcast live from a news helicopter at sea. Hutchins's mother cried. She called her daughter Jacqueline, who dropped the phone, threw on some clothes, and drove to their mother's house. They drove together to Hutchins's home, where Jacqueline called the Coast Guard and said, "I want to know what happened to my brother."

An official-sounding voice told her he couldn't say much right now, but that the men were inside and banging on the hull, and they'd be airlifted to Massachusetts General Hospital. She hung up the telephone expecting they'd be all right. They piled into Bill Fondow's car. Diane sat in front, while Jennifer, Jacqueline, and Hutchins's girlfriend, Jeanne Huberdeau, sat in back. They sped to Boston.

At 7:40 A.M., a few minutes after the Coast Guard helicopter hoisted Hutchins off the deck of the 41-footer, his family sat stuck in commuter traffic on the Tobin Bridge in Boston. Someone tuned the radio to station WBZ-AM. The newscaster said the crew of the *Heather Lynne II* had been removed with no vital signs. The women swore. They cried. They shouted. And then they cried some more.

At 8:07 A.M., Ann Lord, whose husband had called from sea and told her something had happened to the *Heather Lynne II*, called the Coast Guard. She was nearly certain her brother, Kevin Foster, was on board, and she wanted to know what was going on.

"Right now we have three people on board the helicopter, which is about to land at Mass General Hospital," Richard Barone told her, "and, uh, they're doing everything they can for the people."

"There's no vitals?"

"They're doing CPR right now, ma'am."

"All three?"

"Yes, ma'am, and they're dropping them off [to] an advanced life support team at Mass General."

"You don't have the names yet, no identification?"

"No, we don't."

"Do you know what they look like?" Lord asked.

"We don't know that yet, ma'am. They're gonna be at Mass General within minutes."

"Do you have a phone number for Mass General?"

Barone gave Lord the phone number, which she wrote down on a neon orange piece of paper. Later, she tucked it into a small wooden box labeled Mom's Recipes on the kitchen counter beneath the phone, where it would remain years later because she couldn't bring herself to throw it away.

Barone asked Lord if she knew how many people were on board the *Heather Lynne II*. She said she didn't know because she didn't see the boat get underway. She only knew that her brother was supposed to be one of them.

SINCE 6:50 A.M., Barone had been trying to line up a trauma center to provide emergency care to the fishermen once they were removed from the *Heather Lynne II*. He first called Massachusetts General Hospital and said they hoped to fly three survivors to them.

"We don't have them yet," he told the emergency room doctor, "but I want to give you a heads-up. What we got is a fishing vessel about ten miles off of Gloucester. It was run over by a tug and barge, and it's upside down on the surface. And we can hear people knocking on the hull. We've been trying to rescue them for quite some time. We finally got ahold of some divers to get them—hang on a second, it's sinking right now. It's a possibility we might have to fly some of these survivors in. I just got word that it's sinking, so I gotta run, but I'll keep you updated, sir." It was 6:53 A.M., and Barone had just been told that the *Heather Lynne II* had rolled forty-five degrees.

At 7:21, Barone called Air Station Cape Cod to ask if the helicopter, when it flew injured mariners to Mass General, usually landed on the pad on Nashua Street. The Air Station told him the helicopter always landed on the roof. At 7:42, Barone called the emergency room at Mass General to confirm that they'd be flying in three fishermen. Because there had been a shift change since his last call to the hospital almost an hour earlier, he had to brief the new staff. He said three fishermen were being hoisted aboard the helicopter and were undergoing CPR with no vital signs. He planned to fly all three to Mass General.

"All three?" the emergency room person asked.

"Yes, that's about the [only] option that we got," Barone said. "Got to get them to a trauma center. Is that feasible?"

"The treatment, if they're getting CPR, is to put them on a heart and lung machine. I'm not sure we'll be able to mobilize one, much less three."

Barone said he'd try to work something out with Boston City Hospital. He suggested that maybe they could drop one fisherman at Mass General and two at Boston City Hospital. At 7:46, Barone called the emergency room at Boston City Hospital.

"We've got a situation where we medevaced three victims, or patients, into Boston. Basically, CPR is being conducted. They were underwater for a short period of time," Barone said, explaining that he'd like to bring two fishermen to them. The doctor wasn't sure Boston City Hospital could handle all three.

"We really don't have many options," Barone said. "We want to get them to a trauma center."

"I understand," the doctor said. "[Mass] General said they can take only one?"

"They said, yeah, and try to work it out with you. You know, we have to do what we have to do. We're kind of hoping you can handle two."

The doctor said he'd check and call Barone back. At 7:53, a representative from EMS, an ambulance company, called Barone and said he had heard three fishermen were being flown in. Barone asked his advice on whether it would be faster to land at Boston City Hospital and have an ambulance take the third fisherman to Mass General, or whether they should fly the last one to Mass General after dropping two at City. The ambulance representative said the helicopter would probably be faster, although at Boston City Hospital the helicopter would have to land on a pad across the street and not on the roof.

Just before 8 A.M., Barone called the helicopter and said he wanted it to take two fishermen to Boston City Hospital and one to Mass General. The helicopter pilots wanted to take all three to Mass General because they were unfamiliar with the location of Boston City Hospital's helicopter pad. Barone explained that the fishermen had to be split up due to a shortage of medical equipment at Mass General. But the pilots were almost out of oxygen. They recommended dropping off the men at Mass General. If the fishermen then had to be moved, the ambulance crew moving them would have the appropriate medical equipment.

In the middle of this conversation, EMS called Barone and reported that Mass General would take two fishermen. Barone told EMS the helicopter had run out of oxygen and wanted to land on the roof at Mass General. EMS told Barone that would be a nightmare, because then they'd have to carry the fisherman destined for Boston City Hospital all the way through the hospital, down the elevators, and out to a waiting ambulance. Flying straight to Boston City Hospital and then transporting two by ambulance from the street-level helicopter pad would be a lot easier. Barone asked if someone from Mass General could ride in the helicopter and direct the pilots to Boston City's landing pad. EMS said the pad was obvious; all the pilots needed to do was to follow Southeast Expressway to the Massachusetts Avenue on-ramp. The helo pad was right there. But Barone convinced EMS to find someone to jump aboard the helicopter at Mass General. EMS nevertheless gave Barone latitude and longitude coordinates for the pad to pass along to the pilots.

At the same time, Boston City Hospital called and asked how many fishermen would be arriving. The watch-stander who answered the call said they weren't sure yet.

At 8:05, a doctor from Boston City Hospital called again and asked Barone's colleague, Lieutenant LaBrec, how he could help. LaBrec explained that a doctor at Mass General had said the fishermen would need heart-lung machines and that he only had one. They were hoping City would have two.

"That's fine," the doctor said. "So the point is, are you coming by [helicopter]?"

"We're trying to figure that out right now," LaBrec said. "We're trying to get the helo to drop one person off at Mass General and the other two off at you guys. The thing is, that particular pilot is not familiar with your helo pad."

"Well, I sent to [Air Station Cape Cod] two weeks ago a whole description of our pad with 'lat' and 'lon,' " the doctor said. "So it's over there. . . . Do we know anything more of the condition of these guys?"

"No, we're hoisting them now into the helicopter," LaBrec said, not realizing that the helicopter was, at that point already halfway to Boston. "None of them have been breathing, and they've been doing CPR on them as they could."

"Fly two to us, and we'll take care of them from here on," the doctor said.

"OK," LaBrec said. "We're gonna try to get them to you."

At 8:08, Barone called the helicopter, gave them the latitude and longitude coordinates of the Boston City Hospital landing pad, and said someone at Mass General would be willing to ride there with them. The helicopter pilots said that if Mass General could only take one, then they'd be willing to go to Boston City Hospital first, but they needed to know right away because they were only five minutes out from Mass General.

"We're gonna drop them all off there," the pilots told Barone, "unless you tell us different."

Barone told them to go to Boston City Hospital. A pilot from Cape Air—a regional airline that flew passengers from Boston to Cape Cod, Martha's Vineyard, and Nantucket—overheard this conversation and offered to talk the pilots into the helo pad. He said it was in the corner of a softball field just north of the Massachusetts Avenue–Southeast Expressway interchange and just south of the South Station tunnel.

At 8:13, EMS called Coast Guard Group Boston and reached Chief Rick Arsenault, now working the case with Barone, who told them the helicopter was going to Boston City Hospital right away. EMS said they were ready and waiting for the helicopter at Massachusetts General.

"At the General?" Arsenault asked.

"Yeah," EMS said. "You've been telling us to go to the General. We're all set up at the General."

Arsenault asked him to hold on. After a pause, he returned to the phone and told EMS that the rescue team had had to stop CPR on one of the guys. (Later there would be no record of which one, and Beverly divers McCadden and White would insist that they had never stopped. They only wished they could have stopped and offered more attention to the other two, they would say, but they gave each the same attention.) Arsenault confirmed that the helicopter would be going to Boston City Hospital. EMS said they'd try to get an ambulance there to meet them.

At 8:16, the helicopter pilot called Barone.

"We're at the pad now," he said. "No ambulance."

Barone asked him which pad they were at. He said they were on the pad located at the coordinates he had given them.

"This is [the] northwest corner of a softball field?" Barone asked.

"I don't see a softball field," the pilot said, though he knew he was in the right place. The gathered news crews left no doubt of that.

Barone immediately called EMS, now one hour after Jeffrey Hutchins had been removed from the *Heather Lynne II*, and said, "We got a helo on deck and no ambulance."

"Yeah, we were expecting you at Massachusetts General. Full cardiac arrest teams were waiting for you."

"We sent them to Boston City," Barone said. "They said they can handle them at Boston City."

"Are you gonna go to Mass General now?" EMS asked. "You got two full cardiac arrest teams waiting on the roof."

"We can go to the General," Barone said. "They stopped CPR on one person, I understand. Might as well do that."

"OK," EMS said. "Are you unloading somebody at the City right now?"

"No, there's no ambulance," Barone said.

"They told me to wait at [Mass General] . . . and you've got two [cardiac] arrest teams waiting on the roof."

"Well, they stopped CPR on one patient already."

"Right," EMS said, "So you can probably have them load two patients at City Hospital."

"How long will it take an ambulance to get there?"

"Momentarily."

"OK, we'll have them stay there," Barone said.

EMS said it would tell the team at Mass General to stay on the roof.

"OK," Barone said. "Do you want us to drop two off at the City Hospital? We only have two that CPR is being done on, so I need to know whether we should drop two off at the City or get them over to General."

"City's expecting two and General's expecting two," EMS said. "So whatever ones you feel are most critical [unload] at the City."

Barone said he'd drop two off at the City Hospital. EMS said they could then load more oxygen on the ambulance and take the last fisherman to Massachusetts General. At 8:19 A.M., the helicopter called Group Boston. The ambulances had arrived within minutes of the previous call and were transporting all three drowned fishermen, followed by news cameras: Kevin Foster and Jeffrey Hutchins to Boston City Hospital, about a block away, and John Michael Lowther to Mass General.

AFTER HANGING UP with the Coast Guard, Ann Lord called her father at his home in Concord, New Hampshire. "The *Heather Lynne* is underwater," she said, "and they don't know how Kevin is."

She knew her mother had a dentist appointment, so she called there, but her mother had already left. She was on her way to Lord's house for some other reason and did not yet know what had happened to her son. Lord called her sister-in-law, who came over and started making calls. Lord called Boston City Hospital. The man on the end of the phone said the family should come immediately.

"Somehow he worded it in a way," Lord later remembered, "that I thought he was still alive."

THE HUTCHINS FAMILY reached Massachusetts General after 8:00 A.M. only to find out the Coast Guard had sent them to the wrong hospital. Jacqueline called the emergency room nurse at Boston City Hospital, who asked her if Hutchins was taking any medications. The nurse said they were working on him; Jacqueline took the conversation to mean her brother was still alive. A policeman offered to drive them to the hospital. He sped them around traffic and nearly onto sidewalks. His haste hit home. They began to realize things were not all right. When they reached the emergency room, Jacqueline screamed, "I want to see my fucking brother!"

Jeffrey Hutchins's mother, stepfather, two sisters, and girlfriend were ushered into the "family room," where they waited for a doctor, who would soon tell them there was nothing he could do. Jacqueline and Jennifer insisted on seeing their brother. They found him in a messy room smelling like diesel fuel. His belly was bloated. He had a small cut across the bridge of his nose.

Meanwhile, at Massachusetts General, John Michael Lowther's grandfather, mother, aunts, and cousins faced similar news. A member of the emergency room team told them, through tears, that they had tried and tried but could not revive him. Both Lowther and Hutchins had multiple 2- to 16-inch-long diagonal scrapes on their backs—possibly from the collision, possibly from contacting exposed nails when they were pulled through the torn pilothouse roof. Hutchins had a scraped left arm and internal lacerations, but not ruptures, on his heart. Lowther had scrapes and bruises around his collarbone, and his left knuckles were beat up pretty badly; his family attributed this to his banging on the hull for so long. Besides having pulmonary edema (bloody fluid in their lungs), all three men showed no other evidence of trauma, no broken bones or deep cuts, and their deaths—none of them quick—were later attributed to accidental drowning. Very likely all three men had survived the violent collision, the tumble of gear and bodies as the boat was rolled over and down by the oncoming barge, the fierce in-rush of water as she was pushed deck first at nine knots into the dark ocean, and the prolonged cavernous silence upside down under the barge—a half minute or more that must have seemed an eternity—punctuated, perhaps, by the intermittent jarring and scraping of steel on the *Heather Lynne II*'s bottom as the barge passed overhead.

Ann Lord stood outside on her deck in Rye, New Hampshire, and waited for her parents to arrive. She remembered the last time she had seen Kevin. He had sat with her at her kitchen table on Tuesday night, upset with his girlfriend. She'd been upset by a family conflict. They'd had a good talk.

The ringing telephone broke her thoughts.

"Annie, it's Jacqueline," came the voice on the end of the line. "Kevin's dead."

Lord dropped the phone and collapsed on the deck.

» Aftermath

A T THE SCENE of the collision, with the sun higher in a milky, overcast sky and the wind barely alive enough to break the thick hot air and cast ripples across the sea—after Kevin Foster, Jeffrey Hutchins, and John Michael Lowther had been pulled from the wreckage of the *Heather Lynne II* and hoisted into the Coast Guard helicopter—Mike Goodridge climbed aboard the *Retriever* to talk with Ted Rurak. Despite the tangle of emotions swirling through his mind, Rurak was responsible for his empty boat, still tied alongside the *Houma*. Captain Breen was anxious to be free of her. He wanted to retrieve his barge *Essex* and be on his way.

The somber fishing fleet had begun to disperse. Some, like Richard Burgess on board the *Scotia Boat Too*, would attempt to spend the rest of the day tuna fishing. Later that afternoon while headed home, Burgess would return to his log and write, "Sept. 5, '96. Calm. Heather Lynn[e] Hit By Barge. Up Side Down. 5:15 A.M. BAD DAY. ALL 3 GONE." Other fishermen abandoned their efforts to catch a giant bluefin tuna and headed home to the Merrimack River and their waiting families, who hugged them a little tighter. Even though boats in peril were Goodridge's specialty, he wished to go home, too. He'd seen enough for one day.

"Just take care of it, Mike," Rurak told Goodridge as they both wept.

"I wish it would just sink," Goodridge said.

"Me, too." Rurak said.

But the stricken fishing boat could not just be cast adrift. She was leaking diesel fuel. She would be a hazard to navigation. Just as cars can't be left at the side of the road, boats can't be abandoned. Besides, the *Heather Lynne II* had done nothing wrong. As more than a few fishermen would say after the accident, it wasn't the boat's fault.

While they were talking, Kevin Angerstein on the 47-footer had been following a search pattern to look for a possible fourth crew. He passed close by Goodridge and several other boats that had rafted up together and threw a large wake, which caused the rafted boats to bang into each other. Angry at the unnecessary disturbance, Goodridge called Coast Guard Group Boston and said, "You want to ask the 47 if that was intentional, or that's just them not paying attention?"

"They've got to make a couple more loops here," one fisherman added, "to find out which way they're going."

A few minutes later, Angerstein called Goodridge and said he had heard Goodridge was trying to call him.

"You throw a 4-foot wake when the guys are rafted together here," an upset Goodridge said. Angerstein told him he was allowed to travel at that speed when he was conducting a search pattern.

At Rurak's request, the *Heather Lynne II* was now Goodridge's responsibility. The scene that had been controlled by the Coast Guard during the rescue phase was now under Goodridge's control for the salvage phase. But before Goodridge could start thinking about how to right the overturned *Heather Lynne II*, pump her out, and tow her home, he had to give the Coast Guard some answers. It was now almost 10 A.M. Men in blue coveralls from the Coast Guard's Boston Marine Safety Office had arrived on board the *Houma* to begin an investigation. They asked Goodridge on the nearby *Retriever* to survey the *Heather Lynne II*'s immediate condition. They wanted him to look for structural damage as well as any obvious clues as to what had happened in the minutes before the collision.

Goodridge, still dressed in his wetsuit, put his scuba gear back on, took a few deep breaths, and dropped alone beneath the surface. He swam first along the outside. He noticed no damage to the boat's hull other than some fresh splintered wood on her port stern quarter. Besides a few scrapes, there were no other dents or holes. He swam along her bow. He saw no damage except for a one-inch abrasion in her stem about four feet up from the waterline, which the Coast Guard would later conclude had been caused by the *Houma*'s towing cable. He saw a line—like a harpoon line—trailing off into the water. He followed it for about sixty feet, but it continued on. He could not pull it in, so he cut it.

Then he swam inside.

He could hear the tug's generator running, an amplified deep rattle like a lawn mower in a thundershower. There was enough light to make out objects and identify shapes. Although Steve Smith had seen a wall of gillnets hanging down when he first came upon the turtled boat, Goodridge did not—maybe they'd fallen out. He saw just one small net trailing off the stern. Since she had rolled onto her starboard side just before 7 A.M., Goodridge wiggled in through the hole in the port forward corner of the roof through which Sirois and Atherton had pulled Hutchins and Lowther. He swam a few feet farther and closer to the small wooden steering wheel on the opposite side, where Foster had been found. He shivered to think the men had just spent their final hours in there.

Above him, diesel-soaked debris fought for space. Plastic bags, empty cans of Diet Coke, charts, a package of fish hooks, buckets, denim jeans, a white T-shirt, an orange rubber rain jacket, a black boot, a blue hat, a plastic spoon, a lightbulb, a sleeve of Ritz crackers, and a bag of Halls Plus cough drops bobbed. Gear and equipment swirled amidst the chaos of an overturned boat. A brass ship's clock on the pilothouse wall had stopped at 5:36 A.M.

He noticed the engine controls. The red-knobbed throttle was a touch above idle, and the black-knobbed gearshift was in forward, indicating that the boat may have been making way at a snail's pace. Of course the positions of the boat's controls, switches, and keys as Goodridge found them may not have accurately represented their positions and setup at the moment of collision. Gear tumbling around during the collision and rolling, the electrical system shorting out and tripping switches, and prolonged struggles of the trapped men all could have altered settings.

Many people would later wonder how an experienced crew—and a captain who feared collision at sea—could have failed to notice the unmistakably bold target of a tug and barge beaming in on the radar and taken appropriate actions to avoid it. A postcasualty inspection of the *Heather Lynne II*'s radar unit conducted by personnel at the Coast Guard's Research and Development Center in Groton, Connecticut, discovered that it did not have any internal saltwater damage and thus may have been in an air pocket. The internal battery had failed, however; if that had occurred before the collision, the report concluded, it "may have caused the radar to malfunction or fail to retain operator-entered parameters."

The dials on the radar indicated that someone had tuned it so as to reduce sea and rain clutter—both of which create smudges on the screen that can conceal targets—and the "gain" control had been turned all the way down, which tends to block out some targets on the screen. Together these settings—opposite to what would be expected on a calm and settled morning—suggest the possibility that someone had been trying to isolate the most distinct and significant targets from a screen filled with clutter. Also, radar plotting aids such as the variable range markers and the electronic bearing line had been engaged, indicating that someone might have been tracking a target. When inspectors turned the radar on, they found that it was set at a three-mile range and displayed a low-battery warning. It's entirely possible that the *Heather Lynne II*'s radar was not operating properly and may not have given the crew an accurate representation of the vessels surrounding them in that predawn darkness.

Many in the local fishing community would speculate that the crew of the *Heather Lynne II* had not been paying attention, despite the fact that Hutchins's first standing order to his crew was to do exactly that. Some even suggested that these men, who knew how to have a good time, must have been drunk and fallen asleep while the boat sped along on her own at full speed, notwithstanding that her controls were found in the "slow-ahead" position. But autopsies and toxicology reports would show that none of the men had alcohol in their systems, and neither Hutchins nor Foster had any drugs in his system. Lowther had some cocaine metabolites in his blood, but because his blood sample had been mishandled, a forensic toxicologist reported to the Coast Guard that he could not determine how recently before the collision Lowther might have used cocaine, and that, "any determination about cocaine impacting the deceased's ability to operate in the marine environment cannot be made with any scientific certainty." (All of the tug and barge crew passed drug and alcohol tests except for one tug deckhand who tested positive for cocaine; Eklof fired him upon this discovery.) The men of the *Heather Lynne II* crew were not always angels, but on this morning they'd been on the straight and narrow.

Although none of the men were found wearing shoes, it's possible they had been wearing boots, rubber coveralls, or both and had kicked them off while waiting to be rescued. It's unlikely they were all asleep at the time of the collision. Given that the routine on the boat was to wake up several miles ahead of their destination and that Ted Rurak had called about that time, one hour before the collision, and found Lowther alert; given that they needed to catch herring for fresh bait and make other preparations that morning before fishing; given that so much was at stake (the bluefin tuna quota would close for the month just two days later); and given that a speed of 9 knots from the mouth of the Merrimack River would have carried them to the site of the collision some 22 to 27 minutes before it took place, it is unlikely the crew was asleep. If they had all been asleep while the boat forged ahead on autopilot at 9 knots, they would have been more than three miles past the barge at 5:10 to 5:15 A.M., not under its bow.

It is more likely that they were just plain busy preparing for the day ahead.

Goodridge saw an anchor on board that was set up as if ready to be deployed. He knew he could tamper with the scene. He could put the gearshift in neutral. He could toss out the anchor. He could paint a very different picture, a picture that pointed all blame at the tug and left these three fishermen with intact reputations as hard workers trying to make an honest day's pay until they were run down by a tug and barge.

He left the boat and her gear alone.

He really didn't want to bring the boat home. He didn't want to bring a boat home that now, instead of being the pride of the hometown fleet, was a haunting reminder of a morning gone bad, a haunting reminder that three local fishermen had gotten themselves into trouble, and no one, not even the U.S. Coast Guard, could save them. Lowther had been right when he bade his grandfather good-bye that morning—the sea did not take him. A chain of human errors and a web of false expectations had led to his death.

IN THE HOURS immediately following the accident, speculation filled with false rumors rippled along the coastline about how a collision like this could have happened. Mike Simpson on board *Houma* would insist that the *Heather Lynne II* had traveled toward his tug and tow at 10 knots and made no attempt either to avoid the collision or respond to his warnings. The crew of the *Scotia Boat Too*, who were the first witnesses to arrive on scene, insisted that the *Heather Lynne II* had been at anchor, based on the orange ball and line they had observed trailing down into the water, a belief Richard Burgess had relayed to the Coast Guard that morning. The two scenarios could not be more opposed, and those who believed one fervently disbelieved the other.

As had Goodridge, Coast Guard investigators found an anchor, ready to be deployed, stored on board the salvaged *Heather Lynne II*. Some said Hutchins had borrowed an anchor from a friend the day before. Some said he had returned that anchor. Others said it's common to carry more than one anchor aboard, just in case one is lost at sea. The boat also carried three orange balls about sixteen inches in diameter; they were used for the anchor, the bait net, and the harpoon line. The latter would have been attached to a harpoon that the fishermen would throw at a tuna once reeled in close to the boat, thus securing it with an additional line and increasing the chances of hauling it aboard. If the monofilament were then to break, a fish might flee the surface and take all of the harpoon line with it. If that happened, the ball would deploy from the boat to be towed by the tuna. The boat would follow until the tuna tired or expired, then the men would haul in their catch. The *Heather Lynne II*'s harpoon and anchor balls were found on board following the accident, leading most to conclude that the boat had not been at anchor. The third ball, belonging to the bait net, appeared in photographs taken of the scene early on and then, as the morning progressed, was no longer visible. Simpson said the ball just drifted up from under the boat and floated away; alternatively, it was the tug that was drifting, while the ball stayed put, perhaps attached to the mass of gillnets that had fallen from the *Heather Lynne II*.

On the morning of September 6, the day after the collision, the 41-footer from Coast Guard Station Gloucester returned to the accident scene. The *Scotia Boat Too* crew, who were out trolling for tuna that morning, had come across the submerged orange ball with the *Heather Lynne II*'s name on it. They reported it to the Coast Guard. The course from the collision site to the ball was 215 degrees true—the course the *Houma* had been following on its trip from Maine to Cape Ann the day before—for a distance of one-tenth of a mile. According to a written statement by Glen Beaulieu, he and his crew aboard the 41-footer began to haul in the line. After hauling in thirty feet of ½-inch-diameter nylon line, they found it attached to 3-inch, three-strand yellow-and-blue polypropylene line. He also found a 2-foot-long wooden two-by-four attached to the line. They hauled on the line some more and came across three more lines tangled with the main line. After hauling in about a hundred feet, the crew could not haul in any more. They feared the line was snagged on the bottom or on a foreign object.

Beaulieu said that he then hailed the crew of the fishing vessel *Theresa R II* to see if they could haul the line up any farther. After hauling up another fifty feet, a clear monofilament net came up entangled in the line. They could not determine if the net was attached to—or tangled in—the line. It was, Beaulieu said, a real rat's nest. The captain of the *Theresa R II* believed there was no way he could get the rest of the net and lines up without damaging his own boat, so upon Beaulieu's concurrence, the captain cut the lines. Beaulieu saved what they had retrieved, and the rest sank to the bottom.

This effort to retrieve—and the very existence of—the orange ball was not made public until eighteen days after the accident, when *Scotia Boat Too* deckhand Stephen Smith testified at the Coast Guard's Board of Inquiry hearing. Ted Rurak, when asked by investigators to identify the recovered ball and associated items, believed they belonged to the bait net. No one, however, could figure out where the attached massive, 3-inch polypropylene line had come from.

Bill Dobson, a private marine investigator working in Mandeville, Louisiana, had not heard of the collision when he agreed, for purposes of this book, to review the evidence gathered after the collision and form an opinion as to the most plausible chain of events. Dobson owned a consulting firm that specialized in marine accident reconstruction. Formerly he had worked as a police chief, commanded a special operations division for the sheriff's department, served as founding chairman of the Southeast Louisiana Search and Rescue Organization, encompassing 130 federal state and local agencies that worked together on search and rescue, and worked as assistant director of emergency preparedness for a local parish (county). He had retired from the St. Tammany Parish Sheriff's Office as a lieutenant colonel, Special Operations Division, after thirty years of public service and was a nationally recognized expert in marine accident reconstruction, investigation, and search and rescue. He had testified as an expert witness in more than a dozen marine accident cases. In 1991 he helped develop and participated in an official training film in boating safety and marine accident reconstruction used by the Coast Guard.

After Dobson and an associate looked at testimony, photos, and videotapes related to the *Heather Lynne II* accident five years after the fact, he could reach no definitive conclusion as to what happened in those early morning hours. He said the damage done to the *Heather Lynne II* and the barge *Essex*, the paint transfer and striation marks seen on both vessels in photographs and videotape, "are consistent with those that occur when vessels impact at right angles to each other, and when both are moving, one straight ahead and one crossing," as Mike Simpson had claimed.

He remained troubled, however, by the possibility that the *Heather Lynne II* was at anchor at the time of the collision, as Burgess had thought. He acknowledged that tuna boats in New England habitually drop anchor, tie the anchor line to a ball on the surface, and then hang back forty to fifty feet from the ball on a bow line that can be released in a hurry when maneuvering the boat to fight a fish. In this case, Dobson says, "it *could* be possible, if the tug made contact with the anchor line ahead of the buoy, it would have pulled the *Heather Lynne II* in the direction of the barge."

He noted that there was "a pretty good strike area"—one foot square, according to the Coast Guard—on the port stern gunwale of the *Heather Lynne II*, indicating that she may have been hit first from behind. The tug may have run harmlessly in front of the ball, but then the hawser ran along the bow of the *Heather Lynne II*, tangled the pendant in her rigging, and swung her into the path of the oncoming *Essex*, which would have then first hit her stern before pushing her on her side and rolling her over in a matter of seconds. Given the plausibility of this second scenario, Dobson could not be sure of what had happened.

And there is a third scenario, one that fits the evidence most closely and is perhaps the most compelling of all.

Robert Higgins, a Commercial Fishing Vessel Safety specialist for the Coast Guard's First District, who assisted in the investigation, said the investigators themselves and others close to the investigation spent many hours talking through the evidence and trying to figure out what exactly had happened. Higgins, a former commercial fisherman who had known and respected Hutchins, formed a scenario in his mind that gave him nightmares for several nights thereafter.

He believed John Michael Lowther, the last known operator, checked the radar, saw several targets on the screen, and felt he was clear enough of other vessels to pull the throttle back to headway speed, alert the crew below, and begin to prepare the deck for a day of fishing.

"The crew wasn't asleep," Higgins said, disputing rumors to the contrary, "because the stove was found on high, the rods were not in the wheelhouse, the bait net was tied off to the net lifter, all of the decklights were on, the throttle was found to be at headway speed, and they were approaching their destination."

While the accident scene bore 110 degrees true from the Merrimack River, the *Heather Lynne II's* autopilot was found set at 105 degrees true. A setting of 105 could have been a course correction—to adjust for current set and drift—entered at some point during the trip out there, but another possibility is that Hutchins deliberately set a course from the river mouth that would take the *Heather Lynne II* two miles north of his assumed destination. Perhaps he intended to reach the eastern, seaward edge of Jeffreys Ledge, then follow it south while searching for live bait with the fish-finder. If so—and if he left the Merrimack River at 2:30 to 2:40 A.M.—Lowther, at the helm, could have reached the point for the turn south as early as 4:45. It's quite possible that at 4:50, the time when Mike Simpson said he first spotted an oncoming boat on radar some five miles away—and when Branimir Viducic on his scalloper watched a blip closing rapidly with a tug and barge on 12-mile radar range—Lowther had just waked Hutchins and Foster, and Hutchins was taking the helm off autopilot (which would leave the setting of 105 degrees true in place) and turning south while cutting the throttle.

From there the *Heather Lynne II*, over the course of the next 20 to 25 minutes, would have had to travel at a speed of about four knots on a southeasterly heading to find itself in the same small patch of water as the barge *Essex*—one mile northwest of Hutchins's assumed destination and directly over the high ground on the eastern edge of Jeffreys that all the boats were fishing—at 5:10 to 5:15 A.M. This scenario would support Mike Simpson's suggestion that the *Heather Lynne II* altered course to the southeast prior to the collision, but earlier and at a slower subsequent speed than Simpson testified.

It's possible that Hutchins planned to set a bait net to the north and let it fish for an hour or so while he cruised down the edge of the ledge to anchor on the northern end of the fleet that had set up in a north–south line. His assumed destination was one-half mile north of the *Scotia Boat Too*; he would have been just north of the *Blue Heron* in the line of anchored boats. Later he would leave his anchor ball long enough to retrieve the net. If he were engaged in this plan, it would support the idea that the crew of the *Heather Lynne II*, in the minutes before the collision, was awake but busy.

The way Higgins figured it, Kevin Foster may have been below, responding to Lowther's wake-up call and putting on the coffee. Lowther, meanwhile, may have been carrying the tuna rods out of the cabin and placing them into the rod holders set around the stern. He may have prepared one bait net for deployment off the stern with its orange ball and rigged another net to the net lifter so that they could fish it directly from the boat while at anchor. Hutchins may have been helping him, and he may have left the wheel just long enough to miss the tug and barge closing in on them on the radar screen.

It would not have taken long. Moving at 9.5 knots, the tug and barge would have traveled from outside the *Heather Lynne II*'s three-mile radar range to the point of impact in 19 minutes. Nineteen minutes would go fast while the *Heather Lynne II*'s crew scrambled in preparation for the day ahead. Hutchins also could have been watching the fish-finder for a school of herring. Perhaps he even found one—their lucky day—and Lowther was deploying the net that Goodridge, on his initial descent later that morning, noticed hanging off the stern.

If the radar was giving false or intermittent returns—and if their visibility over the deck was somewhere between a half mile, as the *Houma* later reported, and two miles, as others would remember—they could have had less than 19 minutes to react to the tug and barge. It's even possible that their first image of the barge was a massive and baffling shape emerging from the background clutter of the radar screen at the last instant.

Then, suddenly, the wheelhouse was flooded with intense, blinding light from the *Houma*'s spotlight.

"Jeff and John must have been in the wheelhouse and seen it," Higgins said, although it's also possible that Lowther was aft just before the collision and rushed to the wheelhouse in response to the *Houma*'s spotlight and horn. "So there they are, standing there looking at the light, trying to figure out what the hell is going on, and then they are hearing the horn, and seconds later the barge comes up behind them. The rake of the barge and bridle make first contact with the rigging over the wheelhouse, and the next thing they know, they are getting run down by a barge. I think the last thing Jeff saw was the light. That floodlight is so bright, those guys must have thought they were getting invaded. They probably never knew what hit them."

GOODRIDGE SWAM DEEPER into the forward cabin of the empty *Heather Lynne II*. He felt his way through dark water amidst diesel-soaked foam cushions and blankets, a white pillow with small blue flowers, soggy cardboard boxes that had once held spare oil filters, fanned pages of a thick novel, and a large white electric stove. Goodridge felt the boat shift.

Now that the crew was gone, was she herself about to go to her own watery grave? Was Goodridge about to ride her all the way to the bottom? He was ready. Not willing, but ready. While working in the Cayman Islands, he had dived without air tanks to over a hundred feet. With air, he'd been down to two hundred feet before. It wouldn't be a pleasant dive, but he could do it. He turned his thoughts away from the men, whom he had waved to on plenty of occasions in the past. He focused on his breathing. He knew as long as he could breathe, he'd be able to save himself. He just had to keep breathing.

He noticed that the Lexan hatch leading from the forward cabin ceiling to the foredeck was fastened shut. Three of its four knobs had been loosened and removed. The last one took just two turns from Goodridge to open. Whoever had loosened those knobs had had to grope around several feet underwater to do so and then, at the last minute, may have decided against trying to swim down through the hatch to freedom. Goodridge understood this decision. The last thing you would want to do, he thought, is to swim farther down to escape. Or perhaps the attempt had been abandoned from lack of air or from the rational fear that opening the hatch would flood the boat's remaining air pocket. Of course it was possible that the hatch knobs had been loosened prior to the collision—perhaps Kevin Foster was in the process of opening the hatch to ventilate the forward cabin when the *Houma*'s horn sounded and the hawser struck. But if so, would the hatch have remained shut while the barge collided and the boat was plowed into the sea, rolled over, run over, submerged, and trapped upside down in turbulent water for as much as a minute?

As Goodridge swam around inside the capsized fishing boat, he realized that even he probably couldn't have escaped without scuba gear, and he'd been inside plenty of overturned boats. He felt the cold, slick, diesel-soaked water ooze past his face. It crept into his wetsuit and began to burn his skin. By day's end, he'd be covered in rashes and burns that would still plague him several years later.

Down below in the cabin, he also noticed a thin metal fork stuck into the edge of a floor hatch, its tines bent, as if someone had tried to pry the hatch open to expose a hidden air pocket in what had been a bilge compartment. Did the same man who loosened the knobs on the foredeck hatch also do this, or had more than one man been in the forward cabin after the collision? Had Kevin Foster been below at the time of collision, as Robert Higgins would suggest, and only later made his way out to the wheelhouse where he was found? Or did someone swim in from the wheelhouse on a last lungful of air after the boat rolled at 6:53 A.M., find the fork while loosening the three knobs on the hatch, then swim upward with his breath expiring to pry at the bilge hatch before, in the end, swimming down and out to the wheelhouse once again? Other scenarios, too, invaded Goodridge's imagination from that dark flooded cabin; any of the men could have made these attempts, and at any time. Now that's desperation, those who saw the bilge hatch later would say, trying to claw your way out of a 3-inch-thick fiberglass hull with a dinner fork.

Goodridge thought about what he would have done had he arrived on scene in time to save these men. He would have had to stabilize the boat while simultaneously soothing the men inside. He knew that if he just leapt in and tried to help them out, they'd probably end up killing him out of uncontrollable panic.

"There was no way one person would have been able to say, 'I'm taking him out and leaving you, but I'll be right back,' " Goodridge said. "You would have had to have gotten some lights and some air and soothed them enough to go in and get them."

As one fisherman had suggested before 6 A.M., shine some lights on the boat. As a deckhand on the tug had suggested, stick an air compressor hose from the tug under there and feed air into the air pocket. As the Coast Guard manuals advised, let the trapped men know that steps were being taken to get them out. This was all common sense based on salvage practices. In Goodridge's mind, the tug and gathering fleet of fishing boats had possessed plenty of equipment to save her crew. He had the ability to orchestrate their use to effect a rescue, while the Coast Guard had opted to keep bystanders away until divers arrived. It was a case where cooperation among many could have made the difference between success and failure. It was a case where, had everyone pooled their resources under the leadership of someone with the experience to know what needed to be done, they might have made a difference. At the very least they would have been able to say they had tried.

Goodridge especially wished the Coast Guard had thought to call him when it was searching for divers. Rear Admiral John Linnon, who was commander of the Coast Guard's First District at the time of the accident, would later say he wished the same.

"He could have helped us with the *Heather Lynne* if only we'd called him," Linnon said during an interview. "If only we knew what his capabilities were and knew enough to call him, it could have made a difference. There's no way to know for sure, but it sure would have been good to try. Someone in the organization should have known enough to call upon Mike."

GOODRIDGE SURFACED, removed his face mask, and spat the diesel fuel from his lips. He looked up at the crowd of saddened fishermen, exhausted Beverly Fire Department divers, and Coast Guard investigators. He looked at the tug's distressed crew, and at Ted Rurak. He gave the investigators their answers. Satisfied, they left him to salvage the boat.

Goodridge climbed out of the water and stepped aboard the *Houma* while news helicopters grated overhead. He looked at the *Heather Lynne II* tied alongside the tug. He, like firefighter White, noticed the strain on the nylon lines that held her on her side, tight to the tug. The *Heather Lynne II* seemed itching to move. The top of her white deckhouse pressed beneath the black tires on the tug's starboard side. Each vessel held the other captive, it appeared. Goodridge knew that once the lines were let go, something would happen. Once freed from the tug, the *Heather Lynne II* could take a nosedive to the bottom, just as Billy Muniz and others had expected. She could disappear in less than a minute and settle into the muddy gray sand more than 180 feet below. Maybe that would be best.

Goodridge told the tug's crew to loosen the lines.

The tug's gearshift hissed air as her diesel growled astern. Simpson loosened the thick, dirty line that had been wrapped around her skeg several hours earlier. Untethered, the *Heather Lynne II* was left alone to choose her fate. Around her, everyone fell silent. The surface of the calm sea, soaked in an opalescent sheen of her diesel fuel, nudged her. She teetered in the small swell. Her keel dropped to the right. Her deckhouse rolled to the left. She righted herself. Although her bow was weighed down by seawater and she needed Goodridge's care, she hung on the surface and refused to sink.

At day's end, under the sadness of nightfall and the spotlight of the press, Goodridge, alone in his *Unity*, towed the empty *Heather Lynne II*, now pumped out and steady on her waterline, up the Merrimack River, past the vacant dock she had called home, and into the canvas slings of a Travelift at Bridge Marina. He tied up his towboat and walked up the pier, past Hutchins's parked truck. As he slipped away from the tearful crowd of family and fishermen and the press who lined the bridge above and drove home, the *Heather Lynne II*, now dry-docked and suspended in clear night air, shed her last drops of seawater.

»Epilogue

AMERICAN PHILOSOPHER George Santayana is credited with saying, "Those who cannot remember the past are condemned to repeat it." While it is unlikely that the morning of September 5, 1996, will ever drift out of the minds of the fishermen and family members Kevin Foster, Jeffrey Hutchins, and John Michael Lowther left behind, it has dropped off the radar screen of the Coast Guard and the public at large. As of summer 2003, much has changed since that September morning, and yet, in an unsettling way, much remains the same.

Like many of the bystanders who gathered around the *Heather Lynne II* or monitored the morning's events from afar, I have my own thoughts about what I could have done to make a difference and what I would do if I had it to do over again. I awoke that morning to the sound of growling diesel engines as fishing boats raced down the Merrimack River. It was 3 A.M. Eyes closed, I listened as my then-fiancé, Rob, went through the familiar routine of gathering up his gear for a day of tuna fishing with his father, Bob Yeomans. The September night air was heavy and warm. No wind slipped through the open windows. I opened my eyes just long enough to see that it was not foggy; the green flashing light at the top of the Plum Island lighthouse, a mile and a half away, caught my gaze. I would have gone out with him that day except that it also happened to be the day before our wedding. I bade him a sleepy farewell, whispered "good luck," and shut my eyes. As I heard his truck crunch out the gravel driveway, I fell back asleep, thinking more of the white dress in my closet than the dangers that awaited him at sea. In fact, with more than ten years of experience on the water, I never worried that I or anyone I knew might not return from a day at sea. Now I know just how lucky we had been.

At 5:49 A.M., just as the *Houma* approached the turtled *Heather Lynne II* to put a restraining line on her, the ringing telephone awoke me. As I picked up the receiver, I heard the *Erica Lee*'s diesel roaring before I heard Rob's voice. I expected another of our routine "good morning" phone calls. Instead, he asked, "Are you listening to what's going on?" He said a barge had just plowed into the *Heather Lynne II*, and they could hear the guys banging inside. No words came to me.

With VHF radios chattering in the background, their volume turned up high above the engine, Rob said he and his father were going to go and see if they could help. I hung up, raced barefoot downstairs, and turned on the radio scanner. I heard the urgent voices of fishermen discussing what had happened and what they should—or could—do. I was still trying to make sense of it all when, fifteen minutes later—fifteen minutes that I now know might have made a difference—Rob called again at 6:04 A.M. He said, "Get Mike's number."

I pushed aside bridal magazines and RSVP postcards to reach the dusty phone book buried in a basket by the couch. As I thumbed through the pages, I asked why his father wanted Mike Goodridge's phone number. I had heard on the scanner that the Coast Guard was en route and had called a dive team, so I expected they'd be able to take care of it. I also figured Goodridge would already be out there or at least have heard about it. Though I had seen him around the Merrimack River many times, I did not know him and had no real understanding of how he'd be able to help. I read his phone number to Rob, who then hung up, dialed Goodridge's number, and handed the phone to his father. It was 6:05 A.M.

Alone in my living room, I listened to the radio conversations that morning while the rising sun cast shadows across the wall. I turned on the television and stared at live pictures of the scene broadcast from press helicopters hovering overhead. I remember for a long while expecting that the men would be pulled out alive—and what a story they would have to tell—but then, as time wore on and daylight brightened, I began to realize that might not be the case. I remember, amidst it all, being struck by how focused Goodridge sounded in his radio transmissions. He seemed to be the only one who had a real strategy for helping these men beyond just waiting for divers. Following the accident, and through six years spent researching and writing this book to understand fully what happened, I would come to regret that I had not thought to call Goodridge right away, fifteen minutes earlier than he was called. On September 6, 1996, my wedding day, I would read in the *Boston Herald* that all Goodridge could say about that tragic morning was, "I was fifteen minutes too late."

IN THE YEARS that followed, Goodridge had a lot to say about that morning. He wanted to be sure that, above all else, fishermen thought to call him sooner rather than later. He printed business-sized plastic cards and stickers with the Coast Guard phone numbers for Groups Portland, Boston, and Woods Hole on one side and his own contact information on the other. His message, as he handed them out to boaters and fishermen, was simple: "If you need help, call us both."

The Coast Guard revisited its dive team policy, reasserting that there was not enough demand for dive services to merit developing, training, and maintaining its own dive teams, particularly when there were readily available teams in local communities. In the unlikely event diving services were needed again, the Coast Guard said, it would contact the state police first. Other municipal agencies, like the Beverly Fire Department Dive Team, would be a second choice. Private volunteer dive teams such as the new Cape Ann Dive Team, which had been formed as a direct result of this accident, would be lower on the list. Commercial salvage divers like Goodridge would be a last resort. The Coast Guard told Goodridge they "were not in the salvage dispatch business."

Each summer following the accident, the Coast Guard conducted training for helicopter deployment off the Massachusetts coast with municipal dive teams, including the Beverly Fire Department Dive Team, but neither Goodridge nor any other commercial salvage diver was invited to participate. Repeatedly, Goodridge attended Coast Guard meetings and asked what qualifications he needed to be at the top of the Coast Guard's call list, but the Coast Guard would not answer him. Goodridge would become more and more convinced that should an accident like the *Heather Lynne II* happen tomorrow, the Coast Guard's rescue response would not be any different.

Goodridge, with his son Jake, also a licensed captain, continues to assist more and more boaters off the northeast coast of Massachusetts. Although he recognizes that in emergency search and rescue cases other public service agencies will respond, he has vowed to do all he can to help and will not back away, or sit and wait, until the situation, as he sees it, is under control.

"Remember the last time we all stood down?" he asked a reporter who was writing about a controversy that followed his response to a marina fire, in which the fire department said that once they were on scene, Goodridge should have ceased his efforts to help. "That's what happened with the *Heather Lynne [II]*. They stood down and three men died. That's not going to happen again in this area."

WHEN THE COAST GUARD crews returned to Coast Guard Station Gloucester on the afternoon of September 5, 1996, the story was all over the television news and the afternoon papers. The fishing community from Portsmouth, New Hampshire, to Gloucester wanted to know what had taken the Coast Guard so long to bring divers to the scene. The Coast Guard and the Beverly Fire Department Dive Team were shocked to face such criticism so quickly. Both believed they had done a good job.

Kevin Angerstein said his crew had expected a favorable outcome and were just as disappointed as the local fishing community at having failed in their rescue attempt.

"I did [cry], when we first got back to the station," Angerstein said in 2002 when reached by phone in Michigan, where he was finishing out his Coast Guard career as a SAR controller for Coast Guard Group Detroit. "The first outpouring of emotion happened when we got back to station, because that's when you realize the finality of it. This was the first case ever in my years in the Coast Guard, and my only case since, by the way, that we went out there fully expecting to bring at least one of those guys back alive, and it didn't happen."

Angerstein said the crew of the 41-footer, who he mistakenly believed had listened to the banging from inside the hull, was the most upset.

"My first crew on scene, plus the rest of us hearing about it on the radio, had to listen to this poor guy begging and pleading for help and there literally was nothing they could do," he said. "That's not normal for us in our line of business. Usually people cry for help and we can get to them, and we can help them. Or the people aren't crying for help for obvious reasons, but we still do what we can do. Here we got people crying for help and we literally cannot help them. . . . So imagine our feeling for an hour and a half, doing our best to secure the scene. . . . We're sitting there and we can't help this poor guy for an hour and a half. We got all the resources coming, but nothing's happening as fast as we want it to happen. . . . I can say that's what affected me the most."

Angerstein said the immediate criticism that fell on the Coast Guardsmen only compounded their sense of loss. It felt like the whole community of Gloucester had turned on them.

"I'm going to tell you right now that that really hurt the crew," he said, "because we've always had a good relationship with the community of Gloucester. . . . I remember us as a crew going to our senior chief at the time saying, 'somebody needs to go and talk to the press, or talk to some type of community committee and tell them the facts.' "

Angerstein, like others in the Coast Guard involved in the case, said he wouldn't have changed anything about the way the case was handled.

"As far as I'm concerned, I was there," Angerstein said. "I was intimately there. The people involved, whether they were in the Coast Guard, whether they were from the Beverly Fire Department, whether they were Good Samaritans on scene, everybody did an outstanding job. Outstanding."

Angerstein said he knew Mike Goodridge and believed the Coast Guard had a good relationship with him, adding, "We always did good business together and, you know, we thought highly of him." But when asked if the thought had entered his mind to call Goodridge that morning, he replied, "Not at all.

"We knew we had someone alive, so we weren't looking—all these commercial divers, you know, wanting to assist. Nobody stopped them from going to assist. None of them were requested, though, because we didn't want a commercial diver. Commercial divers are trained to go pick up anchors off the bottom and maybe weld something here or get lines out of props. We needed a trained rescue and recovery dive team that knew how to get out of hazardous spaces, that knew how to help and treat and take action on patients when they discovered them in that environment. That's what we needed. That's exactly what we got [with the Beverly Fire Department Dive Team], a full-blown trained, rescue and recovery—not a recovery dive team, but a *rescue* and recovery dive team."

Angerstein said of that day, "I know I'll never forget it."

Several members of the Beverly Fire Department Dive Team said they'd take the horrors of September 5, 1996, with them to their graves. Jeff Sirois, Mike McCadden, and Frank Kavanaugh left the team shortly afterward, in part because of scars left by the day's events.

While few area fishermen talk about the accident anymore, it remains on their minds. Some have started fishing in pairs, making sure they have another boat nearby in case they run into trouble. Others, like Richard Burgess, carry underwater flashlights close by their helms. Many believe they can't expect the Coast Guard to pluck them from peril. Several have vowed that the next time—and it's only a matter of time, they say—they'll call Goodridge first.

As *Scotia Boat Too* deckhand Stephen Smith told the Associated Press on the day of the accident, "Any sense of security we had about being rescued—that kind of slipped away."

THE LOSS OF THE *Heather Lynne II* rippled through the North Shore maritime community in other ways, too. On the day after the accident, Jeanne Lane, who had abandoned her son John Michael Lowther when he was about eleven years old and had had little contact with him since, filed a $10 million wrongful-death suit against tug and barge owner Eklof Marine, claiming that Lowther, due to Eklof's negligence, had experienced great pain and suffering, that there was great pecuniary loss to his estate, and that his mother was left with the loss of companionship of her son. Three weeks later she amended her complaint to include Ted Rurak and his *Heather Lynne II*, alleging that its unseaworthiness also contributed to Lowther's unnecessary pain and suffering and his estate's great pecuniary loss. A month later, Lowther's grandparents, with the support of his half-sister, protested Lane's claim to be the personal representative of Lowther and insisted that they, having raised him as their own son, had a stake in suits filed on his behalf. This was later resolved in probate court, control of his estate being left to his mother and his aunt.

Meanwhile, the estates of Jeffrey Hutchins and Kevin Foster filed similar wrongful-death suits. Rurak also filed a claim against Eklof seeking compensation for the loss of his fishing boat and subsequent fishing revenues; Rurak's insurance company would eventually pay him $148,000 for damage to the boat plus another $18,000 to pay Goodridge for his salvage. Eklof requested a limitation of liability to the value of the tug *Houma*, $620,000. By the summer of 1998, most of these suits had been settled. Foster's family settled with Eklof for $150,000 and released Rurak from any liability. Hutchins's family settled in the same manner for $550,000. The Lowther family settled with Eklof for $425,000 but did not release their claim against Rurak; this claim was finally settled for an undisclosed amount in May 2000. Meanwhile, Rurak, who had not carried any liability insurance to cover claims from the estates of his lost crew and owned few assets other than his house, paid $175,000 to Eklof—essentially reimbursing Eklof for what it paid Rurak's insurance company—in exchange for Eklof dropping any counterclaims against him that could expose him to as much as $500,000 if the *Heather Lynne II* were found to be 50 percent at fault for the collision.

The winter of 1996–97 was a hard one for the Newburyport-area seafood co-op. At a meeting on April 1, 1997, Tri-Coastal Seafood Co-Op, located on the Newburyport waterfront and servicing the area's commercial fleet with bait and ice, decided to go out of business. The co-op included seventy members and had been in business for twenty-four years, but its profits had fallen to about a quarter of what they once had been. Contributing to this drop in revenue was the decline of the groundfish stocks in the Gulf of Maine, which had compelled some fishermen to fish part-time or leave the industry altogether. By 1996, only about ten boats were supplying the co-op with fish to sell. Then came the loss of the co-op's top two producers, the *Heather Lynne II* and the *Sara Jean*, the latter having been sold to the government and destroyed as part of a federal effort to reduce the fleet size. Both boats had helped sustain the co-op through the winters. Bob Campbell, manager of the co-op, told one reporter that revenues had been declining, but the loss of the *Heather Lynne II* was the final straw. He called it "a big slap in the face."

On the morning of the accident, Campbell had sat at his desk at Tri-Coastal and served as a clearinghouse of information on the progress of the rescue. Campbell had once worked on the *Heather Lynne II*, and Lowther had once worked for him at the seafood dock. He knew and liked these men. Family members, concerned fishermen, and the press called him for news; he placed calls to the Coast Guard to learn what he could and relay any information he had. Afterward he organized a fundraising drive to erect what would become a $25,000 memorial, the first the city had ever built despite its long seafaring history. It would be dedicated to the crew of the *Heather Lynne II* and all who left the Merrimack River and did not return.

IN THE DAYS LEADING UP TO the memorial dedication ceremony on Sunday, May 28, 2000, Jeanne Huberdeau would drive her truck to the Newburyport waterfront and look out at the Merrimack River. To her left she could see where the *Heather Lynne II* had once tied up. To her right she could see where the river met the ocean. Every day, everywhere she looked, she was reminded of Jeffrey Hutchins, whose name she had tattooed in a scrawl of ivy leaves across her foot.

She had caught his eye as she tended barrels of flowers and window boxes for businesses throughout Newburyport. She was slim and of medium height with long, dark hair, sharp features, dark eyes, and a bright smile. He had watched her for about two years until, one September day in 1994, he drove up to her in his truck and struck up a conversation that lasted about a half hour. She had seen him once before and thought: "Wow. Who's that?" And now there he was, chatting it up with her. A few weeks later, as she waited to cross State Street in downtown Newburyport, she spotted him driving up the one-way street. He slowed down and she walked over to him.

He said he had built a new house, had just moved in, and wanted her to come see it. She wasn't sure it was such a good idea to go to a strange man's house alone, so she hedged. "If I'm not there by 7 P.M. Saturday night, I can't make it." He told her he would have a few friends at the house, too. That night she felt a giddy nervousness, like a schoolgirl on a first date, even though she was seven years older than he. She pulled up his gravel driveway shortly before seven o'clock. He took her hand and gave her a tour of his house, which was so new the electric stove had not yet been plugged in. He told her about all the intricacies of building the house, like the challenge of trying to lay tile in the corner of the counter so it would mesh just right. He handed her a beer. She felt right at home.

Over the next two years they'd drive around town in her new truck and sing aloud together to songs on the radio. When he wasn't fishing, he was either with her or out hunting. That's where he was headed, way up into the woods of Maine, on a Sunday afternoon in January 1995, while Huberdeau was home riding a horse named Genie. Her own horse—Blue Promise—had cancer. Huberdeau and the borrowed horse were walking on a road when the horse slipped. She fell off and lapsed into a coma for five days. When Hutchins learned what had happened, he turned around and traveled four hours back home to be by her side and help in her recovery.

When they were apart, he'd always call, sending her cell phone bill up to $400 a month. When she wasn't home, he'd leave messages on her answering machine. In a whisper, he'd ask, "Do you miss me?"

If he only knew, now, how much she missed him. As she stepped out of her truck and walked over to the water's edge, she remembered sitting in a car on the Tobin Bridge, banging her head against the window, tears streaming down as the AM radio announced that fishermen had been removed from the *Heather Lynne II* with no vital signs. She had kept trying to send Hutchins a message that morning. She kept thinking, "Use Blue's power." She had known he'd need all the strength he could muster, and she prayed the power of her horse combined with Hutchins's own strength would pull him through. For a while, she'd expected he'd be OK, but once they reached the Tobin Bridge and she heard that radio report, she had a sinking feeling.

When she last saw him in the hospital, she walked over to him and leaned down close to his cheek. She lifted an eyelid. She had to look into his eye and see death for herself, to see that he was really gone. He smelled as if someone had poured diesel fuel over him. Something compelled her to cut a lock of hair from the back of his head. It would forever rest on red velvet inside a round pewter box with an angel on top. Standing in the hospital room beside him, she just wanted to climb under the covers and look him all over, to see that death had really come.

As the days rolled into years following the accident, she tended landscaping jobs as if on autopilot. She made it through the days with her work, mapping out her own schedule, not talking to clients but heeding their requests left on her answering machine. She had to keep going. She had flowers to weed and water, or else they would die.

But the worst, she remembered, was shopping for groceries. Hutchins had loved to eat and was thrilled whenever anyone cooked him a nice meal. She would shop in tears, unable to compose herself. One day she broke down in the frozen food aisle when a friend said hello.

Time doesn't heal all wounds, she'd say, but it dulls the pain. Sometimes, she swears she can smell him. Or she'll catch a glimpse of him out of the corner of her eye. She'll smile and say aloud, "I know you're over there."

Hutchins's old friend and crewmate Jimmy Bashaw had a similar experience. Not one to believe in ghosts, he woke up one night to see a greenish figure sitting on the end of his bed. He called out to Hutchins as the figure moved out of the room. After that, sometimes Bashaw would go to his bedroom with the lights out and lie on the bed and say, "Hey, Hutch, you in here? Do something so I know you're OK."

But he never returned.

Huberdeau walked over to the granite base that would hold the bronze memorial, made in Italy, that would be dedicated to the crew of the *Heather Lynne II*. As she began to plant forget-me-nots and other flowers around the base—choosing them so something would always be in bloom—she recalled that Hutchins had wanted to be remembered as a good family man. He had always wanted a garden, so she built one at his grave, erecting a trellis over the dark stone with a deer by a stream etched on it. She planted climbing vines. And she planted more forget-me-nots.

JUDGE SARIS ISSUED HER DECISION in favor of the Coast Guard later in the summer of 2000. She noted that, according to Congressional mandate, the "Coast Guard may perform any and all acts necessary to rescue and aid persons and protect and save property." As the Third Circuit Court of Appeals had stated, however, "This legislation falls short of creating a governmental duty of affirmative action owed to a person or vessel in distress." Judge Saris agreed with Department of Justice attorney Stephen Campbell's argument that the Coast Guard, in its rescue operations, is held to the same standard of care as a private person, a standard spelled out in the Good Samaritan Doctrine. A Good Samaritan who undertakes a rescue is subject to liability only if his actions increase the risk of harm to those in peril or if "harm is suffered because of the others' reliance upon the undertaking."

While Judge Saris criticized some of the Coast Guard's responses that morning, she did not find enough evidence to prove that the agency made the situation worse or impeded the efforts of would-be rescuers. She also heeded other courts' warnings not to be an "armchair admiral." "The court must consider the Coast Guard's actions and decisions in the dawn light of the information known during the rescue, and not under the bright light cast by nearly four years of hindsight," she wrote. She noted that other court cases had established that "conduct that might ordinarily be negligent may be non-negligent in the pressure cooker circumstances of a rescue."

She then addressed each of the plaintiffs' allegations.

On the issue of whether the Urgent Marine Information Broadcast (UMIB) should have been updated, Judge Saris agreed that the UMIB consisted only of standard language, but felt that, due to the numerous communications broadcast that morning on VHF channel 16, anyone listening would have understood the situation. She noted that Richard Burgess, who arrived first on scene aboard his *Scotia Boat Too*, also put out a call for divers on VHF channel 10. Therefore, Saris wrote, "Any deficiency in a lackluster UMIB was more than cured by the dramatic radio broadcasts regarding the dire race against time."

Judge Saris noted that Billy Muniz, who had been on two fishing boats that had sunk within minutes, said his primary reason for not responding was a belief that the *Heather Lynne II* would sink. She determined that, "Muniz's forbearance was induced by long odds and not reliance on the Coast Guard's involvement."

Black and his colleagues had argued that the Coast Guard misinformed fishermen and other bystanders at the scene that a helicopter with divers was en route as early at 5:34 A.M., according to partially unreadable radio transcripts. But Saris wrote, "Whatever the unreadable portion contained, the Coast Guard communication, heard in its totality, could not have left the misimpression that the helicopter or [Coast Guard's 41-footer] was bringing divers to the scene."

As for what Saris called "the elusive scalloper"—Branimir Viducic, whom the attorneys were unable to identify—the judge concluded that although several fishermen recalled hearing the offer, only fisherman Mike Leary could identify who declined it. Further, she wrote, because there was no indication when that help was offered, there was no way to determine if it could have reached the scene on time; therefore, "plaintiffs have not [proved] that the scallop boat was a would-be rescuer which would have been successful or that the Coast Guard induced the scallop boat's forbearance."

Turning to the question of whether the Coast Guard adequately stabilized the boat, Judge Saris found this "the more serious argument, and perhaps, the most troubling one in the case." She asked in her ruling, "Why didn't a surface swimmer grab the bow line and secure it to the tug?" Though she credited Coast Guard Captain Adrian Lonsdale, the plaintiffs' expert, with suggesting that the Coast Guard had erred by not tying its 41-footer alongside the boat and attempting to pass lines under the hull to stabilize or lift the boat, she also considered the testimony of Petty Officer Christian Smith, coxswain of the 41-footer, who said he made no such attempt because he believed the boat was secure and he feared tying lines to it could jeopardize its stability if, by tilting to port or starboard, it lost its air pocket. "Smith's decision not to risk rocking the boat when it seemed stable was not unreasonable in light of the circumstances he confronted," Saris wrote, adding that, "this court must distinguish between true negligence and hard choices under pressure."

Weighing the plaintiffs' assertions that the Coast Guard should have called more than one dive team, Saris agreed that "it was negligent for Group Boston not to have a comprehensive list of rescue divers." Nevertheless, she concluded that this negligence didn't cause the fishermen any further injury because Station Gloucester had its own list (from which it called the Beverly Fire Department Dive Team) and because the lawyers did not prove any other dive teams could have arrived at the scene faster, such as those near Logan Airport or Air Station Cape Cod. Although Peter Black and Brad Henry had argued that the Coast Guard should have alerted nearby commercial salvage teams with dive capabilities as soon as possible, Saris determined, "it was reasonable to rely on the Beverly Dive Team because it had immediately available divers who knew how to work as a team, and was an entity the Coast Guard was familiar with." She conceded it was "troublesome that the Beverly Dive Team," which she determined was contacted at 5:37, "did not begin to arrive until about 6:23 [divers' recollections and radio logs suggest 6:20]. In a race against time, that delay turned out to be critical." Ultimately, she wrote, "Perhaps [the Coast Guard officers] were too sanguine in their reliance on one dive team, and a perfect SAR operation would have had them searching for back-ups. However, the standard is reasonableness, not perfection, and the courts have cautioned against second guessing."

As for whether or not the Coast Guard should have helped Good-ridge get to the scene faster, Saris believed that had the two joined forces, "it is extremely unlikely that the divers would have been on scene and in the water in time to save the trapped fishermen." Further, she declared, even if this was the wrong decision, the Coast Guard "did not worsen the situation for the accident victims because the Coast Guard in no way impeded or discouraged the divers from getting to the scene as quickly as possible."

Regarding the helicopter's involvement, Judge Saris agreed that helicopter pilot Craig Lindsey should have been diverted to Gloucester as soon as possible, or, at the very least, should have been updated on the status of the rescue. Saris also believed, however, that the divers were not ready to depart Gloucester before the helicopter arrived. (It was unclear why she drew that conclusion, since the divers assigned to the 47-footer were underway by 6:24, and the helicopter did not arrive at Station Gloucester until 6:36.) Therefore, she concluded, "an early diversion would not have made a material difference in the timetable for arriving at the accident scene."

As for whether the Coast Guard should have transported the Beverly Fire Department Dive Team to the scene in the 24-foot rigid-hull inflatable, "perhaps [the Coast Guard] erred in not taking the [rigid-hull], even if it were not an ideal rescue vehicle. Whether it would have made a difference is too close to call."

After considering the Coast Guard's failure to take steps that could have sustained the fishermen's lives, Judge Saris concluded, "There is no evidence that the surface swimmers could have directed the victims to safety without entering the hull." She noted that Petty Officer Barone had said: "The air pocket is very delicate, there was a line on the boat, it was stable. And we had divers en route. The risk of interrupting the air pocket and having the boat shift and go down and people run out of air would have been great." Judge Saris determined Barone's calculation was not unreasonable, and, she added, "even if the failure to take these actions was negligent, the Coast Guard cannot be held liable because these omissions did not worsen the position of the trapped mariners. Injecting compressed air might have increased the chances of a successful rescue, but the failure to do so did not increase the risk of harm."

Because, in her opinion, the Coast Guard did not, as Good Samaritans in a voluntary rescue attempt, make the situation worse for the men trapped in the hull, and because the plaintiffs did not prove that the Coast Guard prevented would-be rescuers from attempting to save the men's lives, the judge ruled that the Coast Guard could not be held liable for the men's deaths.

Joe Hutchins, Jeffrey Hutchins's father, believed there was a lesson in all this for fishermen who head to sea.

"You have to depend on yourself and have a seaworthy vessel and be on your toes," he said. "Because you know you're not going to get any type of help from the Coast Guard."

John Michael Lowther's grandfather, John Lowther, said he hadn't expected a federal judge to find the federal government negligent. He only hoped fishermen would realize that they need to watch out for each other even more. "Fishermen now are taking matters into their own hands," he said. "Fishermen now have to protect themselves."

Ann Lord, Kevin Foster's sister, said she was disappointed to hear about the judge's ruling. "I wish the families could have gotten somebody to admit it just wasn't done right," she said. "But that will never happen."

Richard Burgess felt the same way. He believed the Coast Guard screwed up that morning, and since he had to tell the truth when he testified, he believed the Coast Guard should have been more truthful, too. He said, "[The Coast Guard] frigged up, and they should say so."

Branimir Viducic, captain of the elusive scalloper, thought that if Judge Saris had heard from him, she might have ruled differently. He found the Coast Guard's assertion that it was not required to perform a rescue and that mariners should not rely upon it particularly troubling.

"The Coast Guard is there to protect our coast," he said. "That's what they do. They say they don't have to rescue us. Well, I say if you're not ready for us, who are you ready for?"

The Coast Guard, in response to Saris's ruling, expressed its condolences to the families and said, "We always learn from things that happen."

Plaintiffs' attorney Brad Henry hoped that was true. Following the ruling, he said he hoped the Coast Guard would look at its deficiencies and its relationship with mariners on the North Shore of Massachusetts.

He told the *Newburyport Daily News*, "We hope that the case will serve the purpose of highlighting to the Coast Guard the clear deficiencies in their performance. We hope it's not just a wake-up call, but one that the Coast Guard will pick up and answer."

He expressed similar concerns to me.

"There are fishermen out there with dozens of years of experience, some even with Coast Guard experience, that have ways of helping," Henry said. "And here you have young and well-meaning Coast Guardsmen who, in accordance with their training, believe themselves to be more policemen than firefighters. So long as the Coast Guard considers itself more as law enforcers and not firefighters and rescuers, we will continue to have deaths on the waters of the North Shore."

Following the terrorist attacks on September 11, 2001, the Coast Guard's law-enforcement missions indeed shifted to port security, while at the same time it insisted that SAR remained among its top missions. The administration of President George W. Bush pushed for a major budget increase to address the readiness woes the agency faced while handling the cases of the *Heather Lynne II*, *Northern Voyager*, and *Morning Dew*. As one Coast Guardsman said, throwing money at the Coast Guard won't solve its decades-old readiness problems, but it's a start.

In early 2003, when the agency was transferred to the new Department of Homeland Security, its larger budget started funding such improvements as new boats, a modernized communications system, and an increase in personnel. While these new assets and an increased presence on the water could benefit recreational boaters and commercial fishermen, the Coast Guard advised in spring 2003 that the war in Iraq—where the Coast Guard cutter *Adak* was deployed to help escort the first humanitarian aid shipments into the port of Um Quasar—and elevated security concerns at home had shoved SAR into the backseat of Coast Guard priorities.

"Homeland Security is our number one mission now," Commander James McPherson told an Associated Press reporter in March 2003. His comments were echoed by the commander of the Portsmouth New Hampshire Coast Guard station, who added, "Before it was all about boater safety, and search and rescue. Now it's all about Homeland Security."

ON SUNDAY, MAY 28, 2000, Jeanne Huberdeau took her place in a solemn crowd gathered at the water's edge in Newburyport. Up to four hundred people had attended the fishermen's funerals, and as many had gathered again. They sat before the bronze memorial depicting an anchor and a ship's wheel—modeled after two gold charms Jeffrey Hutchins had worn on a gold chain around his neck. It rested on a granite base on which was mounted a plaque dedicating the memorial to all fishermen who lost their lives at sea and to Jeffrey Hutchins, Kevin Foster, and John Michael Lowther: "Never will they be forgotten."

The afternoon's service opened under blue skies that cleared, strangely, from the east. Sunlight washed over those who gathered, including Mike Goodridge. No uniformed Coast Guardsmen attended.

Tears fell as fourteen-year-old Caitlin Williams sang Sarah McLachlan's "Angel": "You are pulled from the wreckage / of your silent reverie / you're in the arms of the angel / may you find some comfort there."

Jacqueline Hutchins, who had an image of her brother tattooed on her back, put her arm around her mother as they sobbed together. Across the river at Bridge Marina, the *Heather Lynne II* was being painted black, her deckhouse shortened and an A-frame installed on her aft deck, transforming her from a gillnetter to a dragger. To the clap of thunder one July day, she would return to the water with a new name, *Lisa Ann*, and head out fishing once again. Huberdeau believed Hutchins would respect the hard work the new owner had put into the *Heather Lynne II*.

After prayers were read, Rob Yeomans rang a bell after each fisherman's name was spoken. The memorial was blessed with water from the Sea of Galilee, where Jesus is said to have walked on water, filled Peter's empty net with fish, chosen four fishermen to be his disciples, and calmed a storm to the amazement of his shipmates. Then John Michael Lowther's grandfather and family; Jeffrey Hutchins's mother, sisters, and family; and Kevin Foster's sister, Ann Lord, and her family walked to the water's edge and cast three wreaths and twenty-four white roses into the Merrimack River. Two wreaths broke as two women sang:

"Spirit of the wind, carry me,

"Spirit of the wind, carry me home,

"Spirit of the wind, carry me home to myself."

Clouds returned as the ceremony concluded. A single pink rose swayed to the whim of the water current, tossed in a silent dance between wind and tide as it fled seaward. As the crowd dispersed, Huberdeau looked at the forget-me-nots she'd planted around the memorial. She understood that the pain would never go away. Time does not heal all wounds.

IN EARLY SUMMER 2003, as this book was going to press, a fishing boat named *Damariscotta*, once known as the *Heather Lynne II*, and then the *Lisa Ann*, was settling into her new home in Gloucester. Matt Russo, her new owner, planned to fish her as a dragger and maybe one day paint her midnight-black hull red, since his last name in Italian means red and his family owns three other red boats in Gloucester harbor. Russo is the son of a fisherman who was born in Sicily and first fished out of a small rowboat when he was nine years old. After making his way to the United States via California, Russo's father settled with his wife and three sons in Gloucester.

When reached via cell phone on a beautiful morning in late May, Matt Russo was aboard his *Damariscotta*, fishing fifty miles east of Gloucester on his third trip aboard—a trip that had taken him through the waters where, almost seven years before, his boat had been run down by a barge. He explained that his family was deeply religious and, in keeping with maritime tradition, had had the boat christened when her name was changed just a few days earlier to an ancient Indian name meaning "gathering place of many fish." He knew what had happened to her on the last day she had gone fishing as the *Heather Lynne II*, but he said that while it was tragic, her history didn't bother him. He wasn't superstitious and had even bought a house across the street from a cemetery. He was used to having spirits around, he said.

After a few minutes our conversation ended. Russo hung up the cell phone and settled back into the chair by the helm. His *Damariscotta* plunged onward under bright sun and a royal-blue sky, the calm sea rippling off her bow as a net that he hoped was filling with fish dragged behind her.

IN THE DAYS AND weeks and years after the memorial was dedicated,

Jeanne Huberdeau would return alone to tend her plantings at its base. As she worked to keep the spirits of the crew alive and shining through the bright petals, season after season, she would never lose her belief that it wasn't just three people who died that day. When the trapped fishermen were taken from the small Newburyport fishing community, something inside the community died too. Left in its place is a bronze memorial that catches glints of sunlight, a mute reminder that, for those who work at sea, a safe return is never guaranteed.

Notes

THIS IS A WORK OF NONFICTION. My desire to tell this story began with an overnight writing assignment—write a scene based almost entirely on dialogue—given by Lee Gutkind while I was enrolled in the Master of Fine Arts in Creative Nonfiction program at Goucher College in August 1997. I returned to class the next day with a scene built around the radio conversations from the morning of September 5, 1996, more than a year earlier, still fresh in my mind. To my own surprise, I had recounted the radio communications nearly verbatim from memory. The Coast Guard had just issued its investigation report, and like many of those who cared about what happened that day, I didn't find it satisfying. So many unanswered questions haunted me.

I spent six years trying to assemble the events and expectations that collided on the waters off Cape Ann in the early morning of September 5, 1996. But, as with the best mysteries, the more answers I learned, the more questions I found. In so many ways, this story is soaked in controversy, and just about the only fact anyone could agree on was that the *Heather Lynne II* had a green hull. For this reason, I have tried to steer clear of speculation. In addition to interviews with eyewitnesses, whose recollections I tried to verify with alternate sources when possible, I relied heavily on 2,363 pages of transcripts from the Coast Guard Board of Inquiry hearings, since many of those who testified did not want to be interviewed. I also relied on 1,070 pages of trial testimony transcripts, hundreds of pages of associated documents gathered for both the Coast Guard's investigations and the pretrial discovery, as well as several hours of video tapes and audio tapes. In addition, I spent a few years shadowing Michael Goodridge and logged more than 300 hours with him aboard his towboats, where I got a firsthand view of what happens off the coast of Massachusetts when a mariner calls for help. Additional source material included court documents, press accounts, and web research.

And yet, after so many years of research, some answers remain elusive.

Prologue

An excellent source of information on cusk and other New England groundfish is *Bigelow and Schroeder's Fishes of the Gulf of Maine*, 3rd ed. (Washington D.C.: Smithsonian, 2002). For the story of what happened to the *Starbound*, I relied on various press accounts, including those that appeared in the *Portland Press Herald*, *National Fisherman*, *Boston Globe*, *Associated Press*, and *Boston Herald*.

The Collision

For background on the design and construction of the new courthouse, I referred to the website of architects Pei Cobb Freed and Partners (www.pcfandp.com), "United States Courthouse and Harbor Park," and "Favorable Verdict," which appeared in *Building Design & Construction* (January 1999).

Richard Burgess's story is constructed around several conversations with him both on the telephone and around the Gloucester waterfront, as well as transcripts of his testimony at the Coast Guard Board of Inquiry hearing, his trial testimony, and a copy of his logbook from September 5, 1996.

The dialogue from September 5, 1996, that appears in this chapter and throughout the book was taken from audio tapes of VHF radio communications recorded by the Coast Guard and cross-referenced with transcripts of those communications. Other dialogue was taken directly from testimony or from interviews.

10   **as Burgess sped toward it.** James Vaill was aboard the *Sharaban* anchored right behind the *Scotia Boat Too*. Vaill told investigators at the board of inquiry hearing that after hearing the tug's horns, he saw the tug, about ¾ of a mile away, start to turn hard to port, and that if it had not, the *Sharaban* would have had to get off its anchor and get out of the way. They had started their engines and were prepared to move.

13   **flashed under the surface.** Smith believed the pulsating light from the EPIRB was the only way anyone would have seen the boat and not hit it in the morning darkness.

15   **might be deadly.** Rurak, according to his board of inquiry testimony, also considered jumping in the water but feared swimming around gillnets. He abandoned any other ideas, like chopping a hole in her hull, and instead decided to wait for the Coast Guard to arrive, as promised, with divers.

16   **Frawley shouted back.** John Frawley believed there were at least two alive.

16   **out of here!"** Joe Cyr, deckhand aboard the *Jan Ann* that also arrived on scene, believed he heard Lowther at one point say the same thing, according to his conversation with a private investigator, October 9, 1996.

18   **banging on the hull under the galley."** Stephen Smith had reported voices and tapping from the forward end of the wheelhouse, John Frawley from the "forecastle." The galley was at the aft end of the forward cabin, or forecastle, and all these locations were within a few feet of one another.

22   **inside Courtroom Thirteen,** The interior blue, red, and dark wood color scheme of Courtroom Thirteen, one of twenty, was intended to resemble that of the Essex County Superior Courthouse, Massachusetts's oldest courthouse in continuous use. Built in 1805 in Newburyport, it was designed by Charles Bulfinch, who designed the State House in Boston and the central section—including the rotunda—of the Capitol in Washington, D.C. This historic courthouse overlooks a one-way street leading down to the water's edge of the Merrimack River, where the *Heather Lynne II* once tied up.

The Crew

A detailed background on the bluefin tuna fishery can be found in Eugene H. Buck, Congressional Research Service (hereafter called CRS) Report 97-588 ENR (March 8, 1995), *Atlantic Bluefin Tuna: International Management of a Shared Resource*, as well as past issues of *Commercial Fisheries News.*

29 **a 2001 tagging study),** For most of the twentieth century, scientists mistakenly believed that there were two distinct populations of Atlantic bluefin. One large school lived in the eastern Atlantic and Mediterranean while a second, smaller school lived in the western Atlantic and spent summers off the New England coast.

29 **handful of nations** The other nations were Japan, South Africa, Canada, Ghana, France, Brazil, and Morocco. See "About Us" at www.iccat.org.

29 **minimum size limits.** Not all of the twenty-two member nations in 1996 took ICCAT's recommendations seriously, however. U.S. fishermen believed that many eastern Atlantic and Mediterranean fishermen were ignoring management measures, to the detriment of the western Atlantic population.

29–30 **eastern Atlantic and Mediterranean.** ICCAT, believing the eastern Atlantic population to be larger than the western Atlantic population (and resolving to manage them separately), suggested in 1996 that U.S. fishermen be allocated a total harvest quota of 1,311 metric tons, whereas eastern Atlantic fishermen were allowed 39,331 metric tons. New England fishermen regarded this as unfair.

30 **five main groups.** The five categories: harpoon fishermen; purse seiners; sport anglers; incidental-category fishermen (mostly longliners) who caught tuna while targeting other fish; and general-category fishermen. Harpoon fishermen used harpooning techniques similar to whaling. Purse seiners used a large net to encircle schools of fish. The angling category was predominantly sport fishermen who were allowed to catch and keep—but not sell—small, sexually immature fish. The incidental-category fishermen occasionally caught bluefin tuna and preferred to sell rather than discard them. The general-category fishermen were both commercial fishermen and recreational fishermen with a permit to sell tuna.

30 **for the 1996 season.** January 1996 opened with a surprisingly booming fishery off the Carolina coast as sport anglers—who were not permitted to sell—tagged and released as many as 10,000 tuna through mid-March, reporting that they could barely get their hooks into the water and that the fish were just about jumping into their boats. When the time came to establish the rules for the 1996 season, set to open June 1, NMFS was under pressure by North and South Carolina fishermen to let them in on the fishery. New England fishermen were vehemently opposed; they had been paying their dues by adhering to management regulations for years and didn't want a new fishery to take a piece of their pie. Tuna fishermen and local congressmen also criticized the NMFS for not effectively monitoring and managing sport anglers, who repeatedly and without consequence caught more than their allotted quota.

30 **actually caught a tuna.** According to the CRS report, in 1992, 6 percent of the 10,879 general-category permit holders caught a fish, and many of them only a small number at best.

31 **so small a quota,** The general-category quota was 541 metric tons, or about 3,000 fish, based on an average tuna weight of 400 pounds (a metric ton is 2,204.62 pounds).

31 **September and October.** Good-quality fish are football shaped, about 400 pounds, with greasy, light pink flesh.

31 **Sunday, September 1.** A special exception was made to allow fishing through the Labor Day weekend.

31 **take additional risks.** Derby-style fishing is a management measure that critics argue puts fish ahead of safety. Louisiana fisherman Tim Torrence, who fished in the derby-style red snapper fishery in the Gulf of Mexico, said, "When we're forced to fish derbies, that's not promoting safety, that's forcing us on a suicide mission." In the former "suicidal halibut derby" fishery in Alaska, fishermen there would push the envelope, too, by fishing through bad weather, hoping it would break the next day and that nothing would go wrong in the meantime. The halibut fishery in 1995 changed to an individual fishing quota system, in which fishermen were designated their own quotas and could fish when they believed was the optimum time—in terms of weather and fishing conditions—and not in accordance with calendar days designated by the National Marine Fisheries Service. Kate Yeomans, "Regulatory Hazards," *National Fisherman* (May 2000).

32 **19 to 24 fathoms** A fathom equals 6 feet, so he was marking fish from 114 to 144 feet beneath the boat.

32 **a Domino's pizza.** Background information on the crew of the *Heather Lynne II* and a reconstruction of their last days on the water were based on interviews with Dean Holt, Joseph Hutchins, Jennifer Hutchins, Jacqueline Hutchins, Diane Fondow, James Bashaw, David Morse, Bob Campbell, Jeanne Huberdeau, Ann Lord, John Lowther, Ric Littlefield, Richie Twomey, John Frawley, Nelson Beideman, Jimmy Ford, and Bob Higgins; cell phone records of the *Heather Lynne II* and the *Retriever*; witness statements; press accounts; Newburyport High School yearbooks; probate court and Registry of Deeds documents; board of inquiry testimony by Ted Rurak, Charles Wojcicki, and Joe McKechnie; Coast Guard accident investigation reports; and a marine surveyor's report.

33 **community in the commonwealth."** A good book on the maritime history of Newburyport, among others, is Benjamin J. Stone, *Captains, Clams and Cobblestones: A Collection of Papers on Life in Newbury and Newburyport in a Bygone Era* (Historical Society of Old Newbury, 1977), as well as Liz Nelson, *Newburyport: Stories from the Waterside* (Beverly MA: Commonwealth Editions, 2000).

37 **he went longlining** Longlining uses one several-miles-long submerged line and from it extends several baited hooks.

40 **is often compromised."** A good reference for safety issues in general, and collisions at sea in particular, is Kathy D. Ruhle and James A. Ruhle, "Near Miss or Collision: What Can Make the Difference," *Proceedings of the Marine Safety Council*, USCG Journal of Safety at Sea, Fishing Vessel Safety, vol. 58, no. 2 (April–June 2001).

42 **"Pyro" after him.** In the late summer of 1996, Hutchins had picked out a golden retriever puppy and planned to name him "Dog." Pyro is Dog's brother. Jennifer Hutchins chose to keep Dog after Jeffrey's death, and Ann Lord chose to buy Pyro as a reminder of her own brother and his friend, Hutch.

45 **started up the generator** McKechnie found the generator key in the on position. Rurak said that Hutchins turned the generator on at night to power the big halogen lights and that the boat was always extremely well lit.

46 **just after 2 A.M.** In its investigation report, the Coast Guard determined that the *Heather Lynne II* probably left the dock at 2:30, traveled down the Merrimack River, and exited the mouth at 3 A.M. This was based on Jennifer Hutchins's belief that Jeffrey Hutchins left his home at 2 A.M.; the Coast Guard suggested he would have arrived at the boat at 2:15 and spent 15 minutes preparing to get underway.

However, Jeanne Huberdeau recalled the alarm clock sounding in Hutchins's home at 1:30 A.M. and Hutchins and Foster departing shortly thereafter; John Lowther recalled that John Michael had told him he needed to be at the boat by 2 A.M. It is more likely that the crew mustered at the boat by 2 A.M., spent minimal time preparing to get underway, traveled at about 8 knots 3 miles downriver against the tide, and exited the mouth of the Merrimack by 2:30 A.M.

50 **monofilament line.** "300-pound-test" is a measurement of breaking strength but can successfully be used to catch fish heavier than 300 pounds.

Codseeker, May 9, 1877

The facts of this story were taken from and verified in various sources, primarily Allan Easton, *Terror of the Coast: The Wreck of the Schooner Codseeker* (Nimbus, 1992). Other sources included Edward Rowe Snow, "Trapped Aboard the Codseeker," *Tales of Terror and Tragedy* (New York: Dodd, Mead, 1979), and Patricia Stoddart Terry, *Lost Mariners of Shelburne County*, vol. 2 (Shelburne County Genealogical Society, 1991).

56 **some of her buoyancy.** Some forty years later, historian Edward Rowe Snow noted, a four-masted sailing ship was rumored to have done the same thing off Cape Hatteras.

The Tugboat Mate

None of the tug and barge crew testified during the trial; quotes attributed to them were taken from their testimony at the Coast Guard Board of Inquiry hearings. Further, K-Sea Transportation Corp.'s Richard Falcinelli, on behalf of the tug and barge crew, declined interviews for this book. Michael Simpson, however, did agree to be interviewed and was very cooperative.

This chapter is constructed around transcripts of board of inquiry testimony by Michael Simpson (including drawings he made under oath), Shawn Richter, and Captain Allen Breen; press accounts; copies of merchant mariner licenses; Simpson's written statement; and three interviews with Simpson.

61 **9 to 9½ knots** Although Breen and Simpson testified that the tug and barge traveled at 8.5 knots, time and distance calculations made from fixes placed on the chart that had been in the wheelhouse showed a speed of 9 to 9.5 knots.

61 **without waking up Breen.** Simpson, however, disputed this when he told investigators he would have to wake Breen to discuss changing the route that Breen chose.

63 **at $3.6 million).** According to the NTSB report of the Eklof Spill, 5,200 towboats working with 37,000 barges comprised the U.S. towing vessel industry in 1996. In 1994, the Coast Guard published a report that determined a majority (58 to 62 percent) of accidents involving towing vessels from 1981 to 1991 were caused by human errors and not equipment failures.

63 **steel tug *Houma*.** Simpson actually said, "any maneuver that I made would have caused a problem either with the *Heather Lynne [II]* . . . or other . . . vessels in close proximity."

76 **five miles of the *Houma*.** Kelly's estimate of *Heather Lynne II*'s course at 111T (111 degrees true) contradicts the course of 105T that Hutchins at some point that morning had set the autopilot to, as investigators later discovered. Kelly's 111T is an educated guess based on reconstructing an assumed direct course for the *Heather Lynne II* under autopilot, from the Merrimack River entrance to the point of collision. A setting of 105 could have been a course correction—to adjust for set and drift—entered at some point during the trip out there, which would mean Hutchins was

awake for a part of the trip, since he would have been the only one to adjust the autopilot. If this course of 105T began at the mouth of the Merrimack River, it would
have taken the *Heather Lynne II* about two miles to the north of Hutchins's assumed
destination. It's possible that was his plan—set the bait net to the north and then
cruise down the edge of the ledge to anchor up on the northern end of the fleet that
had set up in a line spanning north–south. If this was his plan, it would support the
idea that he was in some way following Simpson, that he had changed course and
was headed more to the south after having followed a more easterly course. If this
were true, it would also suggest that the crew of the *Heather Lynne II*, in the minutes
before the collision, were awake but busy setting out a bait net and getting their day
started, as one Coast Guard investigator would suggest.

Linda E, December 11, 1998

This chapter is constructed around the Coast Guard's two investigation reports and numerous press accounts of the events from the *Linda E*'s loss to her discovery to the present
lawsuits, as well as video taken of the sunken boat. A useful reference on admiralty law is
Thomas Schoenbaum, *Admiralty and Maritime Law*, 3rd ed. (St. Paul: West, 2001).

The Barge Crew

This chapter relies on Berretta and McLernan's testimony, including drawings, given at the
Coast Guard Board of Inquiry hearings as well as e-mail correspondence with Rick Fal-
cinelli, a representative of K-Sea Transportation Corp., and phone conversations with
Mike Simpson, as well as VHF radio tapes.

90   less maneuverable when full. Simpson said the difference between towing a full
  barge versus an empty barge was like towing a deep-V boat versus a light, flat-bot-
  tomed skiff.

90   asleep in his chair. Officials at K-Sea Transportation, formerly known as Eklof Marine Corporation, would not comment on whether sleeping on watch aboard a
  barge under tow was standard practice.

91   a hard right turn. This is the picture he drew for Coast Guard investigators.

94   the capsized boat. A maneuver like this resembles a "Williamson turn": when there
  is a man overboard, the helmsman turns the wheel hard over to the side that the
  person fell over (to keep the propellers away) and then, once 60 degrees from the
  original course, turns the wheel to the opposite direction until the vessel is back on
  a reciprocal course. In this instance, *Houma* would have turned from her course of
  215 true (southwest) to 275 true (or west) and then turned to port. This may be
  why the barge crew saw the tug to the starboard side of the barge while the crew of
  the *Scotia Boat Too*, who came on scene minutes later, saw the tug on the port side
  of the barge, at which point the tug was on more of a reciprocal course.

99   three inches thick. Simpson remembered, "The boatowner was right there, and he
  said don't do it." Ted Rurak was afraid air might escape through a small hole before
  it was big enough to pull the men free.

The Gathered Fleet

Sources for this chapter include testimony at trial and at the Coast Guard Board of Inquiry
hearings, related statements and exhibits, interviews with Bob Yeomans, Mike Leary, Billy
Muniz, Charlie Rine, Dean Holt, and David Yerman, related press clippings and Coast
Guard accident investigation reports *(Sara Jean* and *Lady Lynn)*, as well as the cell phone
record for *Meghan and Ryan* and a statement made for private investigator by Mike Leary
on October 3, 1996.

The Search and Rescue Mission Coordinator

To view the morning through Richard Barone's eyes, given his unwillingness to be interviewed, I relied on telephone transcripts, testimony transcripts and Barone's witness statement. Additional source material included e-mail correspondence with Coast Guard Commander Keith Algernon; the Coast Guard's First District website; a phone conversation with SAR controller Tim Carton; an August 27, 1996, e-mail sent from Station Gloucester to Group Boston; and two phone interviews with Kevin Angerstein.

128 **trapped in a hull."** A few days after the *Heather Lynne II* collision, Barone found this addressed in the Coast Guard's addendum to the *National Search and Rescue Manual* and flagged it for future reference.

134 **willing to assist.** The Coast Guard has never had its own rescue divers and only began carrying rescue swimmers on its helicopters after a 1984 Congressional mandate to do so. The Coast Guard does, however, have a limited number of divers on board its buoy tenders, as well as those who assist with hull inspections and cleanings, research, and light salvage work.

142 **heading out there."** Barone also feared that the dive team, upon viewing the situation, would decide it was too dangerous, that they "may say no-go after evaluating the risk. As it turned out, they got there much faster than expected." Barone, signed statement, November 13, 1996.

143 **Barone said, later adding,** According to the Coast Guard's transcript of the telephone conversation, Angerstein then said, "The 47, with [missing word(s)] you're gonna blow this guy's doors away. I'm doing 50 miles an hour in my rig." Barone then replied, "Yeah, are the divers there?" To which Angerstein, continuing his earlier thought, said, "Doing about thirty-six or so." Barone then said, "Even if the divers were on scene, where [are] you at, you know?" Barone then concluded, "Let's let him keep trucking down there at 20 knots."

144 **and swim inside.** *CG Addendum to the National SAR Manual:* "Rescue and surface swimmers shall not enter capsized or submerged objects—they may reach inside while maintaining a grasp on a reference point on the exterior of the object." Section 4-I, p. 2.

148 **absorption of oxygen.** For more on hypothermia and hydrocarbon poisoning, see "Hypothermia: Surviving in Cold Water," University of Wisconsin Sea Grant, www.seagrant.wisc.edu, Alfred P. Fishman's, *Pulmonary Diseases and Disorders* (1980), and *Taber's Cyclopedic Medical Dictionary*, 18th ed. (Philadelphia: F. A. Davis, 1997).

Barbara and Gail, December 19, 1961

159 **thought he was headed.** I based much of the account of the loss of the *Barbara and Gail* on district court Judge Caffrey's written ruling as well as on press accounts from the time of the accident. Additional background information was found in the *Coast Guard Addendum to National SAR Manual* and in Frank L. Maraist and Thomas C. Galligan Jr., *Admiralty in a Nutshell*, 4th ed. (West Wadsworth, 2001). The loss of the *Lark* was also based on contemporary press accounts and Coast Guard accident investigation records.

161 **lower court ruling.** The Court of Appeals held that, "To expose the men in the Coast Guard to the double jeopardy of possible loss of their own lives and loss of status in their chosen careers, because they failed . . . to select the most desirable of procedures, or their skill was not equal to the occasion, is unthinkable and against the public interest."

This appeals court ruling was not unanimous. In a dissenting opinion, Chief Judge Biggs believed the court lacked the authority to make such a determination. The Supreme Court had already answered the question when it held that under the 1925 Public Vessels Act, suits brought against the United States would be heard and decided in the same process as a suit between private parties. Judge Biggs insisted that the court should not create special rules of exemption for Coast Guard vessels: "I cannot believe that Congress," Judge Biggs wrote, " . . . intended to relieve the United States for liability for the torts [of] the Coast Guard vessels."

Biggs believed that finding the cutter *Mohawk* not liable for navigational errors that forced the barge onto the breakwater was "almost incredible." He wrote, "Here is a towing vessel which puts herself as well as her tow on a breakwater and the majority say that she was not at fault. . . . I am astonished that an experienced admiralty court should hold that her navigation was without blame."

164   services on demand." To back up this assertion, Judge Caffrey noted a contemporary case *(United States v. Geraldine Gavagan)* in which a widow had successfully sued the Coast Guard—and an appeals court affirmed the ruling—for its failure to rescue her husband. A Florida district court judge determined the Coast Guard's shoreside crew negligently failed to implement the National SAR plan, and as such the U.S. could be held liable for a failed Coast Guard rescue. The Florida judge wrote: "The Government in its approach persists in compressing this into the mold of private salvage at sea, so that it is a case of maritime salvage, neither more nor less. This note is the opening theme of its brief: 'This case is the first one in which a District Court has held the United States liable for the failure of its employees to reach a vessel in distress in time to save her crew . . . ' This implies that the attempted rescue failed because of negligent acts of those in command of the two Coast Guard vessels . . . and that liability was imposed because one or both of these vessels made mistakes in the execution of the attempted salvage. This is far from the case. . . . [T]he neglect was not in the failure of these two ships to reach a vessel in distress in time. The neglect was that of persons ashore who were directing the whole operation."

Judge Caffrey, when looking at whether the Coast Guard should be held accountable for failing to rescue the *Barbara and Gail* and five of her crew, insisted that, as had already been established in the cases of *P. Dougherty Company v. United States* and the appeals case of *United States v. Geraldine Gavagan*, when it comes to search and rescue, the Coast Guard is anything but a private entity that should be regarded as a Good Samaritan.

164   failure to use sound judgment. Chief Judge Aldrich noted an unsuccessful Massachusetts lawsuit in 1951 *(D. Lacey v. United States)* where the family of Daniel Lacey sued the Coast Guard because, while it had decided to aid the passengers of a small plane that had crashed in Cape Cod Bay, it failed to reach them while they were still alive. Lacey family attorneys had argued that the Coast Guard is required by law to save lives at sea. The district court judge disagreed. He determined that nowhere is there a law that creates "a right to be rescued . . . [and] it is not for the Court to create this right." Instead, the Coast Guard must be regarded as a Good Samaritan. Once the Coast Guard voluntarily decides to respond to a vessel in distress, it must do so with due care, the judge wrote, because, "the rationale is that other would-be rescuers will rest on their oars in the expectation that effective aid is being rendered."

The Officer of the Day

I spoke to Kevin Angerstein by telephone on two occasions, though much of this chapter is based on his testimony at trial and a statement he made November 14, 1996.

178 **and the 47-footer.** Barone said, "So as far as assets go, to send [a boat] towards the Merrimack River away from the scene, the only one we really had available at that moment would be the 47-footer. And the 47-footer wouldn't do much faster than 20 knots." He later testified, "I didn't have any resources available to send to pick them up. The only resource would have been the 41 to proceed towards the Merrimack River, pick up the divers and make almost the same speed back to the scene."

The Salvor

This chapter is based on more than 300 hours spent shadowing Michael Goodridge, and his testimony at trial; press clippings; interviews with Jeff Smith, John Andrews, and Joseph Frohnhoefer; Congressional reports and testimony pertaining to the creation of the Marine Assistance industry; the Coast Guard's *Local Notice to Mariners* dated August 30, 1983; telephone and e-mail correspondence with Admiral John Linnon; and a phone interview with Captain Gabe Kinney, then chief of SAR for the entire Coast Guard.

By late 2002, the network of towing companies across the country had blossomed into a $35 million-a-year industry that by some estimates annually saved $200 million in property.

193 **Committee for Private Offshore Rescue Towing.** In 2002, it changed its name to Conference of Private Operators for Response Towing.

194 **to meet budget cuts.** Jeff Smith's remark would prove true. During the week surrounding the Fourth of July in 2000 and 2001, Sea Tow International estimated that through responding to 2,200 calls for help—and considering it cost about $900 per hour to operate a Coast Guard vessel and that the average assistance case took about three hours—Sea Tow's services had saved the Coast Guard and taxpayers about $5.5 million in just seven days.

199 **known as a stern trawler)** An Eastern-rigged dragger hauls nets over its side, rather than the stern, and is also called a side trawler.

The Race Against Time

Sources for this chapter include the hours spent with Michael Goodridge, interviews with David Swiss and Jay Lesynski, radio tapes and transcripts, Coast Guard documents, and Goodridge's trial testimony.

208 **get on scene faster.** This was at least his second notification to the Coast Guard of his efforts. By 5:45 A.M., he had called Station Merrimack and asked if it would give them a ride in its faster rigid-hull inflatable. He was told that the boat was not available.

Northern Voyager, November 2, 1997

Sources for this chapter include firsthand reporting (during several hours spent with Michael Goodridge) of the *Northern Voyager*'s search and Goodridge's subsequent dive. I also relied on the Coast Guard's investigation report and associated documents (including video and audio tapes, and witness statements), court documents (including telephone and radio logs and cell phone records), informal conversations with attorney Michael Rauworth and an interview with John Schwind.

226 **Coast Guard Auxiliarist,** Auxiliarists sometimes stood watch as part of the Coast Guard Auxiliary's broader goal of augmenting Coast Guard missions. Julia Tiernan, who also worked as a certified public accountant, had been qualified to stand watch at the Gloucester Station since 1995. Phone conversation with Petty Officer Ronald Simoneau, April 3, 2003.

230 **Chief Warrant Officer Wesley Dittes,** Dittes had twenty-four years of service in the Coast Guard.

230 **working with Goodridge.** Wesley Dittes, deposition, December 7, 2000: "The question of whether Mike Goodridge was going to change the situation was nullified when we had the progressive flooding in the engine space and I removed people from the vessel. From the Coast Guard perspective, it was unsafe for our crew members to be on board the vessel at that point and so I didn't consider having a commercial salvor arrive on scene was necessarily going to make that safer."

230 **Haggerty was looking for.** David Haggerty, deposition, November 6, 2000: "So I'm requesting more pumps and I'm, you know, just hoping somebody is going to bring us more pumps."

232 **boat of 490 gross tons.** Gross tonnage is a measure of volume rather than of weight.

232 **not appear to be in peril.** Observation made by viewing a video of the sinking. On my initial request for the video, CG Public Affairs officer Jay Lipinski said the video probably wouldn't be of much help since it showed the boat in the distance for about an hour and "You really wouldn't be able to tell the ship was sinking. It would take a trained eye to see that the vessel was in distress."

233 **Coast Guard personnel—** According to the CG's watch-stander's notes taken by Auxiliarist Julia Tiernan, the 41-footer had a crew of four, the 47-footer had a crew of six, and the *Adak* typically sailed with a crew of fourteen. Two of the 41-footer's crew went aboard the *Northern Voyager* while two Coast Guardsmen filmed the scene.

233 **officers with far more experience** Rear Admiral Linnon's report stated that "the Coast Guard . . . failed to use its most experienced people on hand to evaluate the buoyancy and stability situation on board the *Northern Voyager*; despite their ready availability, neither the station commander, his executive petty officer, nor any of the experienced crew of the cutter *Adak* ever boarded the vessel to observe the situation first hand."

234 **this frequency clear."** During a deposition given in preparation for the case, Tiernan was asked why she told Goodridge that the Coast Guard needed to keep the radio frequency clear—one that was not being used for the case. She explained that he had called at a tense moment when they weren't sure exactly what was happening on scene, and that they needed to listen to the communications rather than take time to talk to Goodridge. Plaintiffs' attorneys insisted that this had the effect of telling Goodridge he couldn't communicate with anyone on scene, particularly Haggerty.

A Good Samaritan

I talked with Captain Branimir Viducic on two occasions, once by telephone and once in person in Portland, Maine, aboard his boat.

251 **Number 7 Pullmaster winches.** She didn't have a stern ramp as the fishermen who remembered her offer for help thought she had. Her captain, Viducic, never testified at trial because neither the plaintiffs' nor the defendant's attorneys could identify the scallop boat that had offered to help since the offer is not recorded in the Coast Guard's transcript of radio communications. Only upon carefully reviewing audiotapes from that morning after the trial was I able to learn the boat's name and then locate Viducic.

252 **permission to assist.** The owner doesn't remember the call.

253 **no one answered him.** Viducic said, "I said two or three words to the CG on channel 16 or 22, but they never respond[ed]."

The Helicopter Pilot

This chapter is based on Lieutenant Commander Craig Lindsey's deposition, statement, and court testimony as well as on his military service record and an interview with copilot Bill Bellatty at Air Station Cape Cod.

255 **into a life raft.** Officially known as a Stearns Coldwater Immersion Suit, and unofficially referred to as a gumby suit, a survival suit, if worn properly, offers flotation and protection against hypothermia and greatly extends the life expectancy of someone tossed into frigid water.

258 **during the mission.** Peter Black, e-mail to the author, April 8, 2003: "True air speed is a term that is used to distinguish between what shows on an air speed indicator and how fast the aircraft is going through the air." He explained that indicated air speed varies depending on altitude and that most aircraft have instruments that can calculate the difference. Actual speed adds or subtracts the speed of the wind from the true air speed. Black said that a pilot's flight plan will include a true air speed, which is the speed at which a pilot calculates the aircraft will go based on the power setting and forecast conditions; cruise speeds compromise how fast the aircraft should go at full power versus how slowly one should fly to get maximum range—the faster you go, the more fuel you burn. Black concluded, upon reflecting on September 5, 1996, "The distances that day, being short, would have allowed using maximum sustainable power and hence much faster speeds than one would get from 'normal' cruise power."

264 **directed to launch.** There is a discrepancy as to the exact time of launch. Coast Guard records for the most part use 5:55 A.M. The flight mechanic, however, logged the departure time as 5:58. Coast Guard guidelines suggest that a helicopter should depart within 30 minutes of being called. Barone had requested the helicopter at about 5:25 A.M.

Morning Dew, December 29, 1997

The story of the *Morning Dew*'s fateful voyage is based on the NTSB report, Coast Guard investigation report and associated documents/exhibits, numerous press clippings, court documents and rulings, and a phone interview with Libby Cornett. Source material for the Coast Guard's history and budget woes included numerous press accounts, Congressional reports, and transcripts of several speeches made by Admiral James Loy during his tenure.

283 **vessels in distress.** The secretary of the treasury asked the Revenue Cutters to patrol during the winter for the specific task of assisting any vessels in peril.

284 **the nation's coastline.** After about ninety years, the government got involved in funding and management oversight via supervision by Revenue Cutter officers, which led to the creation of the U.S. Life-Saving Service.

284 **in time of war.** A good source of background on Coast Guard history is Robert Erwin Johnson, *Guardians of the Sea: History of the United States Coast Guard* (Annapolis: Naval Institute Press, 1987).

285 **a thousand people too many.** Although the Coast Guard was equivalent in size to 41 of the world's navies, it ranked 39th in average age of its fleet.

Admiral Loy offered these promising words to a reporter for *Boating* magazine, however: "I would ask you to make sure that boaters understand that our first order of business is search and rescue, and that we'll always take whatever steps are necessary to interrupt whatever we're doing anywhere else to address SAR requirements on the high seas or coastal areas. That is our core business, our raison d'etre."

Loy said that despite its budget shortfalls, the agency had begun building new

47-foot rescue boats to replace its slower 44-foot workhorses. Under his predecessor's initiative, the Coast Guard had launched what it called a Deepwater Project, a multibillion-dollar plan to replace several of its cutters and aircraft.

286 **since fiscal year 1998,** The Coast Guard's fiscal year runs from 1 October to 30 September.

286 **increased by 225 percent.** In fiscal year 1998, there were 40 accidents; in fiscal year 2000, there were 130 accidents.

The On-Scene Commander

This chapter is based on Christian Smith's statement made after the accident, his deposition, and his trial testimony, as well as on an interview with Kevin Angerstein and testimony of Angerstein and Richard Barone.

295 **telling me what to do."** During the deposition, Smith stated that, "it's up to the helicopter and Group Boston what they want to do. It's not for me to tell the helicopter to get divers."

298 **six recommended procedures.** Kiely skipped the last procedure: "Only if no rescue is possible, may you consider righting the vessel."

The Experts

This chapter is based largely on the direct testimony of Coast Guard Captain Adrian Lonsdale and Coast Guard Commander Robert Walters (including Walters's Hampton Roads Change of Command Speech, July 7, 1998). Background on the motto of the U.S. Life-Saving Service as described on the Coast Guard historian's website.

312 **I can't remember exactly."** The quote was from Eric Fischl, an American artist known for provocative postmodernist paintings, 1948.

Kavkaz, January 30, 1999

While I was fortunate to interview Anton Sanarov by telephone, I also relied on Coast Guard press releases; contemporary press accounts that appeared in the *Juneau Empire*, *Anchorage Daily News*, and *Alaska Fishermen's Journal*; and the Coast Guard's investigation report.

The Rescue Divers

Sources for this chapter include the testimony of Robert Atherton Jr. at both the Coast Guard Board of Inquiry and at the trial; Atherton's dive log and statement; the dispatcher's log and interviews with the dispatcher; long one-on-one interviews with dive team members; interviews with James Bashaw, Kevin Angerstein, and Michael Goodridge; board of inquiry testimony by Ted Rurak; press accounts; online research; and VHF radio tapes and logs.

331 **little further information.** At the Coast Guard Board of Inquiry, Atherton recalled: "I don't think he knew exactly what the situation was. I knew that he knew that it was a capsized boat, but he didn't elaborate too much information other than that they were the transport boat for us to the scene."

336 **the calm, cold water.** In his dive log, Atherton estimated the water temperature to be about 50°F; the Coast Guard logged the water temperature on scene at 65°F.

337 **a life-or-death difference.** "During the critical Golden Hour after a . . . serious accident, the race by helicopter or ambulance to the nearest shock-trauma center . . . can make a life-or-death difference." Commentary, Neal Barnard and A. R. Hogan,

"Raising the Golden Hour Training Standard," Physicians Committee for Responsible Medicine, www.pcrm.org (January 1999).

340 **hoisted Foster up.** Ron Simoneau, who was aboard the 47-footer and videotaped the events that morning, recalled that while Goodridge performed CPR rescue breathing on Foster, fellow Coast Guardsman Steve DesRosiers joined him by doing chest compressions and, after a few minutes, Brett Beatty offered Goodridge a pocket mask, since they realized Goodridge had probably ingested diesel fuel, seawater, and vomit. Simoneau said that, in his opinion, Goodridge was personally involved with the fishermen and that Goodridge, "knew what he needed to do," so the crew members on the 47-footer did their best to assist him. This portion of the video was not included in the Coast Guard video I received via a Freedom of Information Act request.

The Families

Sources for this chapter include interviews with Jeff Hutchins's mother (Diane Fondow) and two sisters (Jennifer and Jacqueline), Jeanne Huberdeau, and Ann Lord; a statement made by Jennifer Hutchins; transcripts of telephone calls made by and to Richard Barone at Group Boston; autopsy reports and death certificates.

348 **Boston City Hospital.** In 1996, Boston City Hospital merged with Boston University Medical Center to become Boston Medical Center.

353 **attributed to accidental drowning.** Their time of death, noted as due to drowning, was recorded as near 9 A.M.

Aftermath

Sources for this chapter include interviews with Michael Goodridge; phone conversations with Bill Dobson; Dobson's written report; videotape taken by Coast Guard investigators of the scene; a statement made by 41-footer crew, September 6, 1996; VHF radio tapes and transcripts; Kevin Angerstein's statement, November 14, 1996; board of inquiry testimony by Ted Rurak and Lieutenant Joseph McKechnie; a statement made by John LaFlamme, MSO investigator; and a phone interview with Rear Admiral John Linnon.

356 **the salvage phase.** In a January 21, 2000, statement to a private investigator working for the plaintiffs' attorneys, Goodridge said, "The Coast Guard told me [that] when the boat was released by them that we could begin the salvage."

357 **and tripping switches,** A postcasualty inspection found the batteries in the engine room had fallen out of their mounts and wires had melted or been torn, leading one investigator, McKechnie to conclude, "There was obviously an electrical short ongoing with salt water."

358 **filled with clutter.** The "sea clutter" dial was at the 3 o'clock position, and "rain clutter" was set at 2 o'clock—settings that would normally be used on a rough and rainy day.

359 **unlikely the crew was asleep.** The *Heather Lynne II* left her dock at 2 A.M. or within a few minutes after and would have reached the mouth of the river against the flood tide by 2:30 to 2:40. The distance from there to the collision site was 20 miles, which at 9 knots she could cover by 4:43 to 4:53. The collision took place between 5:10 and 5:15.

359 **preparing for the day ahead.** As a mariner at the Hinckley Yacht Brokerage firm in Newport, Rhode Island, told one reporter: "My speculation is that the crew was elsewhere, readying the boat for fishing. It's normal—it's all too normal." David

Arnold, "Evidence in sinking points to towline collision," *Boston Globe*, September 10, 1996.

361 **sank to the bottom.** I was unable to verify this story with the captain of the *Theresa R II*, because I could not locate the boat.

Epilogue

372 **was the most upset.** When reached at Station Gloucester on April 3, 2003, Petty Officer Ronald Simoneau, who was on board the 47-footer with Angerstein, declined to comment on his experiences, saying he still had emotional issues associated with that day and that the events that unfolded were "the most devastating for some of us on that crew." He believed Angerstein could speak for the whole crew.

375 **Goodridge for his salvage.** The $18,000 was divided among those who assisted Goodridge, including David Swiss, Jay Lesynski, and a crew of divers from Dave Stillman's Cape Ann Divers.

Acknowledgments

THIS IS MY BOOK but not my story, and I hope those who agreed to talk with me, many of them through tears, find I have recounted their experience with accuracy, fairness and compassion. I am especially grateful to the families of the lost crew of the *Heather Lynne II*: Diane Fondow, Jacqueline Hutchins, Jennifer Hutchins, Joe Hutchins, Jeanne Huberdeau, Ann Lord, and John Lowther. And to their friends: Nelson Beideman, David Morse, Jim Bashaw, Bob Campbell, and, especially, Dean Holt. I owe many thanks to the fishermen who helped bring me back to the day many of them have spent so many years trying to forget, especially Richard Burgess, Stephen Smith, John Gilson, Billy Muniz, Charlie Rine, Bob Yeomans, Mike Leary, Jimmy Ford, and Ric Littlefield. I am also truly grateful for the chance to meet all of the members of the Beverly Fire Department Dive Team—their candor and compassion were refreshing.

On more than one occasion, I requested interviews with Coast Guardsmen involved in this story, but only two complied—Lieutenant Bill Bellatty and Kevin Angerstein. I greatly appreciate their assistance and willingness to help me to see the morning's events through their eyes. While I found that the more a particular Coast Guard person knew about the case, the less they were willing to talk about it, Robert Higgins, Commercial Fishing Vessel Safety Specialist for the Coast Guard's First District, was a tremendous help. Other Coast Guardsmen who offered assistance included Rear Admiral John Linnon, Captain Gabe Kinney, Captain Russ Webster, Captain Jim Olive, Eric Young, Wesley Dittes, Andrew Shinn, and the crew at Coast Guard Station Merrimack River, who let me tag along with them for a few days during the fall of 1997.

I asked the Eklof Marine Corporation, now known as K-Sea Transportation, to make the crew of the *Houma* and *Essex* available, but they declined. However, Rick Falcinelli, vice president of administration, was a gracious help, as was Joe Koch. I especially appreciate Mike Simpson's willingness to share his side of the story; he made himself available to be interviewed on at least four occasions.

In addition, several others made great contributions to the research and writing. In particular, Susan Jones and Lorelei Stevens at *Commercial Fisheries News* were excellent sources of background information on the bluefin tuna fishery. Attorneys Peter Black, Brad Henry, and Michael Rauworth were extremely gracious with their time and offered critical insights, and Marie Cloonan was a great help. Anton Sanarov was an inspiration to speak with after what he had endured. Libby Cornett was also gracious with her time. It was a pleasure to get to know several members of the marine assistance industry, particularly Terri Parrow, formerly of TowBoatU.S., Joe Frohnhoefer of Sea Tow, John and Pete Andrews of Safe/Sea, as well as the staff of C-PORT.

On the Merrimack River, I enjoyed talking with Jay Lesynski and David Swiss. I am deeply grateful for Mike Goodridge's persistence and patience, and for his agreeing to let me tag along with him on so many occasions, day and night, easy jobs and hard. Without his willingness to be a gracious host while under the zoom lens of a reporter who observed but never stepped in to help, as well as his unending patience with my hundreds of questions, this book would not have been possible.

I am also grateful to the editors of *Boston Magazine*, particularly Jon Marcus, who published a version of this story in November 2000, under the title "Caught Off Guard."

I am lucky to have had a few dedicated readers who were willing to pore through shaky early drafts of this book. Many thanks to Charlie Ess, Karin Round, Betsy Haggerty, Jean Gard, April Doss, Charlie Doane, and Molly Mulhern, as well as the faculty at Goucher College—Lee Gutkind, Jeanne Marie Laskas, Lauren Slater, and Julie Checkoway—and at Breadloaf Writers Conference—Dana Sachs and Ted Conover. Rebecca Taylor offered a keen and compassionate editorial eye, which was a great gift, and Charlie Doane read the book again in its penultimate draft and spurred me to make more improvements. Jonathan Eaton proved to be a brilliant editor who was willing to take a chance on a young writer with a story that deserved to be told, and Deborah Oliver managed the copyediting with a deft touch. Three cheers for my friends and family, who coaxed me through so many drafts, when I waffled between wanting to know all I could about what happened to the crew of the *Heather Lynne II* and then not wanting to know anymore. Finally, my most heartfelt thanks to my husband, Rob, who would not let me change course, and to Jack—you were a great copilot.

"More people die every year on commercial fishing vessels than in any other profession. Kate Yeomans' well-written and riveting book graphically shows the dangers of those who go down to the sea. Anyone interested in the sea should read this book."

—DR. DENNIS L. NOBLE, author, *Lifeboat Sailors: Disasters, Rescues, and the Perilous Future of the Coast Guard's Small Boat Stations* and *The Rescue of the Gale Runner: Death, Heroism, and the U.S. Coast Guard*

"A compelling and complex piece of work."
—*Chesapeake Bay Magazine*

"In *Dead Men Tapping,* Kate Yeomans captures the suspense and the terror of *The Perfect Storm* while dramatizing and documenting a series of riveting mysteries that casts an unforgettable shadow over the U.S. Coast Guard and the eccentric rules of the open seas."

—LEE GUTKIND, author, *Forever Fat: Essays by the Godfather* and *The Art of Creative Nonfiction*